~ Federal Fish Files ~

Affidavits, Natural Resources, And Northwest Treaty Rights From The Edward Swindell 1942 Report

Dr Jay Miller, editor

Report on source, nature, and extent of the fishing, hunting, and miscellaneous related rights of certain Indian tribes in Washington and Oregon together with Affidavits locating usual and accustomed fishing grounds and stations

E.G. Swindell Los Angeles: U.S. Department of the Interior
Office of Indian Affairs, Division of Forestry and Grazing
1942

Edward G. Swindell Jr. (31 May 1909 - 3 Aug 1974) – an attorney for the U.S. Department of the Interior, Office of Indian Affairs, Los Angeles – skillfully investigated the location of "usual and accustomed" [U&A] Indian fishing sites in Washington and northern Oregon as background research for the case of *Tulee v. Washington*, which was decided in 1942 when the United States Supreme Court reversed a decision of the Washington Supreme Court to declare that the state could not require Indians to purchase fishing licenses to fish at their usual and accustomed places, a right guaranteed in their treaties with the US, and still being fought over and defended in the Northwest "fish wars". Swindell's 323-page report covered traditional fishing sites from the Washington coast to the Columbia Plateau. During WW II, the BIA moved from DC to Chicago, where this report was submitted.

Changes made to that report include:

Current tribal names are replaced herein, especially Yakama for the people & tribe, Yakima for
    river, town, and county.
Footnotes once marked as #/ no longer restart with #1 per each page but are now continuous and
    marked between double right strokes for clarity, as /#/, with original #/ placed at the start.
Swindell's own offensive remarks are marked [!!]
Wildly irregular punctuation and spelling has been revised, allowing for a few representative
    examples of his usages.
All native words, correct or attempted, are in *italics*, as a sign of respect.

[To aid research, editor's additions, clarifications, commentary appear between square brackets,
    with original page numbers at 8 point type. Yet unknowns are so [?*?] marked].

No copies of the original report with pasted in photos have been located [known copies are now missing] so images were trimmed from the 1952 mimeographed version at Whitman College Archives and Tacoma Public Library. Please contact Dr Miller if you know of any originals still in the Northwest since the aim is to add anthropological value to a legal report.

I   1

II   63

III 180 > 280 <originally 483>
added   281 Chehalis Meeting Notes
            291 Tacoma Library & Whitman College Transmittal Letters
            292 Name Index 296
            297 Place Name Sources
            298 Portraits at Walla Walla = 305

footnotes #1-#88

PDF is https://www.sos.wa.gov/library/publications_detail.aspx?p=116

© 1919

FEDERAL FISH FILES

REPORT
ON SOURCE, NATURE, AND EXTENT
OF THE
FISHING, HUNTING, AND MISCELLANEOUS RELATED RIGHTS
OF
CERTAIN INDIAN TRIBES IN WASHINGTON AND OREGON
TOGETHER WITH
AFFIDAVITS SHOWING LOCATION
OF
A NUMBER OF USUAL AND ACCUSTOMED
FISHING GROUNDS AND STATIONS

UNITED STATES DEPARTMENT OF THE INTERIOR
OFFICE OF INDIAN AFFAIRS DIVISION OF FORESTRY AND GRAZING
LOS ANGELES, CALIFORNIA
JULY, 1942

Forestry and Grazing
13223-41-931

1358 Federal Building
Los Angeles, California
August 26, 1942

The Commissioner of Indian Affairs
Chicago, Illinois

There is respectfully submitted herewith a report covering an investigation pertaining to the fishing, hunting, and related miscellaneous rights of certain tribes of Indians in the Pacific Northwest under the previsions of a group of treaties executed in the period between December 26, 1854 an January 25, 1856.

The investigation was undertaken pursuant to your instructions of March 3, 1941, as modified by your letter of November 18, 1941. Actual preparation of the report itself was deferred in accordance with your instructions of December 31, 1941, pending the decision in the Tulee case.

It will be evident therefrom that in so far as fishing and hunting activities outside their reservations are concerned, the present day rights of the descendants of the tribes who were parties to the treaties in question are extremely limited with only two general exceptions of any significance, both pertaining to fishing. The decision of the Supreme Court of the United States in the Tulee case unequivocally disposed of any further question as to the right of the states to control and regulate non-reservation hunting and fishing activities as long as (1) the restrictions imposed are of a purely regulatory nature looking to the conservation of fish and wild life resources and (2) such restrictions are applicable to Indians equally with others. [ii]

Despite what the parties may have intended to reserve, the very limited extent of the Indian's non-reservation rights must now be recognized in the light of the judicial interpretation of the treaties in accordance with well established legal principles. Such principles inhibit action on the part of the Federal Government looking to the enlargement of such rights. Action with that end in view is a matter solely within the province of the legislature of Washington and Oregon. In the past, these bodies have given recognition to the plight of the Indians by granting limited special privileges to them to in part compensate them for the restrictions placed upon the exercise of their treaty rights. There would appear to be no reason why in the future the grant of such privileges cannot be supplemented and enlarged upon, at least in so far as subsistence fishing and hunting are concerned.

It was with that possibility in mind that the preparation was undertaken of those portions of the report covering the Indian's prediscovery manner of life and the natural or inherent rights they then enjoyed and continue to enjoy until conservation measures became necessary. If in any manner, therefore, this report with its exhibits consisting of the minutes of the treaty councils in which are recorded the solemn promises and assurances given to the unsophisticated and trusting ancestors of the present generation, is of service to those interested in their welfare by enabling them to justify further statutory recognition of the rights intended to be reserved, it will have well and fully served that particular object of the investigation.

Sincerely yours,
Edward G. Swindell, Jr.,
Associate Attorney

EGS:lg
Attachements

Table of Contents

Part III

APPENDICES "A" and "B" CONSISTING OF MINUTES OF TREATY COUNCILS AND A DIGEST OF TREATY PROVISIONS

INDEX OF MAPS AND DRAWINGS

PHOTOGRAPHS

CASES CITED
[not checked or updated]

VOLUME I
REPORT COVERING AN INVESTIGATION PERTAINING TO THE
FISHING, HUNTING AND RELATED MISCELLANEOUS RIGHTS
OF TRIBES OF INDIANS IN THE PACIFIC NORTHWEST
[Treaties of] DECEMBER 26, 1854 – JANUARY 25, 1856

INTRODUCTION

This report has been prepared as a result of the situation which was created and. which has continued to exist in the States of Washington and Oregon since the inception of the first conservation measures looking to the preservation of their respective wild life resources. Of these resources, it is generally recognized that the principal one both in extent and financial value is the world famous salmon fishing industry, sport as well as commercial.

The existing situation came into being as the direct result of the enactment of fish and wild life conservation legislation which in effect constituted a limitation on the exercise by Indians of certain hunting and fishing rights reserved by them through appropriate provision in the several treaties concluded between the United States and various of the Indian tribes in the Pacific Northwest during the period from December 26, 1854 to January 25, 1856.

The treaty provisions referred to, it must be assumed, were inserted as a recognition on the part of the treaty negotiators representing the United States of the mode of life of the native populations in the area involved, for certainly neither the instructions given to Territorial Governor and Superintendent of Indian Affairs Isaac I. Stevens or the specimen treaties furnished as a guide, contained & suggestion of such a provision.[1] The provision in question is peculiar to the extent that with apparently only one exception[2] a similar provision or that of similar import was not included in any ratified treaties with the various Indian groups throughout the entire United States. The provision in the particular group of treaties with which this report in part is concerned is substantially the same and for convenience as well as ready reference, it is quoted: [2]

"The right of taking fish, at all usual and accustomed grounds and stations, is further secured to said Indians in common with all citizens of the Territory, and of erecting temporary houses for the purpose of curing, together with the privilege of hunting, gathering roots and berries, and pasturing their horses on open and unclaimed lands;
Provided, however, 'That they shall not take shellfish from any beds stated or cultivated' by citizens, * * *" /1/$^\beta$ " "

---

[1] 1/ [This classic clause was inserted into most of these treaties at the insistence of George Gibbs who saw the devastation of native Californians unable to feed themselves when aggressive mining polluted and destroyed many salmon runs, while Stevens liked saving federal funds since people could feed themselves.

[2] 2/ Art. 3, Treaty of June 16, 1820, with the Chippewa Indians, 7 Stat. 206; 2 Kap. 187, reserving a perpetual right of fishing as well as the right to use camp grounds at the Falls of St. Marys.

[3] 1/ Medicine Creek Treaty with the Nisqually, et al, Dec. 26, 1854; 10 Stat. 1132; 2 Kap. 661. Note, however, last proviso for obvious reasons not included in non-tidal area treaties. See Appendix B.

It is true many other ratified treaties contain a reservation of hunting rights for the benefit of various Indian groups /2/[4] and also several unratified treaties concluded in the Washington and Oregon territories contained a reservation of fishing rights /3/[5] but such reservations were not in the broad all inclusive language of the treaties herein discussed. One can safely and without any implication of exaggeration say that the rights thus reserved literally covered innumerable fishing grounds, all of which were well known and effectively used by the native inhabitants for after all the entire area teemed with fish of all species, and fish; with the multitudinous salmon predominant, was the mainstay in the diet of all tribes in the area involved.

It is a logical conclusion then that, with the settlement of the Pacific Northwest and the civilisation of its native inhabitants followed by the discovery of the possibilities of preserving fish by canning and the subsequent birth and rapid and enormous growth of that industry, which today it is estimated returns an annual total of $10,000,000 /4/[6] from the Columbia River fisheries alone, conflicts involving Indian treaty rights inevitably would arise. The indicated provision of the treaties, the [3] changes brought about by settlement, the general agricultural and industrial development of the area, and the many legal pronouncements which have recognized state rights with respects to the enforcement of conservation measures as being superior to the reserved rights of the Indians to fish and hunt outside of their reservations, have resulted in many perplexing administrative problems, and have had a profound effect on the way of life as well as the mental attitude of the remaining Indian population.

The field work upon which this report is based had for one of its primary objects the ascertainment of the location of usual and accustomed fishing grounds as such were referred to in the treaties. After initial preparation and studies had been completed, it was evident that it would be impossible to accomplish that objective in its entirety at this late date. The memory of man is notoriously short lived and since the aboriginal inhabitants had no way accurately to record in detail the data relating to their antecedent history, it was apparent that that feature of the report must depend solely on hearsay testimony passed along from generation to generation by word of mouth. It is conceded, of course, that some such places were and are today so well known, and appropriately described by Lewis and Clark, as well as contemporary writers and explorers, that there could be no question as to their authenticity and very little question as to their precise locations. However, the manner of life of the entire native population was such that of necessity there must have been at least one and in most instances many more such places utilized by each of the numerous separate and distinct groups inhabiting the region in question. Quite a few of these groups have lost their tribal or group identity and in the case of many others, there are no survivors. It follows, therefore, that the location of many such places cannot now be discovered and, consequently, it is not contended that the places which could only be more or less generally described in this report constitute more than a small fraction of these in use prior to and at the time of the several treaties. An illustration of this is provided through comparison of the number and location of Indian fishing establishments along the Columbia River and

---

[4] 2/ For extended list, see footnote 171, p. 265 — <u>Handbook Federal Indian Law</u> — Cohen, U.S.C.P.O. 1941.

[5] 3/ e.g. Treaty of Aug. 7, 1851, (unratified) with the Waukikm [Wahkiakum] Band of Chinooks reserving the right to fish on the Columbia River and two small streams entering the Columbia from the north.

[6] 4/ Includes value of the Columbia River salmon taken from ocean fisheries – Bureau of Fisheries Bill. #32, U.S. Dept. of Interior.

portions of some of its principal tributaries, as such are noted in the Lewis and Clark journals and the affidavits of the Indian descendants of the tribes in habiting the area at the time of the expedition. As a [4] consequence of the change in their manner of life, the present day Indians are primarily interested in those places where a portion of their catch can be disposed of to canneries so that money for necessities of civilized life can be obtained. Then again many of such places are no longer of value since the fish populations have been decimated or completely destroyed as a result of any one of a number of causes not attributable to the Indians.

Hunting rights under these treaties are also of concern to the Indian groups in this area and appropriate reference thereto will be made in due coarse. It is unfortunate from the standpoint of the 'Indians that the provisions of their treaties relating to hunting rights outside of the areas reserved to their exclusive use was so closely tied into those for fishing. It has been pointed out that the reservation of fishing rights is considerably broader in scope and, consequently, of greater value than the usual treaty reservation of hunting rights for any of our American Indian tribes. Hunting rights under the treaties here involved, as well as others throughout the country, did not contemplate they could be exercised in perpetuity, whereas the language concerning non-reservation fishing did contemplate that the rights thus recognized would be continuing ones. It has been and still is difficult, therefore, for them to distinguish between the two rights and, accordingly, they still cherish one equally with the other and have been considerably less prone than other not so fortunate tribes in accepting and submitting to the limitations of state conservation statutes and regulations.

An effort has been made to appropriately refer to the recorded decisions of any consequence of the various courts having a bearing on the Indians' rights under the treaties in question. At the present time there no longer seems to be any question of importance which could be submitted to the courts and upon which a favorable decision could be expected. Under the existing decisions, including those of the Supreme Court of the United States, the plenary power of the states over the control of their wild life resources has been upheld time and again provided, of course, the exercise of such power is consistent with other legal doctrines. Where considered pertinent, [5] quotations from recorded cases have been included although the use of such excerpts has been limited since the report is not intended to be a brief of authorities. Citations to the leading, cases have been included, however, for reference purposes.

There has been included as Appendix "A" the complete records and minutes of the several councils at which the treaties in question were negotiated. It is hoped that they will be of value to those friends of the Indians who may at some future time be interested in obtaining special dispensation for the exercise of non-reservation fishing and hunting rights for purely subsistence purposes or of even more importance to those concerned with the protection from further infringement of such few rights as they still retain from the unlimited number enjoyed by their ancestors.

When one has read the earnest and apparently sincere statements of the treaty commissioners on the one hand and of the chiefs and head men of the Indians on the other, the Indians' position can be infinitely better appreciated. Although the existence of such records apparently was not known or thought of at the time the various cases involving these treaty rights were before the courts, until quite recently, it is rather doubtful whether they would have favorably affected the outcome of the considerable body of litigation instituted to test and determine the extent of such rights. Despite the sincerity of the high contracting parties, it is clear, and it has been so held, that they could not by their previously conceived act limit the police power of the then unforced sovereign states of Washington and Oregon, to regulate and control their wild life resources in order that the benefits therefore would accrue to all of their citizens — both Indian and non-Indian alike.

There has also been included for convenience and ready reference Appendix "B" consisting of a digest of the provisions of the nine treaties concluded during the above-mentioned period including references to the dates of execution and ratification, the names of the various tribes involved in each treaty and appropriate citations to the United States Statutes-at-Large and Vol. III of Kappler (2nd Edition), Treaties. [6]

The locations of a number of "usual and accustomed" fishing grounds are described in a general fashion in affidavits taken from a number of the older members of tribes who were parties to the treaties. In most instances, the affiants were children of individuals present at the treaty councils and by reason of their age many of them were personally familiar with the locations of the ancient fishing grounds through the having visited them and either fished there or saw other members of their tribe engaged in such activity. The locations of the villages or temporary fishing camps were necessarily generalized since it was not feasible to visit them all for the purpose of surveying same to obtain the legal descriptions thereof.

Where factual statements are included, brief references to the authority or authorities therefore are shown either in footnotes or at the end of each topical division of the report. The complete citations to such reference works will be found in the bibliography, which has been included for the convenience of those who may wish to pursue the matter further. [7]

COLUMBIA RIVER – WASHINGTON-OREGON

Picture of Indians fishing on one of the small islands in the Columbia River near the north bank (Washington State) immediately above the "Big Eddy". Indian in foreground has just netted a good haul of salmon with a "bag net", one of the types of primitive fishing gear used at this place from time immemorial and still in use at the present time. Note large wooden boxes to receive the anticipated catch.

A downstream view of Indians fishing at the same spot pictured above. The fisherman on the platform is holding his bag net in the water awaiting for a salmon to enter. In the lower left foreground note the large number of eels on the rocks. The Columbia River eels, like the salmon, are anadromous. When they are caught by the Indians in their nets they provide a welcome addition to their larder.

Above two pictures were taken in 1887 and were furnished through the courtesy of Louis Gunnier, a Yakama Indian. Sampson Tulee, the defendant in the now famous "Tulee case" was arrested on the far side (Washington) approximately opposite the lower fishing stand in the upper picture. [7A] 2 photoz [8]

GENERAL AREA DESCRIPTION

The area covered by the several treaties under discussion is often referred to as the Pacific Northwest. For convenience that designation is used throughout this report to refer to the area in question. Since that designation, however, is a generic one embracing a far larger area than we are concerned with here, it seems desirable to provide a general description of the area covered by the several treaties. At the time the treaties were negotiated, the northwest section of the United States was comprised of two vast territories — Washington and Oregon — which embraced all of the present day states of Washington and Oregon and sections of what are now the states of Montana and Idaho. The Columbia River and its many tributaries traversed the greater part of this vast wilderness and since the salmon frequented this stream in tremendous numbers and spawned in its numerous tributaries, it played an important part in the life of the native population long prior to the coming of the whites. In addition to this stream system, however, there were the coastal waters and numerous rivers and streams teaming with salmon situated west of the Cascade Mountains in what is now western Washington and Oregon. Included in this section were waters of Puget Sound and Hood's Canal.

The two territories were traversed from north to south by the Cascade Mountain range which, in addition to constituting a physical separation and barrier through practically its entire length, generally speaking constituted a line of demarcation between the arid and semi-arid eastern section and the temperate western section with its ample rainfall. Native life and culture in consequence on each side of this barrier was patterned in keeping with the prevailing climatic and physical conditions. On the west the natives were more inclined to be indolent and sedentary in their habits with their principal travel being accomplished by canoes over the ocean and the many existing rivers and streams. Such waters constituted their principal highways of travel, inasmuch as large sections of the western area were densely forested and covered by a thick almost impenetrable growth of underbrush. This was particularly true of the west [general area of treaties map 9] [10] Washington coast and the entire Olympic Peninsula. To the east the country was more open, consisting of a succession of unforested plains and table lands and the forests and undergrowth, where such existed, were not so dense. As a consequence, travel of the population was much more conveniently accomplished.

The area ceded by the Indians as described in the nine treaties covered a very large portion of the two territories. That area, however, does not coincide with the area which today still remains subject to the rights established in favor of the Indians by the fishing clause in their treaties. There are two reasons for this; first, some of the tribes have been held to have lost their treaty rights, as for example the Nez Perce and the group of tribes described in their treaty as the "Tribes of Middle Oregon", and, second, some of the tribes belonging to the western group and known as the "fish eating Indians" either were not parties to a ratified treaty containing the fishing clause reservation, as for example the Chinooks, Chehalis, and Cowlitz, or else had failed to comply with the several other provisions of their treaties with regard to removal to reservations to be established for them, etc. In this latter category fall the Clallam Indians of the north Olympic Peninsula.

Reference to sheet 1 of the General Area Map will give an idea of the area with which this report is principally concerned, as well as indicate the area about which there is no present question as to their being still subject to the rights established by the treaty provision.

Before going on, it is wished to point out that in no circumstances should the above reference to the Nez Perce, Tribes of Middle Oregon, and the Clallam Indians be construed as conceding the extinguishment of the rights reserved to them in their respective treaties. Such determination is solely a matter within the province of courts of competent jurisdiction.

HISTORICAL BACKGROUND

The Pacific Northwest although presently well settled and highly developed was the last American frontier to be discovered and explored. Our knowledge of it dates [11] back less than 150 years. However, the history of this area including its discovery; the extent and nature of its native populations, its natural resources, and its development down to the present day is fully covered in the many reference works available in most libraries.

To appreciate the existing situation resulting from the rights reserved to the Indians by their treaties, one necessarily must have a general idea of the conditions which existed at the time the country was discovered and explored. History records that sporadic contacts had been made by Spanish and other navigators at various points on the unknown and dangerous northwest coast commencing with the visit of Juan de Fuca in about 1592 and continuing at various intervals until the expeditions of George Vancouver (1792-4) and Robert Gray, who, in 1792, upon entering an unknown river, named it after his boat, the Columbia. The recorded references of these visits, however, so far as the native inhabitants were concerned were meager and ordinarily devoted to the treacherous and warlike disposition of the few isolated groups with whom the early explorers came in contact.

It wasn't until the overland expedition of Lewis and Clark (1804-6) that detailed information was obtained concerning the location of and the communal and dietary habits of the various linguistic families represented in the northwest United States by numerous divisions or tribal groups which in turn were comprised of many smaller bands or clans. Subsequently, the entire area was thoroughly explored by missionaries and adventurers interested in exploiting the natural resources of the country and, as a result, a considerable volume of additional information was compiled. While it would be repetitious to endeavor in a report of this nature, which is not intended in any sense to be an ethnological study, to outline in detail the habits and culture of the various groups, certain general information, however, was obtained from a study of the various works listed in the bibliography.

Since it has a bearing on the present situation, certain of that general information is summarized. [12]

NATIVE FOODS

As previously indicated, the area was physically divided into two main sections by the Cascade Mountains — on the -west lived the so-called coastal and Puget Sound tribes, who, in the early days were quite often referred to as "fish-eating Indians" — on the east lived the more nomadic groups who, although relying to a great extent on fish, and in particular salmon, for food generally speaking had a more varied diet resulting from their greater freedom of movement and their ability to pursue and capture the game which abounded in the open eastern area. This latter accomplishment was facilitated as a result of the introduction of the horse through pre-discovery contact and intercourse with the tribes adjoining on the south and east.

It is probable that prior to the coming of the whites and the resultant improvement of their weapons of the chase, that the fish eaters of the coast used game only in vary small quantities. In some instances taboos militated against the extensive use of the flesh of wild animals among the fish eating groups. It is pointed out, however, that the affidavits which form a part of this report and which were obtained from the immediate ancestors of the coastal tribes represented at the treaty councils, contain specific references to the hunting of bear and elk as well as smaller game both by the affiants as well as by their progenitors, who, it appears, told the affiants of the mode of life of themselves as well as their own ancestors. The use of game by some of the more inland of the Sound Indians exceeded that of fish.

In addition to the abundant and varied kinds of fish found in the ocean and tidal waters of the area, the tribes residing along such waters in western Washington were blessed with an abundance of other species of sea food such as lobsters, crabs, clams, oysters, and shrimp, all of which comprised no inconsiderable part of the food supply and which were used to good advantage both in a fresh state, as well as cured for future use. Clams and other shell-fish were cooked and then dried by being strung on cords made of cypress bark and hung in the dwelling houses for winter use. [13]

Some of the tribes of the Pacific coast of Washington and in particular the Quileute and Makah were adapt in the capture of the large marine animals such as seals and whales, the blubber and oil of which were highly esteemed as articles of food. Other coastal tribes not so proficient in this respect, however, also utilized the blubber and oil of these ocean creatures but were dependent for their supply on nature which, as a result of the severe seasonal storms of this area, frequently stranded whales along-the beaches of the several tribal domains.

Although dried salmon and other dried fish were not the most palatable food, they played a very important part it the diet of these tribes. To make it more palatable the Indians of the northwest coast were accustomed to supplement dried fish with whale oil or oil which was obtained from a small fish found along the coast in enormous numbers and known to the natives as uthlecan or olachen [candlefish].

Salmon and herring spawn were also considered a delicacy of the tribes in the western area. Although large quantities of these items were consumed fresh, considerable, additional quantities were dried for winter use.

Salmon, however, both fresh and cured, was the great staple in the food supply of the Indians of the Pacific Northwest. In fact, it has been referred to as the staff of life of the numerous tribes inhabiting that area. It has been estimated that the aboriginal population of the tribes within the limits of the Columbia River watershed at the time of the Lewis and Clark expedition was comprised of 50,000 Indians /1/[7] and that a not unreasonable estimate of their average daily per capital consumption of salmon at that time was one pound. On the basis of those estimates the annual salmon catch would have amounted to 18,000,000 pounds. No doubt equivalent or even larger amounts were consumed by numbers of the coast "fish eating" tribes not within the Columbia watershed. In this connection, it is interesting to note and compare the present day importance of salmon for subsistence purposes as indicated by the results of a recent survey covering the Indians under the jurisdiction of the Yakama, Umatilla, and Warm Springs jurisdictions situated within the interior or mid-Columbia River watershed.   These results obtained from interviews with the heads of 55 representative families   [14]   show that the estimated annual consumption of fresh and cured salmon for 795 families in which salmon was important in their diet, was equivalent to 1,281,045 pounds, or an average of 1611 pounds per family per annum./1/[8] Although the average size of the family unit is not given, the annual per capita consumption of the members of the 795 families, assuming the family unit as being comprised of five members, would equal 322 pounds. While this figure might appear high in view of the fact that the diet of the present day Indians is considerably more varied than that of their aboriginal ancestors, it is pointed out that the consumptive use for subsistence purposes covered both fresh and cured salmon, but the total poundage shown represented the weight of the fish in its fresh state, the weight of the cured salmon having been converted to its fresh weight equivalent. This was done in order to obtain uniformity with as well as to permit comparison with the figures of the Indians' mid-Columbia River commercial catch which is compiled from the-weight of such catch in a fresh state. Consequently, the poundage of the per capita consumption (322) would be reduced by the amount the weight of the cured product consumed is less than the weight of the fresh fish required to furnish the cured product. The amount of fresh fish required to obtain an equivalent amount of cured fish is considerably greater since the curing process results in a considerable loss of weight. The figures used in the survey representing the respective weights of the fresh and cured salmon were not available to the writer.

Estimates not predicated on actual surveys but made by the staff of one of the agencies having jurisdiction over the remnants of a number of the coastal tribes covering 1937 - 1940, inclusive, indicate that only 13% of the total annual catch was used for subsistence purposes. Since these estimates are predicated on the value of the catch and not the weight thereof the annual per capita consumption cannot be here elated. In the opinion of the writer it is probable that the present consumption of fish for subsistence purposes in the western area is less than in the interior for the reason that the natives have been considerably more disposed to adopt the white man's diet and manner of living. [15]

Although neither the eastern or western groups were agriculturally inclined prior to the coming of the white man and their subsequent settlement on restricted reservations, they supplemented their fish and game diet with mixtures of the many varieties of esculent roots, and berries which were indigenous in large quantities throughout the entire area.

Despite the prediscovery natural abundance of the various food items forming the diet of these Indians, circumstances necessitated that large quantities of fish, fish oil, roots and berries be cured in adequate quantities to insure sufficient and balanced diet for these periods of the year when the fresh supply of these commodities was noticeable by its absence. Consequently it was

---

[7] 1/ Sen. Ex. Doc. No. 57, 75th Cong., 1st sess, p. 18.

[8] 1/ Letter of July 22, 1942 – "Fish and Wildlife" from Superintendent, Yakima Indian Agency, to Commissioner of Indian Affairs.

customary for all tribes to anticipate and prepare for each seasonal periods of want. Quantities of fish in considerable numbers were preserved for future use either through smoking or drying in the sun and open air. The choice of the method by which the supply was cured depended on prevailing climatic conditions and the available supply of firewood. In the more temperate and relatively high humility area west of the Cascades where an adequate supply of firewood was readily available, fish and animal flesh were preserved principally by the use of wood smoke. Ordinarily the supply was dried from smoke of the cooking fires in the dwellings of the natives. To the east, however, the principal and usual method of the particular groups, having treaties with which we are here concerned, consisted of filleting the flesh and then drying the resultant thin strips in the open air. This method was the usual one practiced in this area for the reason that at the principal fishing places along the Columbia River firewood was scarce and the natural action of the air with its low percentage of moisture and the extreme temperature developed by the hot summer sun was adequate to properly cure the fish in this manner.

It was customary for the tribes along the Columbia River to manufacture pemmican. This was accomplished by pounding the dried strips until quite fine and packing the resultant mass into baskets lined with fish skin. Clark reports that each basket contained between 90 and 100 pounds, and reference is made to the fact that 107 of these containers were counted at one group of lodges. [16]

Salmon were utilized in the fresh state either by boiling or roasting. It has been reported that the Walla Wallas consumed fish without the formality of cooking.

<u>References</u>

Handbook American Indians, Vol. 1 p. 570.
Bancroft, Vol. 1, pp. 163, 185, 187, 212, 213, 233, 234, 261, 266, and footnotes.
Caughey, pp. 33-35, 39.
Gibbs, "Western Washington — 193-7.
Irving. pp. 150, 453.
Lewis and Clark. Vol. 3, 148 and 107-242; also Vol. 4, 243 - 347.
Swan, N.W. Coast – 26-7, 58, 82-91.
    Cape Flattery — 19 – 30. [17]

FISHING GEAR

When first discovered, the natives had little if anything to learn about fishing from the white man; in fact, they were and in a large measure have continued to be independent of the white man for the method of catching fish and other seafood best suited to the particular physical conditions existing at the various fishing grounds and places where other seafood was obtained. The most that it can be said that the native inhabitants acquired as a result of contact with white people was in the method of operation of the gear which had already been developed by the various tribes. By that it is meant that as a result of the acquisition by the natives of tools and other implements common in civilized communities, they have been able to facilitate the manufacture of the various types of gear which were familiar to them in the first instance. This was accomplished trough the use of such implements and the materials such as steel, iron, and rope also made available to them through introduction by the whites.

The similarity in the several types of fishing gear used by the several tribes both east and west of the mountains is surprising when it is considered that a great many of the groups never came into direct contact with each other. Certainly this is persuasive evidence indicating that through devious channels arising from intertribal trade and intercourse hereinafter discussed, the several individual tribes learned of the successful operation of particular types of gear by other-tribes whose holdings were not necessarily contiguous to each other. Such exchange of ideas in this connection parallels the manner in which the horse was introduced to the various tribes throughout the entire United States west of the Mississippi River, including those in the Pacific Northwest.

With the exception of the spear, gaff and other gear which to a great extent depended on the skill and dexterity of the individual operator, one cannot help being impressed with the efficiency of the various types of fishing apparatus conceived and developed of necessity by the uneducated and unskilled aborigines. From accounts of early explorers and others who visited in this area, it is evident that the various types of gear were ingeniously constructed [18] without satisfactory tools or equipment solely from the limited materials that nature made available in the locality of the various villages and fishing grounds.

TRAPS. Various kinds of traps were common to all tribes. These traps were developed for use not only in the capture of fish but also the capture of both small and large game, and the snaring of birds and migratory fowl. Since we are principally concerned with the fishing activities of the Indians in the Pacific Northwest, our description of the traps will be limited to those developed for use in fishing.

An excellent example of native ingenuity and workmanship is depicted in the drawing of a fish trap which accompanies this section. Although submitted as an example of Snoqualmie craftsmanship, it is representative of fish traps of this type used throughout all of north-western Washington west of the Cascade Mountains. The similar trap developed by the Clallam Indians of the north Olympic Peninsula required even less energy in its operation inasmuch as provision was made for the retention of the trapped fish in an appropriate recess thus obviating the necessity of having an operator at the trap at all times. Such traps were emptied daily. Primary objective of this type of trap as well as many of the others developed for use under different physical conditions was to block completely the upstream passage of the salmon and other anadromous fish on the way up to their spawning grounds ordinarily located on the headwaters of the main streams or their tributaries. The trap show in the drawing ordinarily was used in the deeper water at the mouth of the relatively narrow streams common in the western Washington area, although not necessarily limited to use at the mouth of the stream, i.e., if the requisite water conditions were found up-stream, such traps were utilized.

Another type of trap commonly used in relatively shallow water, which consisted of a series of pickets across the stream, either led the salmon to points where openings had been provided and in which were located nets operated by a member of the tribe, or else completely blocked the stream and directed the fish to a point where they could be conveniently speared or netted with large dip nets. [18a]

SNOQUALMIE TRIBAL FISH TRAP

This tribes most important method of fishing utilized the large tribal trap, "*tee-loe-sit*".[9] It was erected principally for the taking of King salmon and steelhead which served to feed the whole tribe. The trap was constructed annually by hand without nails or wire and with no tools except primitive elk horn chisels and stone axes.

At a meeting of the tribe there was elected a head man who directed the building of the trap which was rather an important and difficult operation. The order in which the various operations were carried out was as follows: First, the tripod, "*skee-ok*", was erected with a long pole, "*spul-kit*" down stream extending possibly fifteen feet above water. About ten feet down from the top, poles, "*chee-lah*", were lashed across this tripod extending beyond the tripod poles upstream. Using these cross pieces as supports, the "*s-p-ti-kweel*" or foot-log, was laid across the entire width of the stream. Suspended from the foot-log was a second row of timbers across the stream above the water line called "*hkla-da-bat-sit*". From these two logs used as a foundation, poles approximately 4" in thickness, "*tla-bat-sit*", were shoved down into the bed of the river at a down stream angle so as to lean against the two legs described above. Across these shove-downs were placed a number of fir poles, "*ptda-la-bat sit*". Finally upon this framework was placed a finely woven cedar and willow bough network, "*a-a-qual*", or screen. This completed the weir or trap which constituted an effective bar against the further upstream passage of the fish. Upon the "*chee-lah*" described above was constructed a platform, "*suf-a-jockh*" where the operator stood holding two poles to which were attached a bag-like net held open by a large ring of cedar or willow twigs. To the center of this net was attached a trigger string, the other end of which was held in the hand of the operator. When he felt a fish hit this trigger string, he quickly pulled up the poles and the hoop, bringing the fish up in his net.

These traps were removed from the stream as soon as a sufficient supply of fish was obtained to satisfy the needs of the tribe, and in any event were removed before high water which would have carried away the weir and destroyed a valuable amount of material which was difficult to replace at that time.

Similar traps were operated by other coastal and Puget Sound tribes. See "Fishing Gear" in text. [19]

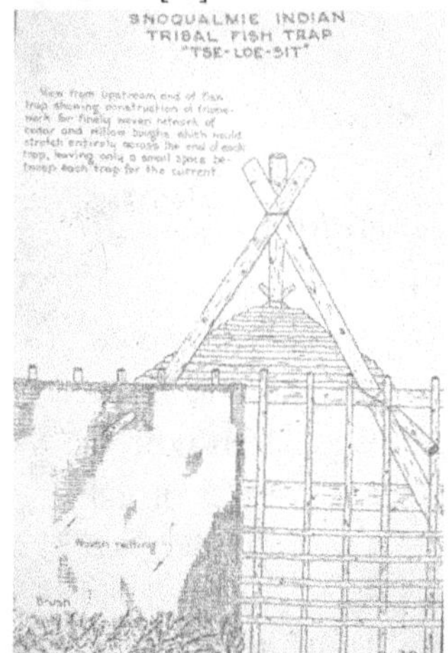

SNOQUALMIE INDIAN TRIBAL FISH TRAP
"TSE-LOE-SIT" [cǝlosǝd]

View from upstream end of fish trap showing construction of framework for finely woven network of cedar and willow boughs which would stretch entirely across the end of each trap, leaving only a small space between each trap for the current. [20]

Detailed description of the fish weirs or traps used by the Walla Walla and Shoshone Indians is set forth in the journals of the Lewis and Clark expedition. Since it is indicative of the abilities of the natives to obtain an adequate supply of their food prior to the coming of the white people and having been recorded in detail by what is probably the first whites to come in contact with them, it is reproduced for reference:

---

[9] [Arthur Ballard 1957 The Salmon-Weir on Green River in Western Washington. *Davidson Journal of Anthropology* 3: 37-53]

Shoshone Weir

"This morning early Capt. resumed his march; at the distance of five miles he arrived at some brush lodges of the Shoshones inhabited by about seven families. Here he halted and was very friendly received by these people, who gave himself and party much boiled salmon as they could eat; they also gave him several dried salmon and a considerable quantity of dried choke cherries. After smoking with them he visited their fish wear (weir) which was about 200 yards distant. he found the wear extended across four channels of the river which was here divided by three small islands. three of these channels were narrow, and were stopped by means of trees fallen across, supported by which stakes of willow were driven down sufficiently near each other to prevent the salmon from passing. about the center of each cilindric [cylindrical] basket of eighteen or 20 feet in length terminating in a conic shape at its lower extremity, formed of willows, was opposed to a small apperture in the wear [rear] with it's mouth up stream to receive the fish. The main channel of the water was conducted to this basket, which was so narrow at it's lower extremity that the fish when once in could not turn itself about, and were taken out by untying the small ends of the longitudinal willows, which form the hull of the basket. The weir in the main channel was somewhat differently contrived. There were two distinct wears formed of poles and willow sticks, quite across the river, at no great distance from each other. Each of those were furnished with two baskets; the one wear to take them ascending and the other in descending in constricting these wears, poles were first tyed together in parcels of three near the smaller extremity; these were set on end; and [21] spread in a triangular form at the base, in such manner, that two of the three poles ranged in the direction of the intended work, and the third down the stream. two ranges of horizontal poles were next lashed with willow bark and wythes to the ranging poles, and on these willow sticks were placed perpendicularly, reaching from the bottom of the river to about 3 or four feet above it's surface; and placed so near each other, as not to permit the passage of the fish, and even so thick in some parts, as with the help of gravel and stone to give a direction to the water which they wished. the baskets were the same in form of the others. this is the form of the work, and disposition of the baskets." /1/[10]

Walla Walla Weir

"This wear consists of two curtains of small willows wattled together with four lines of withes of the same materials extending quite across the river, parralal [parallel] with each other and about 6 feet asunder. Those are supported by several parrelals of poles placed in this manner. Those curtains of willows is either roled [rolled] at one end for a few feet to permit the fish to pass or are let down at pleasure. they take their fish which at present are a mullet only of from one to 6 pounds wt. with small seines of 15 or 18 feet long drawn by two persons; these they drag down to the wear and rase [raise] the bottom of the seine against the willow curtain, they have also a small seine managed by one parson, it bags in the manner of the scooping nets; the one side of the net is confined to simi-circular [semi-circular] bow of half the size of a man's arm and about

---

[10] 1/ Lewis and Clark, Vol. III, pp. 5-7.

5 feet long, the other side is confined to a strong string which being attached to the extremities of the bow forms the cord line to the semi-curcle." /2/[11]

The Clallams [S'Klallams] also constructed a basket like trap fifteen to twenty five feet in length. The trap was with a relatively large opening in one end and tapering to a point at the other. This is operated by placing the large end upstream [22] below a fall or other favorable spot where the salmon can be driven into the upper end by poles and subsequently removed through a gate in the lower smaller end.

NETS. From time immemorial practically all tribes utilized nets in one form or other for catching fish. The prediscovery inhabitants were familiar with the gill net as well as sets similar to the modern day haul seine. Other nets consisted of either dip nets or bag nets, both of which were attached to hoops made of willow or cyprus [cypress] at the end of a long pole. The latter two types of nets are still in use today at many places along the Columbia River and its tributaries. The dip net is smaller in size than the bag net and requires considerable labor in its operation inasmuch as it is necessary for the operator to manually sweep the net through the water in the hope that during the course of its sweep, a fish will be encountered. The bag net, however, aside from its construction, was simpler in operation. Being larger in size, it was not possible to sweep it through the water. Consequently all that is required of the operator, who stands on a platform or rock, is to submerge it in "white water" and patiently wait for a fish to enter the net and betray its presence to the operator through a jerk on the line which runs from the net to his hand.

Small shallow dip or scoop nets were used for the scooping up the uthlecan (candle fish)/1/[12] or herring during the seasons they were available along the coast or the lower reaches of the coastal streams.

At the mouth of the Columbia River the Indians obtained their supply of salmon through the use of large nets reportedly varying in size from 100 feet in length to as much as 100 fathoms or approximately 600 feet. In depth they ranged from seven to sixteen feet and were held in place through the use of a so-called float or cork line at the top, consisting of pieces of dried light wood attached for the purpose of keeping it afloat. The bottom of the net was held in place vertically through the use of weights or sinkers consisting of stones tied to the bottom line of the net itself. The manner of operation was similar to a haul seine with the exception [23a] that man power was used for operation until the introduction of more modem machinery. Swan in his book states that these particular nets were made of twine spun by the fishermen from the fibers of cyprus roots especially prepared for that purpose or from a species of grass obtained from other Indians. It is interesting to note in connection with this particular type of net that after the coning of the white man and the commencement and development of the commercial salmon canning industry, the Chinook Indians along the lower reaches of the river were employed by the canneries in catching the vast quantities required for utilization by the numerous canneries which quickly sprung into existence.

SNOQUALMIE FISHING GEAR
JUMP BASKET

____
[2/] Lewis and Clark, Vol. IV, p. 537.

[12] 1/ This name derives from the fact the flesh was so oily it was often used by Indians, as well as early settlers, for lighting purposes by inserting a dried twig or wick.

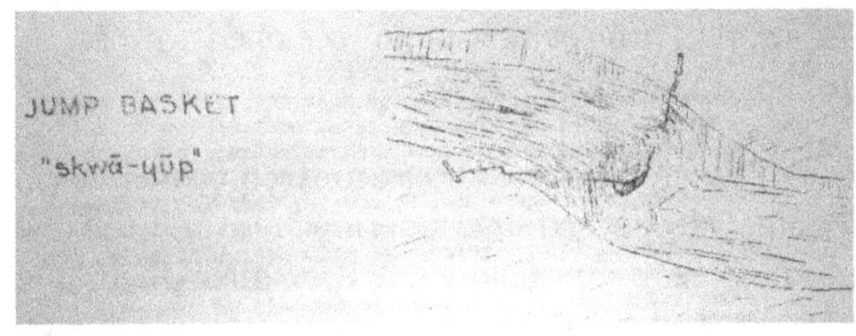

Such baskets, "*skwa-yup*" were used only on the smaller creeks. The trap consisted of a basket made of interwoven willow varying in size and length with the size of the stream. It was hung under small falls for the purpose of catching trout and other small fish descending the streams.

SMALL RIVER TRAP

This type of gear was used in small rivers and consisted of a trap, "*ska-loch*". It was made with a circular mouth of woven cedar limbs and willow twigs. From the mouth wings stretched out to either bank as guides to lead the fish to the opening. Gills of limber boughs extended from the opening into a large bag-like structure made of the sane material.

    1. Guides
    2. Bag
    3. Gills of limber cedar limbs

DIP NET SEINE

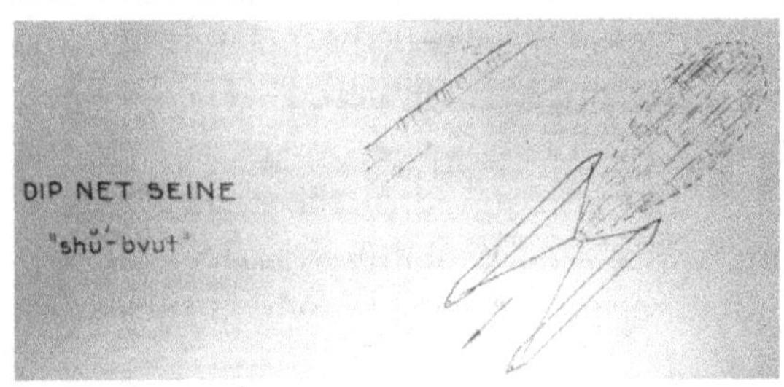

This was a fairly large seine, "*sku-bvut*", ?*? consisting of a long net bag made of "*kag-wahl*". The mouth of the net was held open by a ring of willow or cedar twigs fastened to two upright poles held in the stern of two canoes operating on each side of the bag. To the lower end of each pole was a heavy cord extending to the prow of the canoe in which the pole was held. Since fishing with this type of gear was principally practiced at night, a burning torch of pitch wood was affixed to the prow of each canoe. The canoes were paddled down stream by the prow operators with the stern operators pushing the poles down toward the bottom. When a fish was felt to enter the net bag, the cords in the prow of the boat were pulled up thus raising the mouth of the net out of the water, after which the fish was then dumped into the boat. This system was used in the large rivers and a variation of this type was also operated by one canoe and one man.

This type of gear was commonly used by the coastal and Puget Sound tribes. [24]

In all instances until the coming of the whites it was necessary that the nets be manufactured from materials available in the particular locality or, as indicated by Swan, obtained through trade with other tribes. Along the Pacific coast of the Olympic Peninsula the nets were usually manufactured from cedar bark which was shredded and woven into twine and then formed into the mesh of the net./1/[13] To the east of the mountains where such material was not available, the Indians principally used & twine manufactured from a weed common throughout the entire eastern area and known nowadays as "Indian hemp". The outer covering of the weed was dried and shredded, then woven into the required twine. The Indians assert that irrespective of which of the various materials was used in the manufacture of nets, the material when properly prepared permitted the manufacture of twine as strong if not stronger than the commercially manufactured and more conveniently obtainable twine now used by the Indians in the manufacture of their nets.

---

[13] 1/ The Lummi Indians used willow bark. United States vs. Alaska Packer's Ass'n, 79 Fed. 152, 154. Other tribes were dependent on local material, e.g., the Clallams and Makahs often used dried kelp.

SPEARS, GAFFS, HOOKS, ETC. Such gear was commonly used by practically all tribes. The use of spears and gaffs, however, was limited to those places where the fish could be plainly seen by the fisherman as distinguished from the place of use for dip and bag nets where it was necessary that the water be swift and foaming so as to prevent the fish from seeing the net. Due to the size and strength of the salmon obtained from the various stream, the spears and some gaff hooks had to be so constructed that the weight and struggles of the fish would not snap the slender staff to which the spearhead or hook was attached. The head of the spear was constructed of deer or elk horn securely fastened with native twine in a socket made from a bone found in the foreleg of [25] either of those animals. The end of the shaft was fitted into the socket in such a manner that after the spearhead had penetrated a fish, it became detached and turned sideways in the wound. The head, however, was still firmly attached to the body of the shaft by a length of twine. The spearsman was then enabled to play the fish, somewhat similar to a present day rod fisherman, until it tired sufficiently to permit it to be taken from the water.

Harpoons used in the pursuit and capture of the large marine animals were constructed in the same manner although the line attached to the head was quite often several hundred feet in length, on the other end of which was fastened the bladder of a sea otter or seal filled with air. This device floated on the surface of the water and enabled the hunters to follow the course of the wounded animal as well as ascertain its location after it tired out or died.

Fish rakes, consisting of a pole to which many sharp bones were attached, were used by coastal and Sound groups to take herring when the enormous schools of that fish appeared in the coastal waters.

Hooks and their use were also known to a great many of the tribes especially in the waters along the coast and Sound. The following excerpts are taken from Bulletin 30, Handbook of American Indians, B.A.E., under the headings "Fishhooks" and "Fishing", Vol. 1, pp. 461 and 463:

"Fishhooks — Starting from the simple device of attaching the bait to the end of a line, the progressive order of fishhooks used by the Indians seems to be (a) the gorge nook - a spike of bone or wood, sharpened at both ends and fastened at its middle to a line; (b) a spike set obliquely in the end of a pliant shaft; (c) the plain hook; (d) the barbed hook; (e) the barbed hook combined with a sinker and lure. Material used was wood, bone, shell, stone and copper. * * * The Makahs had a modified form of gorge hook consisting of a shank of wood, a splint of pinewood lashed at an angle of 45° to its lower end, and a simple or barbed spike of bone, wood, iron or copper lashed or set on the outer end of the splint. * * * In some regions as on the northwest coast, a trawl consisting of a [26] series of hooks attached by leaders to a line, was used for taking certain species of fish."/1/[14]
* * * though the natives of the Pacific Coast used fishhooks of wood and bone combined * * * another ingenious device employed along the North Pacific Coast, consisted of a straight pin, sharp at both ends and fastened to a line at the middle. * * * Artificial bait, made of stone and bone combined, was used as a lure and was quite as attractive to fish as is the artificial bait of the civilized fishermen."

---

[14] 1/ The references to copper and iron as materials used in the manufacture of these articles relate to such usage after those materials were available as a result of contact with the whites. [Native copper was widely traded and valued for millennia.]

Probably the most primitive method of obtaining sea food in any fashion was practiced by some of the coastal tribes in obtaining soles end flounders. These were taken by hand after the tide had receded leaving shallow pools in which the fish could be located by use of their feet.

Due to the tremendous numbers of salmon ascending some streams, quite often a sufficient supply was obtained by using a club to knock them on the head.

Clams, cockles, and other shell fish were dug and taken by hand by wading or diving.

*****

References:

Affidavits of descendants of several of the original tribes.
Bancroft - 185-6, 212-3, 233, 261-2 and footnote.
Eells, pp. 655-5.
Goddard. - pp.
Irving - 455, 514.
Lewis and Clark – Vol. 5, pp. 107-242; inc., and Vol. 4, 243-547, inc.
Swan – N.W. Coast, 38-41, 104, 264.
        Cape Flattery, 19-30.
Wilkes - Vol. 4, 345, 380, 384.   [2 falls pix 27] [28]

ANCIENT INDIAN FISHING GROUNDS ON THE COLUMBIA RIVER

Kettle Falls, Columbia River

Illustrating type of aboriginal fishing gear used by the natives long prior to their discovery by the whites. The Indians using this type of gear were known as *"Quiarlpi"* (basket people), having derived their name from their use of this gear. Wilkes (1845) advises that the basket was made of wicker and supported by long poles and that the fish in attempting to jump the falls struck the broad frame and would fall back into the basket. This site has been destroyed by the waters impounded behind the Grand Coulee Dam.

Celilo Falls, Mid-Columbia River

Indians fishing from the same rocks and with the same gear employed by their ancestors prior to discovery by the Americans. There are several rocks and islands at the falls and on each is located a number of "fishing stations". Each station was recognized as belonging to some family or group of families and had its own particular Indian name. The fishing stations shown are covered by water in the spring of the year and are only available after the peak flow of the river has passed. Note salmon enmeshed in bag net in center of picture; also, safety ropes attached to each Indian as a result of regulation by the Indian Celilo Fish Committee. Dip and bag nets were and still are employed at this place. Use of the spear has died out. During the height of the run it is not uncommon for the fisherman to find two or three fish in his net. Reproduced from Bulletin No. 32, U.S. Bureau of Fisheries. [27 2 images]   [28]

TRADE AND INTERCOURSE

From the accounts of the early explorers and settlers it is evident that a considerable volume of trade was carried on between the several tribes in the Pacific Northwest. Since with rare exceptions/1/[15] money or its equivalent was non-existent, the inter-tribal trade was carried on through the primitive method of barter – the exchange of one commodity or artifact for another. Generally speaking, the various staples such as game, fish, roots and berries, which comprised the more important items in the prevalent diet, were the principal articles of trade although it was not uncommon for the tribes to barter for other articles. The various articles of food as previously indicated were found in abundant quantities throughout the entire area. Due to its size, however, it was only natural that the type or species of such items varied considerably in the domains of the several tribes. On the coast all kinds of shell fish and the many salt water varieties of fish were readily available to the natives as was the flesh, blubber, and oil of the larger marine animals. Such species of course were not found in the inland fresh waters. It has been recorded, however, that the interior tribes highly prized such items which provided a pleasant change from the limited standard diet prevalent in their own territory. They, the interior tribes, in turn possessed skins of animals and different varieties of fish, roots, and berries which were desirable to the coastal tribes. Barter between the adjoining tribes, therefore, involving the exchange of scarce or nonexistent commodities was inevitable.

While there is evidence that some tribes may have traveled hundreds of miles for the purpose of trading or to wage war, it does not follow that such long journeys were the customary practice. That is, contact between the coastal and Puget Sound tribes and those of the eastern sections of the northwest area was not necessarily direct. The principal system which appears to have existed is readily described as one of infiltration where tribes in contiguous areas exchanged their respective [29] commodities, which in turn were traded with other contiguous tribes and thus gradually found their way across the country. It has been reported that in the burial grounds of the tribes of the mid-Columbia River area, there have been found buttons from the uniforms of the Imperial Russian Navy, as well as other items such as iron kettles and knives, indicating early contacts with members of civilized communities comprising the various expeditions which explored the northwest coast in the latter part of the 18th and the early part of the 19th centuries. The mid-Columbia River area, of course, is situated far above the mouth of the river and both banks in the intervening distance were inhabited by a number of separate and distinct tribes. They were, however, considered as component units of the Chinookan, Shahaptian, and Athapascan-Tlatskanai {*Swaal*} linguistic families which inhabited both banks of the Columbia River from the mouth of the Snake River to the mouth of the Columbia. Since these groups, which have often been referred to as Columbia River Indians, were not noted for far-ranging travel aside from their annual visits to the mountains in their own particular locality to obtain roots and berries in season, or to meet and trade with other tribes at major aboriginal trading centers along the river or at some of the jointly used root and berry grounds, it is logical to assume that the items found in the burial grounds came into the possession of the upper river groups through infiltration extending over many years of barter between the intermediate tribes./1/[16]

---

[15] 1/ Shell money of some of the coastal tribes, e.g., the Makahs and Clallams.

[16] 1/ As to the buttons, there appears to be no record of Russian discovery of the Columbia. In any event, passage beyond the Cascade Rapids was not possible. [??]

Numerous references to the existence of a well defined and long established system of trade are found in the works of early explorers and settlers, as well as later day historians. By reason of the fact that most of the early accounts were written by travelers using the Columbia River and its tributaries as their highways, the majority of references to prediscovery trade amongst the Indians deal with such activities concluded at what might be termed the major Indian trading centers along the banks of the main stream and principal tributaries. These centers appear to have been frequented by representatives not only of the bands residing along the rivers but in addition appear to have quite often been visited by groups from the Rocky Mountain [30] >>

CELILO FALLS, OREGON

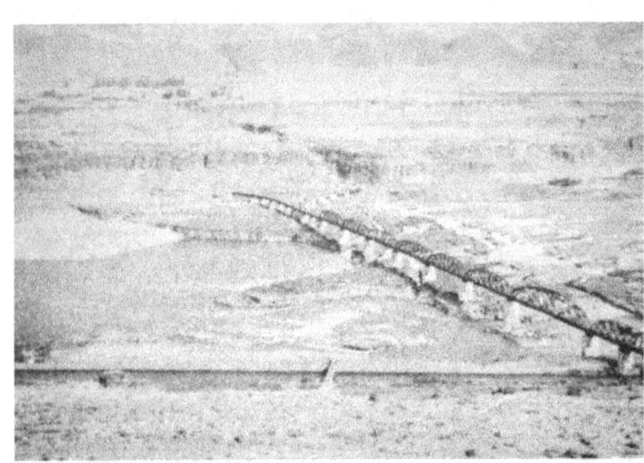

Fall Bridge across the Columbia River just below the falls, showing a number of the rocks from which the Indians fish during the annual salmon runs. The sandy appearing area in the extreme left center was the location of the ancient village of the Skein Indians who derived their name from the fact that the land on which their village was located is in the shape of a "cradle board".

View of Celilo Falls on the Columbia River showing the principal rocks and islands from which the Indians engage in commercial and subsistence fishing. In the right center between the railroad tracks and the highway, as well as to the right of the highway, are the houses which form the present Indian village of Celilo. This is the modern day counterpart of the ancient village of Wishram. The original village was located at the point where the Army canal takes out from the river downstream from the white tower.

Another view of Celilo Falls. On the large island in the foreground are located numerous "custom fishing stations" known to the Yakama Indians as *Wah-peaa-ush*. Transportation to the large island as well as to the smaller islands at the extreme right hand side of the picture is accomplished through the use of cable ways. Prior to the acquisition of such means of transportation the Indians reached the fishing stations by swimming downstream with the current. Needless to say, a safety line was attached to the swimmer.

>> [31] region. The principal of these major trading centers on the main stream, commencing down stream, were those located at Cascade Rapids, The Dalles, the mid-river falls of the Columbia River, known as Celilo Falls and at Kettle Falls on the upper Columbia near the

Canadian border. Near The Dalles was located the well-known trading center of Wishram (*Nixluidix*) of the Tlakluit tribe at the Chinookan family. This place is now known as Spearfish, Washington, and here today reside a few descendants of the original inhabitants. The trading center at the main falls of the Columbia at the time of the discovery was known as *Wyam* and occupied by members of a tribe of the same name belonging to the Shahaptian family. Similar centers were located on the tributary streams of which the better known were those located at the falls of the Willamette River, where Oregon City, Oregon, now stands, the falls of the Spokane, River near Spokane, Washington, and Salmon Falls on the Snake River.

In the accounts of the Lewis and Clark expedition will be found that is probably the earliest recorded reference to the trading activity of the Indians at the mouth of and along the banks of the main stream and some of its tributaries. In addition to referring to several or the above-named places, specific, reference is made to a very large number of other Indian villages and fishing places located on both the north and south banks of the stream. The situes {sites} of such places is indicated on sketch maps /1/[17] showing the main stream from a short distance below the entrance of the Snake River to the Pacific Ocean.

During the period commencing April, 1811, with the founding of Astoria, the first settlement on the Columbia River, until the establishment of the Hudson Bay Company's post in 1824, it is reported that the Indians located at *Wyam* were the cause of a great deal of trouble as a result of their control of the portage which the presence of the falls in the river made mandatory. They are reported as having practically prohibited members of other tribes from passing downstream to the lower reaches of the Columbia. It is further stated that they acted as traders in that they purchased commodities from the tribes located upstream or east of their village as well as from the tribes located downstream or west thereof. In this fashion they acted as [32] intermediaries both buying from and selling to the tribes from east and west, thus realizing a profit on both ends of the transactions. Due to their position at the falls and their ability to defend themselves, they retained this trade as a tribal enterprise.

Wilkes, in his narrative report of the United States exploring expedition, after referring to the method followed by the Indians' in catching the fish at the main fishing spots along the Columbia River, as well as the way in which the surplus quantities of salmon, were preserved for future use or trade, states that after the fishing and trading season was over they (referring to the visiting Indians) retired to their villages and passed the rest of the year in inactivity.

Washington Irving in his "Astoria", after giving a detailed account of the manner in which the Indians obtained their fish and preserved them, goes on to describe the trade carried on at Wishram in the following language: "We have given this process at some length, as furnished by the first explorers, because it marks a practiced ingenuity in preparing articles of traffic for a market, seldom seen among our aboriginals. For like reason we would make especial mention of, the village of Wishram, at, the head of the Long Narrows, as being a solitary instance of an aboriginal trading mart, or emporium. Here the salmon caught in the neighboring rapids, were "warehoused", to await customers. Hither the tribes from the mouth of the Columbia repaired with the fish of the sea-coast, the roots, berries and especially the wappatoo, gathered in the lower parts of the river, together with goods and trinkets obtained from the ships which occasionally visit the coast. Hither also the tribes from the Rocky Mountains brought down horses, beargrass, quamash, and other commodities of the interior. The merchant fishermen at the falls acted as middlemen or factors, and passed the objects of traffic, as it were, crosshanded;

---

[17] 1/ Lewis and Clark Atlas, Vol. VIII. Maps Nos. 32, Pts. 1, 2, and 3; 33 and 34, and 35, Pt. 4.

trading away part of the wares received from the mountain tribes to those of the rivers and plains, and vice versa; their packages of pounded salmon [33] entered largely into the system of barter, and being carried off in opposite directions, found their way to the savage hunting camps far in the interior, and to the occasional white traders who touched upon the coast." /1/[18]

Later on in the same work he refers to the annual run of the uthlecan which occurs only in the lower part of the river and which constituted a valued article of trade amongst the Indians. A similar reference is made by Caughey where it is stated in effect that the oil obtained after these fish had been cooked was highly prized for the purpose of making dried salmon palatable and the tribes that did not have access to waters in which these fish were found, obtained their supply by trade over trails appropriately known as "grease trails". Numerous other references are contained in works of contemporary writers with regard to the nature and extent of the trade that did exist among the Columbia River tribes and the tribes in the areas both north and south of the banks of that stream.

While the foregoing specific references are primarily limited to the interior inter-tribal trade, similar trading activities were carried out between the various Indian groups at the mouth of the Columbia River as well as north and south on the coast. In this connection it is interesting to note that the Chinookan tribes at the mouth of the river traded both with the coastal tribes to the north and south as well as with the river tribes to the east, or interior.

Swan, in his very interesting work on the Northwest Coast, makes reference to the oyster fishery at Shoalwater Bay on the west Washington coast in which he indicates that hundreds of Indians came to this point from tribes to the north and that some of the Indians prosecuting the oyster fishery came from as far as the regions around Puget Sound. In the same work he refers to the fact that clams were taken in great quantities and that after they were dried, they formed an esteemed article of trade with the Indians of the interior inasmuch as quantities annually were carried from Shoalwater Bay up the Columbia. Other shellfish and salt water fish were similarly treated and used for trading purposes. He also points out that the nets of the Indians residing [34] at the mouth of the Columbia were made from the fibers of spruce roots obtained from Indians to the north; also, that the flesh of the salmon caught at the mouth was used in trade with interior Indians after being prepared through pounding into the form of pemmican and stored in baskets containing 10 to 12 pounds each. While the exchange of salmon of the same species between tribes on the same stream having access to the source of supply might appear odd, such trade existed for the reason that although the salmon caught at the mouth of the river was of the same species as that caught farther upstream, the taste of the flesh or products therefrom was entirely different. This results from the fact, well known to ichthyologists, that salmon are in a prime condition at the time they leave the ocean to return to the spawning grounds on the headwaters of their native streams. Since they do not feed after leaving salt water, the energy required for the tortuous upstream journey is derived from the oil stored up during that part or their life spent in salt water. Consequently, the flavor and texture of the flesh deteriorates the farther upstream the fish travels until finally when the spawning grounds are reached, the once abundant supply of oil is exhausted.

It is true that Swan's observations covered the three year immediately before and after the negotiation and execution of the treaties with the several tribes. There is no reason to believe, however, that such intertribal trade was not carried on in the same fashion prior to the time the Indians were first *discovered*.

---

[18] 1/ p. 150.

Bancroft, in his work on native races, also referring to the Chinook Indians residing on the lower Columbia, states that before the arrival of the Europeans, they annually repaired to the region of the Cascades and The Dalles where they met with the tribes from the interior with whom they exchanged their few articles of trade such as fish, oil, shells and wapato for the skins, roots, and grasses of their eastern neighbors. In speaking of the interior Indians, such as the Nez Perce, Palous, Walla Walla, Yakama and Klickitat, and others, he states that few tribes live altogether without salmon inasmuch as those dwelling on streams inaccessible to the salmon by reason of intervening falls are accustomed to obtain their supply by annual migrations to the fishing grounds or by trade with other nations. [35]

Although the preceding references concern trade as carried on between the Indians prior to the advent of the whites, they did engage in a considerable volume of trade with the whites after the latter arrived and settled in the territory. This trade in increasing proportions continued to be carried on up to and beyond the time of the treaties.

The early settlers, in lieu of catching their fish themselves, obtained salmon for their own subsistence through trade with the Indians, inasmuch as sufficient quantities could be obtained in return for various articles coveted by the natives but of negligible value to the white owners. The volume of inter-racial trade gradually increased with the increase in the population and the establishment of white trading posts, including that of the Hudson Bay Company. In due course as the food value of the product became appreciated, a demand arose for salmon to be cured for commercial export purposes. At first, and until in the course of time whites almost completely replaced the Indians as operators in the major fisheries, the actual fishing operations were almost entirely in the hands of the Indians as a consequence of their knowledge of the fishery, their available equipment, and their undeniable skill in the use thereof.

References to the Indian participation in the early fishing is found in the Lewis and Clark journals and David Thompson's account of his explorations in Western America. The former expedition, of course, throughout its entire journey along the Columbia River from the mouth of the Snake River to the Pacific Ocean was to a great extent dependent on the generosity of or barter with the Indians for food, including fresh and cured salmon. Thompson, in his narrative, refers to the fact that at the time of his visit to the first white settlement at Ft. Astoria, the traders were having difficulty in establishing a standard of barter for salmon with the Indians. Apparently a satisfactory standard was not established until some 20 years later or at about the time the first commercial operations looking to the export of salmon were initiated. An interesting account of trade between natives and The Hudson Bay Company on the Frazer River in Canada is contained in the History of the Salmon Industry, Commonwealth Review - 1932-33, by Mildred Vera Hayden, which is quoted: [36]

"The Hudson's Bay Company was the first to engage in salmon fishing. Salted and pickled salmon were staple food products at the Hudson's Bay Company's posts during their entire stay in the Oregon country. In the late twenties they began a commercial trade in salmon. In 1829, at Fort Langley, on the Frazer River, the Company bought 7,544 salmon of the Indians at a cost of a little less than a cent a piece. By 1846, 2,000 barrels of salmon were being cured annually for the Company's use and exportation. The salmon were caught by the Indians and traded to the Company; then cured and made ready to ship. Dunn gives the following description of the mode of curing salmon.

"'As soon as a cargo of salmon is caught, the natives bring it to the trading post in their canoes. A number of Indian women are employed by the trader, seated on the beach with knives, ready to cut up the fish. The fish are counted from each Indian, for which a ticket is given for the quantity, large or small. After the whole of the salmon are landed, Indians congregate around the trading shop for their payments, and receive ammunition, baize, tobacco, etc.'"

"In 1834 Nathaniel Wyeth organized The Columbia River Fishing and Trading Company, intending to carry on the fur trade and salmon trade jointly. The Indians were so under the control of the Hudson's Bay Company that he could not buy from them and was obliged to give up his enterprise and selling his goods to the Hudson's Bay Company."

The reference to Dunn is to the work of John Dunn published under the title ·"The Oregon Territory and the British North American Fur Trade". Although his description, as well as that of Miss Hayden, concern trade between other than the natives with which we are here concerned, the situation in the early days in the Pacific Northwest was substantially the same. It is reported that the Wyeth enterprise established at the mouth of the Willamette, and referred to in the above excerpt, failed for the reason that the Hudson Bay Company was both willing and able to offer the Indians more goods [37] or money for their fish. Reference ill also found to the fact that one of the early exploiters of the industry paid the Indians three leaves from a twist or knot of tobacco for each fish.

As settlement of the territory continued the demand for salmon both for subsistence and export purposes increased. When the value of the commercial industry, then limited to salt curing or pickling of the fish, increasingly interested White interests, the early Indian monopolization of the fishing operations gradually went into a decline until ultimately the great majority of the Indians acted only as employees of the commercial interests. That situation, however, related principally to the lower reaches and mouth of the Columbia, which area was the first to be thickly settled. Elsewhere trade between the Indians and whites continued.

Additional references to such trade are found in practically all accounts concerning the early history of the area. Swan frequently refers to it. In one instance, he, in talking of Shoalwater Bay,/1/[19] states in effect that the bay and all streams entering it are well stocked with large numbers of several varieties of salmon, which in addition to being taken for their own food, were also used "for trading with the whites". This it will be remembered was within the period during which the treaties were negotiated and signed. (1854-56). Territorial Governor Stevens when negotiating with the Quinaielts, Quileutes, Cowlitz, Chehalis, and others in February 1855, among other things advised the assembled Indians "* * * if any of you want to go to Shoalwater Bay to dig oysters for pay, we want you to do so".

References:

Affidavits of descendants of several of the tribes.
Bancroft, pp. 163, 273 and footnote pp. 273-4.
Bureau of Fisheries Bulletin No. 32, 147-8.
Irving, p. 150.
Lewis and Clark, Vol. III, pp. 107 - 242; Vol. IV, p. 243-347.
Swan, p. 26.
Thompson, p ?? [38]

SUMMARY OF NATIVE FOOD, FISHING GEAR, AND TRADING ACTIVITIES

---

[19] 1/ p. 26, 37.

The foregoing discussion, it is appreciated, is fragmentary in scope and by no means complete in so far as it would be possible to cover the subjects if such were the primary object of this report. It was included for the purpose of giving the reader a general idea of the conditions affecting aboriginal life in the Pacific Northwest prior to, at the time of, and subsequent to the discovery and settlement of the area.

It should be evident therefrom that the natives of the area although not considered as being as far advanced in the arts of civilization as other previously contacted natives of the North American continent, were sufficiently advanced in the art of living to the extent that they readily obtained an adequate subsistence from the abundant, though limited in variety, natural food resources of the region. This was true even though at times through the improvident use of reserve supplies, some groups were on the verge of starvation. It should also be evident that the requisite food supply was obtained through the use of implements devised by the native mind and constructed with the most primitive tools from the limited materials which nature placed at their disposal.

Finally it should be clear that during the period prior to discovery, variety in the diet could be and was provided for through trade and intercourse with neighboring tribes, and, further, that such trading activities were carried on with the N1ites after discovery and. settlement of the country.

The fact that such were the exacting conditions has an important bearing on the interpretation the Indians have placed on the nature and extent of the rights reserved to them in their treaties, and, especially so with regard to fishing rights. Of particular importance in connection with the protection of what rights are still possessed by the Indians is the fact that inter-tribal and [39] racial trade existed throughout the entire area. Efforts have been and no doubt will continue to be made to limit such rights ill so far as commercial fishing is concerned. The fact that the treaties made no mention of the right of the Indians to dispose of fish by sale or barter apparently carried considerable weight with the United States Circuit Court of Appeals for the Ninth Circuit in its opinion handed down June 12, 1942, in a case involving the fishing rights of the Makah /1/[20] tribe. In reversing the judgment of the District Court enjoining the authorities of the State of Washington from interfering with the Indians in the sale of their fish, the court said:

> "Such an injunction is unwarranted for there is no allegation of the pleadings which mentions a threatened interference with regard to the sale of fish taken by the Makah tribe and the treaty is silent on the right of the Indians to dispose of the fish by sale or barter after they have been taken." (Emphasis supplied.) [40]

SOURCE OF HUNTING AND FISHING RIGHTS
PAST AND PRESENT

From time immemorial the natives were accustomed to hunt, fish, and acquire other articles 'of food both for subsistence and trading purposes without such pursuits being subject to any limitations other than those imposed by nature. This freedom from restrictions continued until the coming of the whites in such numbers, and the industrial development of the area

---

[20] 1/ B.P. McCauley, et a1 vs. Makah Indian Tribe, 128 F (2d) 867.

resulted in the depletion of the fish and wild life resources to such an extent as to necessitate the enactment of legislation looking to the protection and conservation of those resources.

Hunting, fishing, and other activities were carried on, in season, at the will of the individual or tribal unit as necessity demanded. The aboriginal mind had no concept of rights to pursue activities along these lines, as such rights are recognized to exist today. Their activities in this connection were motivated solely by the natural law of self-preservation rather than any desire to engage in such pursuits for the purpose of sport. In no way were the natives' activities governed or limited as a result of any man-made law.

This unrestricted use by the natives of the available natural resources, represented by the teeming fish and wild life populations, continued for quite some time after discovery of the region and exploration and settlement had brought countless thousands of Americans to reside therein. In common with the natives these newcomers also hunted and fished without regard to any manmade regulations.

This state of affairs continued until a considerable time after the treaties with the several tribes had been negotiated. Consequently, at the time the treaty negotiations were being carried on, conservation measures limiting hunting and fishing activities were unknown to the Indians. It is quite probable that the same can be said for the representatives of the Government, although conservation of such natural resources then not entirely unknown in the east. In any event, it does not [41] appear unreasonable to assume that at the time the treaty councils were held, little if any thought was given to the possibility that the limiting of hunting and fishing activities other than for the protection of private property rights, might some day become an established reality./1/[21] At that time the known supply of fish and game which had served as the principal source of food for countless generations, appeared inexhaustible.

The foregoing assumption is not illogical despite the fact that at that time a large number or settlers had already arrived in the region and it was anticipated that these would be followed by even larger numbers in the immediate future, resulting in an appreciable increase in the population of the area over that estimated as residing therein at the time or its discovery. It hardly seems that the extent of the present day development of this area with its many industries was then anticipated. Least of all is it reasonable to beli.tw, that it could then be foreseen that the discovery and subsequent improvement in the canning industry followed by its tremendous growth, would result in the serious depletion in the supply of the various species of fish which inhabited the local waters in incredible numbers, inasmuch as prior unrestricted utilization of such resource from time immemorial had apparently not seriously affected the supply. This is true even though the fishing by the Indians was accomplished with types or traps and weirs which, it has been charged, completely blocked the upstream passage of the annual runs; Although in sane respects the natives were improvident, they certainly should not be charged with such failing in connection with their fishing operations certainly the existence of large numbers of fish in practically all streams of the area at the time of discovery furnishes ample proof that their fishing operations were not wantonly destructive and carried on without thought to their future welfare.

From the foregoing then it is evident that at the time the treaty councils were held, the inhabitants in the area – Indian and non-Indian alike – [42] enjoyed what might be termed natural or inherent rights to hunt and fish without restrictions other than those imposed by nature or for

---

21 1/ <u>New York ex rel Kennedy v. Becker</u>, 241 U.S. 551, 563; 60 L. ed. 1166, 1172.

the protection of property rights. The Supreme Court of the United States in describing the pretreaty rights of the Indian stated the extent of such rights in the following language:

> "The right to resort to the fishing places in controversy was a part of larger rights possessed by the Indians, <u>upon the exercise of which there was not a shadow of impediment</u>, and which were not much less necessary to the existence of the Indians than the atmosphere they breathed"/1/[22] (Underscoring supplied.)

With the above in mind as describing the conditions existing up to the time of the treaties, the next step to be considered concerns the Indians' rights under the treaties as ·such have been construed by the courts as being limited by fish and wildlife conservation measures. Before examining such rights, however; one would do well to bear in mind the circumstances which motivated the Government in entering into the treaties in question.

It will be recalled that throughout the first seventy years or so of the 19th century and in particular the period from 1810 to 1855 considerable friction developed between the natives and the settlers in the Pacific Northwest area. It was only natural that after the initial awe and bewilderment, arising from contacts with the *up-to-that-time unknown* white race, the natives should resent the encroachment upon their ancestral holdings by the ever growing tide of immigrants, a great many of whom were thoroughly unscrupulous and who did not hesitate to rob and personally exploit the natives. It no doubt became apparent to the Indians that the ever increasing white population threatened to engulf the native population, which during the years immediately following the establishment of Astoria had been enormously reduced in numbers due to the ravages of smallpox and other diseases introduced by the whites and to which the natives were extremely susceptible. [43]

Consequently, friction between the two races rapidly developed as the result of numerous incidents which frequently culminated in sanguinary massacres. The whites although originally inferior numerically, enjoyed greater success in the outcome of their clashes with the natives due to their superiority in weapons with which the natives could not contend. The Federal Government, therefore, adopted the previously formed policy of concentration and resettlement of the natives on compact areas considerably smaller than those formerly claimed by them. Since at that tine it was still the policy of the Government to treat with the natives on the basis of its recognition of the various tribes as being independent nations endowed with the quality of sovereignty, the Government's aims were to be achieved through the assumption of reciprocal obligations on its part and that of the several tribes. The primary objectives of the government were twofold: first, it was considered politic to extinguish through purchase the Indians' recognized title or right of occupancy /1/[23] to the lands claimed by the several tribes, and, secondly, to resettle the several tribes on reservations to be set aside and reserved for their exclusive use and benefit. It was thus hoped that the principal cause of the unsatisfactory relationship between the races; viz, unrestricted contact and exploitation of the unschooled natives by unscrupulous whites, would be removed. The ceded area then would be available for settlement and developnent without the people living in fear of constantly threatening Indian uprisings. With these primary objects in mind the representatives of the Federal Government held a number of councils at various points throughout Washington and Oregon Territories which meetings were attended by the tribes inhabiting the vicinity of such council grounds.

---

[22] 1/ <u>U.S. v. Winans</u>, 198 U.S. 371, 381; 49 L. ed. 1089, 1092.
[23] 1/ <u>Johnson v. McIntosh</u>, 21 U.S. 543; 5 L. ed. 681.

After having the objectives of the Government explained to them, the Indians, among other things, were assured that within ·the boundaries of the lands to be set aside for their exclusive use and benefit, they could continue to hunt and fish as they always had./2/[24]   Under the conditions then existing such a right presumably need not have been mentioned since it no doubt was contemplated such exclusive privilege would inure to the Indians. [44]

In addition to the assurance of such right within the reservation other assurances were given them concerning fishing, hunting, root digging and berry gathering, which activities could be engaged in beyond the boundaries of the reserved lands. It is with this class of rights that we are particularly concerned with at the present time inasmuch as state fish and wild life conservation measures are not applicable to Indians while engaged in hunting or fishing on Indian restricted or tribal lands within their reservations.

At the time provision was made in the treaties for such non-reservation rights, it must not be overlooked that they constituted an entirely different character of right than what we nowadays consider the right to hunt or fish under the laws of the several states. The rights provided for in the treaties differed from our present day conception of such rights in that the right intended to be reserved in reality consisted of the privilege of leaving the confines of the areas which were to be set aside for the Indians' exclusive use. The Supreme Court in the Becker case, supra, succinctly stated this difference when it said:

> "But it is idle to suppose that there was any actual anticipation at the time the treaty was made of the conditions now existing to which the legislation in question was addressed. Adopted when game was plentiful - when the cultivation contemplated by the whites was not expected to interfere with its abundance - it can hardly be supposed that the thought of the Indians was concerned with the necessary exercise of inherent power under modern conditions for the preservation of wild life."

Unlike the Indians whose rights were at issue in that case, however, our Indians of the Pacific Northwest at the time of their treaties, were not aware of the existence of state sovereignty and all that was necessarily implied therein as was pointed out by the court. [45]

Aside from that consideration, however, it was important that the Indians retain the right to leave the reservation for the purpose of obtaining food from their traditional tribally owned sources of supply. Accordingly, the treaties provided that the Indians were "secured" in the right of taking fish

> "at all usual and accustomed grounds or stations" * * * "in common with all citizens of the Territory, and of erecting temporary houses for the purpose of curing, together with the privilege of hunting, gathering roots am berries, and pasturing their horses on open and unclaimed lands *** "/1/[25]

The foregoing provision, therefore, constitutes the source of any special rights the Indians may possess at the present time. Just what such rights are is hereinafter discussed. It is to be noted, however, that the only restrictions on the rights was that the right to take fish was to be exercised "in common with all citizens of the territory;" and that hunting and the other activities were only to be engaged in upon open and unclaimed lands.

---

[24] 2/ See minutes of treaty councils, Appendix "A".

[25] 1/ Medicine Creek Treaty of Dec. 26, 1854, 10 Stat. 1132; 2 Kappler 661, with Nisqually Tribe, et al. All treaties, however, contained substantially the same provision.

In construing the similar provision in the treaty with the Yakama Indians, the Supreme Court in the Winans case, supra, in its discussion of the source of the Indians' rights pointed out that the treaty

"was not a grant of rights to the Indians, but a grant of rights from them, - a reservation of those not granted. And the form of the instrument and its language was adapted to that purpose." /2/[26]

Other courts have also judicially recognized that the rights of the Indians such as they may be~ are predicated on their reserving them from the grant of lands, etc., to the United States rather than on a grant from the government to them. US v. Taylor, 3 Wash. Terr. 88, 13 Pac. 333; Winters v. US, 207; US 564; 52 L. ed. 340; Seufert v. Olney 193 Fed. 200; US v. Cutler, 37 F. Supp. 724 (1941). [46]

THE GENERAL NATURE AND EXTENT OF THE TREATY RIGHTS

With the exceptions hereafter noted, the rights specifically reserved by the several treaties were substantially the same. An analysis of the treaties shows that such specifically reserved rights as well as those held to have been impliedly reserved, can be conveniently classified and discussed under the following headings:

I. Fishing Rights – Reservation and NonReservation, the latter including the right to erect
    structures in which to cure the catch.
II. Hunting Rights – Reservation and NonReservation
III. Right to Dig Roots and Gather Berries.
IV. Right of Pasturage.

The most important of those rights when viewed in the light of present day conservation measures, of course, are those relating to hunting and fishing, although at the time of the treaties the right to leave the reservation for the purpose of gathering roots and berries was equally important to all tribes. This latter right, however, has as yet not been subject to limitations looking to the conservation of such articles of food and since they still are found in abundance both on the Indian reservations and in the national forests within the area, there is little likelihood restrictions on the gathering thereof will be placed in effect. The only limitation which has occurred with regard to that right has been brought about by settlement and development of some of the areas where the Indians, prior to the coming of the white man, had been accustomed to gathering roots and berries in season.

The right of pasturage was, of course, important to those tribes possessing large numbers of horses and cattle.

While the provisions of the treaties with respect to the right of the Indians to obtain fish, game, roots [47] and berries, etc., were substantially the same, the following variations therein are to be noted:

1. The right of taking fish reserved by those tribes west of the Cascades, residing on or in' the vicinity of the coastal waters, was limited to the extent that they agreed not to take shellfish from any beds staked or cultivated by citizens. In effect this constituted a recognition

---

[26] 2/ 198 U.S. 381, 49 L. ed. 1092.

by the natives of an unqualified right in the citizens to the use and enjoyment of such personally owned property.

2. The treaty with the Makahs specifically reserved to them the right to hunt whales and seals at the usual and accustomed grounds. While such right no doubt would have been considered as having been indicated by implication, specific provision therefore was included to allay the fears of the Makah tribe as to whether after removal to the reservation to be established for them, they could continue to engage in those pursuits in which, as distinguished from other tribes, they were particularly adept. Such a provision was not included in the other coastal area treaties.

The Makah treaty also was different from the others in that it did not provide for the right to pasture horses on open and unclaimed lands as did all of the other treaties.

3. The treaties with the so-called interior tribes, for the most part situated east of the Cascade barrier, specifically provided for: "<u>The exclusive right of taking fish in all the streams where running through or bordering said reservation</u>." /1/[27]

Even though specific provision for such exclusive right had not been included, the Indians nevertheless would have been entitled to enjoy such privilege inasmuch as the treaties provided that. the reserves were to, be set aside for the exclusive use of the Indians. The provision apparently was inserted as a result of [48] the grave concern with regard thereto evidenced by the chiefs and head men· of the numerous tribes assembled on the council grounds at Walla Walla, Washington Territory, where the interior treaties with the exception of that with the "Tribes of Middle Oregon" was negotiated. Their concern, as will be seen from a reading of the minutes of the council (Appendix B), was brought about by the fact that the proposed reserves to be set aside were for the most part situated in the vicinity of or were traversed by the trails and "highways used by the emigrants to reach the new territory and since the interior Indians had had considerable more contact with the whites than most of the coastal tribes, they apparently were desirous of insuring that the right being reserved would. be exclusive in them as distinguished from the fishing right in common reserved for exercise beyond the boundaries of the reservation.

I. FISHING RIGHTS AND PROBLEMS UNDER THE TREATY

The Indian fishing right s coming under the above general classification of the. several rights reserved by them in their treaties are susceptible of further sub-classification as follows:

A. Reservation & B. Non-Reservation

    1. In General

    2. At Usual and Accustomed Grounds

        (a) Importance of such rights

        (b) Usual and Accustomed Grounds Defined

        (c) Present Day Rights and Problems

            1. Easements

---

[27] 1/ Refers to the proposed reserve to be set aside for the exclusive use of the tribes who were parties to the four treaties in the eastern area.

    2. Under State Regulation

    3. Problems

For convenience, therefore, our discussion of fishing rights will follow the above outline.

Before treating with such rights, however, it is pointed out that the discussion regarding fishing rights exercised by Indians within the boundaries of the reservations set aside pursuant to the treaties with which we are here concerned, is equally applicable to [49] fishing by any Indians within the boundaries of their reservations irrespective of whether such reservations were set aside pursuant to a similar treaty, an agreement containing specific or implied provision for the reservation of such rights, or otherwise. The basis for this appears in our narrative discussion of reservation rights.

The same is true with regard to the discussion of non-reservation fishing rights in general inasmuch as the Indians of our treaties have no different standing than other Indians when engaged in fishing in waters coming under the exclusive jurisdiction of the several states.

A. <u>Reservation Fishing Rights and Problems</u>.

The present day right of Indians to fish in waters within the boundaries of their reservation without being subject to state regulation is well defined and ordinarily generally recognized by state enforcement authorities.

As we have previously noted, some of the treaties in the Pacific Northwest/1/[28] contained a specific provision whereby the Indians reserved to themselves the exclusive right to take fish from the waters flowing through or bordering the reservations to be set aside for their exclusive use. The right to engage in such activity to the exclusion of all others, however, was not in any way dependent upon the inclusion of a specific provision to that effect in the treaties in question. The Indians who were parties to other treaties which did not include such a provision, were entitled to exercise the same right in this respect. It is to be recalled in this connection that all of the treaties provided that the reservations to be set aside were to be established for the exclusive use and enjoyment of the tribes and that no whites with the exception of administrative officers of the Government or those obtaining permission, would be authorized to reside thereon. Necessarily, therefore, an exclusive right was reserved by implication· in those treaties where specific reservation therefor was not included./2/[29]

The right thus reserved, however, was distinguishable from what we now consider a fishing right to be [50] under present conservation statutes in that what was intended to be reserved was the right to the exclusive use of the waters and lands within the reservations without interference by or being required to share same with the settlers. The actual taking of the fish was incidental, since our present concept of the right to do so which is dependent upon legislative enactment, was then unknown.

The original exclusive right to utilize the reservation lands and waters, however, is no longer extant, its passing having been accomplished either as a result of (1) the changed policy of the Government under which the intrusion and acquisition of lands or interests therein within the reservations by non-Indians has been sanctioned, which land ownership carried with it the right to fish in the reservation waters as an incident thereto, or (2) the adoption by the Indians on a number of reservations of a policy under which non-Indians are permitted to fish within the

---

[28] 1/ Those with the so-called interior tribes.
[29] 2/ <u>State v. Johnson</u>, 249 N.W. 285, 288.

boundaries of the reservation on Indian-owned lands. Such non-Indian fishing activities, of course, are subject to state regulation as well as those adopted by the tribe even though legal title to the land is vested in the United States. State jurisdiction in such case is founded on the police power vested in the states to regulate the taking of the fish and game found within its borders./1/[30]

The above-discussed original exclusive right originally reserved to the Indians, however, is, for the reasons we have seen, of no present concern under this topic.

Of principal importance is the right the Indians now enjoy of freedom from the operation of regulatory state fishing statutes. Their immunity in this respect, however, does not come about by reason of any special right specifically or impliedly reserved to them by treaty agreement or otherwise. Instead their freedom from such restrictions is brought about because the legal title to Indian tribal and trust lands is held by the Federal government which exercises plenary authority over Indian affairs to the exclusion of the several states. An exception to the foregoing, of course, occurs where lands have been patented-in-fee to individual Indians. [51]

The question as to the exclusive jurisdiction of the Federal Government was effectively disposed of by the Supreme Court when in the case of <u>United States v. Pelican</u>/1/[31] it said, in referring to certain trust Indian lands:

> "Although the lands were allotted in severalty, they were to be held in trust by the United States for twentyfive years for the sole use and benefit of the allottee, or *his* heirs, and during this period were to be inalienable. <u>That the lands, being so held, continued to be under the jurisdiction and control of Congress for all governmental purposes relating to the guardianship and protection of the Indians, is not open to controversy.</u>" (Citing cases:) (Emphasis supplied.)

That case, however, had reference to jurisdiction of the Federal courts in connection with the crime of murder, punishment for which is specifically provided for in the United States Criminal Code.

Alleged 'violations by Indians on their reservations or trust lands of state fish and game statutes obviously, however, are in an entirely different category. The question of whether such acts vests jurisdiction in state courts has been frequently considered. The ultimate answer thereto is very well expressed in an opinion/2/[32] of the Minnesota Supreme Court (1930) which had considered the same question a number of times in the past. In discharging an Indian who had been convicted of violating a state conservation statute by taking a muskrat on his trust allotment within the Leach Lake Reservation, the court said:

> "The jurisdiction of the state extends over Indian country within its borders, except as limited by Indian treaties or Federal laws; but it has no jurisdiction [52] over those persons or those matters which have been placed within the exclusive jurisdiction of the United States by the Indian treaties or the Federal laws. Indians living on their reservations or their allotments held in trust for them * * * are wards of the United States and are within the exclusive jurisdiction of the United States while on such reservation or allotment."

Judicial recognition of the fact that Indians should be protected from interference by state authorities when engaged in fishing or hunting on their reservations has been consistent on the part of both Federal and state courts.

---

[30] 1/ <u>Ex parte</u> Crosby, 149 Pac. 989.
[31] 1/ 232 US v. 442, 447; 58 L. ed. 676, 678. ?*?
[32] 2/ <u>State vs. Cloud</u>, 228 N.W. 611.

State v. Campbell, 55 N.W. 553; 21 L.R.A. 169
Selkerk v. Stevens, 75 N.W. 386
State v. Cooney, 80 N.W. 696
State v. Johnson, 249 N.W. 285
In Re Blackbird, 109 Fed. 139
In Re Lincoln, 129 Fed. 247
U.S. v. Hamilton, 233 Fed. 685
Pioneer Pcks. Co. v. Winslow, 294 Pac. 557
State v. Edwards, 62 P. (2d) 1094
State v. Rufus, 237 N.W. 67

Although the Winans while engaged in fishing and hunting on their reservations are not subject to state regulation of such activities, they are of course subject to regulation and control by the Federal Government. This is true even though by specific or implied treaty provision they reserved unrestricted rights to engage in such activities on their reservations. The doctrine that Congress can limit, alter, or destroy rights even though created by treaty, is so elementary it need not concern us. So far all hunting and fishing rights are concerned, see Ward v. Racehorse, 163 U.S. 504, 41 L. ed. 244, which although it concerned a non-reservation hunting right le equally applicable to both fishing and hunting rights within the reservation. It is well settled, however, that although Congress may supercede or void treaties and agreements, such action is not within the power of administrative officials/1/[33] also, the intent on the part of Congress to abrogate or modify must be clearly expressed./2/[34] [53]

Up to the present time, Congress has not enacted general legislation looking to the control of Indian fishing activities within their reservations. Certain limitations thereon, however, do exist but there were adopted and placed into effect by action of tribal governing units. So far as fishing is concerned, such rules and regulations have been adopted on a number of reservations. Violations thereof are punishable only by the Indians tribal courts —·not by state or federal tribunals.

It is evident from the foregoing that the Indians' present day fishing rights, as distinguished from their original rights, within their reservations are well defined and generally speaking recognized by the courts. As such they present no serious problems in so far as Indians under the control and jurisdiction of the Federal government are concerned. Due to the absence of Federal legislation regulating the exercise of such rights and the inefficacy of state conservation statutes, the only limitations on such rights result from acts of tribal governing bodies. In the first instance such regulations were usually adopted on reservations where commercial fishing is of considerable importance. Their primary object aside from regulating personal rights in the fishery as between members of the tribe, is to provide escapement periods for the ascending fish runs in order to perpetuate the runs for future generations. Such rules and regulations are not concerned with fishing for subsistence as such except as it is incidental to the commercial operation. Whether such tribally adopted measures are sufficient or the enforcement thereof vigorous enough to accomplish the desired for objective is a matter which can only be determined by trained conservationists. In any event it is not of present concern as affecting or defining the Indians' rights.

---

[33] 1/ US v. Carpenter, III U.S. 347; 28 L.Ed.451; 18 Op. Atty. Gen. 141.
[34] 2/ Cook v. US, 288 U.S. 102, 120; 77 L. Ed. 641, 650; US v. Cutler, 37 F. Supp. 724.

Probably the principal difficulty or problem which exists as a result of Indians engaging in fishing activities within the reservation boundaries, arises when Indians are engaged in fishing either for commercial or subsistence purposes, on land over which the state is entitled to exercise jurisdiction. The right of the state in this connection comes into existence when the legal title originally [54] held by the United states in trust for the Indians has been extinguished. In such instance the weight of authority is that the land is not "Indian country" within the meaning of federal penal statutes./1/[35] Accordingly in such case, the state has jurisdiction over certain offenses including violations of fish and game statutes which are not in violation of the criminal statutes of the United States. Consequently, Indians though they be wards of the Government become subject to the same restrictions as non-Indians engaging in similar activities in violation of those state statutes.

Due to the inherent difficulties presented by the checkerboarded pattern of landownership within most reservations, however, instances where Indians are cited for Violating fishing laws and regulations mile engaging in such activity on fee patented land within the boundaries of their reservation, are comparatively few in number. Where commercial fishing within the reservations is carried on, such activity almost without exception takes place on lands and in waters not subject to state jurisdiction.

The situation is quite different, however, where after allotment, reservations have been thrown open to settlement and entry and many of the Indians after receiving allotments have in turn disposed of their holdings to non-Indians. Such is the situation which exists in connection with the subsistence fishing and hunting rights and activities of the Indians of the Grand Ronde and Siletz Reservations in Oregon. Although the Indians of these reservations were not parties to the treaties herein discussed, the situation which there exists has been cited as an extreme illustration of the problem which could exist upon other reservations where only a small percentage of the lands have passed to non-Indian ownership and the greater portion remains still subject to the constitutional scope pf exclusive federal jurisdiction over Indian offenses.

Such situations can only be relieved through: (1) education of the Indians as to the precise extent of the rights they are entitled to enjoy, and (2) prompt [55] and energetic defense of Indians cited for alleged violations of state fish and game regulations either as the result of over zealousness on the part of the state enforcement officials or a tendency to limit the right of the Indians to participate in such pursuits through persecution in the form of prosecution. The success of such a program, of course, is entirely dependent upon the local administrators, who in addition to acting as advisors to Indians, should confer and cooperate with state enforcement authorities to the end that such situations can be avoided.

B. <u>Non-Reservation Fishing Rights and Problems</u>.

1. <u>In General</u>. Since we are concerned with rights provided for in certain treaties under the provisions of which a rather unusual right was reserved to the Indians in connection with "usual and accustomed" fishing grounds or stations, discussion of their rights at such traditional places will be handled as a separate topic. Our discussion herein as to their rights at other than such traditional fishing places has been included solely for the purpose of presenting the complete picture of the non-reservation fishing rights now enjoyed by the Indians.

So far as the treaties are concerned, no provisions were included therein for a general right to take fish outside the boundaries of the land to be set aside for their exclusive use. The

---

[35] 1/ Cf. <u>Eugene Sol Louie v. US</u>, 274 Fed. 47; <u>State v. Monroe</u>, 274 Pac. 840.

specific provision for a non-reservation right has limited to the use of certain ancient fishing grounds where fish could be taken. Unquestionably the object of the Government, as previously noted, was to restrict the Indians to residence on their reservations as much as possible in order to avoid conflict with the settlers./1/[36] In addition to that consideration, both the Indians and the Government representatives no doubt were of the opinion that the reserving of the right to take fish at traditional grounds was sufficient for the Indians' needs. In fact, the minutes of the treaty councils show that that particular feature was all that the Indians desired. [56]

There should be little if any question, however, that by implication the treaties reserved to the Indians the right to fish at other than traditional grounds for immediate food purposes during the long and arduous journeys that would be required to reach the main fishing and camp grounds. That right was of only secondary importance and is of no consequence under present conditions and the exclusive jurisdiction of the state in proceedings against all Indians involving the protection of its fish and wild life resources under its conservation statutes./1/[37]

It follows then that at the present time an Indian fishing at a place other than the traditional grounds of his tribe, pursues such activity without the benefit of any special right or privilege reserved by treaty, such as the easement right he enjoys at his ancient tribal fisheries. The fact that he is an Indian does not preclude him from engaging in fishing outside his reservation for he, as a citizen of the United States, is entitled to exercise the same rights and privileges as any other citizen/1/[38] provided, of course, he complies with the formal requirements of the state law and regulations, such as licenses, etc. He is entitled to and fully protected from discrimination in the exercise of his right as a citizen. In other words, he engages in fishing on the same basis and under the same right as any other citizen with exemption from discrimination in the exercise thereof. Consequently, he is subject to the same restrictions imposed by the states as is any other person who is <u>sui juris</u>.

The nature of the Indians' right of fishing at the present time at other than traditional grounds of his tribe as distinguished from his treaty reserved easement right at traditional places, is stated by the court in the case of <u>Seufert v. Olney</u>, 193 Fed. 200, 202-3 (1911). Although the case did not involve a violation by an Indian of any state conservation statute or regulation, the court in its opinion in referring to the easement recognized in the Winans case (hereafter discussed), stated that: [57]

"The court further held that this right could not be abrogated by state laws or state regulations. The court, however, was there speaking of ancient fisheries, "the right of taking fish at all usual and accustomed places"; and I am not aware that the government has ever asserted in behalf of the Indians the right to take fish at any other places, except in accordance with state laws. <u>United States v. Taylor</u>, supra; (3 Wash. T. 88, 13 Pac. 333); <u>United States v. Alaska Packers' Ass'n</u> (C.C.) 79 fed. 152."

With regard to the rights to use other than traditional places, the court said:

---

[36] 1/ See also Chap. 3, Indian Treaties, Handbook of Federal Indian Law – Cohen, U.S, G.P.O., 1941; also <u>State v. Towessnutte</u>, 154 Pac. 805, 808; <u>U.S. v. Alaska Packers' Assn.</u>, 79 Fed. 152, 155.

[37] 1/ <u>Begay v. Sawtelle</u>, 88 P. (2d) 999.

[38] 2/ <u>Geer v. Connecticut</u>, 161 U.S. 519; 40 L. ed. 793; <u>Patsone v. Pennsylvania</u>, 232 U.S. 138; 58 L. ed. 539; <u>LaCoste v. Dept. of. Conservation</u>, 263 U.S. 545, 549; 68 L. ed. 437, 439, <u>Tulee v. Washington</u> 315 U.S. 681; 86 L. ed. 778.

"Indeed, the mere assertion such a right outside of these accustomed places would be disastrous in the extreme. While by the common law all persons had a common and general right of fishing in the sea, and in all other public navigable waters, under modem methods and modern conditions that right cannot be enjoyed in common. * * * * In my opinion, therefore, the true construction of the treaty is this: The Indians are granted certain fishing rights, and privileges in their ancient and accustomed places, which they are entitled to enjoy under and by virtue of the treaty, and of which they cannot be deprived by state laws or state regulations. <u>On the other hand, the treaty confers no rights upon them in other waters or in other places, and if they seek to fish there they must do so in conformity with the laws of the state, and on an equal footing with the rest of mankind</u>." (Emphasis supplied.)

Other cases with reference to the present d~ Indians I rights off their reservations are as follows:

<u>Ward v. Racehorse</u>, 163 US 504; 41 L. Ed. 244
<u>State v. Towessnutte</u>, 154 Pac. 805 [2/4/1916 89 Wash 478 ruling that treaty Indiens fishing at U &A off reservation were subject to state regulations]
New York ex rel Kennedy v Becker, 241 U.S. 557; 60 L. Ed. 1166. [58]
<u>State v. Tulee</u>, 107 P (2d) 42 <u>and cases therein cited reversed in Tulee v Washington</u>. U.S.; 86 L. Ed. 778 on ground that state license statute therein involved was invalid as not being indispensable to effectiveness of state conservation program.

The problems under this topic are comparable to those suggested under the previous heading. Their solution is also dependent upon the same factors.

2. <u>At usual and accustomed grounds and stations.</u>

(a) Importance of such rights. The right provided for in the Pacific Northwest treaties whereby the Indians were to be permitted to resort to their ancient tribal fishing grounds or stations for the purpose of taking fish and erecting temporary curing houses, was at the time of the treaties probably the most important consideration in the minds of the Indian chiefs and head men. It was, of course, closely related to the right to leave the reservations for the purposes of hunting or gathering berries and roots, which subjects will be hereinafter separately discussed.

In substance and effect the particular provision with which we are here concerned provided that (a) the Indians were secured in the right of taking fish at all usual and accustomed "grounds and stations" or "places", such right to be exercised "<u>in common with</u>" the citizens of the "Territory" or "The United States and (b) together with the right "of erecting temporary" or "suitable houses for curing the same". We have underscored the language limiting the right to take fish at such places for the reason that the Indians nowadays feel that the right reserved to them at such places was intended to be exclusive.

The concern of the Indian leaders with regard to this particular provision of the treaties is clearly evidenced by the tenor of their speeches as contained in the minutes of the treaty councils (Appendix B). The Government representatives time and again assured the assembled Indians that they would be permitted to continue to leave their reservations and return to [59] their ancient fishing grounds without interference by the whites. The importance placed upon this right by a number of the coastal tribes is evidenced by the fact that they refused to enter into treaties with the Government. Their refusal was predicated on the fact that the Government representatives in keeping with the policy adopted in Washington proposed resettlement of a number of different tribes on one or two large reserves rather than on a larger number of smaller reserves which the Indians desired to have set apart for them within their own respective territories so that they would continue to be able to use the traditional fishing grounds dear to the hearts of their people. It was their feeling that concentration of a number of different tribes on a large reserve would result in ill-feeling and that the Indians who had used the fishing grounds within and immediately adjacent to the large reserve would bar them from participating in the fishing. So far as they were concerned the then existing limitations on travel would make the long arduous journeys to and from their own fishing grounds unattractive.

A further indication of the value placed upon the fishing clause of the treaty is found in the statement made by an Indian of the Warm Springs Reservation in connection with the controversy which arose as a result of the treaty of November 15, 1865 (14 Stat. 751; 2 Kappler 908) whereby the Confederated Tribes of Middle Oregon relinquished the right of taking fish from their traditional grounds./1/[39] Although the statement was apparently taken sometime in the early part of 1886, it has reference to a discussion amongst the Indians which occurred prior to the negotiation and conclusion of the treaty of relinquishment, which was only a few short years after the original treaty had been entered into. The statement is as follows:

> "Mark then said if Huntington would give us a large ship loaded with solid gold, we would not sell the fisheries; he said we would use all the money up in a short time but the fisheries would stand forever."

It is not difficult to appreciate the universal concern of the Indians with regard to this matter [60] since they were so dependent in varying degrees on fish and especially salmon for their daily food.

(b) Usual and accustomed grounds defined. Before proceeding with a discussion of the rights reserved by the fishing provision in the treaties, it would be well first to consider what was intended by the use of the expression "usual and accustomed grounds or stations. The necessity of having a conception of what was intended will be better understood when, as hereinafter set forth, the limited present day rights of the Indians are discussed.

In the first place, and in keeping with the rule laid down by the Supreme Court,/1/[40] there must be considered the meaning that the Indians themselves would have placed on such expression as it was used during the treaty councils. In this connection, it must be remembered that throughout the treaty councils the Indians were repeatedly assured that after they had moved to and settled upon the lands to be set aside for their exclusive use, they nevertheless still would be permitted to resort to the various and sundry places that they had always used in obtaining their annual supply of fish. There was no limitation placed on the right they were thus being guaranteed. So far as either party was concerned it apparently was intended to cover all such places/2/[41] in existence at the time of the treaties. The Indians were familiar with the location of all such, places as well as the season of the year when fish were available at each for the taking.

---

[39] 1/ P. 7, H.R. Ex.Doc. No. 183, 50th Cong; 1st Sess., Vol. XVIII of Miscellaneous Documents Relating to Indian Affairs.

[40] 1/ US v. Winans, 198 u.s. 371; 49 L. Ed. 1089; Choctaw Nation v. US, 119 US 1, 30 L. Ed. 306; Jones v. Mechan, 175 U.S. 1; 44 L. Ed. 49.

[41] 2/ US v. Alaska Packers I Association 79 Fed., 152; US. v Seufert Bros. 233 Fed.· 579, aff'd. 249 US. 194,·63 L. ed. 5, 55.

In the aggregate the number of such places necessarily was large since it is known that there were very many separate and distinct tribal units native to the territory and that these numerous units in turn were divided into smaller bands or family groups. Each tribe had its own particular fishing grounds and these were scattered throughout the territory inasmuch as in those days salmon frequented practically all of the main and tributary streams within the several watersheds.

This position is supported by the various reference and historical works dealing with the aboriginal [61] life of the territory. It also finds support in the statements contained in the affidavits of the Indians which form a part of this report.

The foregoing is well illustrated by the case of what are now known as the Yakama Indians. At the time of the treaty, 14 separate and distinct tribes, all of whom recognized Kamaiakin, principal chief of the Yakama Tribe, as their leader were designated and referred to as the Yakama Nation. The vast extent of the territory occupied by these 14 tribes will be noted by referring to the general area map. Throughout that entire area were located innumerable fishing grounds. Today, of course, the vast majority of such places are no longer of any value since the salmon, for any one of a number of reasons, are no longer able to ascend the various streams to reach their spawning grounds.

It wasn't necessary, therefore, for the Indians to travel great distances for the purpose of acquiring a supply of fish. What travel they did accomplish was ordinarily for the purpose of visiting the root and berry patches as well as the major trading centers for the purpose of trade with other tribes.   With the exception of the times when war was being waged against neighboring tribes, all travel had as its primary object, the obtaining of food.

Logically, therefore, the thing that was being reserved to the Indians, as they no doubt understood it, consisted of the right to return to any and all of those numerous places which they had theretofore used and where they could continue to take fish and erect the necessary sheds or houses in which the catch could be cured. To them, both the waters in which the fish were caught and the land upon which their camps and smoke houses were erected were the things being reserved for their continued use. [62]

KLICKITAT RIVER COUNTRY – WASHINGTON

One of the fishing grounds of the Columbia River and Yakama Indians located a short distance above the point where the Klickitat River enters the Columbia River. Note Indian fishing platforms precariously perched on the rocks on both sides of the stream.

Another view showing an Indian fishing platform on the Klickitat River, Washington. The net on the platform is the bag net used from time immemorial. The Klickitat River was and. could only be used in the early part of the year when the particular species of salmon frequenting the stream ascended it during the early high water.

Transportation of Indian fishermen and their catch from one bank of the Klickitat River to another is provided by this cable way and cable car.

There have been a number of cases involving Indian treaty fishing rights at particular locations and the courts, after hearing testimony, have either recognized such locations as being "usual and accustomed" fishing grounds within the meaning of the treaty provision, or else denied the Indians' claims. At the time of the [61/63] treaties it was not possible to describe the locations of such places in detail. Consequently, the various waters and tracts of land in which the Indians' rights are vested cannot now be determined by any general yardstick. Each case where a controversy arises must be determined in accordance with the facts and circumstances relating thereto.

In the case of <u>United States v. Alaska Packers' Association</u>, 79 Fed. 152, 154, the Court, referring to the treaty provision and what was probably intended thereby, said:

> "As I construe the treaty, the 5th article was not intended to create a reservation of any particular place for catching fish, in favor of any one of the different tribes or bands of Indians with whom the treaty was made. It is a general provision in favor of all of the Indians represented by signers of the treaty and applies generally to all fishing stations within the territory of Washington;" (Emphasis supplied.)

Another general judicial definition of what in all probability the Indians' understanding was~is found in <u>United States v. Seufert Bros.</u>, 233 Fed. 579, 584 (1916), which involved Indian fishing rights at a particular location along the Columbia River. The court in its opinion defined the expression in the following language:

> "<u>To the Indian mind this would comprise all places where they were wont to take fish</u>. They would not stop to consider any limitation of the territory they were then ceding to the government. It would probably not occur to the Indians that the circumstance of territorial boundary would have anything to do with it, <u>since, to their mind, all such places were being reserved for their benefit anyway</u>. Quite true, some famous chiefs participated in negotiating these treaties; but none of them were trained in the art of drawing contracts, nor were they adept<u>s</u> in the exact use of a language with which they were not familiar. It may well be that they had no intention of depriving themselves of a right to resort to any fishing places where they had previously been wont to fish, and they are in justice and right entitled to the benefit of any doubt on that subject." (Emphasis supplied.) [64]

The above definitions are, of course, only general and they do not furnish a yardstick which would permit one to determine the extent of the area at a particular place to which the Indian rights are attached.

The principal thing the Indians were concerned with at the time of the treaties was the right to continue to take and cure fish at the places they always had and in the same manner. The manner in which the Indians were accustomed to take fish at a particular place is important for the reason that such feature no doubt will be carefully considered by any court in determining the particular area subject to the Indians' rights as they exist today. The principal such right, aside from the easement of ingress and egress hereinafter discussed, consists of the fact that they cannot be required to pay license fees exacted by state statute from commercial fishermen where the imposition of such fees is not indispensable to the effectiveness of the state's conservation program./1/[42]

---

[42] 1/ <u>State v. Tulee</u>, 315 U.S. 687; 86 L. Ed. 778 64.

It is not tended to imply that the Indians are to be limited to the use of gear that was in use at the time the treaties were entered into. In fact, the use of most types of gear employed by the natives has been outlawed by conservation statutes. In the Seufert case, supra, the question was presented as to whether the Indians were entitled to use other methods for catching fish than the more primitive methods employed by their ancestors. The court disposed of the question in the following language:

> "Without discussing the subject at length, I see no reason why Indians may not be permitted to advance in the arts and sciences as well as any other people, and, if they can catch their supply of food fish by a more scientific and expeditious method, there exists no good reason why they may not be permitted to do so. Even more, they ought to be encouraged to adopt the more modern and advanced ways of prosecuting their enterprises." [65]

The question as to the extent of the area subject to the Indians' right is of more importance in ·the area west of the Cascades where commercial fishing by Indians is carried on in a number of non-reservation streams and in the waters of the ocean and Puget Sound. The present day manner of fishing in such waters as practiced by the Indians is in keeping with approved modern practices as distinguished from the fishing activities of the Indians at Celilo Falls on the Columbia River and many of the tributary steams where today the Indians still catch their fish in the same manner and with the same type of gear, viz, dip and bag net, as did their ancestors, the only difference being that the materials used in their manufacture are purchased rather than tediously manufactured from the resources of the region. Weirs and other types of traps can no longer be used outside the reservations nor are they in use on the reservation with the exception of the traps operated by the Swinomish Indians.

The question as to the extent of the area subject to the Indians' right is presented in the pending litigation involving the claimed rights of the Quileute, Makah, and Nisqually Indian tribes, where the Indians have asserted that the right extended to the waters of the stream involved over considerable distances from the mouths thereof. A similar question will occur in any future litigation involving Indian rights at an alleged traditional fishing ground.

c. <u>Present Day Rights and Problems</u>.

Before going on to analyze the present day rights enjoyed under the fishing provision of the treaty, attention is again directed to the fact that the right to take fish as was reserved in the treaty isn't comparable to our present day right to fish whether we be Indian or non-Indian. As previously pointed out, the principal object of including the provision was to reassure the Indians that they would not be limited to obtaining fish for subsistence or trading purposes from the waters located within or immediately adjacent to their reserves. In keeping with this object, specific provision in other articles of the various treaties was made whereby the Indians were assured of access to public highways in order [66] that they could proceed to the fishing and hunting grounds, root and berry gathering districts, and such white communities where they were accustomed to obtaining employment.

So far as the actual fishing was concerned, there was no restriction as to season, limit of catch, or type of gear./1/[43] In the final analysis, therefore, the right intended to be reserved consisted of the right to leave the reserves for the purpose of obtaining food. This conclusion as to the right reserved is supported by the fact that the treaty executed in 1865 by the Confederated

---

[43] 1/ <u>State v. Towessnutte</u>, 154 Pac. 805, 806.

Tribes of Middle Oregon recited in effect that the right to leave the reservation to take fish, erect houses, hunt game, gather roots and berries, etc, was relinquished as a result of the Indians' abusing the privilege to the extent of continuously residing away from the reservation./2/[44]

It is with the subject of the present day rights of the Indians at their ancient fishing grounds that we are principally concerned for in the final analysis such matters are the most important consideration in the minds of the remaining Indian population, although their heritage of the past and its freedom from man-made restrictions is both fresh and uppermost in their minds. Such past privilege, however, does not have any bearing on the limitations which have been placed upon their rights as a result of the decisions of the various courts in connection with the interpretation of their rights under their treaties in accordance with established legal principles.

Although in the first instance there were no restrictions other than those imposed by nature placed upon fishing activities, changed conditions all well as the creation of property rights in non-Indians resulted in litigation instituted to test their rights. The outcome of that litigation has resulted in the judicial definition of the Indians' rights at the present time. [67]

In general their present day rights can be divided into two classes:

1. Easements, consisting of rights of ingress and egress over privately-owned property, including the right to erect temporary curing sheds, and
2. Under state regulation.

1. <u>Easements</u>. It appear that the first controversy presented to a court of record /1/[45] involving the right reserved to the Indians under the fishing clause of their treaties, did not arise until the late 1880's and it concerned their right in real property rather than their right to engage in fishing without being subject to restrictions imposed by the state.

In 1887, the Supreme Court of the Territory of Washington had occasion to consider the treaty provision in question in connection with a controversy involving the refusal of a non-Indian land owner to permit treaty Indians to cross his lands for the purpose of reaching their usual and accustomed fishing grounds on the Columbia River, known as Tun-Water./2/[46] In upholding the Indians' rights under their treaty, the court in effect held that individuals acquiring lands which were embraced within an ancient fishing ground of the Indians, who were parties to the treaties with which we are concerned, acquired same subject to a servitude under which the Indians were entitled to access to their traditional camp and fishing grounds for the purpose of both catching and curing fish. In so far as the writer is aware, that was the first recorded case to recognize the doctrine that the treaties imposed such a servitude upon all lands embraced within the limits of the ancient Indian fisheries. [68]

---

[44] 2/ See Article I of treaty in Appendix B.

[45] 1/ In this connection, however, it is pointed out that it would appear from the statements contained in the affidavits of the Quileute and Queets Indians (q.v.) that controversies prior in point of time had occurred between the Indians and settlers, who in taking up lands for homestead purposes usurped lands upon which Indian villages or fishing camps were located. As usual in disputes between the Indians and the settlers where resort was not had to the courts, the natives were the losers. As a consequence, they were denied access to such traditional fishing and camp grounds.

[46] 2/ <u>US v. Taylor</u>, 3 Wash. Terr. 88; 13 Pac. 333.

Subsequently in 1896, however, a similar question was presented to the Federal Circuit Court for the Southern District of Washington in the now famous Winans case./1/[47] The District Court in its decision (subsequently reversed by the Supreme Court) took a somewhat different view of the property right acquired by settlers under the public land laws. This view although recognizing the right of the Indians to continue to fish in the Columbia River at the particular usual and accustomed fishing grounds involved in that case, denied the treaty right of the Indians to erect temporary buildings on privately owned land on the theory that when the settler acquired such land from the United States, the provisions of the treaty ceased to be effective and the patentee thus acquired an unqualified fee title to the land.

The case was carried to the Supreme Court of the United States where the decree of the lower court was reversed and the case remanded for further proceedings in accordance with its opinion./2/[48] The Supreme Court in discussing the easement rights of the Indians pointed out that the contingency of future private ownership of lands was foreseen and on that basis unequivocally recognized that the Indians' right was a continuing one against the United States, the state, and their grantees. Since the opinion of the court is the basis for the present day right of the Indians to the use and enjoyment of a reasonable right of ingress and egress across privately-owned property for the purpose of reaching their ancient fisheries and to occupy privately-owned land for the purpose of catching and curing their fish, the language of the court recognizing that right is reproduced for convenient reference:

"The remarks of the court clearly stated the issue and the grounds of decision. The contention of the respondents was sustained. In other words, it was decided that the Indians acquired no rights but what any inhabitant of the territory or state would have. Indeed, acquired no rights but such as they would have without the treaty. This is certainly an impotent outcome to negotiations and a convention which seemed to promise [69] more, and give the word of the nation for more. And we have said we will construe a treaty with the Indians as "that *unlettered people*" understood it, and "as justice and reason demand, in all cases where power is exerted by the strong over those to whom they owe care and protection", and counterpoise the inequality "by the superior justice" which looks only to the substance of the right, without regard to technical rules." (<u>Choctaw Nation v. United States</u>) 110 U.S. 1, 30 L. ed. 306, 7 Sup. Ct. Rep. 75; (<u>Jones v. Meehan</u>) 175 U.S. 1, 44 L. ed., 49, 20 Sup., Ct. Rep. 1. How the treaty in question was understood may be gathered from the circumstances.

"The right to resort to the fishing places in controversy was a part of larger rights possessed by the Indians, upon the exercise of which' there was not a shadow of impediment, and which were not much less necessary to the existence of the Indians than the atmosphere they breathed. New conditions came into existence, to which those rights had to be accommodated. Only a limitation of them, however, was necessary and intended, not a taking away. In other words, the treaty was not a grant of rights to the Indians, but a grant of rights from them – a reservation of those not granted. And the form of the instrument and its language was adapted to that purpose. Reservations were not of particular parcels of land, and could not be expressed in deeds, as dealings between private individuals. The reservations were in large areas of territory, and the negotiations were with the tribe. They reserved rights, however, to every individual Indian, as though named therein. They imposed a servitude upon every piece of land as though described therein. There was an exclusive right of fishing reserved within certain boundaries. There was a right outside of those boundaries reserved "in common with citizens of the

---

[47] 1/ <u>US. v. Winans</u>, 73 Fed. 72, rev'd 198 U.S. 871; 49 L. Ed. 1089.
[48] 2/ <u>US v. Winans</u>, 198 U.S. 871; 49 L.Ed. 1089.

territory." As a mere right, it was not exclusive in the Indians. Citizens might share it, but the Indians were secured in its enjoyment by a [70] special provision of means for its exercise. They were given "the right of taking fish at all usual and accustomed places, " and the right "of erecting temporary buildings for curing them." The contingency of the future ownership of the lands, therefore, was foreseen and provided for; in other words, the Indians were given a right in the land, - the right of crossing it to the river, – the right to occupy it to the extent and for the purpose mentioned. No other conclusion would give effect to the treaty. And the right was intended to be continuing against the United States and its grantees as well as against the state and its grantees."

The doctrine thus announced has since been followed by the courts in <u>U.S. v. Seufert</u>, 233 Fed. 579; aff'd 249 U.S. 194, 63 L. Ed. 555 (1919) and <u>US v. Brookfield Fisheries, Inc.</u>, et al, 1938), 24 F. Sup. 712. In the Brookfield case, the court defined the Indians' rights in the following language:

"These treaties have been interpreted in the sense in which they might have been understood by the *red men*. These extended to them the right to fish where they had always fished. An easement was laid down of ingress and egress from such usual and accustomed places. A fishery in gross was attached to all real property and title subject to that description ***. This easement inhered in the title of Brookfield Fisheries ***".

Two other cases of record involving the question of whether the Indians were entitled to an easement over privately-owned property were decided adversely to the Indians' claims on the grounds that the particular places involved were not shown to be ancient fishing grounds of the Indians involved in the particular litigation. <u>Seufert v. Olney</u>, 193 Fed. 200 and <u>US v. McCowan</u>, 2 Fed. Sup. 426, 62 fed. (2d) 955.

In the former case, the court found that the place over which the Indians were endeavoring to assert [71] their right of ingress and egress had not been shown to be a usual and accustomed fishing ground at the time of the treaty. In the McGowan case the Court found that the Indians on whose behalf the case was brought had only used such grounds occasionally and that, therefore, it did not constitute one of the usual and accustomed grounds which was to be reserved to them by the treaty.

2. <u>Under state regulation</u>. In our discussion of Indian fishing rights "In General" while such activity is being engaged in outside their reservation boundaries, it was pointed out that Indians like any other person, <u>sui juris</u>, were subject to the restrictions of state conservation statutes. We further saw that the basis for such was the fact that the several states are vested with exclusive jurisdiction in cases involving violations of laws enacted for the protection and conservation of their fish and wild life resources and that this jurisdiction extended to violations of such conservation laws committed by Indians even though they are wards of the Federal government.

Due to the peculiar nature of the fishing provision of the treaty which, as we have seen, has been construed as far, back as 1887 /1/[49] as creating a property right in the Indians', the questioning of the Indians' right to fish at such usual and accustomed places without interference by state authorities, the same as on their reservations, was inevitable with the coming of fish and wild life conservation measures. There have been a number of cases; in which the question was

---

[49] 1/ <u>US v. Taylor</u>, 3 Wash. Terr. 88.

presented to the courts. Until comparatively recently, however, it had never been squarely presented to our highest tribunal.

It appears that the question as to whether Indians exercising treaty rights were entitled to freedom from regulation was first presented to a court of record in the case of United States v. James G. Swan, 50 Fed. 108 (1892). That case, however, did not involve a violation of a state conservation statute but instead involved a violation of a statute of the United States prohibiting the killing of fur seals within certain specified waters. [72]

One of the defenses interposed in that case was that The James G. Swan[50] was owed and operated by members of the Makah Indian Tribe and that under their treaty with the United States they were especially privileged to engage in sealing in the waters in which the alleged offense occurred. It will be recalled in this connection that the Makah treaty is the only one specifically reserving the "right of taking fish and of whaling or sealing at usual and accustomed grounds and stations". In ordering a decree of forfeiture against the vessel, the court disposed of the Indians' defense in the following language:

> "It is obvious, however, from the language above quoted, that the treaty secures to the Indians only an equality of rights and privileges in the matter of fishing, whaling, and sealing. The guaranty is of rights in common with all citizens of the United States, and certainly such treaty stipulations give no support to a claim for peculiar or superior rights or privileges denied to citizens of the country in general."

Although the question as to the right of states to regulate Indians' fishing at their usual and accustomed grounds was not in issue, the Supreme Court in the Winans case, supra, made the following statement in referring to the treaty provision under which the easement possessed by the Indians was created:

> "Nor does it restrain the state unreasonably, if at all, in the regulation of the right. It only fixes in the land such easements as enable the right to be exercised."

It was this dicta as well as other decisions of the Supreme Court /1/[51] holding that the states held title to the fish and wild life resources within their borders in trust for the people as a whole and, therefore, could, in the protection of that trust under their [73] police power, regulate the taking of such resources, which formed the basis for a series of adverse decisions by the Supreme Court of the State of Washington /1/[52] holding that the Indians even though fishing at traditional fishing grounds were subject to state regulation and control.

Since the question has finally been conclusively decided by the United States Supreme Court, there would be little to be gained by an extended discussion of the reasoning by which the

---

[50] [James G Swan had been Makah Indien agent, author of 1857 The Northwest Coast; Or, Three Years' Residence In Washington Territory; Harpers, New York [UW reprint 1972], who retired to Port Townsend where his exquisite artifact collection remains, while many of his notebooks are at UW, the inspiration of the 1980 novel Winter Brothers A Season at the Edge of America by Ivan Doig. His drawings, including one of his Neah Bay home, are at Yale.

[51] 1/ Geer v. Connecticut, 161 U.S. 519; 40 L. ed. 793 and cases therein cited.

[52] 1/ State v. Towessnutte, 154 Pac. 805; State. v. Alexia, 154 Pac. 810, 155 Pac. 1041; State v. Meninock, 197 Pac. 641; State v. Toulee, 109 Pac. (2d) 280, rev'd on grounds other than those relating to conservation, 315 U.S. 681; 86 L. ed: 778.

state courts arrived at their decisions nor would it serve any ueeful purpose to quote at length therefrom. In brief, however, these decisions were all predicated on the unquestionable strict legal right of the states under the police power with which they were invested to regulate and control the taking of fish and wild life from areas within their exclusive jurisdiction. However, to one interested in equitable considerations and the moral obligation we owe our remaining Indian population, reference is had to the dissenting opinion of Justice Holcomb in the unfavorably decided Towessnutte case, 154 Pac. 809-810.

Inasmuch as the previous adverse decisions of the highest court of the State of Washington had not been appealed to the Supreme Court of the United States, a final and conclusive answer to the question was not obtained until the decision of the latter court was handed down March 30, 1942, in the appeal of the Tulee case. Although the decision therein was favorable to the Indians in so far as was concerned the question of whether the state could require payment by them of a license fee to engage in commercial fishing, which fee was imposed for revenue producing purposes as well as those of partial regulation of the fishing, the more important question as to the right of the state to regulate Indian fishing activities at usual and accustomed places was also disposed of adversely to the claims of the Indians.

In ruling on the question as to the right of the state to require payment of the license fee for [74] a commercial fishing license as required by the state code, the court, after pointing out its responsibility to see that the terms of the treaty were carried out in a spirit which generously recognizes the full obligation of the United States to protect the interest s of a dependent people, said:

"Viewing the treaty in this light we are of the opinion that the state is without power to charge the Yakamas a fee for fishing. A stated purpose of the licensing act was to provide for "the support of the state government and its existing public institutions." Laws of Washington (1937) 529, 534. The license fees prescribed are regulatory as well as revenue producing. But it is clear that their regulatory purpose could be accomplished otherwise, that the imposition of license fees is not indispensable to the effectiveness of a state conservation program. Even though this method may be both convenient and, in its general impact fair, it acts upon the Indians as a charge for exercising the very right their ancestors intended to reserve. We believe that such exaction of fees as a prerequisite to the enjoyment of fishing in the "usual and accustomed places" cannot be reconciled with a fair construction of the treaty. We therefore hold the state statute invalid as applied in this case."

The more important question, however, as to the state is right to regulate the Indians while fishing at ancient grounds, received its ultimate answer when the court in discussing ·the respective positions of the state and the Indian appellant said:

"The state does not claim power to regulate fishing by the Indians in their own reservation. Pioneer Packing Co. v. Winslow, 159 Wash 655, 294 P. 557. Nor does it deny that treaty rights of Indians, whatever their scope, were preserved by Congress in the act which created the Washington Territory and the enabling act which admitted Washington as a state. (March 2, 1853) 10 Stat. at L. 172, [75] chap. 90; (February 22, 1889) 25 Stat. at L. 676, Chap. 180. Relying upon its broad powers to conserve game and fish within its borders (citing cases), however, the state asserts that its right to regulate fishing may be exercised at places like the scene of the alleged offense which, although within the territory originally ceded by the Yakamas, is outside of their reservation. It argues that the treaty should not be construed as an impairment of this right and that since its license laws do not discriminate against the Indians, they do not conflict with the treaty. The appellant, on the other hand, claims that the treaty gives him an unrestricted right to fish in the "usual and accustomed places," free from state regulation of any kind. We think the state's construction of the treaty is too narrow and the appellant's too broad; that while the treaty leaves the state with power to impose on Indians equally with others such restrictions of a purely regulatory nature concerning the time and manner of fishing outside the reservation as are necessary for the conservation of fish (citing cases), it forecloses the state from charging the Indians a fee of the kind in question here." (Emphasis supplied.)

It follows, therefore, that the present day rights of the Indians at their traditional fishing grounds in so far as their freedom from state regulation is concerned, are no greater but instead, are precisely the same as the rights enjoyed by any other citizens. That is to say, state conservation measures are binding upon the Indians when such measures do not discriminate against them and which were adopted for the principal purpose of regulating the fishery so as to conserve the resource.

While such is the general rule, certain exceptions thereto are to be noted.

The legislature of the State of Washington has granted /1/[53] special dispensation to Indians of the [76] Yakama *nation* whereby they are permitted to fish for subsistence purposes at Prosser Falls en the Yakima River, which was one of their ancient fishing grounds. The act was passed to· eliminate the difficulties arising on account of the conflict of certain state laws and the Indians' treaty-claimed rights which had been adversely construed in the Towessnutte case.·

Similar dispensation was provided for the Priest Rapids band of Sokulk Indians at two of their traditional grounds on the Yakima and Columbia Rivers where they now may fish "under conditions not otherwise permitted by the laws of this state" /1/[54] (Washington).

In addition to those special acts, the state legislature has authorized Indian fishing without a license for subsistence purposes with a drag seine or a set net in any of the salt waters bordering any Indian reservation and within one-half mile thereof or with a set net not extending more than one-third across the waters of any stream or river flowing through or bordering on any such reservation and within five miles of the boundaries thereof./2/[55]

The State of Oregon has also made provision for Indians engaged in fishing activities in any waters over which the state has jurisdiction by providing (a) that the operations and rights of "North American Indians who have not severed their tribal relations" shall not be limited by that portion of the state's commercial fisheries code making it unlawful to take fish through the use of spears, gaff, or foul-hook or any other similar device,/3/[56] and (b) that certain prescribed license fees "shall not be required of Indians with treaty rights." /4/[57]

It should be remembered the special privileges granted by such legislation can be withdrawn at the [77] will of the respective state legislatures although since the favorable decision in the Tulee case on the question of the license fee requirement, there would be little to be gained by the repeal of the Oregon statute releasing the Indians from the requirement of paying certain license fees unless, of course, it could be shown that the fees imposed were not for revenue purposes but were intended for conservation of the fisheries through regulation.

---

[53] 1/ L '21, c. 58; Sec. 2451-1, Pierce's Code-Wash.

[54] 1/ L '39, c. 210, Sec. 2451-2, Pierce's Code.

[55] 2/ Sec. 2451, Pierce's Code.

[56] 3/ Sec. 64, Oregon Commercial Fisheries Code - 1941-42, 83-325 O.C.L.A. as amended by C. 131, L. 1941.

[57] 4/ Sec. 134, O.C.1F.C. 1941-2, 83-614 O.C.L.A.

In addition to the above outlined special privileges granted by the state legislatures, one further exception in recognition of the rights of the Indian is to be noted. The Federal Congress when enacting legislation /1/[58] for the protection of fur seals and other fur bearing animals provided that certain provisions thereof should not apply to Indians among others "who carry on pelagic sealing, in canoes or undecked boats propelled wholly by paddles, oars, or sails, and not transported by, or used in connection with other vessels, and manned by not more than five persons each, in the way hitherto practised by the said Indians, * * *". So far as our Indians are concerned; this legislation is not of any practical value for the reason that they no longer engage in such activity to any appreciable extent, if at all, in the inherently dangerous manner and with the unsafe equipment of their aboriginal ancestors. The exception, however, has been here noted solely for the purpose of completing the picture of their present day non-reservation rights.

The principal problem existing on account of non-reservation fishing activities at ancient fishing grounds is the same as exists in connection with any such activities carried on in areas subject to state jurisdiction, namely, the education of the Indians as to the extent of their rights. The Indians have always contended that when fishing at their usual and accustomed grounds they are (a) free from state regulation and (b) entitled to the exclusive use of such places. [78]

Up until the decision in the Tulee case, there may have been some merit to their contention as to their right to fish free from state regulation but that no longer appears subject to question. The court's decision definitely disposed of the claim with the exceptions heretofore noted. Consequently, it now is necessary to explain to the Indians just how limited their right is at such places. It will be a difficult task to accomplish but it is one that must be promptly undertaken and carried to completion in order, if possible, to prevent future violations of the state laws by Indians claiming rights that have been held not to exist. So far as purely subsistence fishing is concerned the state authorities in a few instances are inclined to permit the Indians to fish in their traditional manner at ancient non-reservation fishing grounds provided, of course, the Indians do not too seriously deplete the annual migrations. Such instances in the past, however, have been the exception rather than the general rule. If it could be made the general rule, a number of cases involving the prosecution of Indians violating state fish conservation statutes while fishing for personal subsistence purposes, would be eliminated.

The claim to the exclusive use of such places cannot be supported from the record consisting of the minutes of the treaty councils. It is clear from that record that the non-reservation right was not intended to be exclusive. There exists no logical basis for such a claim for if that had been intended it would have prevented the new settlers from readily obtaining food which they were as badly in need of as the Indians. The courts have had no hesitancy in denying the existence of any exclusive right in the Indians at ancient non-reservation fishing grounds. In the Winans case, the court in referring to the right of the Indians to take fish at their ancient grounds pointed out:

"As a mere right, it was not exclusive in the Indians. Citizens might share it ***"

See also The James G. Swan, 50 Fed. 108; State v. Towessnutte, 154 Pac. 805; US v. Brookfield Fisheries, 24 F. Supp. 712. [79]

In the Brookfield Fisheries case the court after describing the area over which the defendants had exclusive control said:

---

[58] 1/ Chap. 5, Title 16 U.S.C., Sees. 631-659, inc.

"In the channel below that point, defendants will have the right to fish in common with the Indians * * *."

Since the Indians fishing at their ancient fishing grounds are subject to state regulation, the question as to the conservation of the resource does not arise as it does in the case of reservation fishing. It is a matter solely within the jurisdiction of the state with the interest of the Indian Service limited to seeing that in the enforcement thereof the Indians are not discriminated against. Of course, in the interest of developing a spirit. of cooperation, it is up to the Indians themselves to forego the violation of state fish conservation measures under a claim of rights under the treaties which have not and cannot be sustained despite any understanding the Indians may have received from the government's representatives at the treaty councils. The Indian Service field administrative officials can be of considerable assistance in the development of a better understanding between the state authorities and the Indians. In fact, the initiative should be taken by our people by fully advising the Indians as to the restrictions on their fishing right. Ultimately, it might be possible to obtain legislation in the State of Washington similar to that of Oregon under which the commercial fees are not required from certain classes of Indians and the use by them of certain types of gear is permitted.

II. HUNTING RIGHTS AND PROBLEMS UNDER THE TREATY.

Although the same principles of law as governed fishing rights are determinative of the present rights of the Indians to hunt either within or outside of the exterior boundaries of their reservations, the two rights were separated for discussion herein for the reason that the provision regarding non-reservation hunting was not intended to be nor was it as broad in scope as that concerning the right of the Indians to fish outside the boundaries of their reservation. [80]

The Indians' hunting rights under their treaties, as was the case of their fishing rights, are also susceptible of classification for discussion under the headings of: "A" Reservation, and "B" Non-reservation.

The latter classification, however, due to the provisional nature of the right which was intended to be reserved, does not present the same topics for discussion as did the non-reservation fishing rights.

Our discussion of hunting rights like that concerning fishing rights is equally applicable to the hunting rights possessed by the Indians of all reservations irrespective of the manner in which such reservations were created; that is, by treaty, agreement, or otherwise. This situation occurs by reason of the fact that the hunting right intended to be reserved under the Pacific Northwest treaties also had particular reference to the right of the Indians to leave their reservations for the purpose of engaging in such activities on open and unclaimed lands rather than the right to kill game or furbearing animals. We have heretofore pointed out that at the time of the treaties our present day concept of a right to fish or hunt did not then exist nor did it come into existence until the need for the conservation of fish and wild life resources became apparent.

A. <u>Reservation Hunting Rights and Problems</u>.

None of the treaties with which we are here concerned contained specific provision for the right to hunt within the proposed reservation although the matter was a topic of serious discussion at the various treaty councils. It is not unreasonable to assume that it was considered that the inclusion of such a provision would be redundant inasmuch as at that time the right to hunt was an inherent or natural right.

The Indians, therefore, on their reservations continued to possess and enjoy the same right as had been possessed by them prior to the treaty; that is, the unrestricted right to hunt at will. [81]

It is appreciated that the treaty with the interior tribes specifically recognized that the tribes, parties thereto were to have the exclusive right of taking fish within the waters flowing, through or bordering their reserves. In our discussion of reservation fishing rights we endeavored to explain why such a specific provision might have been considered necessary by the interior tribes. There is nothing of record to indicate why a reservation hunting right was not specifically provided for in any of the treaties. It is probable that the Indians were not concerned about their hunting activities being interfered with by the whites as they were with regard to their fishing rights, for fishing activities generally were carried on at fixed locations and the camps and curing sheds were located immediately adjacent thereto. Consequently, the Indians no doubt wished to be assured that the emigrants traveling through their reservations, as such travel was anticipated and specifically provided for in the treaties, would not molest them while engaged in fishing or drive them entirely away from the fishing location.

The question as to whether the failure to include specific provision for either hunting or fishing in the treaties was disposed of in the case of State vs. Johnson, 249 N.W. 285, 288, by the Supreme Court of Wisconsin when it said:

> "While the treaty entered into did not specifically reserve to the Indians such hunting and fishing rights as they had theretofore enjoyed, we think it reasonably appears that there was no necessity for specifically mentioning such hunting and fishing rights with respect to the lands reserved to them. At the time the treaty of 1854 was entered into there was not a 'shadow of impediment upon the hunting rights of the Indians' on the lands retained by them. The treaty was not a grant of rights to the Indians, but a grant of rights from them - a reservation of those not granted, United States v. Winans, 198 U.S. 371, 25 S. Ct. 662, 664, 49 L. Ed. 1089. We entertain no doubt that the rights of the Indians to hunt and fish upon their own lands continued." [82]

The present day rights of the Indians under the changed conditions brought about as a result of the decrease in the fish and wild life populations of the northwest to hunt on their reservations without being subject to restrictions imposed by state statutes, are predicated on precisely the same legal principles and are equally as well defined as are their right to engage in fishing within the boundaries of the reservation. Since those principles were discussed at length in connection with the fishing rights, it is suggested that reference be had to such previous discussion for a statement of authorities.

Although the Indians are not subject to state regulation of their hunting activities such activities are, like their fishing activities, subject to regulation by Congress, except as noted below, or the tribal governing bodies.

Up to the present time regulation by Congress has been limited to the killing of migratory birds, the protection of which is provided for in the Migratory Bird Treaty Act of July 3, 1918 (40 Stat. 755; 16 U.S.C. sec. 703-704). Until recently it had been concluded ·that the restrictive provisions of this act were applicable to Indians even though they were engaged in hunting migratory fowl within the boundaries of their reservation. The theory upon which such conclusion was predicated, of course, was that the act itself, which was passed as a consequence of a treaty between the United States and Great Britain, abrogated the previous right of the

Indians. On March 13, 1941, however, the District Court of the United States for the Eastern District of Idaho, in the case of <u>United States v. Cutler</u>, 37 Fed. Supp. 724, in construing a treaty between the United States and the Bannock and Shoshone Indians containing a reservation as to hunting rights, held that the treaty with the Indians had not been modified and that, therefore, the defendant, who was an Indian exercising his reserved right under the treaty, was not guilty of the charge filed against him. Subsequently, a group of similar cases arose in connection with the hunting of migratory birds by Indians of the Yakama Reservation whose defense likewise claimed immunity from the provisions of the Migratory Bird Treaty Act on the grounds that it did not apply to them while engaged in hunting such birds within the [83] boundaries of the reservation. Until a final and conclusive decision in these or similar cases has been reached, the question as to whether the Indians' rights are subject to Federal regulation in so far as the Migratory Bird Treaty Act under its present wording is concerned, cannot be definitely answered. It is to be noted, however, that the decision in the Cutler case appears to be contrary to the weight of authority.

Restrictions on hunting imposed by tribal authority have been adopted on some reservations. Such restrictions, however, so far as the writer could ascertain, have been limited to the taking of fur bearing animals having commercially valuable pelts. The reason for such limited regulation as distinguished from the more restrictive provisions of the rules and regulations adopted by tribes whose members are engaged in commercial fishing on a substantial basis, is readily apparent when it is considered that with the exception of commercially valuable fur bearing animals, the Indians' hunting activities are for the most part solely for subsistence purposes. It is appreciated that some Indians like whites traffic in game killed out of season. Such illegal hunting, however; it would appear constitutes only a very small percentage of the total annual take of the Indians.

It would be difficult to say the least to induce tribal authorities to adopt restrictive measures which would work a hardship on members of the tribe by prohibiting the hunting of any kind of game for subsistence purposes unless, of course, the reservation game population is so rapidly approaching a state of compete extinction that the future welfare of the tribal group as a whole would prevail over the needs and general welfare of the individual members. Even then it is doubtful whether the tribal councils would by their own act prevent their constituents from procuring food for their families.

In a sense the Indians' hunting activities are limited by their own disinclination to participate in hunting except for the larger animals such as deer, elk, and bear. Unlike the non-Indian hunter, [84] the Indians apparently have no decided urge to participate in the hunting of smaller game. On the large reservations and during the proper period of the year, the bigger game ordinarily is found in sufficient numbers to meet the needs of the Indians. The contrary is true, however, with respect to the smaller reservations where natural limitations curtail Indian hunting under their unrestricted legal right.

Indian subsistence hunting within the reservations presents problems analogous to those of fishing with the exception that the problems created by Indians' hunting on land over which the state has acquired jurisdiction as to game and fish violations, has been more highly emphasized through stricter enforcement of the state law. This exception, however, is occasioned on account of the necessity for resource conservation rather than because of any question as to the interpretation of the Indians legal rights for his legal hunting right on such non-Indian lands is precisely the same as his right to fish on those same lands.

While undeniably important, the conservation of Indian reservation fish resources so far as the enforcement of state statutes for offenses occurring on non-Indian lands is concerned, is of lesser importance to the state except as such reservation fisheries constitute a portion of the state's natural assets. The reason for this would appear to be the fact that substantially all of the various species of fish constituting the commercial fishery on any particular reservation are by nature impelled to return only to the waters in which they were spawned, whereas, game roams at will throughout its native habitat and its presence in any particular place at any time is dictated solely by its immediate food requirements. In other words, game that one day is beyond the boundaries of an Indian reservation may the next day have crossed the boundary where it would no longer be protected by the state's conservation statutes.

State enforcement officials consequently appear to have been more active in apprehending and prosecuting Indians who violate state game laws even [85] though the violation may be unintentional. This has particular reference to cases where Indians legally acquire game, i.e., in the exercise of their right so to do on land not subject to state jurisdiction, but who are apprehended with it in their possession on lands subject to state jurisdiction during those seasons of the year that the state law provides game is contraband and that possession thereof constitutes a criminal offense. The fact that the game is legally taken and for the sole purpose of providing needed food for the Indian's family is not considered by state authorities. While legally the position taken by those authorities in such instances is sound, it is difficult to justify from an equitable or moral standpoint, and especially so when it is considered that in reality the Indians now possess so few of the many rights they were assured they would have when the treaties were being negotiated.

Another somewhat related problem is presented where state enforcement authorities enter and search restricted Indian lands for game thought to be possessed by reservation Indians after having acquired same illegally, i.e., in violation of state law and upon lands over which the state has jurisdiction. Many instances of this occur, as can be testified to by the field administrative officials, and while it is not intended that deliberate violations of state law by tribal Indians should be condoned through encouragement by having government officials vigorously contesting the state's right to thereby enforce its laws, some consideration should be given to the fact that such action by state authorities may in many instances occur as a result of over-zealousness on their part. In any event, the individual Indian is ordinarily not in a position to properly assert his rights and, as a consequence, may be both fined and imprisoned for a deed of which he was not guilty. It should be appreciated that once game has been reduced to possession, the *locus in quo* of the act is generally speaking extremely difficult of definite proof.

Situations such as above-outlined can only be minimized by cooperation on the part of the Indians, the state authorities, and the field administrative officials of the Indian Service. Of course, in the case of game legally taken but found in the Indian's possession on non-Indian lands subject to state jurisdiction, action by state' legislatures would be necessary. This could be along the lines of the special dispensation granted ·the Indians [86] in connection with their fishing activities.

B. <u>Non-Reservation Hunting Rights and Problems</u>.

By the provisions of their treaties the Indians of the Pacific Northwest, among other things, reserved to themselves "<u>the privilege of hunting</u> *** <u>on open and unclaimed lands</u>". This right or privilege was coupled to the provision under which they were to be permitted to leave their reservations to take fish at their usual and accustomed fishing grounds. It is evident from its own terms, however, that it was not intended to be a continuing right as was the fishing right.

As pointed out by the Supreme Court in the Winans Case/1/[59] the contingency of the future private ownership of the lands being ceded by the Indians was foreseen and appropriate provision made therefor.

Obviously then the inclusion of a provision to hunt on the unclaimed public domain was to be only a temporary right, the precarious nature of which was pointed out by the Supreme Court when construing a somewhat similar provision in another Indian treaty. In the case of Ward v. Race Horse,/2/[60] the court defined the right in the following language:

"The right to hunt given by the treaty clearly contemplated the disappearance of the conditions therein specified. Indeed, it made the right depend on whether the land in the hunting districts was unoccupied public land of the United States. This, as we have said, left the whole question subject entirely to the will of the United States, since it provided, in effect, that the right to hunt should cease the moment the United States parted with the title to its land in the hunting districts. No restraint was imposed by the treaty on the power of the United States to sell, although such sale, under the settled policy of the government, was a [87] results naturally to come from the advance of the white settlements in the hunting districts to which the treaty referred. * * * The construction which would affix to the language of the treaty any other meaning than that which we have above indicated would necessarily imply that Congress had violated the faith of the government and defrauded the Indians by proceeding immediately to forbid hunting in a large portion of the territory, where it is now asserted there was a contract right to kill game, created by the treaty in favor of the Indians."

It follows then that Indians engaged in hunting outside of their reservations have no special right but instead possess only the right as any other citizen and, therefore, are subject to the same state game statutes restricting such activities./1/[61]

The problems under this heading are the same as those previously discussed; namely, the education of the Indian as to the limited extent of the right he now possesses.

III. RIGHT TO DIG ROOTS AND GATHER BERRIES

Roots and berries as previously noted formed a considerable portion of the food supply of the pre-discovery natives. Today such articles still are commonly used by members of a number of the tribes, especially the older members.

Under their treaties, therefore, the Indians also reserved to themselves the right to leave the lands to be set aside for than for the purpose of digging roots and gathering berries "on open and unclaimed lands."

Generally speaking, the right was to be exercised in connection with their right to take fish at their traditional grounds since, in many instances, the annual travels from their permanent or winter quarters in the quest for food followed well defined [88] routes which brought them to the fish, root and berry grounds when such commodities were available.

---

[59] 1/ U.S. v. Winans, 198 U.S. 871; 49 L. Ed. 1089.

[60] 2/ 163 U.S. 504, 509-10; 41 L. ed. 244, 246.

[61] 1/ For additional authorities, see those cited under Non-Reservation Fishing Activities, ante pp.??

At the time of the treaties the only limitation contemplated was that which would be brought about as a consequence of the settlement of the lands being ceded to the Government. Up to the present time such private property rights have constituted the principal limitation on the procurement of such food items. It was only natural that with the taking up of the major portion of the ceded lands, that the Indians would in some instances be denied access to areas previously constituting their tribal root and berry patches. However, such commodities are found in considerable abundance on a number of the reservations as well as in the relatively nearby national and state parks and forests, which are scattered throughout the Pacific Northwest. As a result, therefore, those Indians who still desire to include these articles in their daily diet can do so without too much inconvenience to themselves. True, it may be necessary in some instances to travel greater distances than in the early days, but with our present highways and improved means of transportation, which latter have been generally adopted by our Indians, such condition presents no undue hardship.

Other than the limitation imposed by private property ownership, there has been little, if any, interference with the Indians while engaged in gathering their commodities. There, of course, are no laws enacted for the conservation of these resources since their abundance throughout the entire area obviates the necessity for such measures. This is true even though the various species of berries indigenous to the region have proven equally as attractive, as a welcome addition to the diet, to the non-Indians as they do to the descendants of aboriginal inhabitants.

At times the Indians' right in this respect may be said to be restricted when, in connection with the protection from fire of state and national forests, it has been necessary to ban camping in areas constituting a fire hazard. However, it is understood [89] that such restriction has not resulted in the Indian being unable to obtain an adequate supply of such food items.

The right exercised by the Indians, however, would appear to be no greater than the right which could be exercised by non-Indians, as is done in the case of berry gathering. The reason for this is the fact that the treaty specifically referred to "open and unclaimed" lands and it is doubtful whether lands within the parks would be considered as considered as coming within that classification.

IV. RIGHT OF PASTURAGE.

It will be recalled that all of the treaties provided that the Indians were to be also "secured" in the right of "pasturing their horses an open and unclaimed lands". In some instances such right was extended so as to include cattle as well as horses.

This provision varied in importance to the tribes of Indians commensurate with the number of horses possessed by the members thereof. West of the Cascade Mountains and all along the coast the number of horses owned by the Indians was relatively small, whereas the eastern or interior tribes were possessed of considerable numbers of these animals. Consequently, to them it was almost mandatory that provision be made for additional range to that which would be provided by the smaller areas upon which they were to reside.

The reservation of this right; like that of hunting and root and berry gathering also anticipated private property rights coming into existence on the ceded areas, and, consequently, was subject to the same limitation. With the passage of time, however, the numbers of horses and cattle owned by the various tribes was greatly decreased over that owned at the time of the treaty or else the increase in their number anticipated by the government as a result of the hoped for transition of the natives from nomadic or "fish eating" Indians to agriculturists, has failed to materialize. [90]

Although there may be some present need to exercise the right intended to be reserved, there is little likelihood that it could be successfully asserted. With the exception of lands within state and national parks and grazing districts formed under the Taylor Grazing Act, there no longer are any "open and unclaimed lands" in the ceded areas which could be of any value for grazing purposes. As pointed out in connection with the root and berry right, it is doubtful whether the lands included in the parks would be considered as coning within such classification, and there is little question but that the areas within the grazing districts would not be so classified.

So far as could be ascertained, there has been no litigation which involved the question of the Indians' rights under this particular provision of their treaties. Since, generally speaking, the present day Indian holdings are not significant, there would seem little likelihood the question would ever be presented to the courts. [91]

* * * * * * * *

SUMMARY OF PRESENT DAY FISHING, HUNTING
AND MISCELLANEOUS RIGHTS OF THE INDIANS

In the final analysis and with the exception of their rights on their reservations, the Indians are possessed of few of the many rights they hoped to reserve and about which they received repeated assurances. For the sake of convenience and ready reference, the various present day rights of the Indians, as such have been judicially recognized and limited by the litigation herein above referred to and are summarized as follows:

I. RESERVATION RIGHTS

A.   EXCLUSIVE RIGHTS. Tribal Indians, i.e., those who have not severed their tribal relationship, are invested with the exclusive right to fish and hunt o n Indian-owned lands - tribally or individually owned restricted lands. The only limitations on the exclusiveness of that right is brought about either by

(1) cases where non-Indians have acquired land interests within the boundaries of the reservations and consequently, as an incident of their property ownership, can fish or hunt on their lands and can deny the Indians access thereto, or

(2) cases where the tribes have adopted the permit system under which other than members of the tribe are permitted to fish or hunt upon the Indian-owned lands within the reservation.

B. CONTROL AND REGULATION. The exercise of their exclusive right on such lands is in no manner subject to state regulation. It is, however, subject to control and regulation by the Federal Congress or the duly constituted tribal governing body. [92]

II. NON-RESERVATION RIGHTS.

A. HUNTING AND FISHING IN GENERAL. The right of the Indians to hunt and fish outside their reservation is precisely the same as that of non-Indians. It is limited by the same restrictions imposed by state conservation measures which are not discriminatory but are applicable to Indians and non-Indians alike.

An exception to the foregoing is the special privilege given the Indians by Federal law whereby they are permitted to engage in pelagic sealing if using the same equipment and gear as did their aboriginal ancestors. This privilege, of course, covers waters under Federal jurisdiction.

B. FISHING AT USUAL AND ACCUSTOMED FISHING GROUNDS.

(1) REGULATION. The right of the Indians to take fish at such places is also subject to regulation and control· by the states with the exception that the states cannot require the Indians to pay a fee to engage in fishing where such fee is for the purpose of raising revenue and not the ·regulation of the fishery.

(2) EASEMENTS. The Indians who were parties to the treaties reserving the right to take fish at usual and accustomed grounds or stations have a reasonable right or easement of ingress and egress across all property, whether privately or publicly owned, embraced within the limits of such fishing grounds as they existed at the time of the treaties. This easement is a continuing one which inures to the descendants of the various tribes and cannot be defeated through action by the property owner, the states, or the United States. [93]

III. MISCELLANEOUS RIGHTS.

A. ROOTS AND BERRIES. The Indians have a right to obtain these articles of food outside their reservations, limited only by private property rights, or where such right is being exercised in areas under state or federal control such as national or state parks or forests and regulations have been adopted for the protection thereof.

B. PASTURAGE. It is debatable whether the Indians have a right of pasturage since there are no longer any lands which might be considered as being "open and unclaimed" and all grazing areas within parks and grazing districts under the Taylor Grazing Act are subject to governmental lease and regulation. [94]

****

CONCLUSION

The situation lath regard to the fishing and hunting rights of the Indians when viewed from their perspective is indeed discouraging.

Rights that they were assured they would have and that they have always thought they possessed have been denied them as a result of the application by the courts of well established legal principles with which both the aboriginal inhabitants and a large percentage of their descendants are wholly unfamiliar. Although the courts may have been disposed to uphold the Indians' claims upon the basis of the moral obligation owed to these dependent people by both the Federal and State Governments, our system of jurisprudence prevented the definition of their rights solely on the basis of moral or equitable considerations.

The limited nature of the Indians' rights should be recognized by them to the end that their activities will be carried on without contravening regulatory conservation measures enacted for their benefit as well as the community as a whole. It is the problem of the Federal Government to advise the Indians as to the exact nature and extent of the rights they now possess.

It should be evident from the preceding sections of this report that there would be little, if anything, to be gained by further litigation instituted for the purpose of testing the extent of the rights under the treaties, at least in so far as state regulation looking to resource conservation is concerned.

It is more important at the present time for the Indians and the Federal Government to take some steps looking to the elimination of the feeling, widespread in the Pacific Northwest, that the so-called unregulated fishing activities of the Indians is largely responsible for the past injury to the natural assets represented by the various fisheries. To a considerable extent and especially so in recent years, this feeling [95] has been fostered by the litigation brought by several of the tribes to assert their claimed treaty rights at usual and accustomed fishing grounds. This litigation was the direct result of the enactment of conservation measures which outlaws the principal type of gear used by the Indians, viz, set nets, a type which they had used for many years without violating state law. In addition, the legislation in question outlawed all fixed appliances such as traps, weirs, fish wheels, etc.

The measure known as Initiative No. 77 (Chap. 1, Laws 1933) had as its commendable object, the conservation of the declining fish migrations and, of course, was not primarily directed at the Indian fishery. However, its passage constituted a serious blow to the Indian fishing, being carried on at usual and accustomed grounds since due to their extremely limited financial means, their gear necessarily must be obtainable at a minimum of expense. Generally speaking, the Indians are unable to finance the purchase of other more expensive gear and operating equipment, the use of which was not entirely outlawed. In order to continue to provide the necessities of life, the Indians, as a result of the above conservation statute, were literally forced to confine their fishing with such gear to reservation waters. The fact that such was the situation led to considerable agitation in the Pacific Northwest and especially in the state of Washington looking to the further curtailment of the Indians' commercial fishery./1/[62]

In support of this move, statistics were compiled and interpreted so as to throw an unfavorable light on the extent the Indians commercial filshery played in the depletion of the resource. While it is not intended that anything herein said should be taken as an effort to take issue with or exception to such statistics, it is felt that as they have been interpreted, they exaggerate the effect of the Indian fishery. [96]

While there can be no question but that Indian fishing played a part in depleting the early commercial fisheries, and even today in some instances may continue so to do, it is believed that the extent that the Indian fishing participated in such injury has been greatly over-emphasized. Indian commercial fishing activity occurs in three general areas, viz, Puget Sound, Grey's Harbor and the Mid-Columbia River. An analysis made by the Fish and Wildlife Service of the

---

[62] 1/ Indian fishery – A Summary of Present Extent and Nature of Commercial Fishing by Indians on the Columbia River and Elsewhere in the State of Washington – (Mimeographed – Source unknown).

Department of the Interior, of statistics furnished by the Oregon Fish Commission and the Washington State Fisheries Department indicates the extent of the Indians' commercial fishing in these three areas in the relation it bears to the total catch by the entire commercial fishery. The analysis in question shows the following information with regard to the Indian commercial catch in the above-named areas, as follows.

1. Of the total catch in the Puget Sound area, the Indians accounted for only 2.4 percent in 1938, 2.8 percent in 1939, and 6.7 percent in 1940. The percentage is slightly higher if the comparison of the Indian catch is limited only to the other commercial fishing activities in tributary waters and points within the three-mile limit in the Puget Sound area. It is not believed, however, that the latter would give an equitable comparison of the effect of the Indians' catch on the total annual take from the fishery inasmuch as their activities, due ·to their inability to finance non~reservation fishing activities with legal gear and equipment, is very limited.

2. In the Gray's Harbor area, the Indian percentage of the total catch for 1938 amounted to 49.4 percent; in 1939 the percentage was only 26.0; and in 1940 the Indians accounted for 54.8 percent of the total catch. The Indian percentage of the total catch, if compared only with the number of fish taken in tributary waters and waters within the three-mile limit, would be considerably higher. Again, it is pointed out that it would be inequitable to the. Indians to limit the comparison of their catch with that taken within the three mile limit for the same reason as noted above. There are two other factors which have a bearing. On the apparently high percentage of the Indians catch in this area (1) non-Indian [97] fishing with the exception of Grays Harbor proper is limited to only a few places and (2) the catch of sockeye salmon is 100% Indian made since the commercial fishing thereof is prohibited by state law and regulation. It will be recalled that in the case of the <u>Pioneer Pckg. Co</u>. v. <u>Winslow</u>, 294 Pac. 557, it was held that the Indians were the owners of the fish in the Quinaielt River and that even though the disposal or possession thereof was contrary to state law, the state could not interfere with the shipment of same in interstate commerce. (See also, <u>Mason v. Same</u> 5 F. (2d) 255).

In connection with the Indian catch in this area, it is to be noted that 90 percent or more comes from the Quinaielt and Queets rivers located on the Quinaielt Indian Reservation. The Quinaielt river is noted for its large runs of sockeye salmon and has always been a constant source of supply to these Indians as well as their ancestors.

It has been reported that during recent years there has been a tendency toward overfishing on the part of the Quinaielt Indians and that some curtailment of fishing intensity is in order if future runs of salmon are to be insured. In this connection it is to be noted that up to the present time the Quinaielt Indians have probably the most complete set of tribal regulations governing their fishery. See General Remarks attached to the Quinaielt section of Part II of this report.

The remaining Indian catch in this area is of relatively minor importance in so far as its relation to the total take is concerned. Practically all of it is confined to streams bordering or traversing the several reservations located in the area. Whether or not it is excessive when compared to the aggregate of the resource is a matter for further study in each instance.

In the Columbia river area the commercial fishing activities of the Indians are confined principally to the stretch between Spearfish, Washington, and Celilo Falls, Oregon. In the 1938-39 season the Indian commercial catch accounted for only 8.6 percent of the total catch for the entire Columbia [98] river; the percentage for the 1939-40 season amounted to 7.6 for the total for the area. It has been pointed out, however, that if the Indian percentage was computed only on the basis of the fish taken above the Bonneville Dam, it would have accounted for 78.1

percent in 1938-1939 and 54.8 percent during the **1939-1940 season. To compare the Indian catch only with the number of fish taken above the Bonneville Dam for the purpose of showing the unfavorable effect of the Indian fishery on the resource as a whole would be very inequitable to say the least. The fishing places in the area above described are the only remaining places on the Columbia river having any value to the Indians so far as commercial fishing is concerned. The many other places originally used by them have been usurped by the non-Indian industry. There is no reason in the world therefor to suggest that the Indian fishery in this area should be curtailed because of the fact that its location is such that it has a serious adverse effect on future migrations.

The foregoing figures speak for themselves, and in the writer's opinion practically entirely dispel the widespread belief that the Indian fishery is largely responsible for the past damage to the annual fish migrations. Figures, compiled by the Department's Bureau of Fisheries /1/[63] show that from 1927-1934 the dip-net catch on the Columbia River which is almost entirely prosecuted by Indians, did not constitute a significant portion of the total catch, having averaged approximately 2.0 per cent of the total chinook catch, 4.9 per cent of the blue back catch, 2.5 per cent of the steelhead trout and less than 0.5 per cent of the chum and silver salmon catches. It is also to be noted therefrom that the larger percentage of the catch of the several species was accounted for by various types of gear not within the range of the Indians' limited finances. Some of this gear has since been declared illegal by state statutes.

There, of course, may be instances in the past where the salmon population of a particular stream [99] has been seriously depleted or entirely wiped out by regulated Indian fishing activities, but such cupidity is not alone chargeable to the Indian fishermen. The non-Indian fishery was prosecuted equally as avariciously (1) during the' early period covering the development and growth of the canning industry and (2) prior to the enactment of conservation measures outlawing certain highly effective and destructive types of gear.

Aside from the intensity of the fishing during those early periods, however, there were other factors which greatly influenced the decline in the number of the annual spawning migrations. Such factors were the outgrowth of the enormous industrial and economic development in the northwest. Irrigation and industrial development played a large part in the present depleted state of the Columbia River salmon population. Many streams were either wholly or partially diverted for such developments by the construction of impassable dams which denied access to the upstream spawning grounds. In many instances until recent years unscreened irrigation and power diversions accounted for the loss of young salmon on their downstream journey to the sea. In other instances, the activities of the logging industry resulted in irreparable damage to spawning areas.

All in all then it is not seen how the Indians can be charged with a major portion of the responsibility for the present depleted state of the Columbia River salmon population. To deplore past injury, however, without endeavoring to correct and improve the situation would be valueless. Needless to say, steps have been and are continuing to be taken looking to increasing that river system's fish population through appropriate regulation and. control of the fishery itself as well as the other factors which have had a deleterious effect thereon.

Since regulation of the fishery has resulted in the curtailment of the Indians' activities by outlawing their principal types of gear, and since they feel and probably rightfully so, that they

---

[63] 1/ pp. 164-182, Bulletin No. 32, *The History and Development of the Fisheries of the Columbia River.*

were not responsible for the past injury, it has [100] been difficult to get them to accept regulation of both their reservation and non-reservation fishing activities. It is, as we have seen, now settled that outside their reservations they are subject to state control and regulation so long as the measures have been adopted with a view to the conservation of the resource and do not discriminate against the Indians.

The foregoing does not mean, however, that present Indian commercial fishing within the reservations is carried on entirely without some measure of regulation. It is of equal importance to the Indians that their natural assets represented by the annual migrations in reservation streams be protected through the provision of adequate escapement periods to the end that migrations will be insured for the future. Some tribes have already adopted regulations looking to the control of their own activities. Whether such are adequate to achieve their object or whether enforcement thereof is energetic enough is somewhat questionable. Other tribes are considering the adoption of regulatory measures.

Obviously, if their assets are to be protected, some regulation is necessary but in adoption or recommendation of such measures the fact must not be overlooked that the Indians are unable to participate in the commercial fishery on the same basis as the non-Indian with his greater financial resources. This has particular reference to types of gear. While for the benefit of the industry as a whole there may have been justification and merit in the State of Washington declaring all "fixed appliances" as being illegal, the legislation in effect discriminated against the Indian fishermen. Whether resource conservation even though such gear continues to be used on the reservations can be otherwise accomplished by providing adequate and, if necessary, increased escapement periods, limitation of the number of such appliances and strict enforcement of such regulations is a matter for study in connection with the existing conditions on each reservation.

In other words, merely to suggest that through action by the Federal Congress or the tribal governing [101] bodies; the state's conservation measures should be made applicable to the activities on the several reservations, will not necessarily solve the Indians' problems nor would such action improve the situation in so far as the Indians' feeling of their rights being continued to be imposed upon is concerned. In fact, it is doubtful whether the tribal councils would be disposed to adopt such measures which they might consider too restrictive. It is possible of course that study would indicate that in some instances such all restrictive measures are desirable at least until the fish population of a particular stream can be restored to a figure somewhat near its' previous total. ·In other instances study might show that the desired for conservation could be otherwise achieved along the lines previously suggested.

It is believed that the adoption of such measures should in the first instance be the duty of the tribal councils with the assistance and suggestion of federal administrative officials rather than that of those same officials acting under a mandatory statute. In the final analysis the conservation of the asset is a matter involving the respective interests of the several tribes. The depletion thereof directly affects the welfare of practically all tribal members and if the Indians are to achieve self-government of their own interests and property rights under the Indian Reorganization Act, certainly they should be given the first opportunity to act in connection with this matter which is of such vital importance to them. To impose regulation upon them without their cooperation and consent would not be at all desirable from the administrative standpoint or that of the Indians.

It is appreciated that some tribes might not be willing to renounce their present unrestricted reservation rights, either in part or their entirely, and that, therefor, for the protection of their interests the federal government should assume regulation of the taking of their fish and wildlife resources. Enactment of such legislation would present a number of objectionable features, dependent on the form it would take, principal of which would appear to be the matter of enforcement of the measures adopted thereunder. That feature, [102] however, would appear to be a matter for further careful consideration.

In connection with the foregoing the following is quoted from my letter to you of 2/13/42 "Forestry and Grazing" – which states the writer's position regarding reservation control and regulation of fish and wild life resources in somewhat greater detail.

> "It is believed, however, that any legislation proposed by our Department should not overlook the fact that if it apparently ignores, nullifies, or even limits the rights which, as above indicated, the Indians think were unqualifiedly reserved by them in their treaties, they will feel that the Government has once again broken faith by further violating the promises made to their forefathers at the time the treaties were being negotiated. Although explanations of the theory and operation of state legislation and jurisdiction outside the reservations are patiently listened to and apparently assimilated by the Indians, such academic explanations cannot overcome their reliance on the promises reported to them as having been made by Governors Stevens and Palmer during the course of the treaty councils. I have no doubt but that the superintendents of the various interested jurisdictions will agree with me in this respect. Further justification for this viewpoint is found in the constitutions and by-laws of those tribes having adopted same under the Indian Reorganization Act. Ordinarily such documents, under the article defining the powers of the tribal council, provided in effect that such body should have the power to <u>promulgate and enforce</u> ordinances governing the conduct of the members of the tribe, and providing for the maintenance of law and order and the establishment of an Indian court having defined duties, powers, and limitations. For example, see sub-section "i", Section 1 of Article VI of the Makah Constitution, sub-section "k" of Sec. 1, Article VI of the Swinomish Constitution, and sub-section [103] "i", Sec. 1, Article V of the, Warm Springs Constitution.

> Administrative problems in this connection will not be made less difficult if the Indians believe that the Government is arbitrarily regulating their inherent right to hunt and fish for subsistence at will within their reservations, or even commercially where such activities are presently carried on.

> It is my thought, therefore, that the Indian Service, when considering the sponsorship of legislation to provide for Federal control and regulation of Indian hunting and fishing activities, should not minimize this feature of the problem, which ranks in importance with many of the others which must be considered. It seems to me that if any legislation proposed would be drafted so as to provide that control and regulation by Federal authorities would only be resorted to in the event the Indians of a particular reservation failed to provide such regulation <u>as well as adequate enforcement themselves,</u> there would be little justification for the Indians to assert they were again arbitrarily being deprived of their reserved treaty rights. As pointed out by Mr. Presnall, a number of tribes have adopted rules and regulations looking to the conservation of their wild life resources and others are in the course of adopting similar codes. No doubt they will in some respects fail to measure up to the standards established by the authorities governing the taking of fish and game from areas under state jurisdiction.

> Those standards, however, in their present day form were developed only after years of experimentation and study by competent wild life experts. There would appear to be no reason why the Indians could not be educated to such an extent that they would voluntarily adopt such standards to govern their own activities. I state this for the reason that in the past a great deal of the difficulty resulted [104] "from the fact that practically all of the adult Indians had actually enjoyed hunting and fishing prior to the establishment of the strict conservation rules and regulations which are in existence today. The present day generation, however, having not had

such experience, should be more likely to appreciate the necessity for adopting and enforcing conservation practices at least equal to those adopted for the areas under state jurisdiction.

As above indicated, the record shows that some of the tribes have evinced both the desire and willingness to conserve their wild life resources. I would recommend that this privilege of governing their own actions be not denied them unless, of course, it is evident that they are unwilling to conform to conservation practices in keeping with the resources of their respective reservations or that their enforcement of acceptable measures and the penalties prescribed for violations thereof is not sincere or effective. In other words, it is suggested that the various tribes be given a fair opportunity to regulate their own conduct before resorting to direct Federal control.

The writer, of course; has no knowledge or information regarding the situation at jurisdictions other than those in the Pacific Northwest covered by his recently completed field study. From the information thus developed and in view of my belief that such proposed legislation will have an important bearing upon the economic status and lives of those Indians, it is respectfully recommended that any draft of legislation along the general line under consideration be forwarded to the interested superintendents prior to submission to the Congress. While this would result in some delay to the apparently speedy action presently contemplated, it would appear fully justified on the ground that such procedure would permit the office [105] "to ascertain their comments on the draft after studying it in the light of problems peculiar to the situation prevailing on their respective reservations."

In conclusion and in view of my opinion that regulation in some manner, shape, or form is essential, it is hoped that these general comments will not be construed as an effort to delay such regulation solely for the purpose of humoring those individual Indians or groups who under the mantle of the claimed protection afforded by their treaty rights, ignore the need for conservation so that the remaining resources of their tribes can be exploited to their own personal profit."

It is believed that when and if adequate conservation measures regulating the Indian commercial fishery are adopted in accordance with the above views, a great deal will have been accomplished towards alleviating the present ill-feeling with regard to the Indians participating in such activity -- either within or without their reservation. Since the feeling that the Indians are participating in the non-reservation commercial fishery without being subject to any regulation or control, there has been some agitation as to their right to participate therein at all. Such agitation, of course, probably is occasioned more by the fact that there is considerable envy all the part of those interests who are subject to state relations and are under the impression that the Indians are not subject thereto while participating in fishing outside of reservation waters.

In the first place, as we have endeavored to point out; it was never intended that the Indians would be confined to fishing within the boundaries of their reserves or that even though permitted to engage therein outside thereof, they would be limited to taking fish only for their own subsistence use. The minutes of the councils as well as the conditions existing with regard to a well established inter-tribal trade prior to the coming of the whites and the fact that the Indians participated to a very large extent in [106] the early commercial fishery should all act to defeat any such ill-founded argument.

Aside from that, however, our Indians are entitled to participate in commercial fishing on the same basis as any other citizen, irrespective of any alleged special treaty privilege.

In the second place and with the exception of the non-reservation commercial fishing by Indians in the mid-Columbia river area and by the Makah Indians in the waters of the Pacific Ocean and the Strait of Juan de Fuca, the extent of the Indians commercial fishing outside their reservation is wholly insignificant so far as its relation to the commercial fishery in the aggregate is concerned. [107]

******

RECOMMENDATIONS

In view of the situation with reference to Indian fishing and hunting rights as it now exists, there appear to' be but few recommendations in order.

As a result of numerous meetings with the Indians, it was evident to the writer that the most exigent recommendation concerns the education of the Indians as to the precise nature and present extent of such limited non-reservation rights as they now possess. While from personal experience, it is appreciated that it will be difficult, if not impossible, to explain the reason for the present state of affairs to the older generation, who actually fished and hunted prior to state conservation measures, such a program not only should but must meet with more success in so far as the present generation is concerned. Unless such action is taken, the younger Indians, as a consequence of listening to their elders relate of the old rights and the oft-repeated promises of the treaty commissioners, cannot help but become inoculated with the idea that because of the treaties they were endowed with special privileges over those possessed by other citizens. The result is the encouragement of violations of state conservation measures to the ultimate detriment of the Indian population as a whole as well as the perpetrator.

It was also evident that some measure of regulation of hunting and fishing activities within the reservations is in order inasmuch as it is as important to the Indian communities that their tribally owed fish and wild life resources be protected, as the conservation of the similar resources of the state is important to the people of the state as a whole.

Accordingly, and in the light of the within report, it is respectfully recommended that:

1. Immediate steps be taken to fully advise the Indians as to the extremely limited' nature and extent of their non-reservation rights, and the reasons therefor.

2. They be advised there is nothing to be gained to continue to contest the right of the states to regulate and control their activities at non-reservation fishing and hunting areas. [108]

3. Legislation be obtained which will not arbitrarily provide for application of state conservation statutes to Indian reservations, but which in lieu thereof will provide for Federal regulation of reservation fishing and hunting activities consistent with the status of the fish and wild life resources of the several jurisdictions; provided, however, that such legislation be so drafted that no federal administrative action looking to such regulation will be taken unless a tribe fails to act on its own initiative or the steps that it has taken fail to meet the requirements of accepted conservation practice and~or enforcement thereof is inadequate.

4. Efforts be made to obtain the mutual cooperation of state and federal officials as well as the Indians themselves to the end that a better understanding can be had by the parties as to the Indians' claims under their treaties and with a view to obtaining special dispensation, similar to that already in existence, concerning Indian non-reservation fishing and hunting for subsistence purposes.

5. Appropriate investigation be made of the facts with regard to the question as to the ownership of the bed of the Quileute River, with a view to reopening same in the event such

investigation discloses apparent judicial error. (See discussion under General Remarks accompanying the Quileute affidavits.) [109]

****

SOURCE MATERIAL CITED

Bancroft, H. H. The Native Races of the Pacific States of North America - Vol. 1, of five volumes, 1874-1882.

Bulletin No. 32, Bureau of Fisheries, U.S.D.I. The History and Development of the Fisheries of the Columbia River, Joseph A. Craig and Robert F. Hacker.

Caughey, John Walton - History of Pacific Coast, 1933 - privately published by author.

Cohen, Felix S. - Handbook of Federal Indian Law, U.S.G.P.O., Washington - 1941.

Dunn, John - The Oregon Territory and the British North American Fur Trade. G. B. Zieber & Co., Philadelphia, Pa.

Eells, Myron - The Twana, Chemakum and Clallam Indians of Washington Territory. (Smithsonian Report for 1887, pp. 605-81).

Gibbs, George -- Tribes of Western Washington and Northwestern Oregon. (Contributions to North American Ethnology, 1, pp. 157-241, Washington, 1887).

Goddard, Pliney Earl - Indians of Northwest Coast. American Museum Press 1924 (American Museum of Natural History Handbook Series #l0).

Handbook of American Indians - Bulletin 30 (2 parts) Bureau of American Ethnology. - 1910 U.S.G.O.O., Washington.

Hayden, Mildred Vera - History of the Salmon Industry, Commonwealth Review, 1932-1933.

H. R. Ex. Doc. No. 183, 50th Congress, 1st Session (Vol. XVIII, "Misc. Docs. relating to Indian Affairs).

Irving, Washington - Astoria; or Anecdotes of an Enterprise Beyond the Rocky Mountains. Author's rev. 00. - Hudson edition, One Volume, G. P. Putman's Sons, New York. [109A]

Lewis and Clark - Original Journals of the Lewis and Clark Expedition, 8 vols. edited by Ruben Gold Thwaites, 1904. Dodd, Mead & Co., New York, Vols. 3, 4, and 8 (Maps).

Senate Ex. Doc. No. 87, 75th Congress, 1st Session.

Swan, James G.

(a) The Northwest Coast, or Three Years Residence in Washington Territory; Three Years at Shoal-water Bay, New York, 1857.

(b) The Indians of Cape Flattery (Smithsonian Contribution to Knowledge, XVI (No. 220) 108 pp.)

Thompson, David - David Thompson's Narrative of His Explorations in Western America, 1784-1812. Edited by J. B. Tyrrell, The Champlain Society, Toronto.

Wilkes, Charles, Vol. 4 - Narrative of the United States Exploring Expedition During the Years 1838-1842, incl. 5 vols. and atlas, Lea and Blanchard, Philadelphia, Pa. [110]

PART II
AFFIDAVITS

SHOWING THE LOCATION OF
A NUMBER OF
USUAL AND ACCUSTOMED
FISHING GROUNDS AND STATIONS

IN GENERAL

During the course of the field investigation, meetings were held with the older members of a number of tribes who were parties to the several treaties. These people, of their own choise, [choice] then selected two or three of their number who they felt were best qualified from actual knowledge or experience to assist in attaining the objectives of this phase of the investigation.

The objectives to be accomplished through such meetings were to ascertain (1) the location and extent of the usual and accustomed fishing grounds of the several tribal groups and (2) the fishing gear employed in catching their annual supply of fish and the manner of life of their ancestors with especial regard to the various kinds of food they were able to obtain. Such information was to be perpetuated through having the individual Indians execute affidavits in which their testimony was recorded.

The latter information of course was to be supplemental to the data along such lines which had previously been obtained from the source material cited in Part I hereof. With the exception of the various places noted in the accounts of the early explorers as being the location of the more important of the Indian fisheries, there was no record so far as could be ascertained of the location of the countless other such places scattered throughout the Pacific Northwest which were used year in and year out by the numerous tribes resident in that area.

It is appreciated of course that Lewis and Clark made a very complete record in their journals and on the accompanying maps showing the location of the numerous Indian fishing establishments that they came upon during the course of their expedition. The great majority of the places noted in their journals, however, have not been used for many years nor is it probable that under present conditions they will ever be used again. Accordingly and rather than duplicate those records, no effort was made to include the locations of such places in [111] the affidavits in this report with the exception of certain of those places which are still in use today along the Columbia river. Should it ever be necessary to determine whether a particular place comprised one of the traditional fishing grounds of the Indians, it is felt that the information contained in the Lewis and Clark Journals would be acceptable to support any claim to that effect.

It ill doubtful whether such questions will arise for the reason that the older Indians who were familiar with and used such places are rapidly dying out and the younger generation being under the necessity of providing a living under modern conditions for themselves and their families are primarily interested in fishing at those places where a considerable portion of their catch can be disposed of to the commercial canning industry in return for the money necessary to purchase the commodities of civilized life. So far as the Columbia river is concerned, commercial and subsisting fishing activities by the Indians are confined to traditional spots in an area approximately 9 miles in length located between Spearfish, Washington, and Celilo Falls where, as we have seen, the ancient fishing and trading center of *Wyam* was located.

An exception was made in the case of those places for the reason that it is not beyond the realm of possibility that at some future time another great dam will be constructed to the

Columbia river at or near The Dalles, Oregon, in connection with flood control and navigation. When and if this occurs, fewer remaining places in the mid-Columbia river area which constitute the bulk of the commercial Indian fishery on that river, will be inundated by the backwater from such dam. Since they are practically the only places in that area where the Indian's catch can be disposed of commercially, they are of inestimable value to the Indians. The loss of such places would be as calamitous to them as was the loss they sustained as a result of the flooding of a considerable number of commercial and subsistence fishing grounds on account of the construction of the Bonneville and Grand Coulee dams. [112]

With the exception of the affidavits taken from representatives of the Chehalis and Clallam Indians, such feature of the investigation was limited to tribes coming under the treaties which we have been discussing and which are still in I force and effect today so far as the reservation of ancient fishing grounds is concerned. Affidavits were taken from these two groups for the reason that they had heard the field investigation was being made and had received the impression that their rights are also to be investigated.

Affidavits were not taken from the various tribes coming under the jurisdiction of the Tulalip Indian Agency, who were parties to the Medicine Creek and Point Elliott treaties although fishing is still an important activity to them and especially so for commercial purposes. They were not contacted primarily because of the fact that their commercial fishing activities are either confined to reservation waters or when engaged in outside of such waters the Indians have generally speaking, acquiesced to and observed the requirements of the state laws and regulations.

In view of the tenor of the decision in the Tulee case which was not handed down until some several months subsequent to completion of the field work for this report, questions may be presented as to the location of the usual and accustomed grounds of these Indians. They would, of course, only arise in the event the State of Washington endeavored to enforce the commercial license fee provisions of its fisheries code on the grounds that the Indians were not fishing in ancient tribal locations and therefor were subject to such code provisions.

It is doubtful, however, that such questions will present any serious problem should they arise for the reason that the various tribes in the area covered by the two above referred to treaties utilized substantially the same type of gear as did most of the other "fish eating" tribes west of the cascades along the shores of Puget Sound, Hood Canal [113] and the west and northern coasts, or the Olympic Peninsula. Generally speaking, such gear consisted of fish weirs and traps, nets, spears and gaff hooks which were used in the channels of the numerous streams in the area. However, all such activities were not confined to the river channels for these Indians, like the Makah, Skokomish; et al, were reported to have fished for halibut, cod, and other bottom fish in the coastal waters outside the mouths of the rivers. It would be difficult indeed to determine the precise location of those particular places since no doubt, the aboriginal fishermen like their modern counterpart, found it necessary to take such species of fish wherever they could be found.

Affidavits also were not taken from representatives of the Quinaielt Indian tribe for the reason that the members of the tribal council, when contacted with regard to the location of their usual and accustomed fishing grounds advised in effect that the exclusive right now possessed by the Quinaielt Indians to fish in the river of the same name on their reservation without being subject to state restriction is considered sufficient for their present needs. For record purposes, however, the secretary of the Quinaielt tribal council under date of December 3, 1941, furnished information showing that the location of a number of usual and accustomed fishing places extended in a southerly direction, from their present reservation to the mouth of the Columbia River. Their claims in this connection will be discussed under the Quinaielt heading of this part of the report.

Although the Indians of the Warm Springs Reservation were parties to a treaty whereby they reserved unto themselves the right to return to usual and accustomed fishing grounds for the purpose of taking fish and curing same, it will be recalled that such right was relinquished by a later treaty executed some ten years after the original compact. For that reason no affidavits with regard to the location of their traditional fishing grounds were taken, since their subsequent relinquishment acted to extinguish any right under the original treaty provision. However, in order [114] to support the Indians' claim in the event future controversy should arise as to whether the remaining fisheries within the area between Celilo Falls and Spearfish, Washington, on the mid-Columbia River had in pre-discovery times been participated in by the several tribes which were settled upon the Yakama, Umatilla, and Warm Springs Reservations under three different treaties, an affidavit was taken from one member of what are now known as the "Warm Springs" Indians. The affidavit in question supports the statements of the Indians from the other reservations claiming participation in the ancient fisheries there located. The affiant claims descendance from the Tenino Indian Tribe, a member of the Shahaptian family, whose original habitat, it is reported, was the valley of the Des Chutes River (immediately east of Celilo Falls), although the dialect was spoken on both sides of the Columbia from The Dalles east to the mouth of the Umatilla River approximately 100 miles upstream. Since the witness, Isaac McKinley, is recognized as one of the outstanding living members of the Warm Springs tribal organization, his statements should carry considerable weight. His affidavit is included with the Columbia River group of affidavits.

Although the Nez Perce Indians also were parties to a treaty reserving their ancient fisheries for their future use, there is some question as to whether or not their right was relinquished by their subsequent treaty of June 9, 1863 (14 Stat. 647) and the agreement of May 1, 1893 (28 Stat. 326). This particular question has never been litigated; consequently, no authoritative answer thereto can now be given. It would appear to be relatively unimportant, however, in view of (1) the reported minor significance of their present day fishing activities, and (2) their participation in the fishery at Celilo Falls./1/[64] Since in addition many of their ancient grounds no longer have any present value, no effort was made to definitely locate same. Generally speaking, however, their manner of life and methods of taking fish were similar to the other Indians in the interior, e.g., see Yakama and Umatilla affidavits. [115]

The affidavits of the chosen representatives of the Indians of the Yakama Reservation are accompanied by plats showing the general location and legal description of several of the ancient fishing and camping grounds which were used by the Indians at the time of the coming of the white man as well as the area to which they are now confined in connection with their present fishing operations at such places.

Due to the burden of other duties on he personnel of the several agencies, it was not possible to obtain such representative plats covering the other tribal usual and accustomed fishing grounds.

With the group of Yakama affidavits there has been included the affidavits of the representatives of Priest Rapids band of Sokulk Indians, even though such tribe by reason of its

---

[64] 1/ Last paragraph of Superintendent's letter of April 12, 1940, to Frank B. Lenzie, Regional Forester, Spokane, Washington.

failure to participate in the Yakama treaty does not now officially constitute a part of the Yakama nation. The Yakama Indians, however, assert that prior to the coming of the white man, they also participated in the fishing and other activities at the several locations claimed by the Priest Rapids group and described in their affidavits.

There are, of course, numerous other tribes in the Pacific Northwest who prior to the coming of the first white people, lived in the same manner as did the other aboriginals and who also had their own tribal fishing grounds, but who for sundry reasons were not parties to a treaty or agreement containing the provision relative to the right to take fish outside the boundaries of the reservation at their usual and accustomed places. Since such tribes are not entitled to the easement right which inures to the benefit of the members of the tribes having such a treaty provision, there of course would have been no object in identifying their fishing grounds.

The Indian names for a number of the ancient fishing grounds are spelled in accordance with the way the Indian's pronunciation sounded to the writer [!!]. The sound of the Indian dialects is considerably [116] different from the English language, being for the most part guttural, in so far as the majority of the Pacific Northwest tribes are concerned. As a consequence, longer consonant clusters are possible and in a number of instances sounds are produced which have no exact counterpart in the English language.

This feature, of course, varies in degree with the different tribes. Accordingly and rather than endeavoring to indicate the pronunciation of the Indian place names through the use of confusing and not generally understood diacritical markings, the spelling thereof as appears in the affidavit is entirely phonetic. It is believed from the writer's own experience in pronouncing these Indian names when reading the affidavits back to the various Indian groups, that the Indians will be able to recognize the particular place if the name is phonetically pronounced in accordance with the indicated spelling.

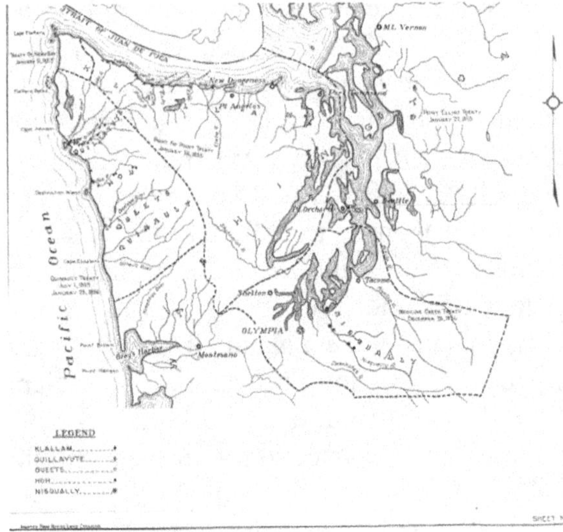

The importance of the Indian name, however, as an identifying feature of any particular fishing location is rapidly passing with the death of the older members of the various tribes who, generally speaking, are the only ones familiar with those names. In some instances it was even difficult for those older people to recall the Indian names of some of the places. Even they; however, in discussing these places amongst themselves, ordinarily use the English equivalent, or the present day name of some nearby identifying place. The English equivalent of any for the Indian names is given in those cases where it could be literally translated.

In this connection, reference is particularly had to the affidavits of the Quileute, Queets, Hoh and Skokomish groups.

The affidavits obtained have been grouped alphabetically by reservation. They are accompanied by a brief general narrative statement concerning the particular reservation.

Where ethnological facts are stated, the source of such information is Bulletin 30 of the Bureau of American Ethnology, familiarly known as the Handbook of American Indians. [117 map of treaties Sheet #2] [118]

CHEHALIS RESERVATION

AGENCY: - Taholah.
LOCATION: - Southwestern Washington, near Cosmopolis.
AREA: - 2,467 acres.
TREATY: - None.
INDIAN TRIBES: - Upper and Lower Chehalis, members of the [Coast] Salishan family.[65]
LOCATION OF "U. & A." FISHING GROUNDS:

Along the Chehalis river and its tributaries as well as the shores of Gray's Harbor and coast of the Pacific Ocean.

PRESENT FISHING GEAR AND REGULATIONS:

Set nets and gaff hooks. This tribe does not have any regulations governing its reservation fishing activities which are relatively minor in scope and carried on in the Chehalis and Black Rivers which traverse the reservation.

PRESENT FISHING ACTIVITIES:

It has been estimated by the Taholah Agency that the total value of fish caught by the Chehalis Indians during the four year period 1937-1940, inclusive, amounted to $9,207 of which $2,800 represented the value used for subsistence purposes. This relatively small percentage is probably, accounted for by the fact that the agency reports nearly all members of the tribe are employed as common laborers in the berry fields, logging and road camps and other activities requiring unskilled labor.

GENERAL REMARKS:

The Chehalis Indians, although attending the treaty council held on the Quinaielt river in 1855, did not become a party to the resultant treaty for the reason that they were dissatisfied with the proposal of the government to concentrate a number of separate and distinct tribes on one or two large [119] reserves. Consequently, even though they, like the other tribes in the territory, were classed as "fish eating" Indians and were dependant primarily on fish and other seafood for their subsistence, which was obtained from traditional fishing grounds, claimed by the tribe, they have no special rights at such places.

The information obtained and set forth in the affidavits was taken and included as a part of this report just because the Indians were under the impression that the investigation was intended to also ascertain the location of their ancient fishing grounds, and secondly, to illustrate, along with the other affidavits, the fact that there were few, if any, streams of consequence in the Pacific Northwest which were not utilized by Indians for the purpose of obtaining their annual supply of food fish.

In order that there would be no misunderstanding on their part, the Indians were very fully advised that the mere fact that their statements were being taken would not in any way give them the right to fish outside the reservation without observing state laws. [120]

AFFIDAVIT

STATE OF WASHINGTON}
COUNTY OF LEWIS }   } SS

Dan Secena, being first duly sworn, upon his oath deposes and says:

---

[65] [See letters re meetings at Chehalis added to the very end of this work.]

That he is 83 years old, a full blood Indian member of the Chehalis Indian Tribe, and a citizen of the United States of America residing on the Chehalis Indian Reservation, Washington; That he was born near Grand Mound, Washington, and lived there up until the time he moved to the Chehalis Reservation where he has lived since, and that his ancestors had always lived and fished in the area in which the various villages of the Chehalis Indians were located prior to the time the white men first came to the country; that he is familiar with the location of a number of the old villages either because he actually visited the sites where such had been located or because he had been told where they had been located by his parents and the elder members of the tribe; that he is also familiar with the number of the places utilized by the Chehalis Indians in fishing for their daily subsistence. Affiant further deposes and says that the places with which he is thus familiar are as follow:

LINCOLN CREEK

There was a permanent Indian village and fishing place at the mouth of what is now known as Lincoln Creek where it enters the Chehalis River; that the Indian name for this place is *Nah-cha-thlah-loat-son* [*nač'ałł* d49][66] and that it means "mouth of creek"; that when he was a small boy he remembers seeing Indians living at this place; that at that time there was a number of houses, one being the big house belonging to the chief and the others to the various families of that community; that there were many people living at that place as he recalls it;

That in addition to this village there were a number of small settlements located all along the Chehalis River; that the Indians obtained fish at all such settlements either with spears, nets, or traps. [121]

That this particular place, however, was one of the principal fishing places of the people who lived there for the late fall run of salmon that the only people who fished there were the people who lived in the community and such of their relatives and friends all might be visiting them at the time the fish were running, that the Indians were able to get enough fish from the fall run to last them all the year; the fish that they did not eat fresh were dried by smoking them over a fire for use during the timed when fresh fish were not available;

That he never actually fished at this place but he did see lots of Indians catching fish there; they caught the fish with a trap, spears, and gaff hooks and sometimes they would use a small net to get the fish out of the water; the trap was so made that the fish in swimming upstream and attempting to get over the trap would be thrown back into a basket; when there were a number of fish in the basket the Indians would take them out.

SCATTER CREEK

That there was an old permanent Indian village and fishing place at the mouth of what is known as Scatter Creek where it enters the Chehalis River; that the Indian name for this place was *Wah-thlah-lin-nah-loat-son* [*wała•ln* 'come loose, open' d33]; that he does not know the meaning of this name in English although the final syllables refer to the fact that it was the mouth of a creek;

That he does not remember ever seeing any Indians living here but understands that the Chehalis Indians did live there prior to the time he was born; that the fact that nobody was living here during his lifetime was probably brought about by the large number of deaths caused by the

---

[66] [d#] = M Dale Kinkade 1991 *Upper Chehalis Dictionary* University of Montana Occasional Papers in Linguistics #7.

smallpox plague which was brought to the country by the white man; that he was told that prior to the plague there was a large number of people living at this village,

That the people who lived at this place caught salmon by spearing them; that to do this they placed pickets across the creek which stopped the fish as they were going upstream and thus gave the Indians the opportunity to spear them while they were trying to get past the picket barrier; [122]

That he has visited the site of this old village a number of times but that when he visited this place he and the Indians who accompanied him used gaff hooks to catch their salmon; that he has not been there for a long time due to the fact that the salmon no longer spawn in the stream;

That although the Indians who lived there before the white men came considered it their permanent home, he and the other Indians that used to go there with him only stayed their temporarily; That the Indians did not sell the fish they caught at this place although sometimes they would give some of their catch to the white settlers as presents.

GRAND MOUND

That there was a very large permanent Village of the Chehalis Indians located on the Chehalis River at a place which is now within the boundaries of the present State school for girls; that the Indian name for this place was *Klah-ky-icklth* [*x̣aqayqł* = 'long prairie' d39] and that in English this meant "long prairie"; that this was the main village of the Upper Chehalis Indians; that it was here that he was born; that he was told that there were many Indians living there before he was born but that the greatest number of them were killed off by the smallpox epidemic;

That the Indians caught the fish here by spearing them and also with a trap constructed in the river; that he does not know whether the Indians ever sold any of the fish they caught at this place but he know he never sold any.

Affiant further deposes and says that after giving the foregoing information in response to questions of Edward G. Swindell, Jr., U.S. Indian Service, on December 4, 1941, at the Chehalis Community House, Chehalis Indian Reservation, he, at Mr. Swindell's request, listened carefully to the questions directed to Andrew Sanders, a member of the Chehalis Indian Tribe, concerning the location of Indian villages and fishing places with which Andrew Sanders was more [123] familiar than affiant; that he clearly heard the answers given by Andrew Sanders and can confirm them as being the truth based on the information about the matters involved that he obtained through his lifetime, and especially when he was a boy and a young man, from his parents and the older members of the Chehalis Indian tribe; that since the Indians could neither read nor write, the only way that they were able to know of the events which had occurred in the past was by each generation telling the people of the new generation of those very things.

That on the 13th day of May, 1942, he was present with Andrew Sanders at the Community House when an affidavit containing the information previously given by Andrew Sanders was read back to him by Mr. Swindell and interpreted by Silas Heck; that the information contained in said affidavit was the same information orally given by said Andrew Sanders on December 4, 1911, and that said Andrew Sanders acknowledged the same to be such and executed the affidavit in his presence as well as that of Silas Heck and Mr. Swindell.

Affiant further deposes and says that the Indians did not always stay in one place; that when they had sufficient fish, or the fish were not running in the streams, they would go to the mountains for berries and to the root patches to gather roots during the seasons when those things were ready for gathering.

Further affiant sayeth not.

(Sgd.) Dan Secena his mark

Dan Secena

Subscribed and sworn to before me this 13th day of May, 1942.

(Sgd.) Frank D. Beaulieu

(Seal) Notary Public in and for the State of Washington,

residing at Hoquiam. [124]

AFFIDAVIT OF INTERPRETER

STATE OF WASHINGTON}
COUNTY OF LEWIS }   }SS

Silas Heck, being first duly sworn, upon his oath deposes and says:

That he is 66 years old, a full blood Chehalis Indian of the Chehalis Indian, tribe, a citizen of the United States of America, residing on the Chehalis Indian Reservation, Washington; That he is thoroughly conversant with the English language and with the language spoken by the Chehalis Indians, and can translate the English language into the Chehalis Indian language and the Chehalis Indian language into the English language; that on December 4, 1941 at the Chehalis Community House, Chehalis Indian Reservation, Washington, in the presence of Dan Secena, deponent in the foregoing affidavit, Andrew Sanders, and Lucy Sanders, husband and wife, members of the Chehalis Indian Tribe, and Edward G. Swindell, Jr., U.S. Indian Service, affiant did, at the request of Mr. Swindell, interrogate Dan Secena with regard to certain matters concerning the location of the permanent villages and usual and accustomed fishing places of the Chehalis Indians, as well as with regard to the way in which they and their ancestors obtained a livelihood; that he translated the questions of Mr. Swindell from the English language into the Chehalis Indian language; which Dan Secena speaks and understands; that he translated from the Chehalis Indian language into the English language the answers of Dan Secena to Mr. Swindell's interrogatories; that at that time Mr. Swindell made written notes of the information given by the said Dan Secena and reduced said information to the narrative form as given in the above and foregoing affidavit of said Dan Secena,

Affiant further deposes and says that on the 13th day of May, 1942, in the presence of Dan Secena and Mr. Swindell, he translated the information contained in the aforesaid affidavit from the English language into the Chehalis Indian language as said affidavit was read to affiant by M. Swindell; [125] that the deponent, Dan Secena, told affiant that the said narrative affidavit contained the information given by him to Mr. Swindell on December 4, 1941 and that he had therefore signed said affidavit because the information contained therein was true.

Further affiant sayeth not.

(Sgd.) Silas Heck

Silas Heck

Silas Heck personally appeared before me this 13th day of May, 1942, and after having the foregoing affidavit read to him in my presence did acknowledge to me that the statements contained therein are true and that he executed same as his voluntary act.

Subscribed and sworn to before; me this 13th day of May, 1942.

(Sgd.) Frank D. Beaulieu

(Seal) Notary Public in and for the State of Washington,

residing at Hoquiam [126]

AFFIDAVIT

STATE OF WASHINGTON}
COUNTY OF LEWIS}   }SS.

Andrew Sanders, being first duly sworn, upon his oath deposes and says:

That he is 77 years old; a full blood member of the Chehalis Indian Tribe, and a citizen of the United States of America, residing at Tenino, Washington; That as a member of the Chehalis Tribe he is personally familiar with the location of a number of the old permanent villages of the Chehalis Indians as well as with the location of the places used by such Indians to obtain their annual supply of fish.

Affiant further deposes that he is familiar with the location of such villages and fishing places as follows:

RAINBOW FALLS

That the Chehalis Indians were accustomed to go to what is now known as Rainbow Falls each year for the purpose of catching eels [lampreys] as they ascended the falls and also to obtain a supply of elk meat; that the Indian name for this place was *Wah-moss* [cəlusid 182],[67] although he does not know what it means; that the Indians used this only as a temporary camping place for about a month of each year; that the eels were caught by hand as they clung to the rocks at the falls; that during his lifetime he can remember Indians up to the number of 20 and sometimes 30 using this camping ground; that he understands that in the early days prior to the time the number of Indians was so greatly decreased this place was used by many more Indians.

MUD BAY

That he has been told there was a permanent village of the Chehalis Indians at what is now known as Mud Bay; that the Indian name for this place was *Squieyelth* [sqʷayaił d103], which was the Indian name for what the white people call the Chehalis Indian Tribe; that this ₍₁₂₇₎ designation included the Indians living at Mud and Eld Inlet; that when he first visited the place when he was a young man there was no village there but he and other Chehalis Indiana would go there quite often for the purpose of digging clams and to catch dog salmon for which this place was very good; that the clams which were not eaten fresh were dried for future use by smoking them; the salmon were caught by hand in the shallow water where they were accustomed to spawn; that he has not been to this place for several years because the game wardens molest the Indians when they come up there to catch fish or dig for clams.

SQUAXIN

That there was probably a permanent village at this place but he is not certain as to this; that the Indian name for this place was *Qui-tse-lay-chen* [kʷacličn = 'middle corner' d111], which in English means "center of where people live"; that this was one of the well known clam digging grounds of the Upper Chehalis Indians and, although he has never been there, he has heard that it always has been used by the Indians to obtain clams.

SKOOKUMCHUCK CREEK

That there was a permanent Indian village called *Tow-a-tin* [te•w'tn' = 'ford place' d52], meaning "fording place" located about a mile above the mouth of the creek on the north side of

---

[67] [l#] = Dawn Bates, Thom Hess, Vi Hilbert 1994 *Lushootseed Dictionary* UW.

the Chehalis River, near the present city of Centralia, which in the old days was known as Centerville, Washington;

That the Indians who lived here fished in the creek, using spears and gaff hooks but could not use a trap as the water was too swift for that purpose; that he has fished there many times, the first time being about 40 years ago; that at that time there was no village there and he does not believe that the Indians have lived at this place for over 80 years or so; that being the time that the white people crowded them out;

The Indians dried the fish they caught at this place to be used at times when fresh fish was not available; they also dried salmon eggs by packing them in the skins of the fish they had caught and this was considered quite a delicacy. [128]

MICHIGAN HILL

There was a temporary Indian fishing place at what is· now known as Michigan Hill; the Indian name for this place was *Wah-lokt-un* [?*?], which means "place to fall down". This place received its Indian name as a result of an old Indian story in which some animals were pushed over the big cliff which is at this spot;

The Chehalis Indians would come to this place early each year from Skookumchuck to catch the fish which could be found resting in the still water preparatory to continuing further upstream; that this place was approximately 6 miles from the Indian settlement at Skookumchuck Creek or about a mile below the mouth of Lincoln Creek; that the Indians used to go back and forth between these two places in canoes.

Affiant further deposes and says that he was present at the Chehalis Community House, Chehalis Indian Reservation, on December 4, 1941 when Dan Secena, a Chehalis Indian, gave certain information to Edward G. Swindell, Jr., U.S. Indian Service, with regard to the location of Chehalis Indian villages and fishing places with which said Dan Secena was more familiar than affiant; that he listened carefully to the questions directed to said Dan Secena; and clearly heard the answers made by said Dan Secena; that he confirms them as being the truth based on information about the matters involved; that he obtained throughout his lifetime and specially when he was a boy and a young man, from his parents and the older members of the Chehalis Tribe;

Affiant further deposes and says that in addition to the things told Mr. Swindell by said Dan Secena, affiant would like to add the following information:

That the Indian village located at Lincoln Creek was the gathering place for Indians of a number of tribes such as the Mud Bay, Squally and Tenino Chehalis; that there were plenty of roots such as camas on the near-by prairie; that in addition to the Fall run of salmon caught at this place he understands the Indians were also accustomed to catching salmon during the [129] spring runs; that they also caught eels [lampreys] at Lincoln Creek and that when the fish and eels stopped running, which was about the month of June, the Indians would move on to Skookumchuck;

That he can recall the Indians fished at Scatter Creek in the winter time for silverside salmon which was usually" available about Christmas time; that he has fished there himself with a spear and a gaff hook; that the Indians would stay at this place about two or three weeks at a time;

That in the early part of the year, in about the month of May, the Indians would fish for trout, using a small trap which they would move from time to time upstream until they reached the outlet from the lake;

That these things occurred during his lifetime; that he has heard that prior to his birth there had been a permanent village at this place, as stated by Dan Secena;

Further affiant sayeth not.

(Sgd.). Andrew Sanders   his mark

Subscribed and sworn to before me this 13th day of May, 1942.

(Sgd.) Frank D. Beaulieu
(seal) Notary Public in and for
the State of Washington,
residing at Hoquiam

AFFIDAVIT OF INTERPRETER

State of Washington}
County of Lewis }   }SS.

Silas Heck, being first duly sworn, upon his oath deposes and says:

That he is 69 years old, a full blood Chehalis Indian of the Chehalis Indian Tribe, a citizen of the United States of America, residing on the Chehalis Indian Reservation, Washington; [130]

That he is thoroughly conversant with the English language and with the language spoken by the Chehalis Indians, and can translate the English language into the Chehalis Indian language and the Chehalis Indian language into the English language; that on December 4, 1941 at the Chehalis Community House, Chehalis Indian Reservation, Washington, in the presence of Andrew Sanders, deponent in the foregoing affidavit, Dan Secena and Lucy Sanders, members of the Chehalis Indian tribe, and Edward G. Swindell, Jr., U.S. Indian Service, affiant did, at the request or Mr. Swindell, interrogate Andrew Sanders with regard to certain matters concerning the location of the permanent villages and usual and accustomed fishing places of the Chehalis Indians, as well as with regard to the way in which they and their ancestors obtained a livelihood; that he translated the questions of Mr. Swindell from the English language into the Chehalis Indian language, which Andrew Sanders speaks and understands; that he translated from the Chehalis Indian language into the English language the answers of Andrew Sanders to Mr. Swindell's interrogatories; that at that time Mr. Swindell made written notes of the information given by the said Andrew Sanders and reduced said information to the narrative form as given in the above and foregoing affidavit of said Andrew Sanders.

Affiant further deposes and says that on the 13th day of May, 1942, in the presence of Andrew Sanders and Mr. Swindell, he translated the information contained in the aforesaid affidavit from the English language into the Chehalis Indian language as said affidavit was read to affiant by Mr. Swindell; that the deponent, Andrew Sanders, told affiant that the said narrative affidavit contained the information given by him to Mr. Swindell on December 4, 1941, and that he had therefore signed said affidavit because the information contained therein was true.

Further affiant sayeth not.

(Sgd.) Silas Heck
Silas Heck

Silas Heck personally appeared before me this 13th day of May, 1942, and after having the foregoing [131] affidavit read to him in my presence did acknowledge same that the statements contained therein are true and that he executed same as his voluntary act.

Subscribed and sworn to before me this 13th day of May, 1942.

(Sgd.) Frank D. Beaulieu
Notary Public in and for
the State of Washington,
residing at Hoquiam [132]

AFFIDAVIT

STATE OF WASHINGTON}
COUNTY OF LEWIS }   } SS.

Lucy Sanders, being first duly sworn, upon her oath deposes and says:

That she is 67 years old and a full blood Indian member of the Chehalis Indian Tribe, a citizen of the United States of America, residing at Tenino, Washington;

That she was born at a Chehalis Indian village located at the mouth of the Black River where it enters the Chehalis River on the upstream or east side of the Black River; that this was the location of an old permanent village of the Chehalis Indians and that it was called *Sah-tsah-ulth*, which in English means "river coming from the lake"; that both the river and the lake had the same name; that when she was a little girl she remembers seeing the Indians fishing there using spears and hooks to supplement the fish which they could catch in a trap constructed at the mouth of the river.

Affiant further deposes and says that when she was a little girl she had been told there was a Chehalis Indian village known as *Thla-qah-mish* [*łakʷamš* 'Blockhouse Prairie' d11], but she does not know what that means in English; that she was told this was a permanent village of the Chehalis people which they had used from time immemorial prior to the time the white people came; that the village was located across from the mouth of Cedar Creek above the city of Cedarville, Washington.

Affiant further deposes and says that she was present on December 4, 1941 at the Chehalis Community House, Chehalis Indian Reservation, Washington, when her husband, Andrew Sanders, and Dan Secena, both Chehalis Indians, gave certain information to Edward G. Swindell, Jr., U.S. Indian Service, with regard to the location of the Chehalis Indian villages and fishing places, and that she listened carefully to the questions directed to both Andrew Sanders and Dan Secena; that [133] she clearly heard the answers given by Andrew Sanders and Dan Secena, and that she can confirm them as being the truth based on her own personal knowledge of some of the things talked about or on information received by her during her lifetime from her parents and other members of the Chehalis Indian Tribe;

That on the 13th day of May, 1942 she was present with Andrew Sanders, when an affidavit containing the information previously given by him was read back to him by Mr. Swindell and interpreted by Silas Heck; that the information contained in said affidavit was the same information orally given by said Andrew Sanders on December 4, 1941, and that said Andrew Sanders acknowledged the same to be such and executed the affidavit in the presence of each other as well as that of Silas Heck and Mr. Swindell.

Further affiant sayeth not.

(Sgd.). Lucy Sanders
Lucy Sanders

Subscribed and Sworn to before me this 13th day of May, 1942.

(Sgd.) Frank D. Beaulieu
(Seal) Notary Public in and for
the State of Washington,
residing at Hoquiam [134]

AFFIDAVIT

STATE OF WASHINGTON}
COUNTY OF LEWIS}   } SS.

Silas Heck, being first duly sworn, upon his oath deposes and says:

That he is 69 years old, a full blood Chehalis Indian of the Chehalis Indian Tribe, a citizen of the United States of America, residing on the Chehalis Indian Reservation, Washington;

That he has lived among the Chehalis Indians all his life and is fully familiar with the way they live at the present time and the way their ancestors lived as such was told to him by his parents and older members of the tribe at the time when he was a boy and a young man;

That on December 4, 1941 he was present at the Chehalis Community House, Chehalis Indian Reservation, Washington, when Edward G. Swindell, Jr., U.S. Indian Service, questioned Lucy Sanders, Andrew Sanders and Dan Secena with regard to the location of the villages and fishing grounds of the Chehalis Indians; that at that meeting he acted as interpreter for Mr. Swindell in questioning Andrew Sanders and Dan Secena;

That at Mr. Swindell's request he listened carefully to the questions directed to all three of the above named individuals and that he clearly heard the answers given by them; that from his own personal knowledge of the things that occurred during his own lifetime he can confirm those statements, and that as to things that happened prior to his birth he can confirm them from the information he obtained from his parents and the other members of the tribe during his youth.

Affiant further deposes and says that since the Indians are unable to make any written records of the events and happenings of the past, the only way such information could be retained would be through the Indian custom of the older members of each generation telling the younger members of the next generation of [135] such things as had occurred in the past.

Further affiant sayeth not.

(Sgd.) Silas Heck His Mark
Silas Heck

Subscribed and sworn to before me this 12th day of May, 1942.

(Sgd.) Frank D. Beaulieu
(Seal) Notary Public in and for
the State of Washington,
residing at Hoquiam [136]

CLALLAM INDIANS

AGENCY: - Tulalip
LOCATION: -

The descendants of the Clallam Indian tribe have no reservation as such. The Government, however, recently has purchased tracts of lands for them along the north coast of the Olympic Peninsula. The largest one of these tracts is located at what is known as Lower Elwha which was the location of one of the prediscovery villages of these Indians.
TREATY: - January 26, 1855, 12 Stat. 933; 2 Kappler 674 at *Hahdskus* or Point no Point.
INDIAN TRIBES: - Clallam [S'Klallam] Indians of the Salishan family.

LOCATION OF "U. & A." FISHING GROUNDS: -

At the mouth of various streams entering the Strait of Juan de Fuca and along Hood Canal commencing at the Hoko River near the northwest tip of Olympic Peninsula east to Port Discovery, Washington. In addition to this area which constituted their perm ant quarters they had summer fishing and camping grounds along the Hood Canal. Many of the present day place names in this area of Washington are derived from the names of Clallam villages upon or near the site of which the non-Indian communities were founded.

FISHING GEAR AND REGULATIONS: -

At the present time fishing is of relatively minor importance to these Indians when engaged in that activity, they use gear which has not been declared illegal by the state of Washington. There are no regulations governing the fishing activities of that portion of this group located on the Lower Elwha reserve. [137]

GENERAL REMARKS: -

The Clallam Indians, although a party to the treaty with the Government, would not when the time came remove to reservation which the Government set aside for them.

At the present time, with the exception of the lands purchased for them at Lower Elwha and one or two smaller areas, not here important, they reside on lands owned by themselves. There is such a community at Jamestown near Sequin, Washington. In view of their refusal to abide by the provisions of this treaty, it is doubtful whether they could successfully assert the easement right at their usual and accustomed fishing grounds. They, like the other Indians, of course would be bound by state conservation measures which do not violate the principles announced in the Tulee case.

There are so few of these people left who have retained their tribal affiliations that there is little likelihood that any controversy with regard to the easement right will arise. At the present time there are two distinct groups and since they like the Chehalis Indians had received the impression that their ancient grounds were to be made a matter of record, meetings were held with both groups. Affidavits, however, were only taken from the chosen representatives of the western group, located at Lower Elwha. Their statements cover only such of the traditional grounds as are located west of Port Angeles, Washington. Had affidavits been taken from the other group, their testimony would have shown that there were Clallam villages and fishing camps at the mouths of the streams entering the Strait of Juan de Fuca from Port Angeles east to Port Discovery where the Clallam country joined that of the Chemakum tribe. These latter also had fishing grounds which the Clallams claim were also used by them. [138]

JOINT AFFIDAVIT OF MRS. SAM ULMER,
JOHN MIKE, AND CHARLEY HOPIE

STATE OF WASHINGTON}
COUNTY OF CLALLAM }   } SS.

Mrs. Sam Ulmer, 66 years of age, John Mike, 80 years of age, and Charley Hopie, 78 years of age, each being first duly sworn and put upon oath severally deposes and says:

That they are members of the Klallam Tribe of Indians, and citizens of the United States of America residing at the Lower Elwha Indian Community near Port Angeles, Washington; that they were born in the country formerly owned by the Klallam Indians which was subsequently taken over by the white people; that they have lived all their lives in the Clallam country and during their lifetimes have had occasion to visit a number of the permanent villages and temporary fishing camps of the Klallam Indians; that as a result of personal observation of the way those places were being used by the Indians at the time of their visits, as well as the information which was given to affiants by their parents and other older members of the Klallam Tribe of Indians during their youth and are familiar with the location of the various places used by the Klallam Indians for permanent village sites west of the present city of Port Angeles, Washington, as well as with regard to the location of the temporary fishing camps used by the Klallam Indians along the Hood canal during the summer month's.

Affiants further depose and say that they are familiar with the location of Klallam Indian villages and fishing places as follows:

HOKO RIVER

That this was the location of one of the old permanent Klallam Indian villages for which the Indian name was *Ho-cho* [*hu'qu'* k631];[68] that there were two big buildings on the west side and two big buildings on the east side of the river and all four of them were located close to its mouth; that there were about eight large families living at this point and that when affiants first [139] remember this place there were approximately 100 people living there; that this was the birthplace of Mrs. Sam Ulmer, one of the deponents herein; that all of the residents of this village were Klallam Indians; that they have either fished there or seen the Indians fishing there and that in the old days the fish were caught with a trap made out of cedar pickets tied together with twisted cedar boughs; that all of the people who lived here shared in the catch; that, sometimes the Indians from further west known as the Makah Indians would visit the people at Hoko River for the purpose of trading with them; that the trap was located approximately seven miles upstream from the mouth of the river because the conditions of the water where the village was located did not permit the construction of the trap there; that in addition to catching fish in this manner, the Indians were accustomed to catching fish with spears where the water was shallow; that they also used what is known as a basket trap which varies in length but ordinarily would be about 24 feet long; that in addition to these methods, the Indians also caught fish near the mouth of the river in nets which were drifted between two canoes and this method of fishing was practiced near the mouth of the river was known as *Tcha-min* [?*?];

SEKIU*

That the Indians from Hoko River used to visit what to them was known as *Sekiu* [ƛa'ƛəways k699] where they would obtain a supply of salt water fish; that they would remain at this place until they had obtained a sufficient supply to take back with them to their permanent village and eat as a change from the fish which were caught in the Hoko River;

CLALLAM BAY

That there was a permanent village located at Klallam Bay which was divided into two parts, the one on the west side being known as *Klah-klah-why-ees* [*čiči'yucx̱əy* k579] and the one on the east was called *Wha-nean-it* [*x̱ŋint* k579]; that there were a number of large and small buildings at these places although the population was smaller than that at the permanent village at Hoko; that at this place the Indians did not have a trap to fish with because there were no streams in which the trap could be constructed; that they caught their fish by trolling in [140]
    *This is located west of Hoko River and should not be confused
    with the present town of Sekiu, Washington.
the bay with Indian hooks made of the crotch of a hemlock limb with a line manufactured out of dried kelp; that the fish they caught in this manner were the spring salmon; halibut and ling cod; that the people at this place were accustomed to going to the village at Hoko for the supply of river fish.

---

[68] [k#] = Timothy Montler 2012 *Klallam Dictionary* UW.

PYSHT

That there were two permanent Indian villages located at *Pysht* [*pəšct* k685], one of which was on the small bay south of what the white people call Pillar Point on the north side of the Pysht River and the other was located on the east side of the river approximately opposite the present town of Pysht; that the Indian name for the one on the north side of the river was *Pee-sht* [?*?] which meant "wind blowing against it all the time" and that the one on the other side was known as *Nee-qho* [?*?]; that there were a number of houses at this place although the Indians have not lived there permanently since the lumber company made them move away about 80 years ago; that they caught their fish in the same manner as Indians who lived at the Hoko River; that the two villages had one trap between them located about two miles east of the junction of the river with the present Clallam Bay Road; that when they remember the Indians fishing at this place they no longer used the trap because there was less effort in catching the fish by buying nets needed instead of constructing the trap, which required a lot of skill and patience;

That the locations for the nets after they had first been established were recognized as the property of the individual families who first started using the place, and that when the trap method of fishing was abandoned, the Indians no longer shared their catch with each other as they did in the old days prior to the coming of the white man when the catch was divided amongst all of the people in the village;

That the Indians of the Clallam Bay villages obtained plenty of roots and berries in the vicinity and did not need to go to the mountains for those things; that they also obtained clams on the beach outside of the bay and in a westerly direction from Pillar Point; that the clams were brought home and cured at their permanent residences.

DEEP CREEK

That there was an old permanent Klallam Indian village located on the east side of and close to the [141] mouth of what is now known as Deep Creek, which village to the Indian was known as *Tse-khun (tse-qhun)* [*c'ix̲ʷəŋ* k591], which means "spit" or "projecting point"; that although this village was not in existence during affiants lifetime they were told that prior to the coming of the white man the Klallam Indians had used this place for a permanent home and that they were accustomed to obtain fish and clams at that point.

Affiants further depose and say that in addition to the above listed permanent villages of the Klallam Indians there were other villages utilized by these Indians prior to the coming of the white people as follows:

1. Twin Rivers: The Indian name for this place was *Nuh-chee-sah-tun* [*nəxʷčəsa'qən* k737] which means "two streams entering ocean at the same place" and that explains the name that was given, to it by the white people.

2. Lyre River: That the Indian name for this place was *qhah-qhah-nah-ah* [*kʷa'x̲ʷa'ma'* k652] but affiants do not know the meaning thereof; that affiants, however, have seen shell heaps and traces of human habitation at this point and were told by their people that this once had been a village site of the Klallam Indians.

3. Salt Creek. That this place was known as *Klte-tun-ut* [?*?] although affiants do not know what this name means; that this place during affiants lifetimes was one of the summer fishing and camping grounds of the Klallam Indians who lived at Elwa; that they would go there each year for the purpose of obtaining the salt water fish that were

native to that area; that they sometimes trolled for salmon while here and if they had enough for their own use, they would sell some of their catch to white people in order to obtain cash for necessities; that at one time there had been quite a large permanent village at this place.

4. Elwha River: That there was an old permanent village located at the meeting place of Indian Creek and Elwa River; that the name of the creek as well as of the village was *Tee-tee-ulth* [*ti'ti'əł* Boston Creek k602]; that the village was located on the south bank of the creek and the west bank of the river; that the site of this village was flooded out from the water backed up by the lower dam constructed by the Puget Sound Power and Light Company; that although, as affiants recall it, there were only a few people living at this place prior to the flooding, [142] it was used by a large number of people who would come to this place from the villages below because it was easy to catch the fish in Indian Creek and the other small streams in the vicinity; that when the people visited this place for fishing places, they would remain for a period of one or two months.

5. Lower Elwha: That there were two villages at what is now known as Lower Elwha Community, one on the east and one on the west bank of the Elwha River [*'e'ḵʷa'* k602]; that their location was approximately one-half mile from the house of Sam Ulmer, a resident of the present community; that there were a number of houses and quite a few people in each of those two sections of the village and that the Indian name for this village was *Elwha* that the Indians were driven from the east side of the river to the west side after the white people came to the country; that the Indians were accustomed to catch fish with all the usual methods employed by the Klallams in obtaining this essential food supply.

6. Morse Creek: That although affiants never did see a village at this place they understood that there was a permanent one there a long time ago and that it was called *Tulth-mut* [*cəłmət* Morse Creek k658], which was also the name of the stream now called Morse Creek by the white people.

Affiants further depose and say that there were a number of other Klallam Indian villages located to the east of the foregoing mentioned places but they would prefer that the Klallam people living in the Jamestown Community give the information with regard to those easterly places.

That the Klallam Indians in addition to their permanent villages located along the north side of what is now known as the Olympic Peninsula and numerous temporary fishing places along the Hood Canal on the west side of Puget Sound to which they went each year for the purpose of obtaining a supply of the fish that were there available and not available at the permanent villages; that these places have not been visited by the Klallam Indians for years due to the fact that they have taken up the white man's way of living and are endeavoring to earn their livelihood through farming and work in the various communities near where they live; that affiants are unable to describe the precise locations where those temporary fishing camps there located although they know the Klallams must have used them because they were situated in the country ceded to the Government by the [143] Klallam Indians;

That the Klallam Indians and the Makahs were accustomed to visiting each others country for the purpose of trading one kind of fish for another kind or whale and seal meat; that although they quite often were at war with each other, they generally speaking considered themselves friends; that sometimes individuals from each tribe would intermarry although this has occurred oftener since the coming of the white man and the breaking down of the old barriers between the tribes.

Further affiants sayeth not.

(Sgd.) Mrs. Sam Ulmer Her Mark
Mrs. Sam Ulmer
(Sgd.) John Mike His Mark
John Mike

Subscribed and sworn to before me this 12th day of May, 1942.

(Sgd.) Frank D. Beaulieu
(Seal) Notary Public in and for
the State of Washington,
residing at Hoquiam

AFFIDAVIT OF INTERPRETER.

STATE OF WASHINGTON}
COUNTY OF KLALLAM}   } SS.

Sam Ulmer, being first duly sworn, upon his oath deposes and says that he is 63 years of age and a member of the Klallam tribe of Indians, a citizen of the United States of America and a resident of the Lower Elwa Indian Community near Port Angeles, Washington;

That he is thoroughly conversant with the English language and with the Klallam Indian language and can translate English language into the Klallam Indian language and the Klallam Indian language into the English language.

That on December 1, 1941, at affiant's home in the Lower Elwa Community and in the presence of Mrs. Sam Ulmer, affiant's wife, John Mike and Charley Hopie, [144] who are the deponents in the foregoing joint affidavit, and Edward G. Swindell, Jr., U.S. Indian Service, affiant did at the request of Mr. Swindell interrogate the said deponents with regard to certain matters concerning the location of a number of the old Klallam Indian villages and fish places in the area formerly owned by the Klallam Indians prior to the coming of the white man; that he translated the questions of Mr. Swindell from the English language into the Klallam Indian language, which the said deponents speak and understand; that he translated the answers of said deponents to Mr. Swindell's interrogatories from the Klallam language into the English language; that at that time Mr. Swindell made routine notes of the information given by the said deponents and reduced said information to the narrative form as given in the above and foregoing joint affidavit of the said deponents.

Affiant further deposes and says that on the 12th day of May, 1942, in the presence of Mrs. Sam Ulmer, John Mike, and Charley Hopie, deponents, and Mr. Swindell, he translated the information contained in the aforesaid joint affidavit of the said deponents from the English language into the Klallam language as said joint affidavit was read to affiant by Mr. Swindell; that the said deponents and each of them told affiant that the said narrative joint affidavit contained the information given by them to Mr. Swindell on December 1, 1941, and they had, therefore, signed said affidavit because the information contained therein was true.

Affiant further deposes and says that during his lifetime he traveled throughout the Klallam country and visited a number of the places referred to by the deponents in the aforesaid joint affidavit; that he has seen with his own eyes, the Indians living and fishing at some of these places; that as to those places which he visited and which the Indians were forced to give up after the coming of the white man, he, when he was a small boy and a young man, was told about how the Indians lived and fished at those places by his parents and the older members of the Klallam people; that he believes the information given him at that time was true because there was no reason why his parents or the other people should have wished to tell him untruths; that he, therefore, can and does confirm the information contained in the aforesaid joint affidavit from his own personal knowledge [145] and the information given him by his parents.

Further affiant sayeth not.

(Sgd.) Sam Ulmer

Sam ·Ulmer

Sam Ulmer personally appeared before me this 12th day of May, 1942, and after having the foregoing affidavit read to him in my presence did acknowledge to me that the statements contained therein are true and that he executed same as his voluntary act.

Subscribed and sworn to before me this 12th day of May, 1942.

(Sgd.) Frank D. Beaulieu

(Seal) Notary Public in and for

the State of Washington,

residing at Hoquiam [146]

COLUMBIA RIVER AREA

AGENCY: - Yakama, Warm Springs, and Umatilla.

LOCATION: - Columbia River from Spearfish, Wash., to Celilo Falls, Oregon

TREATY: - Walla Walla, Cayuse, and Umatilla Treaty of June 9, 1855, 12 Stat. 945; 2 Kappler 694, and Yakama Treaty of June 9, 1855, 12 Stat. 951; 2 Kappler 698. See "Remarks". In re Warm Springs Indians and their treaty of June 25, 1855, 12 Stat. 963; 2 Kappler 714.

INDIAN TRIBES: - Yakama; Walla Walla, Cayuse, Umatilla, and what are now known as Warm Springs Indians from the reservation bearing the same name.

LOCATION OF "U. and A." FISHING GROUNDS: -

Along the main Columbia River from Cascade Rapids to the mouth of the Snake River.

PRESENT FISHING ACTIVITIES, GEAR. AND REGULATIONS: -

In this area are the two places along the Columbia River where the Indians can participate in commercial fishing activities as a consequence of the location of the Seufert cannery near The Dalles, Oregon. Some fish, however, is sold to buyers representing canneries located downstream near Portland, Oregon.

During the season from May 1938 to February 1939, figures furnished by the Oregon Fish Commission show that the Indians of the above named tribes participated in the commercial catch to the extent of 1,639,924 pounds which amounts to 8.6 per cent of the total commercial catch, of salmon in the Columbia River. During the same period of the 1939-1940 season, the Indian catch amounted to 1,397,820 pounds of fish or 7.6 per cent of the total river catch. The value thereof is not given. In [147] addition to the fish of which records are kept, additional large numbers are consumed fresh by the Indians during the fishing season or else cured by drying for use during the winter months as a supplement to the family's food supply. The poundage of the fish used for subsistence purposes cannot be definite ascertained but the importance of this article of food as shown by a survey of 55 representative families is shown on pages 13 and 14 of this report.

With the exception of the spear, the fishing gear used by the Indians in this area is the same kind used by their aboriginal ancestors; viz, dip net and bag nets, the operation of which has been previously described.

Inasmuch as the area is not within any reservation, the Indians while fishing are subject to state law and regulation. In this connection, it is to be noted that fishing activities are carried out on both banks of the river, the north one being in the State of Washington and the south one in Oregon. The latter state in whose jurisdiction is located Celilo Falls has endeavored to recognize the Indians' claimed rights under their treaties as we previously noted on page 76. That state, however, requires that the Indians while fishing commercially observe the closed season in order that appropriate escapement periods be provided for migrating salmon. Until the decision in the Tulee case, the State of Washington, however, did not provide any special dispensation for the Indians as had Oregon, in so far as commercial fishing is concerned.

In addition to the state regulations, the Indians themselves endeavor to regulate their fishing activities as between themselves, i.e., the settlement of disputes as to the right of individuals to use particular fishing locations on the rocks and islands in the river. Regulation of this nature is undertaken by what is known as the Celilo Fish Committee, whose membership is made up of delegates selected by the Indians of the three reservations. [148]

GENERAL REMARKS: -

The Indian fishery in this area in so far as commercial fishing is concerned, is now principally confined to the area immediately adjacent to Celilo Falls on both sides of the river and the Klickitat River which enters the Columbia at Lyle, Washington. It has been reported that the latter fishery, although once of considerable importance, is no longer significant because of the depleted fish migrations entering the river. There are, of course, other spots within the area at which some fishing operations are carried on.

It will be recalled that within this area were located the major Indian fishing and trading centers of *Wyam* on the Oregon side immediately adjacent to the falls and at Wishram (*Nixluidix*) on the Washington side where Spearfish, Washington, is presently located.

According to the affidavits of the Indians, of the several tribes now fishing in this area (q.v.), some of the ancestors of each tribe participated in the fishing at Celilo Falls (*Wyam*) as well as other places along both banks of the river. This is understandable when it is considered that practically all of them are members of the Shahaptian linguistic family or, as in the case of the Cayuse, a Waiilatpuan tribe closely associated with the Walla Wallas of the former family. In some instances the courts have recognized the rights of the Indians of the three reservations to the joint use of same of the various fishing places in the area in question. See United States v. Seufer, 233 Fed. 579, aff'd, 249 U.S. 194, and U.S. v. Brookfield Fisheries, etc., 24 F. Supp. 712.

Although the Warm Springs Indians (Tribes of Middle Oregon Treaty) presently participate in the fisheries in this area, their doing so without being required to observe all state regulations such as license fees and poundage taxes as well as seasons, etc., is really by sufferance since the fishing rights originally reserved by their treaty were subsequently relinquished. (See p. 323A hereof.) [148A]

The principal problem existing in this area is brought about by the fact that there are so many more Indians participating in the fishing than in the early days. This situation has been brought about by two factors, viz, the fact that our present day Indians are anxious to engage in commercial fishing in order to obtain money with which to purchase the necessities of modern life and the fact that fishing for subsistence purposes alone at the majority of the many other usual and accustomed grounds is either no longer possible due to the destruction of the fish runs frequenting such places or else state law prohibits the type of gear (weirs and traps) formerly utilized at such places. It has been estimated that as many as 1,500 Indians are assembled in the area during the height of the season, most of whom reside at Celilo Falls. Since the established locations in this area are recognized as the privately owned property of families whose ancestors allegedly have used same for countless generations, disputes frequently occur when newcomers endeavor to usurp a spot claimed by others. The Celilo Fish Committee endeavors to settle these disputes but inasmuch as it cannot inforce [enforce] its decisions, such controversies present a continuing source of administrative problems. This situation is further complicated as a result of Indians from other jurisdictions as well as non-Indians coming to the Falls to participate in the fishing. However, since the right to utilize the usual and accustomed places was reserved in common with other citizens, there seems to be no effective way to eliminate this phase of the situation outside of acquisition by the United States of title to the fishing and camping grounds. This possibility has been the subject of considerable study by the government during the past several years. [149]

AFFIDAVIT

STATE OF OREGON}
COUNTY OF WASCO}   } SS.

Tommy Thompson, being first duly sworn, upon his oath deposes and says:

That he is 79 years old, a full blooded member of the *Wyam* [*wayam* = 'above' v279][69] Tribe of Indians, and a citizen of the United States of America residing at Celilo, Oregon; that to the Indians, Celilo is known as *Wyam* and the people who lived there in the old days prior to the coming of the white people, were known as *Wy-am-pum* [*wayampam* v279];

That he was born at *Wiyam* and has lived there all his life; that his father and mother told him his ancestors had always lived and fished at that place; that the Chief or Head of the *Wyam* Indians had always been a member of his family; as for example, his father's oldest brother was *Stocket-ly* who representing the *Wyam* Indians at the treaty council with Governor Joel Palmer, signed the treaty on their behalf; that after *Stocket-ly*'s death about 36 years ago, affiant became the Chief or Headman of the Indians still living at *Wyam* and that, as a consequence of the foregoing, and the things that were told him by his parents as well as his own personal knowledge of the situation, he is fully familiar with how the *Wy-am-pum* lived and fished at the falls of the Columbia River, which in Indian is known as *Chee-wan'-a* [*nch'i wana* v356] or "Big Water" in the white mans language.

Affiant further deposes that he first fished at *Wyam* when he was about 14 years old and that ever since then he has fished there each year although that was not the only place where he has caught fish; that when the water was too high at *Wyam* for good fishing, he would go to Tenino where water conditions would permit fishing even though fish could not be caught at Celilo at that time.

That he also fished at what is known as *Skein* [*sk'in* v279], which in Indian means "cradle board" and which is [150] located immediately below the railroad bridge crossing the Columbia River west of the falls; and that the name Skein was given to that place and the group of Indians who lived there because their camp grounds were shaped like the cradle board used by the Indians to carry their babies; that the Indians also called this place *Wah-pykt* [v] and that they used to be able to get a good supply of drift wood on account of the currents of the river there.

---

[69] [v#] = Virginia Beavert & Sharon Hargus 2009 *Yakama Sahaptin ~ Ichishkiin Sinwit Dictionary* UW.

The Indians considered *Wah-pykt* their permanent home and they were about 180 or so in number;

That a long time ago he also fished above the mouth of Rock Creek, which the Indians called *Tampanoe* [?*?], where fishing was carried on by a different method than that used at *Wyam* and Skein; that at the latter two places fish were caught with spears and dip or bag nets, whereas at *Tam-pance*, the Indians were accustomed to catch their fish with a long net;

That his principal fishing activities, however, have always been at *Wyam*, and that when he and the other Indians from *Wyam* would visit the other Indian fishing camps along the river, they would do so primarily for the purpose of meeting the people who lived at those other fishing places since they were all friends and joined each other in participating in Indian ceremonial dances and games of skill and chance;

Affiant deposes that up until the time the Celilo Ship Canal was constructed, the old Indian village and camping ground was located up near where the present upstream or intake end of the canal comes out of the river, and that the Indians did not move to their present location until after they were forced to move by reason of the construction of the canal; that when he was a small boy his parents as well as the other older people told him that *Wiyam* was and always had been a permanent village and that Indians lived there all the year around;

That he was told that prior to the time he was born, there were a large number of Indians living at *Wyam*, probably as many as 600 or 700 individuals; [151] that of this number about 200 were adults; that when he was a boy, there was not, however, nearly as many Indians living at *Wyam* because most of the inhabitants move to the various reservations when he was a young man about 20 years old; that they did this in accordance with their treaty with the Government; that the greatest number of them went to Warm Springs Reservation, a few went to the Yakama Reservation and probably les than 10 went to the Umatilla Reservation; that he did not want to leave his own home and that despite the fact that his relatives are reported to have selected an allotment for him at Warm Springs;

That the *Wyam* Indians were related to those living at Tenino, Skein, and *Wah-pykt* and there was a slight relationship between them and the Indians who lived at Rock Creek; that all these people were friends amongst themselves as well as with the Umatillas, Walla-Wallas, Cayuses, Wascoes and Yakamas, even before the white people first came to the Indian country, although he understands there were times some of the smaller groups would have trouble amongst themselves but this did not last; that since he first began to remember things, it is his recollection that generally speaking all of the river Indians in the area around *Wyam* were good friends and the older people have told him this was true prior to the time he was born;

That in addition to being friends, some members of all of the Indian tribes he has named would visit *Wyam* for the purpose of trading roots, berries, and venison for dried salmon put up by the people who lived at *Wyam* that it the visiting Indians did not have anything to trade for fish, the local people would either give them some of their own supply or else they would lend them the necessary equipment and permit them to catch all the fish they needed from one of the established fishing stations belonging to the local people; in other words, all the Indiana were friends and shared their food and the means of obtaining same with those who were less fortunate.

Affiant further deposes that the fishing platform locations on the banks of the river and on the rocks and islands in the river by the falls, have been used by the local people from as long back as the Indians can remember; that these stations have been [152] handed down from the older to the younger Indians of the same family from generation to· generation; that the Chief of the local Indians was the one who would say who should use a place when there was no one in the family to whom it had belonged capable of making use of it and that the decision of the Chief was final and respected by all the other Indians; that as he remembers it, when he was a boy there were only about 25 or 27 Indians actually who went out to the rocks for the purpose of catching fish, whereas today there are as many as 200 Indians fishing during the heaviest part of the summer run; that in the old days, there were not as many controversies concerning who should use a particular fishing rock as there were plenty of such places for the number of Indians who then fished; that the location of the fishing stations changed as the river would go down after the high water in the springtime; that although a number of new fishing sites have been discovered since the number of Indians fishing has increased, there are still not enough places for all those who wish to fish at *Wyam*; that on account of this, it is necessary to divide the use of some places among those Indians who do not have fishing rocks which have been handed down in the family from generation to generation as long back as the Indians remembered;

That the number of Indians who came to obtain fish at *Wyam* is quite large and that most of them come from the Umatilla, Yakama, and Warm Springs Reservations, although a very few come from the Nez Perce country and Montana; that some of those who come from the first three named places are descendants of the original owners of the local fishing stations prior to their removal to the reservations.

Affiant further deposes that when he was a boy he recalls the Indians lived in houses made of tulles for which the Indian name is *Tee-koe* [*tk'u* v455] and that the same material was used for their drying sheds; that in some of the large houses as many as five or six families would live and in other instances there would be only one family to a house that in the old days some of the houses were partly built underground because they were easier to keep warm and that the [153] people entered them through a small opening close to the ground, after which they descended to the floor by a small ladder put there for that purpose;

That the Indians nowadays and always have dried their fish in the open air in a shed which kept them from the rays of the sun, and that they did not cure their fish by smoking them over fires;

That in the old days, the Indians would dry some of the fish they caught at all times through the spring and fall runs, whereas today most of the drying for their own personal future use is done during the season when the Columbia River is closed to commercial fishing; that the reason for this is the fact that the Indians in order to survive under modern conditions, must sell the largest portion of their catch which is not eaten fresh in order to have money available for the purchase of medicines and commodities, such as coffee, sugar, flour, and like things; that each family of Indians, when he was a boy, would dry and put away for their own future use, about 30 sacks of fish, depending, of course, on the size of the family; that large families would dry more than the average or small sized families; that each sack would contain about 10 or 12 fish which weighed almost 100 pounds, since each fish after it had been cleaned, the head and tail removed, and then dried, would only weigh between 6 and 8 pounds, as he would judge their weight;

That the annual fish runs are not as large as they used to be because he feels the white commercial fishing takes most of the fish from the river before they have had a chance to come up to the Indians' fishing place; that for that reason, as well as the others previously explained, such as the increased number of Indians fishing and the need to sell the major portion of their catch, the Indians as a whole do not obtain as much fish or revenue as they used to;

That the spring run of salmon in 1941 seemed to be quite small and not nearly as heavy as the spring runs of a few years ago; that the fall run for that year was very good and although he did not catch many [154] fish because of personal sickness, grandsons and other relatives were fairly successful in their fishing operations;

That during the 1941 season, he did not dry many fish and that up through the month of September, the number he had thus put away for his own use was only about 27; that this was brought about by the fact that the commercial fishing season opened early and he needed money from the fish he caught to purchase medicines and other necessities of life; that the amount he received for the fish he caught and sold during the spring run was only about $70; that due to his illness he could not fish to any large extent during the fall run.

Affiant further deposes and says that the Indians do not fish with spears nowadays because it is harder to catch them with spears and the canneries will not buy fish that have been caught in that fashion;

That although the main article of food for the Indians in the old days was fish, both fresh and dried, they supplemented this diet with venison and roots and berries; which were obtained at places other than *Wyam*; that he used to hunt occasionally but ordinarily depended upon other Indians supplying him with such articles in return for fish that he caught while they were gathering the roots and berries.

Affiant further deposes and says that since the Indians were not able to record the history of their ancestors, the only way that they knew of for the things that happened before they were born or their parents were born, was the custom of the older Indians of each generation to tell the younger members of the tribe about the things and events that had occurred in the past, and in that manner the history and events relating to the Indians have been handed down from generation to generation and the information set forth herein with regard to the things that happened before affiant was born was obtained in that fashion, that the information set forth herein with regard to the way the Indians lived, fished, and hunted since his birth are matters within his own personal knowledge and relate to things that he actually saw himself. [155]

Affiant further deposes and says that the fishing rights, which were reserved to the Indians by the treaty with the United States, have a value to the Indians which cannot be measured in the terms of dollars and cents of the white man; that the subsistence value to the Indians as a whole is enormous and that were the Indians to be deprived of such rights they would be left without their principal means of support.

Further affiant sayeth not.

(Sgd.) Tommy Thompson His Mark
Tommy Thompson

Subscribed and sworn to before me at The Dalles, Wasco County, Oregon, this 7th day of May, 1942.

(Sgd.) J.W. Elliott
Superintendent of Warm Springs
Indian Agency, Oregon

AFFIDAVIT OF INTERPRETER

STATE OF OREGON}
COUNTY OF WASCO}   } SS.

Isaac McKinley, being first duly sworn, upon his oath deposes and says:

That he is 63 years old, a full blood member of the Tenino tribe of Indians, and a citizen of the United States of America, residing on the Warm Springs Indian Reservation, Oregon;

That he is thoroughly conversant with the English language and with the language spoken by the Indian residents of *Wyam*, otherwise known as Celilo, Oregon, and can translate the

English language into the *Wyam* Indian language and the *Wyam* Indian language into the English language;

That on October 8, 1941, at The Dalles, Oregon, in the presence of Chief Tommy Thompson, deponent in [156] the foregoing affidavit, and Edward G. Swindell, Jr., Associate Attorney, U.S. Indian Service, affiant did, at the request of Mr. Swindell, interrogate Chief Thompson with regard to certain matters concerning usual and accustomed fishing stations of the Indians along the Columbia River, as well as with regard to the way in which they and their ancestors obtained a living; that he translated the questions of Mr. Swindell from the English language into the *Wyam* Indian language, which Chief Tommy Thompson speaks and understands; that he translated from the *Wyam* Indian language into the English language the answers of Chief Thompson to Mr. Swindell's interrogatories; that at that time Mr. Swindell made written notes of the information given by the said Chief Thompson and reduced said information to the narrative form as given in the above and foregoing affidavit of the said Chief Tommy Thompson.

Affiant further deposes and says that on the 7th day of May, 1942, in the presence of Chief Thompson and Mr. Swindell, he translated the information contained in the aforesaid affidavit from the English language into the *Wyam* language, as said affidavit was read to affiant by Mr. Swindell; that the deponent, Chief Thompson, told affiant that the said narrative affidavit contained the information given by him to Mr. Swindell on October 8, 1941, and had, therefore, signed said affidavit because the information contained therein was true.

Further affiant sayeth not.

(Sgd.) Isaac McKinley
Isaac McKinley, Interpreter

Isaac McKinley personally appeared before me this 7th day of May, 1942, and after having the foregoing affidavit read to him in my presence did acknowledge to me that the statements contained therein are true and that he executed same as his voluntary act.

Subscribed and sworn to before me this 7th day of May, 1942.

(Sgd.) J.W. Elliott
Superintendent, Warm Springs
Indian Agency, Oregon [157]

Celilo Falls. Columbia River, Oregon. Picture of John Thompson, a Yakama Indian, standing on a fishing scaffold constructed on Chief's Island (*Zo-wy-chias*) [?*?] trying his luck with a spear. This is a sight seldom seen nowadays due to the skill required on the part of the spearman. The spearing of salmon can be accomplished only in quiet water where the fish can be seen while resting prior to ascending farther upstream, as compared with dip and bag net fishing which require "white water" to prevent the fish from seeing the net.

Big White Salmon River. Washington. Indian fishing camp located at mouth of the river. Note strips of salmon being cured on the racks in the lower center of the picture. This camp is located within the area flooded by the Bonneville Dam and on a stream used by the Government in connection with its White Salmon fish hatchery. The Indians nowadays obtain their fish from hatchery employees who, after stripping the eggs, turn the carcasses over to the Indians. Salmon

obtained at this point and in this manner, although not in the best condition, are particularly good for drying purposes due to the absence of the natural oils.

Indian fishing from a "custom station" located on a rock or island known as Little Ah-teem [*atiim*]. Note the safety rope attached to the fisherman, required by regulation of the Celilo Indian Fish Committee; also the cable way crossing from Little *Ah-teem* to another island. In the upper right hand corner will be seen the cable car used for transporting both the Indians and their catch between the island and the mainland. Picture taken in September, 1941, at a low stage of the river. [158]

CONFIRMATORY AFFIDAVIT

STATE OF OREGON}
COUNTY OF WASCO}　　　} SS

Mrs. Ellen Thompson, being first duly sworn, upon her oath deposes and says:

That she is 74 years old and a full blood Indian member of the Yakama Indian tribe, and a citizen of the United States of America, residing at Celilo, Oregon; that to the Indians, Celilo is known as *Wyam*;

That she was born at what the Indians call *Wish-am* [wiš<u>x</u>am v465], which was located on the north bank of the Columbia River and which is now known as Spearfish, Washington; that her father was a Chief or Headman of the Indians living at that place; that although she has an allotment of land on the Yakama Indian Reservation, she has never lived there, having spent her entire life along the Columbia River.

Affiant further deposes and says that she is the wife of Chief Tommy Thompson of the *Wyam* Indians, residing at Celilo; that she was present on October 8, 1941, at The Dalles, Oregon, when her husband gave certain information to Edward G. Swindell, Jr., Associate Attorney, U.S. Indian Service, with regard to Indian villages and fishing places along the Columbia River and that she listened carefully to all of the answers given by her husband to Mr. Swindell's questions;

That on the 7th day of May, 1942, she was present with her husband when the affidavit containing the information previously given was read back and interpreted; that the information as originally given and contained in the said affidavit is true to the best of her knowledge and belief; that a great deal of the information given by Chief Thompson concerned matters within her own personal knowledge and that as to the information given about matters which were not within her personal knowledge, she understands same to be true, because she had been told the same thing by her parents and the older members of her own people; that she has visited all of the places mentioned by her husband; that she is personally familiar with the situation concerning each of those places as same existed within her lifetime; that as to things that happened [159] prior to her birth, she· has knowledge thereof because the members of the Indians living at those places told her those things which was the way the Indians customarily kept track of the events which had occurred in the past.

Further affiant sayeth not.

(Sgd.) Mrs. Ellen Thompson Her Mark
Mrs. Ellen Thompson

Subscribed and sworn to before me at The Dalles, Wasco County, Oregon, this 7th day of May, 1942.

(Sgd.) J.W. Elliott
Superintendent, Warm Springs
Indian Agency, Oregon

AFFIDAVIT OF INTERPRETER.

STATE OF OREGON}
COUNTY OF WASCO}   }SS.

Isaac McKinley, being first duly sworn, upon his oath deposes and says:

That he is 63 years old, a full blood member of the Tenino tribe of Indians, and a citizen of the United States of: America, residing on the Warm Springs Indian Reservation, Oregon.

That he is thoroughly conversant with the English language and with the language spoken by the Indian residents of *Wyam*, otherwise known as Celilo, Oregon, and can translate the English language into the *Wyam* Indian language and the *Wyam* Indian language into the English language;

That on October 8, 1941, at The Dalles, Oregon, in the presence of Mrs. Ellen Thompson, deponent in the foregoing affidavit and in the presence also of Chief Tommy Thompson, her husband and Edward G. Swindell, Jr., U.S. Indian Service, affiant did at the request of Mr. Swindell interrogate the said Mrs. Ellen Thompson with regard to her age, tribal affiliation, and knowledge of Indian usual and accustomed fishing stations along [160] the Columbia River; also with regard to whether the said Ellen Thompson had carefully listened to the questions and answers thereto of Mr. Swindell and Chief Tommy Thompson, respectively, with regard to details relating to the above mentioned matter; that affiant translated the questions of Mr. Swindell from the English language into the *Wyam* Indian language, which Ellen Thompson speaks and understands; that he translated from the *Wyam* Indian language into the English language the answers of Ellen Thompson to Mr. Swindell's interrogatories; that at that time Mr. Swindell made written notes of the information given by the said Ellen Thompson and reduced said information to the narrative form as given in the above and foregoing affidavit of the said Ellen Thompson.

Affiant further deposes and says that on the 7th day of May, 1942, in the presence of Ellen Thompson and Mr. Swindell, he translated the information contained in the aforesaid affidavit from the English language into the *Wyam* language, as said affidavit was read to affiant by Mr. Swindell; that the deponent, Ellen Thompson, told affiant that the said narrative affidavit contained the information given by her to Mr. Swindell on October 8, 1941, and had, therefore, signed said affidavit because the information contained therein was true.

Further affiant sayeth not.

(Sgd.) Isaac McKinley
Isaac McKinley, Interpreter

Isaac McKinley personally appeared before me this 7th day of May, 1942, and after having the foregoing affidavit read to him in my presence did acknowledge to me that the statements contained therein are true and that he executed same as his voluntary act.

Subscribed and sworn to before me this 7th day of May, 1942.

(Sgd.) J.W. Elliott
Superintendent, Warm Springs
Indian Agency, Oregon [161]

AFFIDAVIT

STATE OF WASHINGTON}
COUNTY OF YAKIMA}   } SS.

Chief William Yallup, being first duly sworn, upon his oath deposes and says:

That he is 75 years old, a full blooded Klickitat (Rock Creek) Indian, sometimes known as Columbia River Indians; that he is a citizen of the United States of America, residing at the village of his people at Rock Creek, Washington, which is near the Goodnoe Hills Post Office, Washington; that the Indian name for this place where he now resides is *Kah-mulkh* [k̲'mił v424];

That he was born at Indian berry patches in the Columbia National Forest where the Indians used to hold their horse races; that at that time his parents were there for the purpose of gathering their annual supply of roots and berries, as well as to meet with the other Indians who annually gathered there for the purpose of exchanging news and to hold dances and other entertainment;

That the permanent home of his parents was located at about the same place where he now lives which is approximately 35 miles upstream on the Columbia from the old Indian village of *Wah-pykt*; that he has always lived along the Columbia River and his father and mother told him that they and their ancestors had always lived along the river; that his father was related to the Indians who lived at *Wyam* now known as Celilo on the Oregon side, and that his mother was related to those who lived at *Wah-pykt* sometimes known as *Skein* situated on the Washington side of the Columbia River; that all of these Indians considered themselves one big family;

That by reason of the facts just recited, as well as the things that were told to him by his parents and his own personal knowledge of the conditions as they existed during his lifetime, he is fully familiar with the fishing places of the Indians along the Columbia River.

Affiant further deposes and says that in addition to the Indian village located at Rock Creek, as above described, there were other Indian villages and fishing [162] places as follows:

1. *Wah-pykt*, sometimes known as Wishram. The Indian meaning for *Wah-Pykt* was "water falls" [x̲apaawish v461] and it was located on the Washington side of the Columbia River.

2. There was another village below *Wah-pykt* known as *Skein* [sk'in v168-9], which was also located on the Washington side of the river. Its name meant "cradle board" and it was so named because the camping grounds of the people who lived there were in the shape of the cradle board used by the Indians.

3. *Wyam*, known to the white people as Celilo [*silaylu* v352]. This was one of the principal villages of the Columbia River ·Indians and it was located on what is now the Oregon side of the river;

That the houses of the permanent homes of the people in these various villages were made out of tulles; that before he was born the principal part of these houses was constructed underground; that since he was born and started to remember things, the Indian houses have been constructed above ground and banked with dirt.

Affiant further deposes and says that at *Kah-mulkh* [k̲'mił v424] there were about 600 people living when he was a small boy; that there were approximately 50 Indian houses in a permanent camp; that since his father was the Chief of the people that lived here, he had the largest house and approximately 10 families lived in it; that the Indians spent about four months at this place during the winter time, after which they departed for the mountains to let the men kill game and permit the women to gather the roots which formed a part of their subsistence; that after these things had been obtained, they were brought back to the winter camp where they would hold their big spring feast which occurred about the time the first salmon returned up the river; that thereafter the Indians remained in their permanent camp until it was time for the various groups to start out to gather the later roots and the berries which would then be coming into season; that some of these groups crossed the river and gathered those things on what is now the Oregon side;

That the Indians caught their fish at *Kah-mulkh* in the same manner as the Indians who lived at *Wyam*; [163] that thereafter when the spring run of salmon had passed, it was necessary for them to go to other fishing places to obtain food because the water was too low and clear for fishing at *Kah-mulkh*; that a large number of the people from *Kah-mulkh* would go to *Wyam* to fish and that the Indians living at that place would not object inasmuch as they as well as the Chiefs were old friends; those that would go to *Wyam* remained there for approximately three months, commencing about the middle of July as time is reckoned by the white man and ending when the salmon passing *Wyam* have turned white.

Affiant further deposes and says that not all of the Indians were fishermen, some were more proficient at hunting and they and their families would go to the mountains for that purpose, as well as to permit the ladies and children to gather roots and berries; that when the fall came, all of these various groups would return to their permanent camp; that this permanent camp was not necessarily in the same place each winter, its location each year would depend on the availability of a supply of food for cooking and heating purposes; that the camp of each group, however, ordinarily was in the same general vicinity year in and year out.

Affiant further deposes and says that the Indians who lived permanently at *Wyam* also used to go to the mountains for their own deer, roots, and berries, although they obtained most of their supply through trading with other Indian;

That *Way-pykt*, Skein, and *Wyam* were all permanent homes of the Columbia River Indians; that he estimates approximately 500 Indians lived at both *Skein* and *Wahpykt*; that this figure was the total for both places and he believes that about the same number or one half of 500 lived at each place; that the people who lived at these three places were true Columbia River Indians and did not include Indians from the Umatilla, Yakama, and Warm Springs Reservation.

Affiant further deposes and says that he is familiar with the various groups of Indians whose tribes form the Yakama nation; that the Indian from that reservation, as well as those that were moved to the Umatilla and Warm Springs Reservations after the treaty with the white man, used to return to the Columbia River each year to their old accustomed fishing stations in order to obtain a supply of fish for their own use; [164]

That in addition to those Indians who had previously fished there, other Indians living on those three reservation would also come to the various permanent villages along the river; that they would come to these places with pack horses loaded with buckskins, roots, berries, blankets, and white men's groceries, which they would trade for salmon caught by the local Indians; that with the exception of the things brought into the country by the white people, the Indians forming these three reservations had always been accustomed to trading with the local Indians for a supply of fish;

That the visiting Indians with the exception of those who had been removed or were descendants of those who had been removed from the Columbia River, did not fish because they did not have enough time and they were not familiar with the methods used by the local Indians to catch salmon; that, however, the local Indians, if the visitors said they wanted to, did permit them to try to catch as much fish as they could to meet their needs; that only a few of those Indians took advantage of that opportunity;

That the number of Indians who came to trade with the local people was quite large and if they had nothing to trade, the river Indians would either let them fish or if they could not do so, they would give them enough fish so that they would not lack for it as food.

Affiant further deposes and says that he first learned how to fish when he was quite a young man; that when the water conditions were not right for fishing at *Kah-mulkh*, he would go with his father's family to the various places heretofore named; that in addition to those places, he also caught fish from what is now known as Big Island;

That when he was a boy, he would think that approximately 130 Indians actually fished from the rocks when the run was the heaviest; that early in the season, however, the number would be considerably less because there were fewer fishing platform locations available; that according to old Indian custom each family had its own place which was used every year and passed down from generation to generation; that in the old days, as well as now, when there were [165] not enough places available for the number of Indians who wanted to fish, they would change places so that all could get enough fish for their needs; that it was customary for the fishermen to tell the widows and the old people that if they would meet them as they were returning from the fishing places, they would be given enough fish for their needs.

Affiant further deposes and says that he has fished in the Columbia River each year since he can remember and that he still fishes at *Wyam* although someone has taken his old accustomed station, which his family acquired many years ago; that there are a great many more Indians fishing at *Wyam*, most of whom are newcomers because their ancestors had not fished there and did not have accustomed places; that he cannot estimate the number of Indians or the number of places available for their use at *Wyam* but he has seen that all available places on the rocks are in use when the heaviest part of the summer and fall run is on;

That when he was a boy there was plenty of fish in the river; in fact, it was thick with fish during the times of the runs; that in those days the Indians only took what they needed for their own use and drying; that during the runs, they would eat fresh fish three times daily and the surplus they caught would be dried for use when no fresh ones were available; that until the establishment of the cannery, the Indians only took enough fish to meet their own needs and for purpose of trade to obtain commodities they could not so easily acquire themselves;

That in those days each family would dry for its own personal use approximately 30 sacks of fish, each of which contained about six large salmon weighing, after they had been cleaned for drying, about six pounds;

That for purposes of trading, each family would put away about 10 sacks of fish, in addition to manufacturing a supply of pemmican [salmon flour] which they also used to trade with visiting Indians.

Affiant further deposes and says that there does not seem to be as many fish available nowadays as there used to be when he was a boy; that he believes the reason for this is the fact that very large quantities [166] have been caught and sold to the canneries and that the Indians do not get the benefit of this; that there are too many Indians fishing nowadays at *Wyam* to permit each to obtain a sufficient quantity for their own use as well as to sell to the Seufert Cannery to obtain money to purchase things that they cannot get along without now and which can only be obtained in the white man's store; that during 1941, he only made three sales of fish to the cannery for which he received only $30; that be sold these fish rather than dry them because he needed the money.

That even though the runs were smaller, probably one third smaller, than they used to be, the total number of fish caught by the Indians at *Wyam* is large when the catch of all of them is added together; that this is true also with regard to the total amount of money received by the Indians; that he feels there are too many Indians fishing at *Wyam* nowadays and that, therefore, none of them get as much money as they should.

Affiant further deposes and says that when he was a boy the Indians caught their fish with dip nets, set nets, and spears; that today there is no difference except that spears are no longer used and that the reason for this is the fact that the canneries will not buy fish that had been stuck with spears, and also there are not enough Indians today who have the patience to acquire the skill to catch salmon using the old Indian spear;

That at Skein, in addition to the above described ways of catching fish, the Indians also used a long net which was weighed down with stone;

That the material used in making all of the nets was made of what is known as "Indian hemp" for which the Indian name is *tah-qhus* [*taxus* v386] that the spear points were made of deer or elk horn, and that the part of the head that held the point was made from the hardest bone in the foreleg of the deer.

Affiant further deposes and says that his parents when he was a small boy told him that they had fished at and knew about all of the places of which he had been talking and that it had always been that way; that his father had shown him the various fishing camps and [167] the locations of the various fishing places at those camps; that his parents and the other old members of the tribe told him that the Indians had always fished in the Columbia River even as they were doing at the time that Lewis and Clark first came through the country.

Affiant further deposes and says that the fishing rights, which were reserved to the Indians by the treaty with the United States, have a value to the Indians which cannot be measured in the terms of dollars and cents of the white man; that the subsistence value to the Indians as a whole is enormous and that were the Indians to be deprived of such rights they would be left without their principal means of support.

Further affiant sayeth not.

(Sgd.) Chief William Yallup his mark
Chief William Yallup

Subscribed and sworn to before me this 11th day of June, 1942.

(Sgd.) M.A. Johnson
Superintendent
Yakama Indian Agency

AFFIDAVIT OF INTERPRETER

STATE OF WASHINGTON}
COUNTY OF YAKIMA } 　 } SS.

Thomas Yallup, being first duly sworn, upon his oath deposes and says:

That he is 56 years of age, a full blood Indian of the Yakama Indian tribe and a citizen of the United States of America residing on the Yakama Indian Reservation, Washington;

That he is thoroughly conversant with the English language and with the language spoken by the Klickitat Indians residing at Rock Creek, Washington, and can translate the English language into the Yakama-Klickitat language and the Yakama-Klikitat language into the English language; [168]

That on October 3, 1941, at The Dalles, Oregon, in the presence of Chief William Yellup, deponent in the foregoing affidavit, and Edward G. Swindell, Jr., Associate Attorney, U.S.

Indian Service, affiant did, at the request of Mr. Swindell, interrogate Chief Yallup with regard to certain matters concerning usual and accustomed fishing stations of the Indians along the Columbia River, as well as with regard to the way in which they and their ancestors obtained a living; that he translated the questions of Mr. Swindell from the English language into the Yakama-Klickitat Indian language, which Chief William Yallup speaks and understands; that he translated from the Yakama-Klickitat Indian language into the English language the answers of Chief Yellup to Mr. Swindell's interrogatories; that at that time Mr. Swindell made written notes of the information given by the said Chief Yallup and reduced said information to the narrative form as given in the above and foregoing affidavit of the said Chief William Yallup.

Affiant further does and says that on the 11th day of June, 1942, in the presence of Chief William Yellup, he translated the information contained in the aforesaid affidavit from the English language into the Yakama-Klickitat language, as said affidavit was read to affiant; that the deponent, Chief William Yallup, told affiant that the said narrative affidavit contained the information given by him to Mr. Swindell on October 3, 1941, and he had therefore signed said affidavit because the information contained therein was true.

Further affiant sayeth not.

(Sgd.) Thomas Yallup
Thomas Yallup, Interpreter

Thomas Yallup personally appeared before me this 11th day of June, 1942, and after having the foregoing affidavit read to him in my presence did acknowledge to me that the statements contained therein are true and that he executed same as his voluntary act.

Subscribed and sworn to before me this 11th day of June 1942.

(Sgd.) M.A. Johnson
Superintendent Yakama
Indian Agency [169]

AFFIDAVIT

STATE OF OREGON}
COUNTY OF WASCO}   } SS.

Willie John Culpus, being first duly sworn, upon his oath deposes and says:

That he is 48 years of age and a full blood Indian member of the Yakama Indian tribe, and a citizen of the United States of America residing at the village of his forefathers located at Rock Creek, Washington, near the Goodnoe Hills Post Office, Washington;

That he was born on the Washington side of the Columbia River at a place just east of the Maryhill Ferry; that he does not consider himself a true Yakama Indian even though his father and mother took allotments for themselves and himself on the Yakama Reservation; that he belongs to the same band of Indians as Chief William Yallup, which are sometimes known as Klickitat Indians; that he follows the customs of the Columbia River Indian people and spends most of his time between his own home at *Wyam* and his wife's home at Rock Creek; that he has spent practically all his life along the Columbia River and as a consequence of the things within his own personal knowledge and the information given to him by his parents as well as the older members of the tribe to which he belongs, he feels that he is fully familiar with the way the Indian people live at the present time and the way their ancestors lived even before the coming of the white man

Affiant further deposes and says that he has fished at his usual and accustomed place at *Wyam* known to the white people as Celilo ever since he was old enough to fish unassisted that the number of fish available to the Indians nowadays is a great deal less than when he first started fishing; that since the white people offered to buy the fish the Indians caught, he has sold some of his catch in order that he could get money to support his family; that the money he received in this fashion does not amount to much; that ordinarily it is as little as $200 a year; that for the 1941 season up until October, 1941, he had only sold enough fish to equal $200 in cash, this despite the fact that both the spring and fall run that year was better than the previous few years; [170]

That during that part of the 1941 season when commercial fishing is prohibited on the Columbia River, the salmon were not available at the Columbia River falls; that this is the time of the year that the Indians ordinarily try to put away their supply of salmon to be. used during the winter months; that his wife tells him that up until October 1941 she had only dried about 18 fish; that he does not know the reason for this but believes they must have closed the gates at the Bonneville Dam;

That he shares his fishing place with one other Indian at all times; that when they have enough fish for themselves, they let other Indians use their place; that in reality he and his partner have two places but can only use one at a time depending on the height of the water in the river; that according to Indian custom these places belong to certain families who have had them for generations and that when the present owner dies the place is given to his closest relative.

Affiant further deposes and says that he was present on October 3, 1941, at The Dalles, Oregon, when the Chief of his tribe, Chief William Yallup, gave certain information to Edward G. Swindell, Jr. U.S. Indian Service, with regard to Indian villages and fishing places along the Columbia River; that he listened carefully to all of the answers given by Chief William Yallup in response to Mr. Swindell's questions;

That on the 7th day of July, 1942, he was present with Chief Yallup when an affidavit containing the information previously given by Chief Yallup was read back to him by Mr. Swindell and interpreted by Thomas Yallup; that the information as originally given and contained in the said affidavit is true to the best of his knowledge and belief; that a great deal of the information given by Chief Yallup concerned matters within his own personal knowledge and that as to the information given about matters which were not within his personal knowledge, he nevertheless understands such information to be true because he had been told the same thing when he was a young man by his parents and the older members of the tribe of Indians to which he belongs; that all of the things told Mr. Swindell at that time by Chief Yallup are true. [171]

Further affiant sayeth not.

(Sgd.) Willie John Culpus his mark
Willie John Culpus

Subscribed and sworn to before me this 7th day of May, 1942.

(Sgd.) J.W. Elliott
Superintendent, Warm Springs
Indian Agency, Oregon

AFFIDAVIT OF INTEPRETER

STATE OF OREGON}
COUNTY OF WASCO}   } SS.

Thomas Yallup, being first duly sworn upon his oath deposes and says:

That he is 58 years of age, a full blood Indian of the Yakama Indian tribe and a citizen of the United States of America residing on the Yakama Indian Reservation, Washington;

That he is thoroughly conversant with the English language also with the language spoken by the Klickitat Indians residing at Rock Creek, Washington, and can translate the English language into the Yakama-Klickitat language and the Yakama-Klickitat language into the English language; that on October 3, 1941, at The Dalles, Oregon, in the presence of Willie John Culpus, deponent in the foregoing affidavit, and Edward G. Swindell, Jr., U.S. Indian Service, affiant did at the request of Mr. Swindell interrogated Willie John Culpus with regard to certain matters concerning usual and accustomed fishing stations of the Indians along the Columbia River; that he also interrogated the said Willie John Culpus as to whether said deponent had heard and understood the information given by Chief William Yallup to the said Mr. Swindell concerning in detail the location of usual and accustomed fishing stations of the Columbia River Indians as well as with regard to the way in which they and their ancestors obtained a livelihood; that he translated the questions of Mr. Swindell from the English language into the Yakama-Klickitat Indian language, which Willie John Culpus speaks and [172] understands; that he translated from the Yakama-Klickitat language into the English language the answers of Willie John Culpus to Mr. Swindell's interrogatories; that at that time Mr. Swindell made written notes of the information given by the said Willis John Culpus and reduced said information to the narrative form as given in the above and foregoing affidavit of the said Willie John Culpus.

Affiant further deposes and says that on the 7th day of May, 1942, in the presence of Willie John Culpus and Mr. Swindell, he translated the information contained in the aforesaid affidavit from the English language into the Yakama-Klickitat language, as said affidavit was read to affiant by Mr. Swindell; that the deponent, Willie John Culpus, told affiant that the said narrative affidavit contained the information given by him to Mr. Swindell on October 3, 1941, and had, therefore, signed said affidavit because the information contained therein was true.

Further affiant sayeth not.

Thomas Yallup, Interpreter

Thomas Yallup personally appeared before me this 7th day of May, 1942, and after having the foregoing affidavit read to him in my presence did acknowledge to me that the statements contained therein are true and that he executed same as his voluntary act.

Subscribed and sworn to before me this 7th day of May, 1942.

(Sgd.) J.W. Elliott
Superintendent, Warm Springs
Indian Agency, Oregon [173]

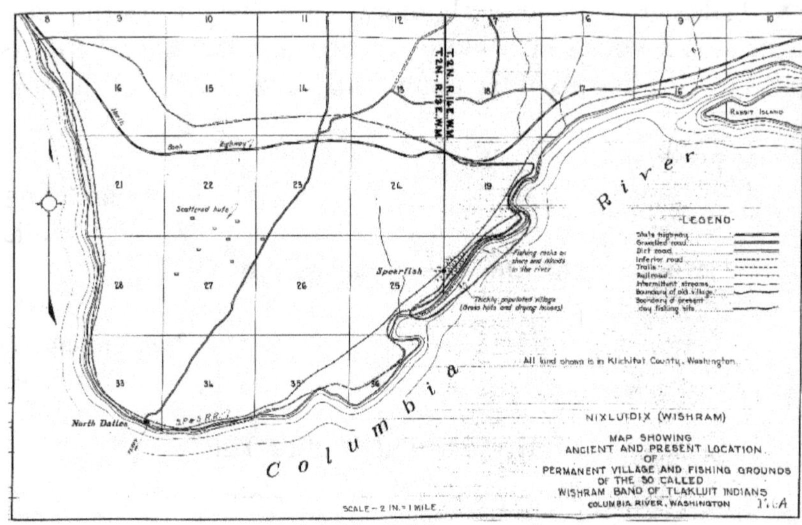

[Nixluidix Wishram map]

AFFIDAVIT

STATE OF OREGON}
COUNTY OF WASCO}   } SS.

Martin Spedis, being first duly sworn upon his oath, deposes and says:

That he is a citizen of the United States of America residing at Spearfish, Washington, and that he was 74 years of age on November 2, 1941;

That he is a member of the Klickitat band of the Yakama tribe of Indians of the Yakama Reservation, Washington, although he does not reside on that reservation; that he was born at what is now known as Spearfish on the Washington side of the Columbia River and has lived there all of his life;

That the Indians name for this place is *Nixluidix**[70] although it is sometimes referred to as Wishram, which is not correct;

That although he is a Yakama Indian, the language of his people was different from the language of the Yakamas; that it is somewhat similar to the language of the Wasco people living on the Warm Springs Indian Reservation in Oregon; that his father was an Indian who had moved to Warm Springs Reservation and his mother was a member of the Indians residing at Wishram, although she received an allotment on the Yakama Reservation; that his mother's mother was also a member of the Indians living at Wishram, although her father was Chief Henninick of the Yakama nation; that he is familiar with the Indian fishing places on both sides of the Columbia River in the general vicinity of Spearfish (Wishram) and that he commenced fishing when he was about 10 years old and continued to fish until about 1937 when he had to stop on account of a paralytic stroke; that he has only fished at places along the Columbia River and then mostly at Spearfish (Wishram); that sometimes his father took his family across the river to the Indian fishing place that was now known as Celilo Falls; that the Indian name for this place is *Wyam*; that as a result of these things [174] immediately above stated, he is personally familiar with the way the Indians used to live at Spearfish, having actually observed them and also having been told about how it was prior to his birth by his parents and the other old people; that he was selected by the Yakama Tribal Council to give information with regard to such things;

Affiant further deposes and says that the Indians have always camped at their present location; that when he was a boy the Indians did not live in houses like they do today but instead they all lived in a big long house; that in addition to being used as living quarters, this house was used for drying fish; that several families lived in this house and each had their own portion thereof for their use;

That in the old days approximately 500 Indians lived at Spearfish and that they lived in big houses, parts of which were built in the ground like a cellar so that they could be kept warmer than would be possible if they had been constructed entirely on the surface of the ground; that the great majority of the houses were located in the same general area as the present homes of the few remaining Indians who have permanent homes at Spearfish, although there were some houses at various places in the area below the main highway*[71] and between the present town of Spearfish and to the bank of the river formed by the big bends in the river on both the east and west sides of the village of North Dalles;[72]

---

[70] */ From under *Tlakluit* [*iɫax̱luit*], p. 762, pt.2 of Bull.30 (B.A.E.) "Handbook of American Indians". Phonetically and as pronounced by deponent, it is "*Nick-a-lowd-icks*".

[71] */ U.S. No. 830 – North Bank Columbia River Highway.

That at the present time there are only approximately 35 Indians now living at Spearfish (Wishram); that the difference is accounted for by the fact that many died and the remainder removed to the Yakama Indian Reservation where they received allotments of land; that in the days prior to the coming of the white people, he understands that the Indians from the other villages along both sides of the Columbia River were accustomed to visiting those Indians living at Spearfish; that when these Indians visited they came for the purpose of trading things that they had for fish and other things that the people at Spearfish had available for trading purposes; that the trade amounted to quite a bit because the Indians at Spearfish had good fishing stations and were able to [175] catch many more fish than they needed or could use themselves; that sometimes the visiting Indians would fish at the local stations when they had nothing to offer in trade and that the local Indians did not object since they had plenty of fish for themselves and there was plenty for all the visitors;

That the various fishing stations were the private property of individual family groups and they were handed down within the family from generation to generation; that it had always been that way and the Indians always recognized their own rights to family stations; That although there are only a few permanent residents at the present time, a large number of other Indians come there each year to fish when the big runs are on; that he would estimate the number who visit this place each year to fish as being 200 and they use all of the approximately 120 fishing stations on the rocks and islands in the river; that quite a bit of the fish caught nowadays is sold to buyers for the canneries although the Indians still dry large quantities for their own use since they still like fish and it forms an important part of their food supply; that the reason they sell considerable quantities of their catch is because they must have money to purchase commodities such as flour, sugar, and things like that which they cannot obtain otherwise;

That the Indians who fish at Spearfish nowadays are mostly the descendants of the old former residents, although quite a few of them are not so descended; that they come mostly from the Yakama Reservation although quite a few came from the Umatilla and Warm Springs Reservations;

Affiant further deposes and says that when he was a boy the Indians caught their fish in dip and bag nets made out of materials they gathered in the fields; that they also used spears and hooks; made of elk horn and these materials were as good as those used today but they were much harder to make;

That some of the Indians at Spearfish used to go to the mountains to gather berries and dig roots although they obtained most of their supply of these things through trading with the visitors who had plenty of such to trade for the local people's dried fish; that when those who did go to the mountains went there, they would stay three or four weeks at a time, and in addition to the roots and berries they obtained, they would also hunt for deer and other game; [176]

Affiant further deposes and says that he has fished at what is now know as Celilo but which place the Indices know as Wy-am, as well as other places along the Columbia River; that he is reluctant to give detailed information with regard to those places since he feels the people who lived there should do so and he understands that they intend to give such information; that generally speaking, however, there were a number of Indian villages and fishing places along the Columbia River located at those spots where the water conditions would permit the Indians to catch the fish without too much trouble; that the Indians who lived at those-places did so in the same manner as those who resided at Spearfish; that most of them moved to the various

---

72 1/ See plat.

reservations when they were-set aside by the Government under the treaties, although those Indians and their descendants continued to use such places for many years thereafter; that a number of such good fishing locations were destroyed when the Government built the Bonneville Dam; that this was a bad thing for the Indians because now they could not fish unless some of their friends at other places along the river would let than use their places.

Further affiant sayeth not.

(Sgd.) Martin Spedis
Martin Spedis

Subscribed, and sworn to before me this 7th day of May, 1942

(Sgd.) J.W. Elliott
Superintendent, Warm Springs
Indian Agency, Oregon [177]

AFFIDAVIT

STATE OF OREGON}
COUNTY OF WASCO}   } SS

Isaac McKinley, being first duly sworn, upon his oath deposes and says:

That he is 63 years of age, a full blood Tenino Indian of the Tenino tribe of Indians, and a citizen of the United States of America residing on the Warm Springs Indian Reservation, Oregon;

That he was born on the Warm Springs Reservation and has an allotment there; that his mother was a Tenino Indian and his father was a Umatilla Indian from the Washington side of the Columbia River, that his father's home was a long way east of Rock Creek probably farther east than the present town of Alderdale, Washington; that both his parents took allotments on the Warm Springs Reservation when the Indians were moved there by the Government; that prior to their taking allotments, however, they had maintained a home at *Wyam*;

That two of his uncles; who were his mother's brothers, had always fished at *Wyam* on the Oregon side and Skein on the Washington side of the Columbia River, although both of them spent most of their lives living at Skein; that he first fished at *Wyam* in about the year 1894 after leaving school at Warm Springs; that from 1894 until 1917 he fished at *Wyam* at various times but not every year; that since 1917 he has fished each year at the usual and accustomed fishing stations belonging to his family;

That because of the foregoing he is personally familiar with the situation along the Columbia River and especially at *Wyam*, that in addition to his personal knowledge of the situation, he was told many things with regard thereto by his parents concerning same as it existed during his lifetime and as it was prior to their life-time, such latter information being predicated on the things that had been told them by their [own] parents.

Affiant further deposes and says that when he first visited *Wyam* the Indians were camped at several places along the present Celilo Ship Canal right-of-way, [178] which was constructed about 1905; that there were three principal places in the area were the Indians lived and that although each of them had its own name, all three of them were known by the principal name of *Wyam*;

That when he first recalls visiting *Wyam* there were about 80 Indians living there; this included men, women, and children, that there were only about 10 Indian families who would visit *Wyam* each year for short periods; that these families consisted of Umatillas and Yakamas; that these families who visited *Wyam* were former residents of *Wyam* and that they returned each year for the purpose of visiting their relatives as well as to obtain a supply or fish;

That some members of the Indian tribes he has named would visit *Wyam* for the purpose of trading roots, berries, and venison for dried salmon put up by the people who lived at *Wyam*; that if the visiting Indians did not have anything to trade for fish, the local people would either give them some of their own supply or else they would lend them the necessary equipment and permit them to catch all the fish they needed from one of the established fishing stations belonging to the local people; that the local Indians would sometimes gather roots and berries but usually they fished at *Wyam* and depended upon trading for their supply of roots, berries, and other things;

That *Skein* and *Wah-pykt* were two names for the same place which was located on the Washington side of the Columbia River at a point just below the present railroad bridge which crosses the river about threes-quarters of a mile below Celilo Falls; that the Indians who lived at *Skein* and *Wyam* spoke the same language as did the Tenino Indians and those which are now known as the John Day Indians; that the language of these four groups was somewhat different from the language of the Wasco Indians who also used to come to the various places along the river to fish;

That when he first accompanied his uncles to fish on the Washington side of the river there were about 15 families of 90 people in all living at Skein; that aside from the Indians who live there all year [179] around this place, as were the others along the Columbia River, was used by former residents who had removed to the reservation; that in the event these people were dead, their descendants would use their same places; that this was customary practice of the Indians along the Columbia River; that old Indian law and custom provided that the fishing stations at the various villages along the river belong to certain families and when the father died the places that belong to that family were passed along to his children; that this was customary practice and is still followed today although it is difficult to keep outside Indians from interfering with the owners of usual and accustomed places;

That his family over the years was accustomed to using two fishing places depending on the height of water in the river; that in the spring of the year he fishes at Tenino from a station which has belonged to his family for many many years; that in the spring the water is too high to fish at his family station at *Wyam* but that after the spring runoff has passed by, the water is too low for good fishing at Tenino and he; therefore, for the summer and fall fishing; uses the family fishing station at *Wyam* located on what is known as Big Inland;

That in addition to himself, his family fishing station is shared with four other Indians whose names are: Charley McKinley; Andrew David, Charley Pete and Wilford Sooksoit; that all five of them fish at this place as a partnership and that all share alike in the catch and the proceeds of that part of the catch sold to the cannery; that the two usual and accustomed places of his family are better than ordinary and that each member of the partnership made about $1,000 for the fishing season of 1941:

That, in addition to the partnership, that uses these places, other Indians who either do not have places to fish from or whose places are not as good, are permitted to use his family's places when no member of the partnership is using it; that some of the Indians to whom this privilege is extended are: Clarence Menias, William Moody, Gibson Moody, and Wilson Menias, all of whom are from the Warm Springs Reservation;

Affiant further deposes and says that, as he recalls it, each family, when he was a boy, dried [180 map] about 25 sacks of fish; each of which would weigh approximately 50 pounds and that all of this quantity would be for his own use; that although this amounts to approximately 1000 or 1200 pounds per family and, therefore, might seem large, the Indians in those days required much more fish than they do now because other commodities were not as readily available as they are now; that, in addition to the amount that the Indians dried for their own use, each family would dry about 400 or 500 pounds of salmon which they used for trading purposes when they needed roots, berries, and other like things;

That when he was a boy and a young man, the permanent population of *Wyam* would be increased by 40 or 50 Indians who would come up from the Warm Springs Reservation during the fishing season; that these were people or descendants of people who formerly fished at the place; that the same situation existed with regard to those few Indians living at Skein and Rock Creek who had moved to the Yakama Reservation;

That nowadays he would estimate that approximately 300 Indians actually fish at *Wyam* during the height of the fall season and that although he believes almost this many Indians fish during the spring season, they are spread out along the river at places like Tenino where the fishing is best when the water is high; that, as he recalls it, there would be only approximately 40 Indians who actually fished at *Wyam* when he was a boy; that there were not nearly as many fishing stations as there are today; that in those days the fishing stations then used were the "usual and accustomed places" mentioned in the treaty and that the same Indians could and did use their places year in and year out without any interference by or trouble from the other Indians; that when the people who had the right to use these places died, their right passed to their children regardless of whether they were male or female and that if they did not have any children, the local chief would decide who thereafter should be permitted to use the place in question.

Affiant farther deposes and says that the Indians have always been accustomed to fish along the Columbia River and that the descendants of those Indians who moved to reservations are principally located either at Umatilla, Yakama, or Warm Springs; that he does not believe that the Nez Perce Indians ever came to *Wyam* for the purpose either of fishing or to trade with the residents of that place. [181]

Affiant further deposes and says that fishing along the river in recent years has been principally good and that in 1941 it has been much better than usual; that he believes the fishing will continue to be good because the state people and others like the Federal Government are trying to protect the fish from being all killed off, that he does not believe that the Bonneville Dam has affected or will affect the fishing of the Indians at *Wyam* and other places above the dam;

That when he was a boy, he recalls the Indians selling quite a number of the fish they caught to the Seufert Brothers cannery for which they only received 1¢ per pound; that nowadays most of the Indians sells the greater portion of their annual catch to the canneries in order that they can obtain money for things that they cannot acquire without having that money; that Seufert does not object to the Indians bringing fish across his land when such fish is to be used for their own subsistence but that he does object to Indians bringing fish across his land when they intended to sell same to other canneries or fish buyers;

That the Indians dry most of their fish from those caught during the fall run and during the season when fishing for commercial purposes is prohibited; that practically all of the fish caught during the closed season are either eaten fresh or dried; that although some fish caught during the spring run are dried and put away for future use; the amount is not large because the fish are then too oily and they do not dry as well as those caught later on in the year; that the oil causes them to spoil before they re fully cured in the air; that that is why the Indians prefer to obtain practically all of their supply of dried fish from the late summer and fall runs;

That in the year 1941, his wife dried about 800 pounds of fish as compared to 1,300 pounds dried during the previous year; that the smaller quantity put away this year is explained by the fact that his wife had been ill and not because they did not want to put away a larger quantity; that of their supply of dried fish; they ordinarily only kept between 400 and 500 pounds and the balance is given away to the old folks on the Warm Springs Reservation who are unable to fish for themselves and who must have this help so that they can live through the winter. [182]

Further affiant sayeth not.

(Sgd.) Isaac McKinley
Isaac McKinley

Isaac McKinley having personally appeared before me and after having the foregoing affidavit read to him in my presence did acknowledge to me that the statements contained therein are true and that he executed same as his voluntary act.

Subscribed and sworn to before me this 7th day of May, 1942.

(Sgd.) J.W. Elliott
Superintendent, Warm Springs
Indian Agency, Oregon [183]

HOH RESERVATION

AGENCY: - Taholah

LOCATION: - West central coast, Olympic Peninsula, northwest Washington.

AREA: - 443 acres

TREATY: - July 1, 1855, and January 25, 1856; 12 Stat. 971, 2 Kappler 719.

INDIAN TRIBES: - Hoh Indians, a branch of the Quileute tribe.

LOCATION OF "U. & A." FISHING GROUNDS: -

From the Mouth of the Hoh River to its source in the Olympic Mountain[s], as well as north and south of the mouth of the river along the Pacific coast. Ordinarily, the villages and fishing places were located where smaller tributary streams entered the main river.

FISHING GEAR AND REGULATIONS: -

Set nets and hand dip nets. These Indians at present do not observe any regulations in connection with their fishing activities.

PRESENT FISHING ACTIVITIES: -

These Indians participate in both commercial and subsistence fishing although no figures as to the value of each are available. It is conservatively estimated that the annual value of the fish taken for commercial purposes would be $2,500.00. The subsistence value cannot be estimated although it is pointed out the Indians almost entirely subsist on fish and sea food.

GENERAL REMARKS: -

The northern boundary of the Hoh Reservation is reported to run only to the middle of the channel of the Hoh River and, consequently, the Indians' fishing activities with set nets which are illegal under Washington law, are confined to that section of the river which forms a part of their reservation. [184]

There are only one or two descendants of the original Hoh tribe. The balance of the few other Indians living on the reservation are Quileutes who in order to obtain a set net fishing location, settled on the Hoh reserve. [185]

AFFIDAVIT OF FRANK FISHER,
HOH INDIAN

STATE OF WASHINGTON }
JEFFERSON COUNTY }   }SS.

Frank Fisher, being first duly sworn, upon his oath deposes and says;

That he is about 77 years of age, a full blood member of the Hoh Indian tribe and a citizen of the United States residing on the Hob Indian Reservation, Washington;

That he was born on the Hoh River and has lived on that river all of his life; that this was the permanent home of his parents and their parents before them and that it had always been the home of the Hoh Indians; that during the course of his life he has had occasion to visit the various places where the Hoh Indians had settlements prior to the coming of the white man; that as a result of his knowledge thus gained from personal observation and the knowledge given him by his parents when he was a small boy as to the location of such places and the way the Indians lived and fished there, he feels he is qualified to give information with regard to such matters.

Affiant further deposes and says that when he was a small boy there were only about 50 members of the Hoh Indian tribe although he was told that long prior to that time there were many more but that they had died on account of the smallpox epidemic which killed almost all of the Indians of the tribe; that the main village of the Hoh tribe was known as *Che* (as in chuck)-*lahk* [*cha•la•t'* j96] and it was located at the site of the present village now being used by the few remaining members; that in the summertime the people who lived in this place were accustomed to visiting what is known as Destruction Island for the purpose of hunting whales; that they also used to fish in the ocean for black bass, halibut, and salmon which they caught by trolling; that they also caught salmon in a trap located about one-half mile up the river from the main village where there was another smaller permanent community; [186]

That a long time ago the Hoh Indians used to go up to what is now known as Ruby Beach for the purpose of catching smelt which they would dry and take back to their permanent homes; that they have not done this since the state required that they must have a license to fish if they were outside their reservation; that when the Indians went to this place to catch smelt, they used to erect temporary shacks in which they lived, and dried their fish; that they ordinarily, would stay at this place about one week or 10 days at time and the various families in the tribe would take their turns in using the houses that were erected at this place; that in the proper season, they would also dig clams which were plentiful at certain times of the year.

Affiant further deposes and says that he is familiar with the location of the following Hoh villages which, however, are no longer used since the Indians that inhabited them have either died off or been driven away by the white people:

1. *Tsay-klay-it* [?*?] which meant "water pushing rock" located about one-half mile upstream from the mouth of the river.

2. *Tse-ohilk-lay-sh-quah* [?*?] which meant "high bank". This place was located a little below the high bank of the Hoh River about one-half mile above Braden Creek.

3. *Tohoe-poe-qwat* [?*?] which meant "and of good country before bad country begins" because when the Indians traveled upstream their journey from this point on was much more difficult than the journey from the mouth up to this place.

4. *Koatse-a-bi-dilkh* [?*?] located about a mile and a half from the preceding village; that he does not know the meaning of this in English.

5. *Due-wuk-a-kah* [?*?] which means "Indians' rhubarb"; that it was located across from the mouth of what the white people call Owl Creek.

6. *Klow-wuk-klulkh* [?*?] which meant "other side of sand bar"; that this place was located above the preceding one at the mouth of a small creek which has no name.

Affiant further deposes and says that there were a number of other places further upstream which were [187] used by the Hoh Indians but such places were used principally for hunting elk, bear, and other game, the surplus meat of which was dried and taken back to their permanent homes to be eaten at times when they want a change from fish; that the Indian, however, would catch fish at these various other places but principally for the purpose of eating them at the time and not for the purpose of curing them to be put away for future use.

Affiant further deposes and says that the Hoh Indians were friends of the Queets and Quileute Indians and that he has fished using the same methods as would those Indians; that their fish traps were the same and made of the same materials; that his spears and nets were also made of the same materials as the spears and nets of the others; that ordinarily each village would have a fish trap to catch fish during those times when the water was low enough so as not to wash out the traps from their foundations; that when the water was too high to construct a trap, the Indians would catch their fish by nets drifted between two canoes or by spears on the upper reaches of the stream where it was not necessary to go to the trouble of constructing the trap;

That the Indians of the Hoh tribe were accustomed to trading with the Indians living to the north and south of them for things that those Indians had which the Hoh Indians could not acquire in their own country; that generally speaking, however, the things that they traded amongst themselves were not fish or food but rather personal possessions and hides of the animals which they caught on their hunting trips.

Further affiant sayeth not.

(Sgd.) Frank Fisher his mark
Frank Fisher

Subscribed and sworn to before me this 8th day of May, 1942.

(Sgd.) Merle Hagmann
(Seal) Notary Public [188]

AFFIDAVIT

STATE OF WASHINGTON}
JEFFERSON COUNTY }   } SS

Joseph Pullen, being first duly sworn upon his oath deposes and says:

That he is 66 years of age, a full blood member of the Quileute Indian tribe, and a citizen of the United States of America residing at the village of La Push, on the Quileute Reservation, State of Washington.

That he is thoroughly conversant with the English language and with the language spoken by the Hoh Indians residing on the Hoh Reservation and can translate the English into the language spoken by the said Hoh Indians and can translate the language spoken by the said Hoh Indians into the English language;

Affiant further deposes and says that on the 8th day of June, 1942, in the presence of Frank Fisher, deponent, and Merle Hagmann, Field Aid at the Taholah Indian Agency, Hoquiam; Washington, be translated the information contained in the aforesaid affidavit of the said deponent from the English language into the Hoh language as said affidavit was read to affiant by Frank D Beaulieu, Clerk at the Taholah Agency; that the said deponent told affiant that the said narrative affidavit attached hereto, contained the information given to Mr. Edward G. Swindell, Jr., United States Indian Service, on October 14, 1941, and that he had, therefore, signed said affidavit because the information contained therein was true.

(Sgd.) Joseph Pullen

Subscribed and sworn to before me this 8th day of June, 1942

(Sgd.) Merle Hagmann
(Seal) Notary Public in and for
the State of Washington,
residing at Hoquiam [189]

MAKAH RESERVATION

AGENCY: - Taholah

LOCATION: - Northwest tip of Olympic Peninsula, Wash.

AREA: - 27,075 acres.

TREATY: - January 31, 1855; 12 Stat. 939; 2 Kappler 682 at Neah Bay.

INDIAN TRIBES: - Makah Indians. Reported to be a member of the Wahashan [Wakashan] family and the only one within the United States. The tribe belongs to the Nootka branch of that family.

LOCATION OF "U. & A." FISHING GROUNDS: -

Various streams entering the Pacific Ocean and Strait of Juan de Fuca, commencing with the Hoko River on the west to Cape Flattery thence south along the Pacific coast to a point south of Ozette Lake. This lake also is claimed as one of the old fishing grounds of the Makah tribe.

Clams, oysters, and smelt were obtained along the coast. In addition, these Indians customarily fished for "Bottom" fish in the waters of the Pacific Ocean. They also engaged in hunting whales, seals, and other marine animals.

PRESENT FISHING ACTIVITIES, GEAR, AND REGULATIONS: -

There is relatively little fishing done in reservation waters and, consequently, up to the present time no formal rules and regulations governing same have been adopted by this tribe. At the present time, however, the matter is receiving study by the tribal council with a view to adopting appropriate regulations.

From records of the local fish buyer at Neah Bay, it has been ascertained that the average annual value of the fish sold by these Indians during the [190] 1937-1940 period amounted to $16,150.00. During the same period it has been estimated the value of the fish used for subsistence purposes amounted to approximately $1,250.00 per-year.

Since most of the fishing by this tribes occurs in non-reservation waters, the gear ordinarily used conforms to the state fisheries code.

GENERAL REMARKS: -

Until state law prohibited it, the Indians fished in the waters of the Hoko River which was one of their claimed accustomed and usual fishing grounds. In order to determine the question as to whether the state had authority to regulate their fishing activities on usual and accustomed grounds, this tribe with its own money engaged counsel to file suit to enjoin state authorities from interfering with their fishing activities in the Hoko River. After a favorable decision from the District Court of the United States for the western district of Washington, northern division, the state appealed the case to the Ninth Circuit Court of Appeals in San Francisco. On June 22, 1942, the Circuit Court rendered an opinion reversing the lower court with leave for an amendment of the bill of complaint. It is considered probable that the ultimate decision in this case it-it be carried any further, will be made in accordance with the principles announced by the Supreme Court in the Tulee case. [191]

AFFIDAVIT

STATE OF WASHINGTON}
COUNTY OF CLALLAM }   } SS

      Joseph Sly, being first duly sworn, upon his oath deposes and says;

      That he is 84 years old, a full blood member of the Makah Indian Tribe and a citizen of the United States of America residing in the village of Neah Bay in the Makah Indian Reservation, Washington;[73]

      That he was born in the Makah Indian village located on the *Sekiu* River; that during the course of his life he has visited a number of places where the Makah Indians used to have their permanent villages and fishing locations; that as a result of the personal information gathered from those visits as well as the information given to him by his parents and the older members of the Makah Tribe when he was a small boy, he is very familiar with the way the Indians lived and obtained food in the old days as well as prior to the time he was born.

      Affiant further deposes and says that the place where he was born was not the permanent home of his parents; that at the time of his birth they had gone to the mouth of the Sekiu River which was a usual and accustomed fishing place of the Makah Indians for the purpose of obtaining fish which they dried and cured for use during the winter time when fish was not as plentiful as at other times of the year; that they were accustomed to go there each year for that purpose and each time they went there they established a camp close to the mouth of the river which was used by four families as well as by any friends who might visit then from time to time; that affiant has not fished in the Sekiu for many many years, probably as many as 50 years, and that at that time there were no white men in this part of the country; that the Indians caught fish-at *Sekiu* with hooks and nets which prior to the coming of the white men, they made theirselves out of nettle fibers; that affiant does not believe the Indians ever had one of the Indian fish traps at this [192] place; that the Makah Indians have always used *Sekiu* as long back as anyone can remember and that affiant was told by his parents that their ancestors had always fished the Sekiu ever since there had been "daylight".

      Affiant further deposes and says that the Makah Indians were also accustomed to going to the mouth of the Hoko River for the purpose of obtaining a supply of fish; that sometimes his parents would visit this place for as long as three months and at others they would stay only for short periods; that other Indians from Neah Bay used to go to this fishing place for the purpose of obtaining their supply of fish; that the names of some of them were: *Kee-chukh*, *Quedessa*, *Yokum*, La Chester, Circus Jim, *Tallacus* and *Hoko* Charley*.

        * Clallam affidavits show this individual a Clallam Indian.

      That the Indians who fished there had permanent homes at Neah Bay but they used to go over to Hoko each year some time in August before the fish started to run so that they could

---

[73] [m#] = Ann Renker & Maria Parker Pascua 1989 *Makah Traditional Cultural Property Study* Olympia: Office of Archaeology and Historic Preservation.

construct the traps and be ready to catch the fish when they first started to go up the river; that the people who fished at this place went there each year because the places belonged to their families and they were handed down from generation to generation; that the Indians who fished this place would do so in canoes and would bring back their supply of fish in the same manner because there were no roads in those days; that the trap they used was constructed a couple of miles from the camping place and that they traveled back and forth to it in their canoes; that the camp itself was located at the mouth of the river where it enters the ocean.

That when the Indians returned from Hoko River they traded the kind of fish they caught at that place for other kinds of fish that the Indians who remained at Neah Bay were able to obtain in the ocean, such as dried whale, dried halibut, ling cod and other bottom fish; that after the white men came they traded some of their fish for white man's food such as pork, bacon and things like that, although sometimes the white men would pay them cash for their fish after they had learned the value of money.

That Hoko and Sekiu were the places with which affiant is most familiar and that he can point out the places where the old Indian camps used to be, as well [193] as where the trap vas located at Hoko; that at times at Hoko the Indians fished along the course of the river using a net which they drifted between two canoes; that they used this method of fishing when the water was too high for the construction of a trap.

Further affiant sayeth not.

(Sgd.) Joseph Sly his mark
Joseph Sly

Subscribed and sworn to before me this 11th day of May, 1942.

(Sgd.) Frank D. Beaulieu
Notary Public in and for
the State of Washington,
(Seal) residing at Hoquiam

AFFIDAVIT OF INTERPRETER

STATE OF WASHINGTON}
COUNTY OF CLALLAM }   } SS.

Luke Markishtum, being first duly sworn, upon his oath deposes and says:

That he is approximately 66 years of age, a full blood member of the Makah Indian Tribe and a citizen of the United States, residing in the village of Neah Bay on the Makah Indian Reservation, Washington;

That he is thoroughly conversant with the English language and with the Makah Indian language, and can translate the English language into the Makah Indian language and the Makah Indian language into the English language;

That on October 15, 1941 at the village of Neah Bay, Washington, in the presence of Joseph Sly, deponent in the foregoing affidavit, and Edward G. Swindell, Jr., U.S. Indian Service, affiant did at the request of Mr. Swindell interrogate Joseph Sly with regard to certain matters concerning usual and accustomed fishing places and camping grounds of the Makah Indians; that he translated the questions of Mr. Swindell from [194] the English language into the Makah Indian language which Joseph Sly speaks and understands; that he translated the answers of Joseph Sly to Mr. Swindell's interrogatories from the Makah Indian language into the English language; that at that time a written record was made of the information given by the said Joseph Sly, which information has been reduced to the narrative form as given in the above and foregoing affidavit of the said Joseph Sly;

Affiant further deposes and says that on the 11th day of May, 1942 in the presence of Joseph Sly and Mr. Swindell, he translated the information contained in the aforesaid affidavit from the English' language into the Makah Indian language, as said affidavit was read to affiant by Mr. Swindell, that the deponent, Joseph Sly, told affiant that said narrative affidavit contained the information given by deponent therein to Mr. Swindell on October 15, 1941 and that he had therefore signed the said affidavit because the information contained therein was true.

Further affiant sayeth not.

(Sgd.) Luke Markishtum
Luke Markishtum

Luke Markishtum personally appeared before me this 11th day of May, 1942, and after having the foregoing affidavit read to him in my presence did acknowledge to me that the statements contained therein are true and that he executed same as his voluntary act.

Subscribed and sworn to before me this 11th day of May, 1942.

(Sgd.) Frank D. Beaulieu,
(Seal) Notary Public in and for
the State of Washington,
residing at Hoquiam [195]

JOINT AFFIDAVIT OF RANDOLPH PARKER, CHESTER WANDERHARD, HENRY ST. CLAIR, LUKE MARKISHTUM, HENRY MARKISHTUM, AND ARTHUR JOHNSON – MAKAH INDIAN TRIBE

STATE OF WASHINGTON }
COUNTY OF CLALLAM }   } SS

Randolph Parker, 67 years of age, Chester Wanderhard, 67 years of age, Henry St. Clair, 67 years of age, Luke Markishtum, 66 years of age, Henry Markishtum, 62 years of age, and Arthur Johnson, 70 years of age, each being first duly sworn and put upon oath, severally deposes and says;

That they are full blood members of the Makah Indian Tribe and citizens of the United States of America residing at the village of Neah Bay on the Makah Reservation, Washington;

That they were born either on the Makah Reservation or in the country owned by the Makah Indians before that country was ceded to the Government; that they have spent their entire life in that country and during the course thereof they have had occasion to visit the various places where the Makah Indians at one time had permanent villages or temporary fishing camps; that they have fished at these places and have seen other Indians fishing there; that such places have, from as long back as the Indians can remember, always been used as a source of food supply; that when affiants were small boys and young men they were told about these places by their parents and the older members of the Makah tribe since it was customary for the Indians to pass such information from generation to generation in such manner; that aside from their personal knowledge gained from actual use and observation of the various places, affiants believe that the things that were told them by their parents were true and confirmed their own knowledge gained during their respective lifetimes;

Affiants further depose and say that in addition to catching salmon and other fish found in the various streams throughout the original Makah country, they and their ancestors were accustomed to go out to the halibut banks for their supply of that kind of fish; that they also caught ling cod and other species of bottom fish, and some of the Makahs also caught seals and whales in the ocean: [196]

That when the Indians fished at the various usual and accustomed places not located at or near their principal permanent villages of Neah Bay, Ozette, Suez and Wa-atch, they lived in temporary homes constructed for the purpose of providing shelter from the elements as well as a lace in which the surplus fish could be dried and then taken back for use when fresh fish was not available;

That some of the better known of these places formerly used by the Indians were those located at the Hoko, Sekiu and Lyre rivers; that in addition there were a number of places along the beach where smelt could be caught in season; that prior to the coming of the white people the Indians fished using equipment designed and manufactured by them out of the available materials; that generally speaking, the salmon, caught in the rivers and streams were captured either with an Indian fishtrap which could only be constructed at considerable effort at a point where the Indians knew the water conditions were just right for this type of gear; when the water was high and a trap could not be used, the salmon were caught in homemade nets which ordinarily were operated from canoes; that some of the Makahs caught their fish by spearing them where the water was shallow; that ordinarily the places where fish were speared were located quite aways upstream from where the trap was located; that the Indians who speared fish would remain sometimes for several days at the spearing places and would dry and smoke their fish before bringing then back to the main encampment; that others would remain only long enough to get a canoe load of fish which they would cure at their main camp;

That after the Indians moved to their present reservation in keeping with the treaty, they continued to use the non-reservation fishing places because at each one they could obtain a different specie of fish, as for example, those that continued to use Osette Lake obtained a very special and good lasting salmon; that all of the Makahs did not use all of the various places and as a consequence those from each place would trade their kind of fish for the kind caught at the other places; that it was customary for the same families to use the same place each year and this would be followed from generation to generation; that the trade amongst the Indians amounted to quite a lot even before the white people first came; that it continued thereafter but it gradually changed from trading amongst themselves to, at first, trading fish to visiting boats in return for which they received the usual trade goods of calico, molasses and such things; [197] that even this changed when the canning of salmon became an established industry and the canneries offered cash to the Indians for their catch; that due to the change in their habits of living subsequent to the coming of the white people, it was necessary for the Indians to sell their fish for money in order to be able to buy necessities such as medicine, flour and other articles of food and clothing.

Further affiants sayeth not.

(Sgd.) Randolph Parker
Randolph Parker
(Sgd.) ChesterWanderhard
Chester Wanderhard
(Sgd.) Henry St. Clair
Henry St. Clair
(Sgd.) Luke Markishtum
Luke Markishtum
(Sgd.) Henry Markishtum
Henry Markishtum
(Sgd.) Arthur Johnson
Arthur Johnson

Subscribed and sworn to before me this 11th day of May, 1942.

(Sgd.) Frank D. Beaulieu
(Seal) Notary Public in and for
the State of Washington,
residing at Hoquiam [198]

NISQUALLY RESERVATION

AGENCY: - Taholah.
LOCATION: - West central Washington between Olympia and Tacoma. -
AREA: - 1,111 acres
TREATY: - Medicine Creek treaty of December 26, 1854,
10 Stat. 1132, 2 Kappler 661. -
INDIAN TRIBES: - Nisqually tribe, a unit of the Salishan family.

LOCATION OF "'U. & A." FISHING GROUNDS: -

Along the Nisqually River and its tributaries as well as the shores of Puget Sound where oysters, clams, and other marine life were taken.

PRESENT FISHING ACTIVITIES, AND REGULATIONS: -

At the present time the Nisqually Indians fish in the Nisqually River both within their reservation as well as outside the boundaries there of. During the period 1937-1940; inclusive, the Taholah Agency has estimated that the total value of the fish taken by the Indians both within their reservation and outside the boundaries thereof as ranging from $1,100.00 in 1937 to $15,350 in 1940, their biggest year of the four years for which the estimate was made. Only a small percentage of the total value was outlawed for subsistence purposes.

This tribe uses set nets, which are authorized by Washington law. It has no rules and regulations governing their fishing activities within the reservation.

GENERAL REMARKS: - The Nisqually Indians were parties to the treaty with a number of related tribes, the names of which are shown in Appendix B. They, however, were reported to have been the most powerful of the group and apparently were the only Indians [199] to settle upon the present Nisqually Reservation. The other tribes to a large extent have lost their tribal identity; in fact, many of them are no longer wards of the government. Fishing activities within the reservation are carried on by the few remaining individuals who consider themselves as true Nisqually Indians and who have been allotted thereon.

The fishing activities outside the reservation are carried on by individuals who although claiming Nisqually rights are descendants of the other tribes that were parties to the same treaty. Their non-reservation fishing activities in the Nisqually River are at present carried on without interference by the state as a result of a temporary restraining order obtained in 1937 in connection with the suit to test the Indians' rights to fish in that river, one of their claimed usual and accustomed fishing grounds, without interference by state authorities. It has been reported, that the Indians within the reservation are of the opinion that the unrestricted fishing activities by the other members who were parties to the treaty has resulted in seriously decreasing the annual fish migrations.

Under the decision of the Tulee case, the Indians fishing activities outside the boundaries of the reservation will, no doubt, be limited to the principles set forth by the Supreme Court. [200]

JOINT AFFIDAVIT OF ALLEN YELLOUT, PETER KALAMA
AND GEORGE BOBB, NISQUALLY INDIANS

STATE OF WASHINGTON }
COUNTY OF THURSTON }   } SS

Allen Yellout, 70 years of age, Peter Kalama, 80 years of age, and George Bobb, 65 years of age, each being first duly sworn and put upon oath, severally deposes and says:

That they are Nisqually Indians and citizens of the United States of America and residents of the State or Washington;

That they have spent all of their lives in the country formerly owned by the Nisqually Indians and sold to the United States pursuant to the treaty of 1855; and that during the course of their respective lives they have had occasion to visit the various places where the Nisqually Indians at one time had permanent villages or temporary camps for the purpose of utilizing their usual and accustomed fishing grounds; that they have fished at these places and have seen other Indians fishing there; that such places have always been used by the Indians from as long back as they can remember as a source of their food supply of fish; that when affiants were small boys and young men they were told about these places by their parents and the older members of their tribe and that aside from their personal knowledge of such places gained from actual use and observation, affiants believe that the things that were told to them as to such places always having been used by the Indians were true and confirmatory of their own knowledge gained during their respective lifetimes.

Affiants further depose and say that they are familiar with the location of old Nisqually village sites and fishing grounds as follows: -

1. WINDY CANYON. - That there was an old Indian village known as *Spooy-ails* [?*?] located on the Nisqually River at a point about 300 yards from the present railroad bridge on the main line between Seattle and Portland; that the Indians caught fish at this place with spears and an Indian fish trap made out of cedar boughs and which stretched all the way across the river; that they heard this was at one time quite a large village; that [201] when the Indians had sufficient fish for their meals they would open the trap so the fish could proceed upstream to their spawning grounds; that when the water conditions did not permit the use of the trap they caught the fish in a net which was operated from two canoes; that this was a good fishing place from which the Indians obtained considerable quantities of fish for immediate consumption as well as for curing and storage for future use.

2. YELM CREEK. - That there was a village located on both sides of what is now known as Yelm Creek where it entered the Nisqually River; that the Indian name for this village was *Dop-shat* [?*?]; that it was not a permanent village but only a temporary village site used during the fall of the year when the dog salmon were running; that the place was used by the Indians of the various permanent villages for about 5 or 6 weeks at a time; that the fish were caught with spears and a trap shaped like a corral which was emptied each morning.

3. WALKER PLACE - That there was a temporary fishing place known as *Keh-culs-duts* [?*?] located on the Nisqually River about 2 miles above the county road bridge on the road between Yelm and McKenna, Washington; that the place was utilized by most of the different Nisqually bands where they would camp and fish for as long as the fish were running which was about 2 weeks.

4. MUCK CREEK -   That there was a permanent Indian village known as *Yell-whahlse* [*yox^walsšabš* s24][74] located about 8 miles above the mouth of the creek which at one time was known as Douglas Creek; that this place was used by Indians from the other Nisqually villages during the time the fish were running; that this village was the home of Leshi, the Nisqually chief, who signed the treaty with Governor Stevens; that Muck Creek along its entire length was a fishing ground of the Nisqually Indians who caught their fish with spears and traps; that at *Yell-whahlse* the Indians caught fish by constructing a small dam; that the Indians have not used this place since the army took over Fort Lewis in about 1918.

5.   McALLISTER CREEK -   That this place was known as *She-nah-dah-dob* [*x^wəda'əb* = 'shaman, Indien doctor, medicine man' [n > b & m > d]] where the Nisqually treaty was signed*; that the Indians fished all along this creek using spears and Indian gaff hooks; that the Indians established temporary camps at the mouth of the creek and from these camps [202] they would go out into the bay when the tide was out to catch flounders and dig clams; that they also used this place as a sort of headquarters from which they would go over to what is now known as Andersen Island to dig clams; that they would stay at the Island for several weeks at a time until they had sufficient clams for their future needs.

    * In English known as Medicine Creek and in treaty referred to as "*She-nah-nam*" [*x^wəda'əb*] = shaman, Indien doctor, medicine man [n > b & m > d].

    Affiants further depose and say that the foregoing were the more important of the many Nisqually fishing places and that they are no longer used as they were in the old days because the Indians can-not fish in their old accustomed manner; that like the other Indians in the Pacific Northwest, fish was their most important article of food although they supplemented the fish with roots and berries which they obtained at the proper places when the time of the year in which they ripened arrived.

    Further affiants sayeth not

(Sgd.) Allen Yellout
Allen Yellout

Subscribed and sworn to before me this 9th day of June 1942.

(Sgd.) Merle Hagmann
Merle Hagmann
(Seal) Notary Public
(Sgd.) Peter Kalama
Peter Kalama

Subscribed and sworn to before me this 9th day of June 1942.

(Sgd.) Merle Hagmann
Merle Hagmann
(Seal) Notary Public
(Sgd.) George Bobb
George Bobb

Subscribed and sworn to before me this 9th day of June 1942.

(Sgd.) Merle Hagmann
Merle Hagmann
(Seal) Notary Public [203]

---

[74] [s#] = Marian Smith 1940 The Puyallup-Nisqually. NY: Columbia University.

QUEETS INDIANS
QUINAIELT [QUINAULT] RESERVATION

AGENCY: - Taholah

LOCATION: - Northwest corner of Quinaielt Indian Reservation situated in the center of the west coast of the Olympic Peninsula, Washington.

AREA: - See Quinaielt Reservation.

TREATY: - July 1, 1855, and January 25, 1856; 12 Stat. 971, 2 Kappler 719

INDIAN TRIBES: - Queets and Quinaielt tribes.

LOCATION OF "U. & A." FISHING GROUNDS: -

Queets River and its tributaries, the mouth and lower portion of which is located within the boundaries of the present Quinaielt reservation. As usual with the tribes in this area the villages and fishing camps were located along the main stream and usually at the mouths of the tributaries where conditions permitted the construction of fish weirs or traps. See attached map of Indian fishing locations on the Olympic Peninsula, Washington.

FISHING GEAR AND REGULATIONS: -

Set nets, drift nets, and hand dip nets. Fishing on the Queets River within the Quinaielt Reservation is carried on under rules and regulations adopted by Quinaielt tribal council. For gist of regulations see Quinaielt REMARKS.

PRESENT FISHING ACTIVITIES: -

The present fishing activities of the so called Queets Indians are solely carried on within the boundaries of the reservation since the gear used by them has been declared illegal by Washington law. The value of the catch for the period 1937-1940, inclusive, of this group of Indians has been included [204] in the estimate of the value of all fish taken from the these streams in that reservation.

GENERAL REMARKS; -

The Queets (*Quaitso*) Indians are also a member of the Salishan family and it has been reported that they probably formed a part of the main Quinaielt tribe. Since there is a separate community located on the Queets River which is some distance from the main settlement of the Quinaielt Indians at Taholah, Washington, the affidavits of this group were taken separately inasmuch as their original habitat was confined to the Queets River and its tributaries. The location of the present village of Queets is adjacent to the spot where the original main village of that tribe of Indians was situated. They are considered a part of the Quinaielt tribe, having received allotments of land on that reservation. [205]

AFFIDAVITS OF JOHNNY SHALE AND JACK SAM
QUILAIELT (QUEETS VILLAGE), WASHINGTON

STATE OF WASHINGTON }

COUNTY OF JEFFERSON}   } SS

Johnny Shale, 68 years of age, and Jack Sam, 81 years of age, each being duly sworn and put upon oath severally depose and say:

That they are full blood members of the Quinaielt Indian tribe, citizens of the United States of America residing at the village of Queets (Quinaielt Indian Reservation, Washington);

That they were born at the old Queets village and have lived all of their lives in the country owned by the Quinaielt (Queets) Indians prior to the time the white man first came to the country; that this country was the permanent home of their parents and their parents' parents before them and that when they were small boys they were told that their ancestors had always lived in that territory; that during the course of their life they have on various occasions visited the sites of the villages of the Quinaielt-Queets Indians which were situated along the streams running through the country originally owned by said Indians; that as a result of their personal observation of the things existing at those places, as well as the information that was given to them when they were small boys and young men by their parents and the older members of their tribe, they are fully familiar with the exact locations of those places as well as with regard to the way the Indians of their tribe were accustomed to obtain their livelihood at the present time as well as prior to the time the white man came to the Indians' country;

That the Quests Indians were accustomed to catching smelt in the Pacific Ocean at a place now called Brown's Point by the white people and that when they were small boys each family that went up there would dry enough smelt so that it would take them three or four trips to carry the dried fish back to the permanent village; that they have fished for smelt at Brown's Point many times during their life but have not done so since the white people passed laws requiring that the Indians have a license. [206]

Affiants further depose and say that the present village of Queets, Washington, is not located on the site of the original village that was in existence when they were small boys; that the old village was located just below the present main highway bridge* on the south bank of the river about a mile from the ocean and approximately 200 to 250 yards from the present village; that the Indians had two names for the Queets village, one of which was *Lee-choe-eese* [?*?] and the other was *Elths-tah-ach* [?*?] which latter meant "on the high bank"; that the village was given this name because it was situated on a bluff on the south bank of the river;

* Refers to bridge on US 101 crossing the Queets River.

That there were six big smoke houses in the old village and that about six families lived in each house making the population, as they recall, about 180 people all told inasmuch as there was an average of about five people in each family; that those houses were used for smoking the fish caught by the people who lived in them; that this was the permanent and main home of the Queets Indians; that the Indians caught their fish at this place by using a trap when the water conditions were right and that they all shared in the catch from this trap; at other times when the water was too high for a trap they caught fish in a net which was drifted in the stream between two canoes; that in addition to the main village there were two other communities in the same general vicinity, one of which was situated about three-quarters of a mile down stream toward the ocean and known as *Yoe-stos-whoh* [?*?]; that this name meant "new river channel" and the community was situated on the -north side of the old channel, that it had one big smoke house and five small ones and in all there were about 16 families, two other smaller houses and six other large ones; that the large houses were also used for social gatherings and that they would estimate the population of this place as being between 85 and 100 people; that they understand from their parents and grandparents that prior to the coming of the white man there were many, many more Indians living at this place but the great majority of them were killed off during the smallpox epidemic; that the other village in the same general vicinity was located on the south bank of the Queets River about two miles above the main village or [207 3] at the spot where the cable now crosses the stream; that the name of this other village was *Queets-nilth* [?*?] which meant "wild crabapple"; that there had been one big smoke house and five small ones and that the people who lived at these places were either killed off or moved to the main village of Queets.

Affiants further depose and say that there was another permanent village of the Queets Indians on the Queets River located about 1½ mile above the mouth of what is now known as the Salmon River or approximately one mile outside of the present boundary of the Quinaielt Reservation; that the Indian name for this place was *Nook-stay-slin* [?*?], which meant "plenty of salmon"; that when they remember this place it was merely a temporary camping place but the old people told them that prior to the coming of the white man it had been one of the permanent villages of the Queets people; that they have fished there but at the time they did fish at this place, the water was shallow and they used spears because it was easy to catch the fish in that fashion and not necessary to build a trap; that when they recall it, they remember approximately three families used to go there each year up until about 40 or 45 years ago when the white people settled the land and did not want the Indians around; that when they recall this place, there were two or three shacks standing there made out of split logs and covered with cedar bark.

Affiants further depose and say that there was an old permanent village of the Quests Indians on the north bank of the Queets River directly opposite the mouth of what is now known as Matheny Creek; that the Indian name for this village was *Poat-tso-itsa* [?*?], which meant "right across from mouth of the creek" or "middle of channel", that the name of the creek was the same and that during affiants lifetime the Indians only used this as a temporary camp although they were told it used to be one of the permanent villages; that just prior to the time the white people settled the place where this village was located, which was about 40 or 45 years ago, there was only one smoke house still standing and that some of the people from the main village of the Quests would go up there each year and stay approximately two months at a time during the months of September and October; that they used to catch black, silverside, steelhead and a few dog salmon by spearing them because at that time of the year the water was shallow at this place and a trap was not required. [208]

Affiants further depose and say that there were three other Queets Villages above *Poat-tso-itse* [?*?] located on the Queets River as follows: one directly opposite the mouth of Sam's Creek known as *Pee-tse* [?*?], which meant "sneeze"; another located opposite what is known by the white people as *Tshletshy* Creek for which the Indian name was *Tsh-lait-shah* [?*?] meaning "elk cooking rock"; and the third one was located on the north bank of the Queets River just below the mouth of Harlow Creek for which the Indian name was *Tsh-stoe* [?*?], which meant "half way between two big mountains"; that these three places were temporary hunting and fishing places of the Queets Indians; that some of them went there each year for the purpose of hunting bear and elk and that at times if the fish were running in the streams they would catch some for immediate consumption and if there was enough left over, they would dry them and take them back to their permanent village.

Further affiants sayeth not.

(Sgd.) John Shale his mark
Johnny Shale
(Sgd.) Jack Sam
Jack Sam

Subscribed and sworn to before me this 11th day of May, 1942.

(Sgd.) Frank D. Beaulieu
(Seal) Notary Public in and for
the State of Washington,
residing at Hoquiam [209]

AFFIDAVIT OF JACK SAM
QUINAIELT-QUEETS INDIAN

STATE OF WASHINGTON}
COUNTY OF JEFFERSON}   } SS

Jack Sam, being first duly sworn, upon his oath deposes and says:

That he is 81 years of age and a full blood member of the Quinaielt-Queets tribe and a citizen of the United States of America residing in the village of Queets, Quinaielt Indian Reservation, Washington;

That he was born in the country formerly owned by the Queets Indians and that he has lived in that country and at the Queets Indian village all of his life; that in addition to the information contained in his affidavit jointly made with Johnny Shale, he is familiar with the location of other Queets Indian villages either as a result of personal observations or by reason of information given him by his parents when he was a small boy and a young man.

Affiant further deposes and says that he is familiar with the following Indian villages located on the Clearwater River:

Poat-tsah-pash [?*?]:

That this means "middle of the channel" or the same as the meaning of the name of the village known as *Poat-tso-itse* on the Queets River; that it was located on the south side of Hurst Creek and the east bank of the Clearwater River and that although he never actually saw this village when people were living there, he has seen the posts which they used in constructing their houses; that he has visited and fished there but never camped there for the reason that when the day was over he and the other Indians would bring their fish home in their canoes and cure them at their permanent village; that they caught the fish at this place but with a spear.

Kah-yah-lay-huts (*T'sum-how-wah*) [?*?]:

That affiant does not know the meaning of this name; that there was one big house there; that affiant saw it during his life time and he and other Indians [210 6] used to go to this place for a few days at a time and spear fish, which they took home with them for the purpose of curing; that the Indians have not used this place for approximately 40 years because the land on which it is located has been settled by the white people.

No-qhy-tsales [?*?]:

That in Indian this meant "dirty rock"; that although affiant has never seen any houses there, he has seen evidence of the fact that houses had once existed at this place; that he has fished here with spears and that the catch would be brought back to his permanent home and the permanent home of the others who fished with him, where they would be cured.

Nah-hah-pish [?*?]:

That affiant never did see any houses here but saw evidence that houses had once existed at this point; that he does not know the meaning of the Indian name for this place and that, although he has fished there with spears, he has never stayed there longer than over night, after which he would return to his permanent home; that it would take two days to reach this place going upstream in canoes and only over night to get back;

Affiant further deposes and says that there were a number of other places on the Clearwater River above *Nah-hah-pish* [?*?] but that the Indians used these places principally for hunting purposes although they were accustomed to catching fish there at the time they would camp there during the hunting season.

Affiant further deposes and says that the Queets Indians dug clams and caught smelt at a place called *Quailth-tails* [?*?], which meant "red rock", and which is now known to the white people as Brown's Point; that the Indians a long time ago when they used this place would live in the caves in the rocks along the beach and that they did not erect houses until after the white people had come to the country; that the Indians would only go to this place during the proper season of the year when the clams could be dug from the sand and the smelt were spawning along the beach; that this lasted about two or three months; [211 7]

That clams were also dug at a place known now as *Kalaloch* [?*?] but that they would return to their camps at Brown's Point rather than spend the night at Kalaloch; that the people from all of the Queets villages were accustomed to visiting the ocean during the clam digging time and the time when the smelt were available in order to obtain a supply to take home. Further affiant sayeth not.

(Sgd.) Jack Sam His mark

Jack Sam

Subscribed and sworn to before me this 11th day of May, 1942.

(Sgd.) Frank D. Beaulieu

Notary Public in and for

the State of Washington,

residing at Hoquiam

AFFIDAVIT OF ROBERT E. LEE

STATE OF WASHIHGTON}
COUNTY OF JEFFERSON}   }SS.

Robert E. Lee, being first duly sworn, upon his oath deposes and says:

That he is 63 years of age, a full blood Quileute Indian residing at the village of Queets, Quinaielt Indian Reservation, Washington, and a citizen of the United States of America;

That he has lived at the Queets village for a number of years or ever since the time that the state prohibited the Quileute Indians from fishing in the Quileute River at LaPush; that he and a number of other Quileute Indians moved down to the Queets village at that time in order that they could fish without being interfered with by the state authorities; that the Quileute Indians and the Queets Indians are in a sense different people although they are all friends and their language is quite similar.

That during his lifetime he has had occasion to visit with his friends, the Queets Indians, a number [212] of the places used by the Quests Indians during his lifetime and prior thereto as the location of their permanent villages and fishing camps; that as a result of his personal knowledge thus gained from actual observations, he is familiar with the locations of a number of such places.

Affiant further deposes and says that on October 14th and 31st he was present at the village of Queets on the Quinaielt Indian Reservation when Jack Sam and Johnny Shale of the Queets Indian tribe' answered certain questions propounded by Edward G. Swindell, Jr. U.S. Indian Service concerning the locations of the old Queets villages and fishing places; that he listened carefully and clearly heard both the questions and the answers given thereto by the said Jack Sam and Johnny Shale and that insofar as he is personally familiar with the things they talked about or is familiar with through having heard about same during the course of his life, he can and does confirm the information-contained in the said answers.

Affiant further deposes and says that on the 11th day of May, 1942, he was present when Mr. Swindell in the presence of the said Johnny Shale and Jack Sam, read back to them an affidavit containing the information previously given by them on October 14th and 31st, 1941, as said affidavit was interpreted by Frank Bennet, that the said Johnny Shale and Jack Sam at that time acknowledged that the information contained in the said affidavit was the same as originally given by them and they, therefore, at that time signed said affidavit in the presence of affiant. Further affiant sayeth not.

(Sgd.) Robert E. Lee
Robert E. Lee

Subscribe and sworn to before me this 11th day of May 1942.

(Sgd.)Frank D. Beaulieu
(Seal) Notary Public in and for
the State of Washington,
residing at Hoquiam

AFFIDAVIT OF INTEPRETER

STATE OF WASHINGTON}
COUNTY OF JEFFERSON}   }SS.

Frank Bennet, being first duly sworn, upon his [213] oath deposes and says:

That he is 51 years of age, a full blood member of the Quileute Indian tribe, and a citizen of the United States of America residing at the village of Queets, Quinaielt Indian Reservation, Washington;

That he is thoroughly conversant with the English language and with the language spoken by the Queets Indians residing on the Quinaielt Reservation and can translate the English language into the language spoken by the said Queets Indians and can translate the language spoken by the said Queets Indians into the English language;

That on October, 14, 1941, at the village of Queets and in the presence of Jack Sam, Johnny Shale, and Robert E. Lee, deponents in the foregoing, affidavits and Edward G. Swindell, Jr., U.S, Indian Service, affiant did at the request of Mr. Swindell interrogate the said deponents with regard to certain matters concerning the location of a number of the old Quests Indian villages and fishing places in the area ceded by the Queets Indians to the United States; that he translated the questions of Mr. Swindell from the English language into the language spoken by the Queets Indians which the said deponents speak and understand; that he translated the answers of said deponents from the Queets language into the English language; that on those days, Mr. Swindell made written notes of the information given by the said deponents and reduced said information to the narrative form as given in the above and foregoing affidavits of the said deponents.

Affiant further deposes and says that on the 11th day of May, 1942, in the presence of Jack Sam, Johnny Shale, and Robert E. Lee, deponents and Mr. Swindell he translated the information contained in the aforesaid affidavits of the said deponents from the English language into the Queets language, as said affidavits were read to affiant by Mr. Swindell; that the said deponents and each of them told affiant that the said narrative affidavits contained the information given by them to Mr. Swindell on October 14 and 31, 1941 and that they had, therefore, signed said affidavits because the information contained therein was true. Further affiant sayeth not.

(Sgd.) Frank Bennet
Frank Bennet, Interpreter [214 10]

Frank Bennet personally appeared before me this 11th day of May, 1942, and after having the foregoing affidavit read to him in my presence did acknowledge to me that the statements contained therein are true and that he executed same as his voluntary act.

Subscribed and sworn to before me this 11th day of 1942.

(Sgd.) Frank D. Beaulieu
(Seal) Notary Public in and for
the State of Washington,
residing at Hoquiam [215]

QUILEUTE RESERVATION

AGENCY: - Taholah

LOCATION: - On the Pacific Coast of the Olympic Peninsula approximately 40 miles south of Cape Flattery.

AREA: - 594 acres

TREATY: - July 1, 1855, and January 25, 1856. 12 Stat. 971, 2 Kappler 719.

INDIAN TRIBES: - Quileute Indians.

LOCATION OF "U. &. A." FISHING GROUNDS; -

Along the Quileute, Bogachiel, Sol Duc, Clearwater and Dickey Rivers and the Pacific Coast north and south of the mouth of the Quileute.

PRESENT FISHING GEAR AND REGULATIONS: -

Since the above waters have been declared to be outside the reservation and subject to state jurisdiction, the Indians' gear has been that which had not been declared illegal by Washington law. No supplemental tribal regulations therefore were necessary.

PRESENT FISHING ACTIVITIES: -

Present day fishing activities are largely confined to the mouth of the Quileute river and the Pacific Coast where smelt are caught where such activities are at present subject to state regulation as hereinafter noted.

GENERAL REMARKS: -

Prior to 1934 or 1935 the members of the Quileute Indian tribe had always fished in the Quileute river without interference by the State authorities inasmuch as it had been contended that the bed of the river was a part of the reservation. At that time, however, the State authorities asserted jurisdiction over the fishing activities in the river, presumably on the basis of (1) the impending initiative amendment to the fisheries code and (2) the decision of the Ninth Circuit [216] Court of Appeals in the case of <u>Taylor v. US</u>., 44 F. (2d.) 531, which held in effect that the bed of the river and the submerged lands below the meander line were not a part of the reservation. Up to that time it has been estimated that the income from fishing by these Indians at times amounted to as much as $25,000 a year. During the period 1937-40, inclusive, the Taholah Agency has estimated that the total value of the fish taken by the Indians dropped to as low as $600 in 1937. In 1938 the estimated value of the catch is $12,750; in 1939, $3,960 and back to $2,500 in l940. In considering these figures it should not be overlooked that the catch for any year is predicated on the cyclic year of the species of fish native to any particular water course.

As a result of the State successfully asserting jurisdiction over the fishing activities in the river, by abolishing the use of set nets, the Indians' annual income was very seriously curtailed inasmuch as they were no longer permitted to fish with such nets which they had been accustomed to using up to that time. Since then, they were only permitted to fish in the river at certain times of the year, and even then they are limited to the use of drift nets inasmuch as the state fisheries code outlaws "fixed appliances". Many of the Indians consequently were forced to move to the Hoh Indian reservation where they could continue to fish with the gear they possessed in Hoh river which is not under State jurisdiction.

It is to be noted in this connection that ever since the decision in the Taylor case there has been a question in the minds of the Indians as well as some of the administrative officials of the Indian Service and others as to whether or not the adverse decision of the Ninth Circuit Court of Appeals was based upon an erroneous as to a material fact. The decision of the lower court (33 F. (2d) 608) which was favorable to the Indians, and which was reversed, in effect held that the Executive Order of February 19, 1889, creating the Quileute reservation, antedated by three days the enabling Act (25 Stat. 676) admitting the Territory of Washington into the Union and that consequently the bed of the river had been included in the grant to the Indians. [217]

In reversing the lower court the appellate court's opinion is of such tenor that it is indicated, it may have had a misunderstanding as to the facts concerning the date of the creation of the reservation and the date of the Enabling Act. This assumed misunderstanding is indicated by the following quotation from the court's opinion:

> "If we recognize the rule that in grants to Indians uncertainties are to be determined more favorably to them than to the Government, we must here recognize that the governmental act is dual in its effect, if so construed, as it takes from the State a right <u>already expressly granted to it</u> and reserves it for a political body, not by express grant or reservation but by mere implication. In other words, so construed, the act of the President extends to a political body, merely because it is a political body, a right which must be taken from another political body to which it has been <u>already expressly granted</u>. It would seem more reasonable that the <u>previous express grant</u> to a political body would take precedence over the implications which would otherwise arise from the reservation of the upland for an Indian tribe. We are inclined to think that the inferences to be derived from the fact that the Quileute Indians for whom the reservation was set apart are overcome by the <u>prior express grant of the tide lands and navigable waters to the State</u>." (Emphasis supplied.)

It would appear from the above that the decision of the court was predicated upon the assumption that title to the tide lands and bed of the river had been granted to the State prior to the creation of the Quileute Reservation. It is not clear however, from the court's opinion when taken as a whole, whether its decision was predicated upon that assumption or whether the above quoted language was merely dicta. Elsewhere in the opinion the court pointed out that the Executive Order creating the reservation did not refer to the navigable waters surrounding and adjacent to the uplands described therein and that in fact there was nothing in the description in the Order which justified an inference that it was the intention "to reserve for the Indians lands below the high tide [217A] line or lands covered by the navigable waters adjoining the lands conveyed". The Supreme Court of the United States denied the government's petition for certicrari [certiorari] (283 U.S. 820; 75; L. ed. 1436). It is not clear whether the original channel of the river traversed the lands described in the Executive-Order. There would seem to be considerable merit to the contention that title to the bed of the river was retained by the United

States in trust for the Indians by the Executive Order, if in fact the description of the lands in the Order was such that it described lands on both sides of the river.

It is possible of course that this particular feature of the case was carefully considered after the unfavorable decision was handed down by the Circuit Court and that in investigating the matter it was determined that the decision of that court was in accordance with law and the facts as they actually existed. In view of the importance of this matter to the Indians of the Quileute reservation; however, it is recommended that the facts with regard thereto be carefully looked into in order to determine whether or not some action should not now be taken in the event the investigation determines the Circuit Court may have predicated its opinion on an erroneous assumption of a material fact. It is believed that the question can properly be considered when and if the State of Washington takes action looking to the dissolution of the preliminary injunction granted by the U.S. District Court for the Western District of Washington (S.D.) under date of May 5, 1941 in the case of <u>Quileute Indian Tribe et al. v B.F. McCauley, et al</u>, No.72. [218]

AFFIDAVIT

STATE OF WASHINGTON}
COUNTY OF CLALLAM } SS

Sextas Ward, being first duly sworn, upon his oath deposes and says:

That he is about 90 [ninety] years old, a full blood member of the Quileute Tribe, and a citizens of the United States of America, residing in the village of La Push, Quileute Indian Reservation, Washington.

That he was born at an Indian village called *Shu-a-wah* [*sho•wat'* ~ *bo'lak*^{w} = 'turbulent' j48][75] located at what the white people now call Beaver Prairie; that this was the permanent home of his parents although after he was born his people moved to the Dickey River which was his home of his

mother's people; that he is personally familiar with the location of a number of the permanent villages and fishing places of the Quileute Indians which he visited at various time during his lifetime; that in addition to information he gathered by actual observation of the way the Indians lived and fished at those places he also was told by his parents as well as the older members of the Quileute Tribe about the way the Indians lived and fished at various villages prior to the coming of the white man and for as long as the Indians kept tract of the things that happened in the past by telling their children so that they could tell their children and thus always know how their ancestors had lived.

Affiant further disposes and says that he is familiar with the location of Quileute Indian villages and fishing places as follows:

SOL DUC RIVER

That there were several villages located along the course of the Sol Due River which receives its water from what the white people call Pleasant Lake; that the Indians lived at these various villages all of the year except for those short periods when they [219] would come to the main Quileute village at La Push to visit with their friends and relatives and also to trade some of their fish for seal and whale meat which the people at La Push were able to obtain from the ocean.

That the villages along the Sol Duc River about which the affiant is personally familiar are as follows:

---

[75] [j#] = Jay Powell 2008 *Quileute Dictionary* La Push [1976]

BAH-QWAT [*bak̲ʷat* = 'junction' j47]
That there was a permanent village of the Quileute Indians known as *Bah-quat*, which means "junction", located on the north side of the Quileute River just below where the Sol Duc and Bogachiel Rivers come together to form the main Quileute; that this village was really in two parts, the other section of which was situated south of the Sol Duc but on the north bank of the Bogachiel; that he would estimate that about 25 people lived in each of the two sections of the village of *Bah-qwat*; that each place had its-own fish trap from which they were enabled to obtain a plentiful supply of fish each year; that these were permanent villages of the Quileutes but they had not been used since the white people homesteaded the land upon which they are located and they would not let the Indians live there any longer; that the Indians have not lived at this place since before his son, Jack Ward, who is about 57 years old, was born.

QUAL-LAH-DIS [?*?]
That there was another permanent village on the Sol Duc located about two miles above *Bah-quat*; that, as he recalls it, he would say approximately 30 or 35 people used to live there; that the Indians stopped living at this village for the same reason they did at *Bah-qwat*, that this was a suitable place for fishing, and the Indians caught their fish with a trap and sometimes with spears and sometimes with nets which were used from canoes.

UCK-QWY-OOT [*ok̲'idok̲ʷat* – ridge j30 *kloshe nanitch*]
That there was another permanent village known as *Uck-qwy-oot* located about two or two and a half miles [220 3] above *Qual-lah-dis*; that the name meant "over the hump" and when he remembers this place there was only one house there being used by one family, even though it was a good place to fish; that prior to the time the white men came to the Indians country there had been more Indians living there but they died during the epidemics or had moved on down to the main village of La Push after the Government set aside the Quileute Reservation; that the Indians got their supply of fish at this place in the same manner as the others.

SHU-A-WAH [*sho•wat'* ~ *bo'lak̲ʷ* = 'turbulent' j48]
That the Indians who lived at *Shu-a-wah* obtained the principal part of their supply of fish from a trap located near the village; that they did not find it necessary to go elsewhere to catch fish because their trap supplied them with all they needed; that they would, however, at various times during the year visit the main Indian tillage of La Push for the purpose of catching smelt and drying them to be taken back to their village to be used as a change in their food supply; that the smelt were caught in the ocean along the shore in front of the main village of La Push; that some of the Indians who were skillful enough would go out in the ocean for the purpose of catching seals or whales; that *Shu-a-wah* was a permanent village of about 20 people or more, with three smoke houses; that it was located just a little bit below the junction of a creek that comes from Lake Pleasant and the Sol Duc River; that he had a smoke house at *Shu-a-wah* until about eight years ago although he did not live there, having moved to La Push a long time before that; that he left his old home at *Shu-a-wah* because the Game Warden told the Indians to stop fishing about 7 or 8 years ago.

DICKEY RIVER

Affiant further deposes and says that there was a permanent Quileute Indian village located at the mouth of the Dickey River ad that the Indian name for this place was *Doe-hoe-*

*dach-tedar** [*dix^w odachtada* j42]; that when he was a [221 4] small boy he remembers quite a few Indians living at this place and he would estimate the number roughly as 75; that so far as he knows this was the only Quileute village on the Dickey River; that the Indians caught their fish in the Dickey River using four fish traps which stretched all the way across the stream; that the Indians who used to live at this village, as well as others from La Push and other Quileute villages, used to go up to the area around Dickey Lake for the purpose of hunting elk which they smoked and brought back to the village to east as a change from the fish that they were accustomed to eating most of the time.

> *Metsker's official map of Washington shows that the east and west forks of the Dickey River join, and from that point on to where the stream enters the Quileute River, about a mile from the ocean, it is designated as the Dickodochtedar River.

Affiant further deposes and says: that these are the villages with which he was most familiar and that other members of the tribe are more familiar with the location of Quileute villages on the other rivers.

That as a matter of general information affiant points out that when he was a boy there were no white people living in the Quileute country; that prior to the coming of the white men the Indians who lived in the villages along the various streams were able to catch much more salmon than those who lived along the ocean, whereas those along the ocean could obtain seal, whale, and smelt; that as a result of this they were accustomed to trade amongst themselves so that they could have all kinds of fish and sea food for their daily subsistence; that after the white man came to the country they would trade fish to the white people for sugar, coffee, molasses and things like that; that the trade amongst the Indians and the white people amounted to quite a bit;

That in addition to the places above mentioned he was told when he was a small boy and a young man that the Quileute Indians used to fish at the lower or south end of Ozette Lake; that the other end of the lake was used by the Ozette Indians who were different people than the Quileute ; that the Indians would go to Ozette Lake and stay about a month at a time for the purpose of obtaining a special kind of salmon that lived in the lake and which could not be obtained from the streams on which the Quileute lived; that the Indians would go to this place in canoes which they paddled in the ocean to a point where the lake was [222 5] closest to them; that from there they would carry their belongings over a trail to the shores of the lake where they established a temporary camp; that they maintained canoes at the lake which were smaller than their ocean canoes which they used when they fished in the lake; that the Ozette Indians were friendly to the Quileute and they did not have any trouble over both of them using the lake to obtain fish; that although he never went to this place himself he used to know a number of Indians who did fish up there at various times and who told him the foregoing; that he understands that when the treaty was made with Governor Stevens the Quileute Indians were supposed to be given the right to continue to use their old fishing place at Ozette Lake.

Affiant further deposes and says that fishing activities at various Quileute villages were substantially the same; that ordinarily each village would have at least one trap and that in addition to the traps the Indians caught fish with spears and nets; that when the Indians had obtained enough fish they would remove the weirs from the river in order that the fish they did not need could go upstream and lay their eggs so that there would be a supply of fish for future years; that the fish traps or weirs were made of fine maple boughs laced together with spruce limbs and they stretched entirely across the stream in which they were build; that the nets used by the Indians were made out of twine which the Indians manufactured from maple vines.

That the Indians stopped using fish traps or weirs many years ago for the reason that after the white men came they could obtain nets which were easier to use and did not require the hard work of constructing the weir;

That he can not estimate how much fish each family dried to be used during those times of the year when fresh fish was not available, but he knows that they always had plenty of fish; that there are not nearly as many fish in the river nowadays as … when he was a young man;

That the Indian houses at all of the places above mentioned in the old days were made out of cedar planks, [223 6] lashed together with twisted cedar boughs; that the roofs of the houses were made of the same material except that the planks were fixed so that they would fit together and be water-tight; that prior to the time the white men came the planks were made by splitting cedar logs with sharpened spruce knots which were pounded with stone hammers.

Affiant further deposes and says that the Hoh Indians were a separate group of Indians from the Quileute although they spoke substantially the same language; that during his lifetime they have always been friendly with each other, many of them having intermarried; that each group recognized the fishing places of the other and did not interfere with their respective use of the same; that he understands that this was the way things were prior to the time the white men came to the Indians' country and always as long as there were Indians living in this country.

Affiant further deposes and says that when he was a small boy he was told that the villages he has talked about used to have many more people than lived there when he first remembered things; that he was told the reason there are so many less Indians nowadays was on account of the fact that after the white men came to the country they brought with them serious diseases which killed off the greater' portion of the Indians.

Further affiant sayeth not.

(Sgd. Sextus Ward his mark
Sextus Ward

Subscribed and sworn to before me this 11th day of May, 1942.

(Sgd. Frank D. Beaulieu
Notary Public in and for
the State of Washington
Residing at Hoquiam

AFFIDAVIT

STATE OF WASHINGTON }
COUNTY OF CLALLAM }   } SS

Benjamin Harrison Sailto, being first duly sworn, upon his oath deposes and says; [224 7]

That he is 69 years old, a full blood member of the Quileute Indien Tribe and citizen of the United States of America, residing, in the village of La Push Reservation Washington.

That he was born at La Push, Washington, which is and always has been the principal and largest village of the Quileute Indians; that this was the permanent home of his parents and it had been their parents home before them, although during one period of his life he had spent some time with his grandfather who had a place located about a mile and a half above La Push which was on land not on the Quileute Indian Reservation; that he has visited a number of the villages and fishing places of the Quileute Indians throughout the course of his life and he is therefore personally familiar with their location as well as with the way the Indians who live there obtain their livelihood; that in addition to his personal knowledge gained from actual observation throughout his life he remembers the things that his parents and the older members of the Quileute tribe told him when he was a small boy, and he believes that the things they told him were true because the things that existed when he was a small boy and a young man substantially confirm the things that were told him.

Affiant further deposes and says that although the principal Quileute village was at La Push, there were a number of other villages located along the various rivers in the country owned by the Quileute prior to the coming of the white man; that some of these villages contained a number of houses, both large and small, and that the larger houses were occupied by a number of families and the smaller ones ordinarily were occupied by more than one family; that these various villages were located at those places on the river where the conditions were favorable for catching fish in the manner the Indians obtained this supply of food prior to the coming of the white men; that in all these villages, he was told, many people resided prior to the coming of the white men but that after that event had occurred many of the Indians were killed off by the epidemics which the white men brought with them; that in some instances whole village were wiped out and there would be no survivors; that where there more [225 8] survivors they were consolidated with other nearby villages or moved down to the main village at La Push in ever increasing numbers after the treaty with Governor Stevens (in 1855);

That the way the Indians caught their fish at these various places was substantially the same; in most instances each village had a trap and they supplemented the fish caught in the manner by using spears and sometimes nets; that the traps were built in shallow water although not necessarily at the mouth of the small streams which flowed past a number of the villages; that most of the villages were permanent although at certain times of the year the people who lived there would visit the Indians at other places or else come down to the main village at La Push for festivities and to obtain a supply of the different kinds of fish food which they could not obtain at their own fishing places; that when they visited thee other places they traded some of the fish they caught for the things that the people had at the places they were visiting; that they would catch smelt in the ocean along the beach in front of La Push as well as far south as the country occupied by the Hoh Indians; that in addition to smelt the Indians who lived at La Push would also catch whales and seals in the ocean;

That when affiant was a boy there were no white men in the country and he did not see one until he was about 25 years old; that after the white people commenced to settle in the country the Indians traded fish to them in return for potatoes and things like that although some of the white people would catch salmon in the small creeks near their homesteads;

That the Quileutes were not related to the Quinaielt Indians although they were good friends;

That the Quileute Indian houses were constructed of long boards which were split from cedar logs and then bound together with cedar boughs.

Affiant further deposes and says that he is personally familiar with the location of Quileute Indian villages and fishing places as follows: [226 9]

BOGACHIEL RIVER

T'CHOE-KLAY-BIQUE [?*?]

That there was a permanent Quileute village located opposite the creek which enters the Bogachiel [*bok͟ʷac'hi'l* j49] River about a mile from the junction of the Bogachiel and Sol Duc Rivers known as *T'choe-klay-bique* [*sa't'a ba'k͟ʷat* j47], which in Indians means "end of the trail from the beach"; that when a small boy he remembers there were two big smoke houses in this village and this approximately30 people or possibly a few more lived there, including men, women and children; that the Indians have no lived at this place since the land was taken over by the white people.

PAY-CHAY-TEE-U [*p'ic'hit'ayo ḵ'a* = 'red gravel creek' j58]

That he was told there was another permanent village situated a short distance. Above where what the white people call Mayfield's Creek runs into the Bogachiel River; that the Indian name for this was *Pay-chay-tee-u*, which means "red rock bottom" because the bottom of the river at this place was reddish colored; that he never saw this village although his mother and father both told him about it, as well as the fact that although a lot of people used to live there they had all been killed off by the smallpox epidemic which happened many, many years ago.

T'SAH-QWAH-LEE [?*?]

That there was a permanent village located on the Bogachiel River about a mile above *Pay-chay-tee-u* which was known by two names, one being *T'sah-qwah-lee* and the other *T'si-t'so-wah-kly*, both of which meant "branches dragging on the water" because there were a number of willow trees located at this point; that there were three smoke houses at this place and 7 adult men and •their families, or approximately 35 peoples; that the Indians moved from this place a long time ago when the land was homesteaded by the white people.

T'SE-DEE [*t'si'dikᵂ* j64]

That there was another permanent village located on the Bogachiel River about six miles below the point where the Calawah river runs into the Bogachiel; that approximately 30 people in four families lived her in ₍₂₂₇ ₁₀₎ two great big houses that they obtained their fish by construction a trap in the river and that when the fishing was not good here they would go farther down stream where they would fish from two canoes pulling a net between the two.

T'CHOE-LOE-YASS-LEE [*c'ho'loyasli* = 'tall reaching tree place' j67]

That there was also a permanent village on the Bogachiel River about one-half mile above the junction with the Calawah, which was known as *Hoke-t'soe*, meaning "burnt ground"; that this village, prior to the coming of the white men and the burning of the timber was known as *Kah-bah*; that this village contained about three houses and probably more than 40 people in ten families; that he was told the Indians moved from this place because they could not get enough fish and the white people were also beginning to take their land from them; that they moved to other villages of the Quileute Indians;

T'SAH-LEE-LAIT [*tsalilitkᵂ* 'going uphill' j80]

That there was also another permanent village on the main Bogachiel River just below the mouth of the creek which enters the river from the north side west of the main highway* between the towns of Bogachiel and Forks; that the Indian name for this place was *T'sah-lea-lait* which meant "over the hill"; that this was the home of the parents of William Penn, a Quileute Indian, and that they and their relatives were forced to leave this place when the white people homesteaded the land.

* This refers to U.S. Highway 101. [228 11]

T'QHOE-LAY-K'AY-LEE [?*?]

That there was one other permanent village that he knows of on the Bogachiel River which was located just above the present town of Bogachiel; that the Indian name for this place meant "leading to prairie"; that he never did see this place but his parents told him about it, but he does not have any idea how many Indians or houses were at this point.

CALAWAH RIVER

Affiant further deposes and says that there was a permanent Quileute Indian village on the Calawah River located about where the present main highway* between Forks and Tyee crosses the river; that the name of this village was *Tse-choke*** [*hac'hal* = 'good fishing' j75], meaning "upper end of the prairie"; that affiant is not personally familiar with the facts about this village, but when he was small he was told that it was a permanent village of the Quileute Indians and that quite a few of them lived there, the number of course being much larger prior to the coming of the white men.

Further affiant sayeth not.

(Sgd.) Benjamin Harrison Sailto his mark
Benjamin Harrison Sailto

Subscribed and sworn to before me this 11ᵗʰ day of May, 1942.

(Sgd. Frank D. Beaulieu
Notary Public in and for
the State of Washington
Residing at Hoquiam

* This refers to U.S. Highway 101.
** This apparently is the same prairie referred to in the village mentioned under the Bogachiel River; that village is almost due south of the one herein discussed.

JOINT AFFIDAVIT OF STANLEY GRAY,
DANIEL WHITE, AND MARK WILLIAMS

STATE OF WASHINGTON }
COUNTY OF CLALLAM }   SS

Stanley Gray, Daniel White, and Mark Williams being first duly sworn, upon their oaths depose and say: [229 12]

That affiants are 78, 70 and 70 years of age in the above named order; that they are full blood members of the Quileute Indian tribe and citizens of the United States of America; residing in the village of La Push, Quileute Indian Reservation, Washington;

That they were born in the country owned by the Quileute Indians prior to the coming of the white men which was sold to the United states Government b the treaty negotiated by Governor Stevens many years ago; that they have lived in the Quileute country all of their life and at various times have had occasion to visit one or more of the old Quileute Indian villages and fishing grounds; that as a result of their travels they are personally familiar in some instances with the actual conditions which existed at some of the places formerly occupied by the Quileute Indians; that aside from their personal information gathered throughout the course of their life they, in common with the other Quileute Indians, were told by their parents and the older members of the Quileute Tribe when they were small boys growing into manhood about the location of certain of the various villages and the way the Indians used to live and fish; that affiants therefore feel that they are familiar with the situation which existed at those various places;

Affiant further depose and say that on October 15 and 30, 1941, at the village of La Push on the Quileute Indian Reservation, Washington, they were present when Sextas Ward and Benjamin Harrison Sailto, members of the Quileute Indian Tribe, answered certain questions propounded by Edward G. Swindell, Jr., U.S. Indian Service, concerning the location of Quileute villages as said Sextus Ward and Benjamin Harrison Sailto recalled them; that they listened carefully, and clearly heard both the questions and the answers given thereto and that they can and do confirm the information contained in said answers insofar as they are personally familiar therewith from actual observation during their lifetime; that so far as things that occurred prior to their lifetime were concerned they can and do confirm them as being true and the same things that were told to them by their parents when they were small boys and young men. [230 13]

Affiants further depose and say that on the 11th day of May, 1942 they were present in the presence of said Sextas Ward and Benjamin Harrison Sailto and Mr. Swindell when an affidavit containing the information previously given by said Sextas Ward and Benjamin Harrison Sailto was read back to them by Mr. Swindell and interpreted by Morton Penn, a member of the Quileute Tribe of Indians; that the said Sextas Ward and Benjamin Harrison Sailto at that time acknowledged that the information contained in said affidavit was the same as originally given by them and they therefore signed said affidavit in the presence of affiants; that the information as originally given and contained in the said affidavit is true to the best of affiants knowledge and belief.

Further affiants sayeth not.

(Sgd.) Stanley Gray
Stanley Gray
(Sgd.) Daniel White
(Sgd.) Mark Williams

Subscribed and sworn to by Stanley Gray, Daniel White, and Mark Williams before me this 11th day of May, 1942

(Sgd.) Frank D. Beaulieu
Notary Public in and for
the State of Washington,
residing at Hoquiam

AFFIDAVIT OF INTERPRETER

STATE OF WASHINGTON }
COUNTY OF CLALLAM }   SS

Jack Ward, being first duly sworn, upon his oath deposes and says;

That he is 57 years old, a full blood member of the Quileute Indian tribe and a citizen of the United [231 13a] States of America residing at the village of La Push, Quileute Indian Reservation, Washington;

That is thoroughly conversant with the English language and with the Quileute Indian language, and can translate the English language into the Quileute Indian language and the Quileute Indian language into the English language.

That on October 15 and 30, 1941, at Affiant's home in the village of La Push and in the presence of Sextus Ward, Benjamin Harrison Sailto, Stanley Gray, Daniel White and Mark Williams, who are the deponents in the foregoing affidavits, and Edward G. Swindell, Jr., U.S. Indian Service, affiant did, at the request of Mr. Swindell, interrogate the said deponents with regard to certain matters concerning the location of a number of the old Quileute Indian villages and fishing places in the area ceded by the Quileute Indians to the United States, as well as with regard to the way the Quileute Indians and their ancestors obtained their livelihood; that he translated the questions of Mr. Swindell from the English language into the Quileute Indian language, which the said deponents speak and understand; that he translated the answers of said deponents to Mr. Swindell's interrogatories from the Quileute language into the English language; that on those days Mr. Swindell made written notes of the information given by the said deponents and reduced said information to the narrative form as given in the above and foregoing affidavits of the said deponents.

(SGD.) Jack Ward.
Jack Ward

Jack Ward personally appeared before me this 11th day of June 1942, and after having the foregoing affidavit read to him in my presence did acknowledge to me that the statements contained therein are true and that he executed same as his voluntary act.

Subscribed and sworn to before me this 11th day of June, 1942;

(Sgd.) Jesse H. Henry
Supt. & Physician [232 13b]

AFFIDAVIT OF INTERPRETER

STATE OF WASHINGTON }
COUNTY OF CLALLAM }   }SS

Morton Penn being first duly sworn, upon his oath deposes and sayeth;

That he is 60 years old, a full blood member of the Quileute Indian tribe and a citizen of the United States of America, residing in the village of La Push, Quileute Indian Reservation, Washington;

That he is thoroughly conversant with the English language and with the Quileute Indian language and can translate the English language into the Quileute Indian language into the English language;

That on the 11th day of May, 1942, in the presence of Sextus Ward, Benjamin Harrison Sailto, Stanley Gray, Daniel White and Mark Williams, deponents, and Mr. Swindell, he translated the information contained in the aforesaid affidavits of the said deponents from the English language into the Quileute language, as said affidavits were read to affiant by Mr. Swindell; that the said deponents, and each of them, told affiant that the said narrative affidavits contained the information given by them to Mr. Swindell on October 15 and 30, 1941, and that they had therefore signed said affidavits because the information contained therein was true.

Further affiant sayeth not.

(Sgd.) Morton Penn
Morton Penn

Morton Penn personally appeared before me this 8th day of June, 1942, and after having the foregoing affidavit read to him in my presence did acknowledge to me that the statements contained therein are true and that he executed same as his voluntary act.

Subscribed and sworn to before me this 8th day of June, 1942.

(Sgd.) Merle Hagmann
(Seal) Notary Public

QUINAIELT RESERVATION

AGENCY: - Taholah.
LOCATION: - West Pacific coast about 35 miles north of Hoquiam, Washington.
AREA: - 175,159 acres.
TREATY: - July 1, 1855, and January 25, 1856; 12 Stat. 971, 2 Kappler 719.
INDIAN TRIBES: - Quinaielt [Quinault], Queets and Quileute

LOCATION OF "U. & A." FISHING GROUNDS: -

Pacific coast and streams entering same from Queets River south to the Columbia River as claimed by Quinaielt tribal, council. (See Remarks below.)

PRESENT FISHING ACTIVITIES, GEAR AND REGULATIONS: -

Present fishing activities of the Indians of this reservation are confined to reservation waters consisting of the Queets, Raft, and Quinaielt rivers; These streams furnish them with an adequate supply of fish both for commercial and subsisted purposes; hence it is not necessary for them at least at this time to fish outside the boundaries of the reservation. The type of gear used within the reservation is set, drift and hand dip nets which, generally speaking, are illegal in Washington. At certain times of the year of course the use of drift nets in certain non-reservation streams is authorized by law. That feature, however, is immaterial inasmuch as that law is not applicable on the reservation. The Taholah Agency has estimated that during the 1937-40 period, the total value of the fish taken from the three streams was $24,720 in 1937; $97,550 in 1938; 44,442 in 1939 and $18,672 in 1940. These figures were obtained from the local fish buyers.

This tribe probably observes more regulations of their fishing activities than any other1. The season for steelhead is limited to the months of December and January and that for blueback [sockeye] salmon from April 1st to July 1st. [234]

On the Quinaielt river, all commercial fishing is closed, from July 1 to September 15, although Indians are permitted to fish for subsistence purposes during that period. In the lower river all fish nets must be out of the river from 6:00 p.m. Saturday until 6:00 a.m., Monday. The upper river fishermen are permitted to set their nets back in the river 6:00 p.m. Sunday.

A -tax of one cent per fish is collected from fish buyers by the treasures of the tribal council and the proceeds in part are used to pay a channel patrolman whose duty it is to patrol the river and enforce the tribally adopted regulations./1/[76]

The secretary of the tribal council reports that the rules are strictly enforced although it is known some violations are bound to and have occurred. Whether these rules are adequate or strictly enough enforced is debatable since it is reported there-has been a tendency to overfish the reservation streams.

GENERAL REMARKS: -

As indicated in the narrative section of, this part of the report, the Quinaielt tribal council advised that their fishing rights within the reservation were sufficient at least for their present needs and for that reason no affidavits were taken with regard to non-reservation usual and accustomed fishing grounds. The tribal council, however, furnished the Indian names and a general description of a number of places which they state were some of the ancient fishing grounds of the Quinaielt tribe.

A brief description of these non-reservation traditional fishing grounds is as follows:

1. *Kla-wa-qu* [?*?] The English name for this place is *Ilwaco* and the fishing place was located along the beach, and shore of the Columbia river at what is now known as

---

[76] 1/ Letter of 12/3/41 to Edward G. Swindell, Jr., from Secretary, Quinaielt Tribal Council and data furnished by Agency.

Sand Island. It is asserted that it was the jointly used place of the Quinaielt, Lower Chehalis, Willipa and Chinook Indian tribes. [235]

2. *Newh-munch* [?*?] This, in English is North River. The fishing grounds extended from the mouth of the river to up above tide water. This also was jointly used by the Quinaielt, Lower Chehalis and Willipa Indian tribes.

3. *Hoquiam* [$\underline{x}^weq^wyamc$ = 'hungry for wood' w173] The fishing grounds were located along the Hoquiam river from the mouth to several miles above the tide water and were jointly used by the Quinaielt and Lower Chehalis tribes.

4. *Hump-tulips* [$x^wəmtulapš$ w175] The English name is the same. The fishing grounds were located from the mouth of the river up to the junction used by the Quinaielt and Lower Chehalis tribes.

5. *Wh-oo-see* [?*?] Now known as Bay Center. The fishing grounds were located from the mouth of the Palix river to several miles above tide water. This was jointly used by the Quinaielt and Willipa tribes.

6. *Klack-spootichom* [?*?] Now known as Long Island. The fishing grounds extended from the mouth of the Nasalle river to several miles above tide water and were jointly used by the Quinaielt and Willipa tribes. It will be recalled that Swan in his book on the Northwest Coast (p. 136) specifically mentions the Indian fishery on the Nasalle river.

There, of course, in the pre-discovery days must have been numerous other; places used by the Quinaielt Indians with which the present descendants are not familiar. None of the above listed places were presently being used for the reason that the type of gear which the Indians used there in the pre-treaty days as well as that which they are accustomed to at the present time is not legal in the State of Washington.

It might also be noted in connection with the Quinaielt tribe that Swan (p. 264) states that the Indians "fish principally by means of weirs which they build with a great deal of skill and also by spears and hooks." As contrasted with present day fishing activities where the Indians, it is reported, take their fish principally with set nets and some drift nets. [235A]

In connection with the fishing in the Quinaielt river, it is to be noted that the Supreme Court of the State of Washington, in its decision in the case of the <u>Pioneer Pckg. Co. v. Winslow</u>, 294, Pac 557, held that the Indians owned the fish in the Quinaielt river and that the State of Washington therefore could not restrict the taking of same nor could it restrict the shipment of same to points outside the State since such shipments constituted Interstate Commerce and therefore were not subject to regulation and control by the State. In the case of <u>Mason v. Sands</u>, 5 P. 2nd 255, the court held in effect that without legislative authority administrative officials of the Government could not interfere or regulate these Indian's fishing activities. [236]

SKOKOMISH RESERVATION

AGENCY: - Taholah
LOCATION: - Head of Hood Canal, north of Shelton, Washington, Olympic Peninsula
AREA: - 3,052 acres
TREATY: - Jan. 26, 1855, 12 Stat. 933, 2 Kappler 674 at Point No Point (*Hahskus*)

INDIAN TRIBES: - Skokomish
LOCATION OF "U. & A." FISHING GROUNDS: -

The Skokomish River and its tributaries; also at the mouths of various streams entering Hood Canal from the reservation north to Dabob Bay, Washington, at the north end of Dabob Bay near Quilcene, Washington.

Clams and oysters were taken from the tide lands along the head of Hood Canal. Bottom fish, such as halibut, etc., were taken in the waters of the canal at the feeding and spawning grounds.

PRESENT FISHING ACTIVITIES, GEAR AND REGULATIONS:

Commercial fishing activities are confined within the reservation boundaries, inasmuch as the set nets used by the Indian fishermen have been outlawed by state statute. From figures furnished by the local fish buyer, the Taholah agency has computed the value of the Indians' commercial catch as being only $200 in 1937; $4,250 in 1938; $3,190 in 1939 and $5,330 in 1940. From these figures it is apparent that the Indians' annual income fluctuated considerably from year to year. The Taholah agency however reports that fishing is only an incidental occupation for the Indians now residing on the reservation.

In 1941 the tribal council under the authority vested in it by the Indian Reorganization Act, adopted an ordinance to govern fishing and trapping on the reservation. It is reported that these regulations are by far the most progressive of any of the tribes under the Taholah agency. Provision therein is made for escapement periods well calculated to perpetuate the supply of fish for the future provided they are energetically enforced. [237]

GENERAL REMARKS:

The Skokomish reservation was set aside by the Executive Order of February 25, 1874, for the joint occupancy of Clallam and Skokomish Indians. We have noted, however ante p. 137 that the former did not choose to remove to the reservation since it was locate a considerable distance from their principal villages and fishing grounds along the north coast of the Olympic Peninsula. The Skokomish tribe claims usual and accustomed fishing grounds all along the west shore of the Hood canal although their permanent habitat, it is reported, was at the mouth of the Skokomish River. It is indicated (see attached affidavits) that they jointly used some of the places with the Clallams. [238]

AFFIDAVIT OF ROBERT LEWIS

STATE OF WASHINGTON }
COUNTY OF CLALLAM }   } SS

Robert Lewis, being first duly sworn, upon his oath deposes and says:

That he is over 100 years of age, a full blood member of the Skokomish Indian Tribe and a citizen of the United States of America residing on the Skokomish Indian Reservation, Washington;

That all of his life has been spent in the country owned by the Skokomish Indians prior to the coming of the white people and during the course of his Life, he has had occasion to visit a number of the places where the Skokomish Indians either had permanent villages or where they were accustomed to go year in and year out for the purpose of obtaining a supply of fish which was the most important part of their food supply; that as a result of the personal knowledge he thus acquired from actual observation of how the Indians lived and fished at such places, he was selected by the Skokomish Indians to give information about such matters to representatives of the Indian Service; that in addition to his knowledge gained from actual observation, he was told about such places, when he was a small boy and a young man, by his parents and the other older members of the Skokomish tribe; that it was customary for the Indians to pass along such information in such fashion from one generation to another in order that the new generation would know where these places were and how they had been used by the Indians ever since anyone could remember.

Affiant farther deposes and says that he is familiar with the names and locations of old Skokomish villages and usual and accustomed fishing grounds as follows:

1. *QUIL-CEED*, [*qʷəlsid* b89][77], which the white people now call Quilcene; that there was a permanent village of the Skokomish located on the north Side of the beach at Quilcene Bay in which there were many houses when he was a young man; that the Indians in the old days caught considerable quantities of fish by using traps in each fork of the river and with spears in the shallow water.[78]

2. TAH-BAAGH [*tabuxʷ* b97], known to the white people as Dabob; that he never say this place but was told hat long prior [239 2] to the coming of the white people; the Indians had lived at this place and caught lots of fish.

3. *DOS-WHAL-LUPS* [*duswa•ylupš* 'thieves' b68], known to the white people as Dosewallips; that there was a large village of many houses located at this place near the mouth of the river of the same name and affiant has fished there many times throughout his lifetime, that the fish were caught with a trap and spears.

4. *QHUB-QHUB-EYE* [*duxʷxabxabay* 'place of horsetail rush' b54], now known to the white people as Hamma Hamma and located at the mouth of the river bearing the same name; that this was a temporary fishing and camp ground at which the Indians would remain as long as the fish were running; that the Indians in addition to catching salmon with a trap and spears, also dug clams from beach and at night time they would spear ling cod from canoes using lighted torches to bring the fish to the surface; that the surplus fish and clams were dried for future use when fresh fish was not available or for trading purposes with other Indians.

5. *DUCQH-YAH-BOOSE* [*duxʷyabus* 'place of crooked jaw salmon' b62], now known to the white people as Duckabush and located at the mouth of and on the south side of the present Duckabush River; that it meant "Wind around the Point" from the fact that it was located at spot not touched by the winds prevalent at this particular place, that although the Indians had houses located at this place, it was only used during the time when the fish were running in the river; that the fish were caught with a trap.

6. *DUE-WAH-TAGH* [*duwataxʷ* b158], now known as Dewatto; that affiant does not know the meaning of the Indian name; that it was the permanent home of a large number of Skokomish Indians and they were able to catch plenty of fish and dig large

---

[77] [b#] = William Elmendorf and A L Kroeber 1992 *The Structure of Twana Culture*, with comparative notes on Yurok Culture. Pre-White tribal lifeways on Washington's Hood Canal. Pullman: WSU Press. [1960]

[78] (1) Tarboo on Metsker's maps of Washington.

quantities of clams; that in the summer the Indians moved upstream from the permanent village at the mouth of the Dewatto River to a place about two miles distant where the river was narrow and fish were caught there with spears and gaff hooks; that he has at various times caught fish there.

7. *LIL-LAH-WHOP* [*sləlawap* 'go into bay' b48] which meant inlet and is now known as Lilliwaup; that there was a permanent village situated on both sides of the creek and located close to its mouth; that a large number of Indians used to live at that place catching fish with spears and gaff-hooks; that in the spring this was a good place to catch herring. [240 3]

8. *DUE-QHAH-WILL-LUP* [?*?], which meant "steelhead salmon stream" and which is now known as Steelhead Creek; "that this was a temporary fishing ground and camp of the Skokomish Indians whose permanent homes were around Hoodsport, Washington; that they spent considerable time at this place which was also food for hunting and berry gathering purposes.

9. *TSCHO-QUAH-LUITH* [*č'oqʷaɬəl* b24] and *YEE-LOUGH-QHOE* [*yila'lqo* b18], which, prior to their being flooded by the water of the City of Tacoma's power dam, were located respectively at the falls and forks of the Skokomish River; that there were a number of small villages on the Skokomish River and the people who lived in them were accustomed to fishing at these places as well as at some of those along the Hoods Canal. [Henry Allen born at #18]

10. *DUCQH-LAY-LAHP* [*duxʷlelap* 'far end' b128], now known as Union River; that there was a permanent Skokomish village about a mile from the mouth of the Union River at the head of Hood Canal near Belfair, Washington, that he has fished there during his life and the fish were caught by trap and spears and gaff hooks.

11. *DUCSK-QHOE-QUAPSH* [*duxʷk'uk'ʷabš* 'where they et salmon backbones' Big Mission Creek b133], now known as Mission Creek; that this was a temporary fishing and camping place for the Indians living at *Ducqh-lay-lahp* and it was located at the mouth of Mission Creek.

12. *TAH-QHOO-YAH* [*ta•xuya* b147], now known as Tahuya, Washington; that this was the permanent home of a group of Skokomish Indians where they caught fish with a trap as well as with spears and gaff hooks.

Affiant further deposes and says that the Clallam and Chemakum Indians were accustomed to fishing at the various villages and usual and accustomed temporary fishing places of the Skokomish people along the Hood Canal; that they were friends and gladly shared their places during the times the other Indians visited the Skokomish; That he understands the expression "usual and accustomed" fishing places to mean those places that the Skokomish Indians used prior to the coming of the white people and had been using ever since they could remember.

Further affiant sayeth not.

(Sgd.) Robert Lewis His mark
Robert Lewis

Subscribed and sworn to before me this 12th day of May, 1942

(Sgd.) Frank D. Beaulieu
(Seal) Public Notary in and for
the State of Washington,
residing at Hoquiam [241 3a]

AFFIDAVIT OF INTERPRETER

STATE OF WASHINGTON }
COUNTY OF CLALLAM }   }SS

Lucy Allen, being first duly sworn, upon her oath deposes and says;

That she is a member of the Skokomish Indian Tribe and a citizen of the United States of America residing on the Skokomish Indian Reservation, Washington;

That she is thoroughly conversant with the English language and with the language of the Skokomish Indians and can translate the English language into the Skokomish Indian language and the Skokomish Indian language into the English language.

That on December 2, 1941, in the presence of Robert Lewis, deponent in the foregoing affidavit, and Edward G. Swindell, Jr. U.S, Indian Service, affiant did, at the request of Mr. Swindell, interrogate the said, Robert Lewis with regard to certain matters concerning the location of the permanent villages and usual and accustomed fishing grounds of the Skokomish Indians, as well as with regard to the way they and their ancestors obtained a livelihood; that she translated the questions of Mr. Swindell from the English language into the Skokomish Indian language which the said Robert Lewis speaks and understands; that she translated the answers of the said Robert Lewis from the Skokomish language into the English language; that Mr. Swindell made written notes of the information given by the said Robert Lewis and said information has been reduced to the narrative form as given in the above and foregoing affidavit of said Robert Lewis.

Affiant further deposes and says that on the 12th day of May, 1942, in the presence of Robert Lewis and Mr. Swindell, she translated the information contained in the aforesaid affidavit from the English language into the Skokomish language as said affidavit was read to affiant by Mr. Swindell; that the deponent, Robert Lewis, told affiant that the said narrative affidavit contained the information given by him to Mr. Swindell on December 2, 1941, and that he had therefore signed said affidavit [242 3b] because the information contained therein was true.

Further affiant sayeth not.

(Sgd.) Lucy Allen

Lucy Allen personally appeared before me this 12th day of May, 1942, and after having the foregoing affidavit read to her in my presence, did acknowledge to me that the statements contained therein were true and that se executed same as her own voluntary act.

Subscribed and sworn to before me this 12th day of May, 1942.

(Sgd.) Frank D. Beaulieu
(Seal) Public Notary in and for
the State of Washington,
residing at Hoquiam [243 3c]

JOINT AFFIDAVIT OF BEN JOHNS, GEORGE ADAMS,
AND CHARLIE CUSH

STATE OF WASHINGTON }
COUNTY OF CLALLAM }   } SS

Ben Johns, 65 years of age, George Adams, 62 years of age, and Charlie Cush, 77 years of age, each being first duly sworn and put upon his oath does severally depose and say;

That are members of the Skokomish Indian Tribe and citizens of the United States of America residing on the Skokomish Indian Reservation, Washington;

That they were either born on the Skokomish Indian Reservation, or in the country formerly owned by the Skokomish Indians and sold to the United States Government pursuant to their treaty negotiated by Governor Stevens; that they have lived in the Skokomish Indian country, or on the Skokomish Indian Reservation all of their lives, and at various times they have had occasion to visit a number of the sites of the old Skokomish Indian villages and fishing grounds; that as a result of their visits to these places, they are personally familiar with the actual conditions which existed at some of these places as a result of actual observation of the Indians living or fishing there; that in addition to the knowledge thus personally gained from actual observation, they when small boys and young men were told by their parents and the older members of the Skokomish Indian tribe as to the location of these villages and fishing grounds and as to the way the Indians used to live and fish there prior to the time of their birth and prior to the time of the coming of the white man; that affiants therefore feel they are familiar with the situation which existed at those various places and can give relevant information with regard thereto;

Affiants further severally depose and say that on October 16, 1941, they were present at the community house on the Skokomish Indian Reservation when Robert Lewis; a member of the Skokomish Indian tribe, answered certain questions propounded by Edward G. Swindell, Jr., US Indian Service, concerning the location of Skokomish villages and fishing ground as said Robert Lewis, one [244 3d] of the oldest living members of the tribe, was able to recall and identify same; that they listened carefully, and clearly heard both the questions, and the answers given thereto and that they can and do confirm the information contained in said answers insofar as they are personally familiar therewith from actual observation during their respective lifetimes; that so far as the information given by the said Robert Lewis related to things that occurred prior to their respective lifetimes, they can and do confirm them as being true inasmuch as the same things were told to them by their parents when they were small boys and young men.

Affiant further depose and say that on the 9th day of June, 1942, they were present when an affidavit containing the information previously given by the said Robert Lewis was read back to them; that the information contained in that affidavit was the same information given by the said Robert Lewis under date of October 16, 1941; that the information contained in said affidavit is true to the best of affiants knowledge and belief.

Affiants furthers sayeth not.

(Sgd.) Ben Johns
Ben Johns

Subscribed and sworn to before me this 9th day of June, 1942.

(Sgd.) Merle Hagmann
Notary Public
(Sgd.) George Adams
George Adams

Subscribed and sworn to before me this 9th day of June, 1942.

(Sgd.) Merle Hagmann
(Sgd.) Charlie Cush, his mark

Subscribed and sworn to before me this 9th day of June, 1942.

(Sgd.) Merle Hagmann [245]

YAKAMA RESERVATION

AGENCY: - Yakama
LOCATION: - South central Washington
AREA: - 1,112,792 acres
TREATY: - June 9, 1833, 12 Stat. 951; 2 Kappler 698 at Walla Walla
INDIAN TRIBES: -   Yakamas and 13 other confederated tribes named in heading of treaty digest, post p. 471

LOCATION OF "U. & A." FISHING GROUNDS: -

The territory claimed by the 14 confederated tribes was the largest area ceded to the United States under the group of treaties we have been discussing. In this connection reference is had to sheet #1 of the General Area Map, ante p 9 on which is delineated the lands ceded by this group of tribes. It has been noted that the entire area was traversed by numerous streams. In pre-discovery days there was hardly a stream of any importance from which fish were taken by the several tribes. Today, however, there are only one or two places where salmon are still caught exclusive of the fisheries situated in the mid-Columbia river area previously discussed.

PRESENT FISHING ACTIVITIES, GEAR AND REGULATIONS: -

Today at the few remaining places fish are still taken with the types of gear used by the ancestors of the present generation, viz. spears, dip nets, and gaff hooks. Weirs of course are no longer used.

Present day activities at these places are confined to fishing for subsistence purposes since salmon, both fresh and dried, still plays an important role in the diet of these Indians.

Regulation of the fishing at these places in so far as conservation objectives are concerned is non-existent. [246]

GENERAL REMARKS: -

In pre-discovery days and up until the agricultural and industrial development in the ceded territory, large runs of salmon frequented all major streams therein, principal of which, aside from the main Columbia, was the Yakima and its many tributaries. They all combined to furnish an inexhaustible food supply for the several tribes. With the development of the area, however, especially that relating to agriculture, many impassable barriers were erected in the several streams to divert all or a large portion of the waters for irrigation purposes. The result was either the loss of large spawning areas or else the loss of considerable numbers of the fingerlings in unscreened irrigation or power diversions as they journeyed downstream to the sea from the remaining spawning grounds.

As we have previously pointed out, no effort was made to ascertain the precise locations of Yakama fishing grounds where they were no longer in use since such would be of no value except from a historical standpoint. At a meeting at the Yakama Indian Agency, Toppenish,

Washington, with the delegates selected by the tribal council to assist the writer in his investigation, the Indians referred to the following as being some of the ancient places:

1. *Soo-Nooks* – located on the main Tieton River below the Rimrock Dam.
2. *Stook* – located on the Naches [*na̱xchiish* v405][79] River below the mouth of Rattlesnake Creek near the present community of Nile, Washington.
3. *Cle-elum* [*tɬyalïm* v354] – located at the mouth of the lake with the same name.
4. *Kachess* [*ḵachiish*] and *Keechelus* [*kichɨl̲x̲s* v393] – also located at the mouth of lakes having the same name.
5. *Swauk* – located on Swauk Creek about 3 miles above its confluence with the Yakima river.
6. *Manastach* [*manashtash* v400] – located on a creek with the same name about four miles above its confluence with the Yakima River.
7. *Selah* [*siila* v430] and *Wenas* [*winaas* v463] – each located in a creek of the same name approximately 1½ and 2 miles, respectively, above their confluence with the Yakima River. [247]
8. A group of places on the main Tieton River and the north and south forks thereof. These places have been inundated by the water stored in the Rimrock Reservoir.

The Yakama Indians as shown by their affidavits continue to catch fish for subsistence purposes at four places, although at the present time two of them are principally used by the few remaining members of the Priest Rapids band of Sokulk Indians. The legal descriptions are shown on the plats accompanying this group of affidavits. In connection with these remaining places, it is to be noted:

(1) That two of them located at the Sunnyside and Wapato diversion dams are partially on the Yakama reservation and the Indians fish on the reservation side of the streams without regulation by state authorities.

(2) That fishing at the other three non-reservation places, two on the main Columbia at White Bluffs and The Horn diversion dam and one at Prosser dam on the Yakima, is carried on through special concessions given by the state legislature. See ante p 76. [248]

AFFIDAVIT

STATE OF WASHINGTON }
COUNTY OF YAKIMA }   } SS

Columbia Wildman, being first duly sworn, upon his oath deposes and says:

That he is 74 years of age and a full blood member of the Yakama Indian tribe, and a citizen of the United States of America residing on the Yakama Indian Reservation, Washington.

That he was born at an Indian village on the Columbia River known as *Tah-koot* [*taq'ʷt* u108],[80] and that the Indians who lived there were known as *Tah-koot* Indians; that this place

---

[79] [v#] = Virginia Beavert & Sharon Hargus 2009 *Yakama Sahaptin ~ Ichishkiin Sinwit Dictionary* UW.

[80] [u#] = Confederated Tribes of Umatilla and Noel Rude 2014 *Umatilla Dictionary* UW.

was located near the present town of White Bluffs, Washington; that he spent the early years of his life at that place, as well as other Indian villages in the same general vicinity; that after his family died, he moved away and since then has traveled quite a bit, during which time he has visited a number of sites where there used to be located permanent villages or temporary fishing camps of the Indians who under the treaty were moved to the Yakama Indian Reservation; that as a consequence of the foregoing, and the things that were told to him by his relatives and other older Indians, as well as his own personal knowledge acquired from actually seeing how the Indians lived and fished, he is very familiar with the way the Indians lived and how they caught their fish both during his lifetime and prior thereto, as the latter was told to him;

That he cannot speak English and that he is not familiar with the way white people keep track of ' time or how they measure distances or describe things, but, nevertheless, he feels he can explain those things in such a way that they can be understood by others who may have occasion to refer to his statements.

Affiant further deposes and says that prior to the tine that the number of fish that were in the river was made so small on account of the activities of the white man in constructing dams and catching very large quantities of same, there were many places utilized by the various Indian tribes making up the Yakama nation for permanent village sites as well as temporary fishing camps; that it was customary for the Yakama Indians [249 2] to travel around within the country with which they were familiar for the purpose of obtaining supplies of fish as well as supplies of roots, berries, venison and other wild animal meat; that nowadays, there were only a few places of that nature that are used by the Indians due to the fact that almost all of old places have been destroyed and are no longer of any practical value to the Indians.

Affiant further deposes and says that he is acquainted with the names, locations, and other pertinent, information concerning the following Indian villages and fishing places;

WY-YOW-NA

That there was a temporary fishing place near White Bluffs – on the Columbia River known as *Wy-Yow-Na* [*wayawna* 'current type' u109]; that this place was located about a mile and a half from the place where affiant was born (affiant indicated this approximate distance by pointing to the location of his birth place from where he was standing at *Wy-Yow-Na* at the time he gave the foregoing as well as the following testimony concerning such place); that although he has never fished here, he has seen many other Indians fishing here and he at times has helped handle the canoe used by some of the fishermen;

That he first remembers seeing Indians fishing here when he was a small boy or about 70 years ago; he has been told that this place always was one of the usual and accustomed fishing places of the Indians roaming the surrounding country; that he understands as many as 500 Indians or more have camped at this place; that this number of Indians was made up of a large number of families; that there were usually seven or more people in each family including the old people;

That *Wy-Yow-Na* was not a permanent village or fishing camp for the Indians who used it; that it was one of their fall fishing places; that the camp ground in the springtime was flooded by the water from the river; that the Indians not only camped on the bank of the mainland but they also had camped directly across on the island (the island in question is shown on the maps as Locke Island); that the Indians used this place to catch fish because it was easy to catch them here because it was one of their spawning grounds, although [250 3] the Indians would not catch the fish until after they had finished spawning; that the Indians when they camped at this place, would remain about a moon and a half (corresponds to approximately six weeks);

That the Indians caught their fish her in two different ways. One way was by using spears. During the day time; they would spear the fish because then they could see them in the water, while at night they would drift downstream in their canoes in which an Indian would be holding a torch to attract the fish and another Indian would be ready to spear it as soon as it was attracted to the light. The other way was with a long net that was about 75 feet long (distance indicated by pointing from where affiant was standing to a pile of rocks approximately 75 feet away) and that it was as deep as from the ground to affiant's chest, (approximately 5 feet); that the fish' would snare themselves in the net, after which they would be removed by the Indians;

That each family would catch on an average of about 300 fish, each of which were about four feet long and two hands high (length was indicated by holding hands apart); that some of the fish, of course, were small but that that size would be the general average; i.e., the fish actually were of all different sizes; that the Indians dried a large quantity of this fish to be used during the times when fresh fish was not available and, also, for trading with other Indians for different kinds of fish or for roots, berries, meat, or buffalo robes.

That large numbers of outside Indians used to visit this place for the purpose of trading with the people who fished here although the visiting Indians did not themselves fish; that these Indians came from all around this area, such as on the other side of the Columbia River from the Nez Perce country and such places so that they could gather with the local people and trade with them and also enjoy their games and ceremonies;

That the last time he was here and helped others to fish was about 37 or 38 years ago although he has been here every year since then but only to visit his relatives and partake in their feasts, and ceremonies that he visited *Wy-Yow-Na* for that purpose last year [251 4] but there were not many fish; that only a few Indians still use this place and that they were really not Yakama Indians since they do not live on the reservation although they are relatives and friends of affiant;

That the Indians made their own fishing equipment and canoes from the available material; that the twine for the nets before the white man came was made from Indian hemp which the Indians call *tah-qhus*; [ta<u>x</u>us v210]; that spear heads were made from elk horn and bone; that the canoes were hollowed out from logs by the Indians taking a sharp rock and digging the inside out;

That fish was an important food, that it was as important to the Yakama Indians as meat; that both the meat and fish were supplemented by roots and berries gathered at the places known to the Indians in the territory roamed by them; that after the white man came, the Indians became accustomed to trading some of the fish they caught and dried for articles like sugar, coffee, flour, and like things.

That there was another place further upstream from *Wy-yow-na* used by the Indians for fishing but which is no longer of any value to them; that this other place is not known as Priest Rapids, where the Indians that still use *Wy-yow-na* still make their winter camp.

WAN-A-WISH

That there was an Indian fishing place known as *Wan-a-wish* [*wanawish* = 'rapids' v388] located near what is now known as the Horn Rapids Dam; that this place is still used by the Indians for fishing although there aren't nearly as many fish as there used to be in the old days; that the Indians who fished at *Wan-a-wish* were the same people as those who fished at *Wy-yow-na*: that the reason for this is the fact that *Wy-yow-na* was a place to catch fish in the fall of the year; thereas, [whereas] *Wan-a-wish* was one of summer fishing places; that the Indians ordinarily fished at *Wan-a-wish* during what corresponds to the white man's month of July;

That *Wan-a-wish* has always been a usual and accustomed fishing place of the Indians that lived in the area in which it is located; that prior to the construction of the dam now in the river the Indians used to fish from the rocks in the river which form [251 5] the rapids; that they used to fish at this place with dip nets which they held in the water where it was foaming and the fish could not see the net; that after the dam was constructed the good fishing places or the Indians were destroyed and since then the Indians have found it necessary to catch their fish when they are running at this place by spearing or hooking them with gaff hooks as they were trying to go over the dam; that they no longer used nets which was the only method used in the old days prior to the construction of the dam the Indians camped at a different place from where they camp today; that although their camp ground in the old days was a considerable distance from where the fish were caught, they used it in preference to a place closer by because there was a good spring of water there; that after the dam was constructed, the man who takes care of it built his house at the place where the Indians used to camp; that the place where the Indians fish today has been used by them continuously every year since they were told they could not use the old original camp ground;

That the people who fished at this place were the same as those who fished at *Wy-Yow-Na*; that in addition to those people, it was used at times by Indians of other bands belonging to the Yakama Reservation; that in addition to those Indians, Indians from over in the Umatilla and Warm Springs country would come over for the purpose of trading roots and berries and other things for the fish that had been caught by the people who use this place; that the camp at this place would remain as long as the run of fish lasted, which affiant estimates to be about 1½ months.

That the Indians when they fished here in the old days would fish at night and they quite often would catch as many as 15 or 20 fish each time they went out to the fishing rocks; that the fish which were not eaten fresh were dried by curing them in the big shed which was erected for that purpose; that the shed that is located at the camp grounds now utilised [utilized] by the Indians is the same type of shed that has always been used for that purpose:

That in the early days a great many more Indians used this place for fishing purposes than at the present time; that in those days there were two drying sheds, both of them longer than the one used nowadays; that [253 6] he is unable to estimate the number of camps that were here in the old days but there were many Indians which used it at that time;.

That when he was a boy the Indians obtained large quantities of fish at this place but since there have been so many dams constructed the supply of fish is now very limited.

WAH-WA-TAM

That there was an Indian usual and accustomed fishing ground near the Sunnyside dam which was called *Wah-wa-tam* [*awatam* Parker v13]; that although he never fished at this place, he has seen many Indians fishing there at various times throughout his life; that he first saw Indians fishing at this place when he was a young boy about 10 years old; that at the time the Sunnyside Dam had not been constructed;

That when he was a boy the Indians caught their fish by using a weir located about half way between the present Sunnyside Dam and the bridge which crosses the river, and is known as Parker Bridge; that more specifically it was located at the upper end of a small island in the river above the dam; that the weir stretched all the way across the river and it was placed at this point because the water conditions were exactly right for the use of a weir to catch fish; that in those days the Indians only caught their fish at the weir since their custom would not permit them to use spears or nets at this point; that the use of spears and dip nets by the Indians fishing at this place did not come into being until after the dam was constructed and the back water therefrom destroyed the place the weir used to be constructed;

That after the dam was constructed and the old fishing grounds destroyed, the Indians could only catch fish by spearing them or dip netting them as they were trying to get over the dam; that the Indians then built platforms in the river the same as they use today and these platforms were used by the various fishermen; that the set net or dip net they used consisted of a medium sized hoop around which the net was woven until it reached a point; that', four strings were fastened to the hoop which extended down the full length of the net so that when the Fish entered the net after it had been placed in the water, the fisherman would feel the strings jerk and he would then take his fish out of the water; [254 7]

That at the time he first saw the camp when he was a small boy, he would say there was approximately as many as 500 Indians camped in the vicinity of the weir; that the camp was only a temporary one used during the fishing season which lasted about a moon or a moon and a half; that the houses in this camp were made of tulle mats and that the people from distant places would build them each year using the same materials which they carried home after the fishing season was over and their houses dismantled; that the Indians came from all the surrounding country for fishing as well as for the purpose of trading and enjoying the entertainment that was always going on; that a long time ago the Indians would make their camp on both sides of the river; that after the dam was constructed the Indians moved their camp grounds closer to where they then were forced to catch their fish; that until they were stopped by the people who are in charge of the dam, they used to fish on both sides of the river; that nowadays they can only fish on the reservation side because the people who are in charge of the dam say that they interfere with their work; that this was an exceptionally good fishing place and the Indians were accustomed to obtain a larger quantity of fish which they would cure and put away for use when the fish were no longer available in the stream; that each family would dry not less than 100 fish and the average length was about 2½ feet long (witness indicated this length by holding his hands apart); that in addition to the fish that were eaten fresh or put away for future use, the Indians would also dry large quantities of fish to trade with visiting Indians; that nowadays, he would say there were only about 20 families fishing at this place although large numbers of the Indians from the Yakama Reservation gather there each year for the purpose of entertainment.

That the Indians cannot get nearly as many fish as they used to.

OW-YEH

That there was a usual and accustomed Indian fishing place near the diversion dam for the Wapato Indian Irrigation Project known as *Ow-yeh*, although he has heard some people refer to it as *Pah-qho-tah-kewt* [*paxutakyuut* v142], [255 8] that this latter name is the wrong name for this place because it means "where two mountains come down together forming a place to get through"; that the white people call that place Union Gap;

That although he never fished there for the same reasons that he did not fish at *Wah-wa-tam*, he has seen throughout his life Indians fishing there; that the first time he saw them fishing there was about the same time he saw them fishing at *Wah-wa-tam*; that the camp here was also only a temporary camp used when the salmon was passing this place; that the Indians did not use a weir at this place because the conditions were not right; that instead they caught their fish with spears and dip net; that the actual place were the Indians fish has changed because the river changed its direction a number of years ago;

That the Indians who used this place for fishing were the same that fished at *Wah-wa-ta*m; that they would come to this place after the run had passed the other place; that on account of the water conditions, one had to be a very good fisherman in order to catch fish here; that all the Indians in the camp shared in the catch which was made by the expert fishermen;

That he understands the Indians no longer camp at this place but that some of them come here and fish when the temporary camp is established each year at *Wah-wa-tam*;

That the old camp grounds covered quite a large area through which a part of the Yakima River now flows.

Affiant further deposes and says that the four places of *Wy-yow-na*, *Wan-a-wish*, *Wah-wa-tam*, and *Ow-ye*h were four of the more important fishing grounds of the Indians prior to the coming of the white man; that the Indians still fish at these places today, although their value to the Indians has been decreased a lot on account of the fact that there are not as many fish in the rivers as there used to be; that in addition to those places, there were many many others used by the Indians both before and after the white man came [256 9] to the country; that these other places have been destroyed for any one of a number of reasons and therefore, the Indians cannot use them.

Further affiant sayeth not.

(Sgd.) Columbia Wildman his mark

Subscribed and sworn to before me this 6th day of May, 1942.

(Sgd.) H.V. Lewis
Acting Superintendent,
Yakama Indian Agency

(Note: For further information with regard to *Wy-yow-na* and *Wan-a-wish*, see affidavits of Johnny Buck and Cy Tahmalwash of the Priest Rapids Indians.)

AFFIDAVIT OF INTERPRETER

State of Washington }
County of Yakima }   }SS

Thomas Yallup, being first duly sworn, upon his oath deposes and says:

That he is 56 years of age, a full blood Indian of the Yakama Indian tribe and a citizen of the United States of America residing on the Yakama Indian Reservation, Washington.

That he is thoroughly conversant with the English language and with the language spoken by the Yakama Indians and can translate the English language into the Yakama Indian language and from Yakama Indian language into the English language;

That on August 26, 1941, affiant visited certain usual and accustomed, fishing places of the Yakama Indians known as *Wy-yow-na*, near White Bluffs on the Columbia river, and *Wan-a-wish* [*wanawish* = 'rapids' v388] at the Horn Rapids Dam on the Yakima River in the company of Columbia Wildman, [257 9a] deponent in the foregoing affidavit and Edward G. Swindell, Jr., U.S. Indian Service; that affiant did at the request of Mr. Swindell, interrogate Columbia Wildman with regard to certain matters concerning said usual and accustomed fishing stations as well as with regard to the way in which the Indians who use them, as well as their ancestors, obtained a livelihood; that he translated the questions of Mr. Swindell from the English language into the Yakama Indian language which Columbia Wildman speaks and understands; that he translated the answers of Columbia Wildman to Mr. Swindell s interrogatories from the Yakama

Indian language into the English language; that at that time a stenographic record was made of the information given by said Columbia Wildman; that the information contained in the said stenographic record has been reduced to narrative form as given in the above and foregoing affidavit of the said Columbia Wildman.

Affiant further deposes and says that on the 6th day of May, 1942, in the presence of Columbia Wildman and Mr. Swindell, he translated the information contained in the aforesaid affidavit from the English language into the Yakama Indian language, as said affidavit was read to affiant by Mr. Swindell; that the deponent, Columbia Wildman, told affiant that the said narrative affidavit contained the information given by him to Mr. Swindell on August 26, 1941 and that he had, therefore, signed said affidavit because the information contained therein was true.

Further affiant sayeth not.

Sgd.) Thomas K. Yallup
Thomas Yallup, Interpreter

Thomas Yallup personally appeared before me this 6th day of May, 1942, and after having the foregoing affidavit read to him in my presence did acknowledge to me that the statements contained therein are true and that he executed same as his voluntary act.

Subscribed and sworn to before me this 6th day of May, 1942

(Sgd.) H.V. Lewis
Acting Superintendent
Yakama Indian Agency [258 9b]

AFFIDAVIT OF INTERPRETER

State of Washington}
County of Yakima }   } SS

Philip Olney, being first duly sworn, upon his oath deposes and says;

That he is 61 years of age, a three-quarters blood Indian of the Yakama Indian tribe, and a citizen of the United States of America residing on the Yakama Indian Reservation, Washington.

That he is thoroughly conversant with the English language and with the language spoken by the Yakama Indians and can translate the English language into the Yakama Indian language and the Yakama Indian language into the English language.

That on October 10, 1941, at the Yakama Indian Agency, Toppenish, Washington, affiant, in the presence of Columbia Wildman, deponent in the foregoing affidavit, and Edward G. Swindell, U.S Indian Service, did at the request of Mr. Swindell, interrogate Columbia Wildman with regard to certain matters concerning *Wah-wa-tam* and *Ow-yeh*, usual and accustomed fishing places on the Yakima River, which are used and have always been used by the Yakama Indians; that he translated the questions of Mr. Swindell from the English language into the Yakama language, which Columbia Wildman speaks and understands; that he translated the answers of Columbia Wildman to Mr. Swindell's interrogatories from the Yakama language into the English language; that at that time Mr. Swindell made written notes of the information given by the said Columbia Wildman;

Affiant further deposes and says that on the 6th day of May, 1942, in the presence of Columbia Wildman and Mr. Swindell, he translated the information contained in the aforesaid affidavit from the English language into the Yakama language as said affidavit was read to affiant by Mr. Swindell; that the deponent, Columbia Wildman, told affiant that the said narrative affidavit contained the information given by him to Mr. Swindell on October 10, 1941, and that he had, [259 9c] therefore signed said affidavit because the information contained therein was true.

Further affiant sayeth not.

(Sgd.) Philip Olney

Philip Olney personally appeared before me this 6th day of May, 1942, and having the foregoing affidavit read to him in my presence did acknowledge to me that statements contained therein are true and he executed same as his voluntary act.

Subscribed and sworn to before me this 6th day of May, 1942.

(Sgd.) H.V. Lewis
Acting Superintendent
Yakama Indian Agency [260 > 261]

WAN-A-WISH

Yakima River, Washington

View of the present day camp grounds and curing shed used by the remnants of the Priest Rapids band of Sokulk Indians. This structure is not located on the site of the original camp grounds due to the fact that such land was taken up in a homestead and is now occupied by the caretaker of the dam. Structure pictured here is located on the river bank immediately above the dam shown in the upper picture. This is the spring fishing ground of these Indians. See affidavit of Columbia Wildman, Yakama Reservation; also affidavit of Priest Rapids Indians.

The Horn Diversion Dam, located immediately upstream from the ancient fishing grounds of the

Priest Rapids band of Sokulk Indians of the Yakama Reservation also claim this as one of their usual and accustomed fishing grounds. (See plat). Prior to the construction of the dam the Indians caught their fish in the downstream rapids through the use of dip and bag nets. Subsequent to the construction of the dam the fish have been caught as they endeavor to go over the dam. Note fish ladder in center of dam as well as one in the immediate right foreground. Since Washington conservation statutes prohibit fishing within the immediate vicinity of dams, present day Indian fishing activities are carried on through special dispensation granted them by Section 2451-l, Pierce's Code, Washington, 1939 Edition. [262]

WAN-A-WISH

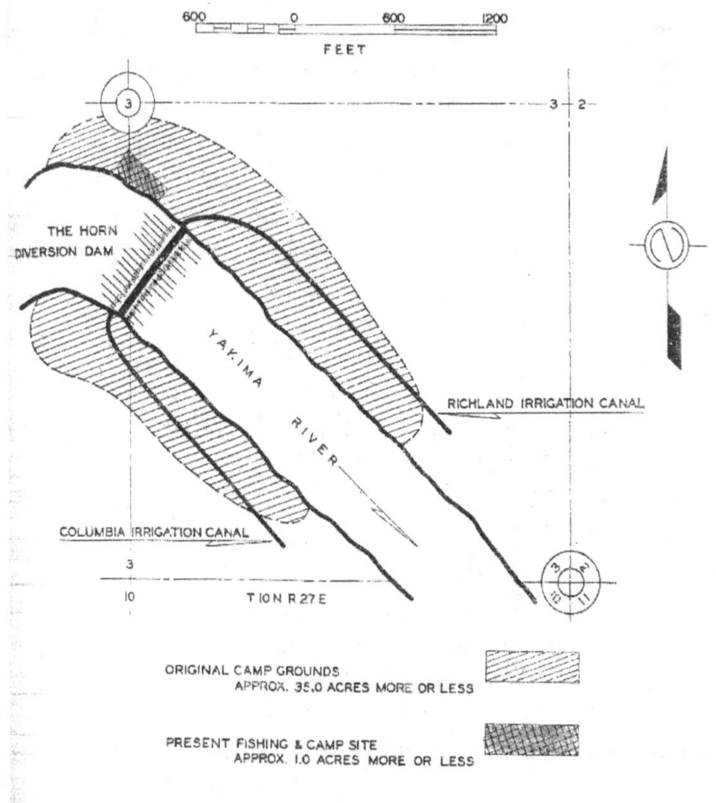

AFFIDAVIT

STATE OF WASHINGTON }
COUNTY OF YAKIMA }   } SS

Moses Sampson, being first duly sworn, upon his oath deposes and says:

That he is about 85 years of age, a full blood Yakama Indian of the Yakama Indian tribe, and a citizen of the United States of America residing on the Yakama Indian Reservation, Washington;

That he was selected by the tribal council of the Yakama Indians to give information concerning usual and accustomed fishing places of the various groups of Indians which comprise the Yakama Nation to the best of his knowledge; that he was selected to give this information despite the fact that he is not a fisherman, because during his life he has seen the various places and visited them for the purpose of obtaining a supply of fish from his friends and relatives and to attend the various Indian ceremonies held each year during the tines the Indians fished at such places; that aside from the knowledge he has personally gathered as a result of his visits to these places, he is in the possession of information with regard to them which was given to him by his parents when he was a small boy; that it was customary for the Indians to tell their children about how their ancestors had lived and the things that they had done because there was no other way the Indians had to pass this knowledge along;

Affiant farther deposes and says that he is familiar with certain usual and accustomed Indian fishing places as follows:

TOP-TUT

That he has visited the usual and accustomed fishing place known as *Top-tut* [*taptat* v417, 'long hair in front, short hair on sides' u105] many times during his life; that it is located at the place where the white people have constructed what is known as the Prosser Dam in the Yakima River near the town of Prosser; that the first time he recalls visiting this place was about 50 years ago which was prior to the time the dam was constructed; that at that time there were many Indians [263 2] camps at *Top-tut* and he would roughly estimate their number to be about 400 and that there were approximately 100 Indian camps at that with about four to six people in each camp;

That he understood the Indians only camped at *Top-tut* during the time the salmon were running at that point in the Yakima River; that it was a good fishing place because the Indians could catch their fish rather easily as they ascended the river and passed through the rapids and over the falls; that the falls that used to be at *Top-tut* were destroyed when the white people constructed the dam that is now in the river and, therefore, the Indians had to change their method of fishing;

That the Indians in the old days fished with spears and dip nets and were very successful in obtaining a supply of fish, some of which were eaten fresh and others dried and either put away for future use or traded off to visiting Indians for roots, berries and other articles; that the average catch, he would judge, was approximately 20 fish each day for each family; that these fish were dried in large drying sheds, of which there were a number at that time;

That although he has not visited *Top-tut* for a number of years he understands that the Indians still go there to obtain fish although there aren't nearly as many as there were when he first visited the place; that in later years after his first visit to this place, the Indians would also catch their fish with a gaff hook; that he understands that they do not obtain nearly as many fish as they did when he was a boy because the fish are no longer as numerous in the river as they were then;

That Indians from all around used to visit this place for the purpose of trading for fish: that there was quite a bit of this trade; that the Indians had their camps on both sides of the river at this point, although in later years they confined their camp grounds to the present site because they were not permitted to cam on the other side of the river by the authorities of the City of Prosser.

WAH-WA-TAM

That there was a usual and accustomed Indian fishing place known as *Wah-wa-tam* [*awatam* = 'deep water' v13, v411] located between what the [264 3] white people call the Sunnyside Dam in the Yakima River and the Parker Bridge, which crosses that river about three-fourths of a mile or so upstream from the dam; that in the old days when he first visited this place and saw the Indians fishing there, they were using the old Indian weirs; that this was before the Sunnyside Dam was constructed; that after the dam was constructed, the place where the weir was could no longer be used and the Indians were forced to catch the fish just below the dam;

That when the 'Indians fished with the weir, it was a sort of community enterprise and all of the Indians camped at the spot would share in the catch each day;

That after the dam was built, the Indians caught their fish with spears and dip nets which they used from platforms built in the river below the dam; that in the old days there were lots of fish but since that dam, as well as the others in the river, have been constructed, the fish are no longer as plentiful as they used to be;

That the Indians who fished at *Wah-wa-tam* were the same Indians who fished at *Top-tut*; that, therefore, the number of Indians who used to camp at this place was about the same as the number he stated he thought camped at *Top-tut*; that the camp used to be on both sides of the river but it is now and has for many years been confined to the reservation side of the stream; that the Indians still use this place each year to obtain a supply of food fish, and that he believes the number that go there now is approximately 100, that the number of fish they can obtain is small compared to what they used to get at this place;

That when the fish were plentiful, the Indians would dry large quantities for their own use or for the purpose of trading with the Indians from the surrounding area who would come to visit them but not necessarily to fish.

OW-YEH

That he is personally familiar with the usual and accustomed Indian fishing places located near what the white people call Union Gap, for which the Indian name was *Pah-qho-tah-kewt*, that the name for the fishing camp site was *Ow-yeh* and that although he has never [265 4] fished there, he has seen Indians fishing there throughout the course of his life; that the first time he saw Indians fishing there would be about 70 years ago, and that at that time the place was used by a large number of Indians; that their camp was not permanent but just used when the fish were running at this point in the Yakima River;

That the first time he saw the Indians fishing there and for a number of years thereafter, there was no dam located in that vicinity; that many years ago the Government constructed a dam to divert irrigation water for the Wapato Indian Irrigation Project; that on account of the construction of this dam, as well as the fact that the river channel changed, this place is not used nowadays as much as it used to be; that he understands that some Indians still fish at this point although they do not obtain many fish; that the old camp ground of the Indians was located in the same general vicinity as the house constructed by the Government to control the operations of the dam and canal; that the Indians who fish there nowadays have their camps at *Wah-wa-tam* and only come up each day to catch fish, which they take back to where their camp is and either dry it or use it in its fresh state.

Affiant further deposes and says that he understands the term usual and accustomed Indian fishing place to have reference to those places that the Indians were using prior to the time the white man came to the Indians' country; that the three places he has been talking about are the more important ones of the old places still used by the Yakama Indians; that in addition to those, however. There are a number of other places which can no longer be used because the fish no longer go there to spawn; that those other places are located all along the Yakima River and the other streams that run into that river;

That the estimates he has given with regard to the number of Indians that camped at the three places he talked about in detail are merely rough guesses because he is not familiar with the white man's way of counting nor when he visited the places did he ever think he would be called upon to estimate how many people or houses were located there at those points;

That in the old days prior to the coming of the white man the Indians were accustomed to roam around all throughout the country which they sold to the white people; that" they were accustomed to catch fish in all [266 5] the streams in that area because at that time salmon could be found in all of them; that those things are no longer true today because the white people have destroyed the fish that used to come up here; that fish is still an important part of the food supply of the Yakama people, even though a large number of them were farming their lands which the Government allotted to them; that these Indian farmers if they do not have relatives who give them fish, will trade some of the things they raise to those who have fish available for such purpose; that this trade is something like the trade that the Indians practiced in the old days before the white man came, except that now they do not have the roots and berries available in such large quantities as they used to;

Further affiant sayeth not.

(Sgd.) Moses Sampson
Moses Sampson

Subscribed and sworn to before me this 6th day of May, 1942.

(Sgd.) H.V. Lewis
Acting Superintendent
Yakama Indian Agency

AFPIDAVIT OF INTERPRETER

State of Washington }
County of Yakima }   SS}

Philip Olney, being first duly sworn, upon his oath deposes and says:

That he is 61 years of age, a three-quarters blood Indian of the Yakama Indian tribe, and a citizen of the United States of America residing on the Yakama Indian Reservation, Washington;

That he is thoroughly conversant with the English language and with the language spoken by the Yakama Indians and can translate the English language into the Yakama Indian language and the Yakama Indian language into the English language; [267 5a]

That on August 27, 1941, at the Yakama Indian Agency, Toppenish, Washington, affiant after having previously visited usual and accustomed Indian fishing places known as *Top-tut*, *Wah-wa-tam*, and *Ow-yeh* in the company of Moses Sampson, deponent in the foregoing affidavit and Edward G. Swindell, Jr., U.S. Indian Service, did at the request of Mr. Swindell interrogate Moses. Sampson, with regard to certain matters concerning said three usual and accustomed fishing places of the Yakama Indians as well as with regard to the way in which those Indians and their ancestors obtained a living; that he translated the questions of Mr. Swindell from the English language into the Yakama language, which Moses Sampson speaks and understands; that be translated the answers of Moses Sampson to Mr. Swindell's interrogatories from the Yakama language into the English language that at that time a stenographic record was made of the information given by the said Moses Sampson; that the information then given has been reduced to the narrative form contained in the above and foregoing affidavit of the said Moses Sampson;

Affiant further deposes and says that on the 6th day of May, 1942, in the presence of Moses Sampson and Mr. Swindell, he translated the information contained in the aforesaid affidavit from the English language into the Yakama Indian language, as said affidavit was read to affiant by Mr. Swindell; that the deponent, Moses. Sampson, told affiant that the said narrative affidavit contained the information given by him to Mr. Swindell on August 27, 1941, and that he had, therefore, signed said affidavit because the information contained therein was true.

Further affiant sayeth not.

(Sgd.) Philip Olney
Philip Olney, Interpreter

Philip Olney personally appeared before me this 6th day of May, 1942, and after having the foregoing affidavit read to him in my presence did acknowledge to me that the statements contained therein are true and that he executed same as his voluntary act.

Subscribed and sworn to before me this 6th day of May, 1942.

(Sgd.) H.V. Lewis
Acting Superintendent
Yakama Indian Agency [268 Ow-yeh] [269]

OW-YEH

USUAL AND ACCUSTOMED INDIAN FISHING
AND CAMP GROUNDS IN THE VICINITY OF
UNION GAP, WASHINGTON, IN YAKIMA COUNTY.

FEET

WAPATO DAM

YAKIMA

TO YAKIMA

STATE HIGHWAY

RESERVATION CANAL

RIVER

RIVER

STATE HIGHWAY

T 12N R19E

ORIGINAL CAMP GROUNDS
APPROX. 15.0 ACRES MORE OR LESS

PRESENT FISHING SITE
APPROX. 1.0 ACRES MORE OR LESS

AFFIDAVIT

STATE OF WASHINGTON }
COUNTY OF YAKIMA }   } SS

Alex Showaway, being first duly sworn, upon his oath deposes and says:

That he is 74 years of age, a full blood Indian member of the Yakama Indian tribe and a citizen of the United States of America residing on the Yakama Indian Reservation, Washington;

That he is personally familiar with the location of a number of the usual and accustomed fishing places of the Yakama Indians which were used by them prior to the time the white man came to the Indian country and some of which are still in use today; that a large number of the old places are no longer used by the Indians for the reason that the fish no longer go to the stream in which such places were located and the reason for their being no fish is the fact that the white people have built so many dams which prevent them from going up to the old and accustomed places; that nevertheless there are three principal places still used by the Indians which were used by them prior to the coming of the white man and as long back as Indian history records same; that the way the Indians record their history is different from the way white man; that since they could not read or write, they were forced to keep track of the things that happened in the past by the older generation telling the younger generation of the things that had been told to them when they were children, that this is how the Indians know that the usual 'and accustomed places had always been used by the Indians in the country.

Affiant further deposes and says that on August 27 he was present at the Yakama Indian Agency in Toppenish, Washington, when Moses Sampson, a member of the Yakama tribe answered certain questions propounded by Mr. Edward G. Swindell, Jr., U.S. Indian Service with reference to the location of usual and accustomed fishing stations of the Yakama Indians, that he listened carefully both to the questions propounded by Mr. Swindell and the answers given by Moses Sampson in response thereto; that on account of his own personal knowledge of the [270] things which Moses Sampson then told Mr. Swindell, he can confirm them as being true and as to those things that occurred prior to the tine that affiant was born and about which Moses Sampson gave information on August 27, 1941, he can confirm as being true because his parents told him substantially the same things when he was a young man;

That he is personally familiar with the three fishing places known as *Top-tut, Wa-wah-tam* and *Ow-yeh*; that he visited all of them many times during his life time; that in each instance he was a very small boy when he first visited them and at that time those places were being used by a great many more Indians than use them at the present time that he has fished at various times during his life at all three of those aforesaid places.

Affiant further deposes and says that prior to the coming of the white man the Indians were able to get plenty of fish for their needs; that in addition to the fish they had fresh or dried and put away for future use, they would trade fish to the Indians who would visit them at the various places; that they received in trade dried roots and berries and sometimes venison and skins of animals; that it was customary for the Indians to trade between the various tribe in order that they could obtain articles of food which were different from those which were available in their own country; that although fish still is used to a large extent by the Indians of the Yakama Reservation for food,, they do not obtain enough because there are so few fish left in the river; that the Indians if the state would permit them, would like to continue to go to their old fishing places off the reservation and catch fish in the old Indian accustomed manner.

Further affiant sayeth not.

(Sgd.) Alex Showaway his mark

Subscribed and sworn to before me this 6th day of May, 1942

(Sgd.) H.V. Lewis
Acting Superintendent
Yakama Indian Agency [271]

AFFIDAVIT OF INTERPRETER

State of Washington }
County of Yakima }   }SS

Philip Olney, being first duly sworn, upon his oath deposes and says;

That he is 61 years of age, a three-quarters blood Indian of the Yakama Indian tribe, and a citizen of the United States of America residing on the Yakama Indian Reservation, Washington

That he is thoroughly conversant with the English language and with the language spoken by the Yakama Indians and can translate the English language into the Yakama Indian language and the Yakama Indian language into the English language;

That on August 27, 1941, at the Yakama Indian Agency, Toppenish, Washington, affiants after having previously visited usual and accustomed Indian fishing places known as *Top-tut*, *Wah-wa-tam*, and *Ow-yeh* in the company of Alex Shawaway, deponent in the foregoing affidavit, and Edward G. Swindell, Jr., U.S. Indian Service, did at the request of Mr. Swindell interrogate Alex Showaway with regard to certain matters concerning said three usual and accustomed fishing places of the Yakama Indians as well as with regard to the way in which those Indians and their ancestors obtained a living; that he translated the questions of Mr. Swindell from the English language into the Yakama language, which Alex Showaway speaks and understands; that he translated the answers of Alex Showaway to Mr. Swindell's interrogatories from the Yakama language into the English language, that at that time a stenographic record was made of the information given by the said Alex Showaway, that the information given has been reduced to the narrative form contained in the above and foregoing affidavit of the said Alex Showaway;

Affiant further deposes and says that on the 6th day of May, 1942, in the presence of Alex Showaway and Mr. Swindell, he translated the information contained in the aforesaid affidavit from the English language into the Yakama Indian language, as said [272] affidavit was read to affiant by Mr. Swindell; that the deponent, Alex Showaway, told affiant that the said narrative affidavit contained the information given by him to Mr. Swindell on August 27, 1941, and that he had, therefore, signed said affidavit because the information contained therein was true.

Further affiant sayeth not.

(Sgd.) Philip Olney
Philip Olney, Interpreter

Philip Olney personally appeared before me this 6th day of May, 1942, and after having the foregoing affidavit read to him in my presence did acknowledge to me that the statements contained therein are true and that he executed same as his voluntary act.

Subscribed and sworn to before me this 6th day of May, 1942.

(Sgd.) H.V. Lewis
Acting Superintendent
Yakama Indian Agency

[273 *Wa-wa-tam*] [274A Sunnyside Dam]
One of the present day fishing grounds of Indians of Yakama Reservation, Washington, which they commenced using when construction of Sunnyside Diversion Dam, Yakima Project, U.S.B.R., (left) caused destruction of the prediscovery usual and accustomed fishing ground. Present fishing place has acquired same name as the original which was located a short distance upstream at the upper end of a small island. Present day fishing is carried on from platform using dip nets or spears instead of the weir annually constructed at the original grounds. Indians are limited to fishing on the near side of stream which is within Yakama Reservation boundaries. Note fish ladder in center of dam. [275]

One of the present day fishing grounds of Indians of Yakima Reservation, Washington, which they commenced using when construction of Sunnyside Diversion Dam, Yakima Project, U.S.B.R., (left) caused destruction of the prediscovery usual and accustomed fishing ground. Present fishing place has acquired same name as the original which was located a short distance upstream at the upper end of a small island. Present day fishing is carried on from platform using dip nets or spears instead of the weir annually constructed at the original grounds. Indians are limited to fishing on the near side of stream which is within Yakima Reservation boundaries. Note fish ladder in center of dam.

AFFIDAVIT

STATE OF WASHINGTON }
COUNTY OF YAKIMA }   } SS.

Jim Keninick, being first duly sworn, upon his oath deposes and says:

That he is about 85 years of age, a full blood member of the Yakama Indian tribe and a citizen of the United States of America residing on the Yakama Indian Reservation, Washington;

That he is descended from the Skein group of Indians who moved to the Yakama Reservation after the treaty with Governor Stevens; that he was selected by the Yakama Tribal Council to give information about the usual and accustomed Indian fishing place known as *Top-tut* because of his personal familiarity with the way the Indians lived and fished at that place during his lifetime, as well as his knowledge concerning same about things which occurred prior to his lifetime, which knowledge was obtained from the things told to him by his parents when he was a small boy and a young man;

That on August 27, 1941, he was present at the Yakama Indian Agency, Toppenish, Washington, when Moses Sampson and Alex Showaway, members of the Yakama Indian tribe gave information about Indian fishing places, including *Top-tut*, to Edward G. Swindell, Jr., U.S. Indian Service; that he listened carefully to the questions propounded by Mr. Swindell to the aforesaid Moses Sampson and Alex Showaway and also to the answers they gave in response to such questions; that the things they told Mr. Swindell are true.

Affiant further deposes and says that he visited *Top-tut* long prior to the time that the dam was built; that he distinctly recalls that there were falls in the river approximately as high as an average size room; that it was for this reason the Indians considered *Top-tut* an especially food fishing place; that he has actually seen the fish going over the falls; that nowadays the falls are no longer there because when the dam was built they apparently blasted them with dynamite; [276]

That the Indians who camped there would only remain as long as the fish were running; that as he recalls it, he would roughly estimate the number of Indians who use this place at about 500 all told; that this was when he visited the place as a young man of about 20 years of age; that since then he has seen the Indians fishing there at various times and that he understands that this has always been a usual and accustomed place of the Yakama Indians; that he was told so by his parents and that his parents were told by their parents; that they had fished there from as long back as the Indians could remember; that the Indians still fish at Prosser, although the number of fish now is very much smaller than when he was a young man.

Further affiant sayeth not.

(Sgd.) Jim Meninick his mark

Subscribed and sworn to before me this 6th day of May, 1942.

(Sgd.) H.V. Lewis

AFFIDAVIT OF INTERPRETER

STATE OF WASHINGTON }
COUNTY OF YAKIMA }   }SS.

Philip Olney, being first duly sworn, upon his oath deposes and says:

That he is 61 years of age, a three-quarters blood Indian of the Yakama Indian tribe, and a citizen of the United States of America residing on the Yakama Indian Reservation, Washington;

That he is thoroughly conversant with the English language and with the language spoken by the Yakama Indians and can translate the English language into the Yakama Indian language and the Yakama Indian language into the English language; [277]

That on August 27, 1941, at the Yakama Indian Agency, Toppenish, Washington, affiant after having previously visited usual and accustomed Indian fishing places known as *Top-tut*, *tlah-wa-tam*, and *Ow-yeh* in the company of Jim Meninick, deponent in the foregoing affidavit and Edward G. Swindell, Jr., U.S. Indian Service, did at the request of Mr. Swindell interrogate Jim Meninick with regard. to certain matters concerning said three usual and accustomed fishing places of the Yakama Indians as well as with regard to the ~ :In which those Indians and their ancestors obtained a living; that he translated the questions of Mr. Swindell from the English language into the Yakama language, which Jim Meninick speaks and understands; that he translated the answers of Jim Meninick to Mr. Swindell's interrogatories from the Yakama language into the English language, that at that time a stenographic record was made of the information given by the said Jim Heninick; that the information then given has been reduced to the narrative form contained in the above and foregoing affidavit of the said Jim Meninick.

Affiant further deposes and says that on the 6th of May, 1942, in the presence of Jim Meninick and Mr. Swindell, he translated the information contained in the aforesaid affidavit from the English language into the Yakama Indian language, as said affidavit was read to affiant by Mr. Swindell; that the deponent, Jim Meninick, told affiant that the said narrative affidavit contained the information given by him to Mr. Swindell on August 27, 1941, and that he had, therefore, signed said affidavit because the information contained therein was true.

Further affiant sayeth not.

(Sgd.) Philip Olney
Philip Olney, Interpreter

Philip Olney personally appeared before me this 6th of May, 1942, and after having the foregoing affidavit read to him in my presence did acknowledge to me that the statements contained therein are true and that he executed same as his voluntary act.

Subscribed and sworn to before me this 6th day of May, 1942.

(Sgd.) H.V. Lewis
Acting Superintendent
Yakama Indian Agency [278]

TOP-TUT

One of the ancient fishing grounds and assembly centers of the Indians comprising the Yakama nation located at Prosser Dam, U.S.B.R., opposite the town of Prosser, Washington. Prediscovery camp grounds occupied land on both sides of the river as well as in foreground. At the present time

Indians are limited to two small areas adjacent to the dam. Prosser Power Canal of U.S.B.R. Yakama Project, appears at lower right. (See plat with Yakama affidavit.)

Close up View of Prosser Dam showing fish ladder in center of dam installed to facilitate

upstream passage of the small remaining salmon run. Prior to construction of dam, Indians fished with spears and dip nets. At the present time fish are taken with gaff hooks and, in a few instances, spears. (See Yakama affidavits.) Although Washington conservation statutes prohibit the taking of fish at dams, the Yakama Indians fish here in their traditional manner under the special authority of Sec. 2451-1, Vol. 1, Pierce's Code – Washington, 1939; Sec 5774, Rem Comp Stats.

[278 text & map of *Top-tut*] [279 2 views] [280]

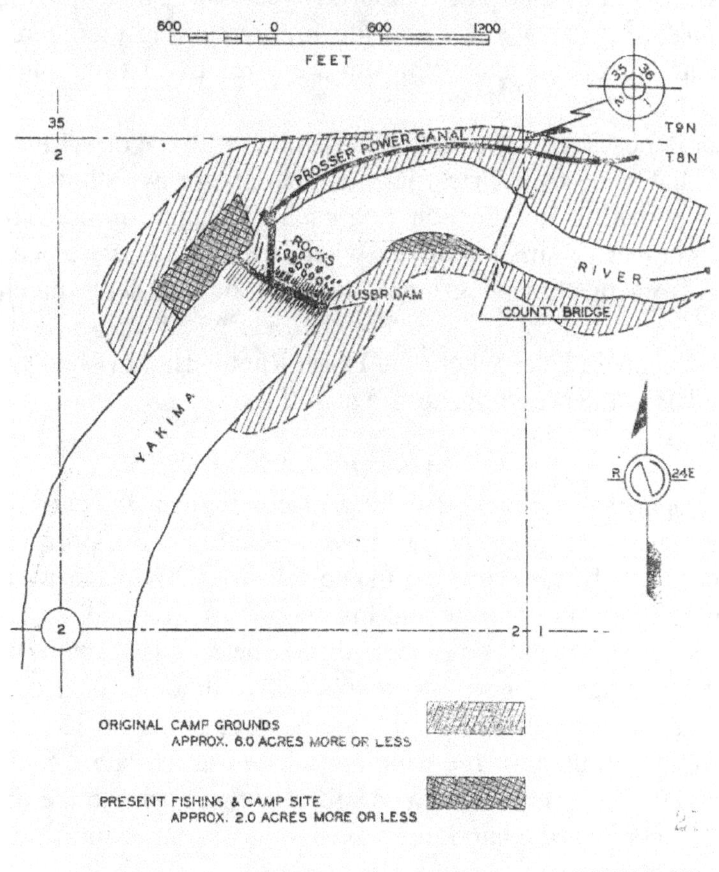

AFFIDAVITS OF JOHNNY BUCK AND TOMANAWASH
PRIEST RAPIDS INDIANS

STATE OF WASHINGTON }
COUNTY OF YAKIMA }   }SS.

Johnny Buck, being first duly sworn, upon his oath deposes and says:

That he is 62 years of age and the head man or leader of what is known by the white people as the Priest Rapids Band of Indians; that he is a citizen of the United States of America and a resident of the State of Washington;

That neither he or his people ever received allotments from the federal government nor did they participate in any of the treaties; that his people still live in the same manner as their ancestors, following the same pursuits and visiting the same places year in and year out for the purpose of obtaining their livelihood;

That the principal village of his people is located near Priest Rapids, Washington, and they use this place for their winter camp; that this is the same place the ancestors of his people used from as long back as the Indians have any knowledge thereof; that when he was a boy, the band consisted of a large number of Indians and that although he is not familiar with the white man's way of counting and things of that nature, he would estimate that there was approximately 100 and 150 Indians in the band when he was a small boy; that at that time his people were accustomed to catching a supply of fish at Priest Rapids but had not been able to do so since the power plant was constructed at that place about 25 years ago; that, nevertheless, when winter comes and the season's work is over, he and the few remaining members of his band, which numbers approximately 50 people including children, return to their old home to spend the winter.

Affiant further deposes and says that he is familiar with the usual and accustomed fishing places of his people; that aside from Priest Rapids, there were two other principal places where they were [281] accustomed to obtain their fish each year; that, in addition to these principal places, there were a number of smaller places where the Indians were accustomed to catching fish as they traveled from the fishing grounds to the root and berry patches and the hunting districts;

That the two principal places where the Priest Rapids Band fished prior to the coming of the white man, as well as at the present time, are as follows:

WY-YOO-NA

That this was one of the principal fishing places [*wayawna* 'current type' u109] of the Priest Rapids Indians where they were accustomed to obtain a large portion of their fish supply during the time when the fish were running in the fall; that this place was located near White Bluffs on the Columbia River and that he and his people, as well as their ancestors, had used it every year as far back as they could remember; that as he recalls it, there would be as many as 500 Indians living at this place when he was a small boy, although only between 100 or 150 of them were members of the Priest Rapids band, the balance being Indians from the surrounding country; that the camping grounds of the tribe are located at the same spot today as they were when he was a boy and he was told the camp was located there prier to the time he was born; that when there were more people in the band, they used to have some camps on the big island in the river;

That according to the Indien custom, fishing at this place could only be done by using spears or a net which was operated from two canoes; that it was only the members of the Priest Rapids Band that fished at this place, the visiting Indians merely attending the camp for the purpose or visiting and trading some of the things they had, such as roots and berries, pueblo robes and the like, for the fish that were caught at this place; that if the visiting Indians did not have anything to trade, the local people would, nevertheless, give then some fish so that they would not go hungry;

That when he was a small boy and a young man, the fish that came to this place to spawn were many in number and that in those days two men could catch about 100 fish at the time they were running, whereas, nowadays, they were lucky if they could catch between [282] five and ten fish during the same length of time; that the fish that were not eaten fresh or given away were dried in the open air or with a fire depending upon weather conditions and then put away for use during the winter; that each family would dry and put away about 100 fish, each one of which was different in size, but affiant estimates that the average one would be between 20 and 24 inches long after the head had been removed and that each would weigh from five to six pounds after dried; that nowadays due to the fact that so many dams have been constructed in the river, the fish are not nearly as plentiful as they used to be;

That the Indians when they camped at *Wy-yow-na* would remain for approximately four or five weeks at a time in the fall of the year corresponding with the white man's month of October; that they did not camp here at other times during the year because it was only in the fall of the year that fish used this place to spawn, and, further, because in the spring of the year the campsite was under water; that the Indians often they fished at this place did not catch fish until after they had spawned because they were anxious to see that the run of fish would continue so that they could have a sufficient supply each year.

WAN-A-WISH

That the principal spring fishing place of the Priest Rapids Indians was known as *Wan-a-Wish* [*wanawish* = 'rapids' v264; 'flow down' u102] and located near where the present Horn Rapids Irrigation Dam on the Yakima River is constructed; that his people have used this place ever since he can remember, and when he was a small boy his parents and other older members of the tribe told him that it had always used by their people; that prior to the construction of the dam the Indians fished in the Yakima River from a point about were the dam is located to a place quite a ways down stream; that at this place in those days they only used dip nets to catch the fish because the water conditions were not right for any other methods; that the fish were caught in the rapids in the river formed by the rocks at this point, and that was why they could only use dip nets;

That in the old days prior to the construction of the dam, the Indians established their camps on both sides of the Yakima River, although the principal portion [283] of the camp was located at a point where there is now constructed the house which is owned by the man who takes care of the dam; that after the dam was constructed and the caretaker for the dam installed in his new home, the Indians were no longer permitted to have their camp at the old place;

That the present camping place of the Indians is located on the bank of the river up close to where the dam was situated; that the Indians have been using this place, he would say, for about 45 years or ever since the dam was built, which was when he was a grown man; that the few remaining Indians prefer to camp at the present site because then they are closer to where they actually catch their fish and where they can obtain a supply of firewood which floats down stream and is stopped by the dam; that the fish are easily caught at the dam as they endeavor to go up to their spawning grounds, although they are not as plentiful as they used to be;

That the fishing grounds and campsite at *Wan-a-wish* is not and never has been a permanent place of the Priest Rapids Indians; that it was only used during the spring and early summer each year when the chinook, blueback and steelhead salmon were going up the river to spawn; that the Indians stayed here for approximately two months; that the fish caught were different from those caught at *Wy-yow-na*, since those caught at that place were what is known as dog salmon to the white people and *metulla* [*mit'ula* v427] to the Indians;

That almost as many Indians used this place for camping purposes as used the camp grounds at *Wy-yow-na*; that large numbers of other Indians used to visit here also for the purpose of obtaining the different kind of fish that were here by trading with the local people; that here as at *Wy-yow-na* they observed rules of the local Indians, which did not permit them to participate in the fishing; that the fish that were not eaten fresh or traded and were dried in the sun only because at that time of the year it was never necessary to dry them through the use of fires; that the fish that was traded to the visiting Indians was mostly for roots and berries although the Priest Rapids Indians obtained large supplies of these things themselves; [284]

That this was a very good fishing place because in the old days lots of fish could be caught very easily in the shallow swiftwater.

Affiant further deposes and says that when he was a young man and prior to the time he was born, the Indians spent their Winters at what is now known as Priest Rapids where they could obtain fresh deer meat; that when spring came; it was the duty of the women to gather roots and that after the roots had been gathered, the camp was moved to the spring fishing place at *Wan-a-wish* until the run was over; that thereafter the Priest Rapids Indians would move to the mountains where they would remain until the fall of the year, gathering roots and berries to be used during the long winter months ahead; that when the fall of the year came, they would then return and establish their camp at *Wy-yow-na* to catch the fall run of fish, which was especially good for drying purposes; that when the run was over at *Wy-yow-na*, they would then return to their winter camp; that this procedure was followed each year and that his people still follow the same procedure with the exception that nowadays they can earn a little money helping farmers harvest their crop and work in the hop yards in the fall of the year;

Further affiant sayeth not.

(Sgd.) Johnny Buck his mark
Johnny Buck

Subscribed and sworn to before me this 6th Day of 1942.

(Sgd.) H.V. Lewis
Acting Supt.
Yakama Indian Agency

AFFIDAVIT

STATE OF WASHINGTON }
COUNTY OF YAKIMA }   }SS.

Cy J. Tomanawash, whose Indian name is *Tah-mal-wash*, being first duly sworn, upon his oath deposes and says: [285]

That he is 42 years of age, a full blood member of the Priest Rapids band of Indians, and a citizen of the United states of America residing in the State of Washington;

That on the 29th day of September, 1941, he was present at the Yakama Indian Agency, Toppenish, Washington, when Johnny Buck, the head man of the Priest Rapids band of Indians, gave certain information to Edward G. Swindell, Jr., U.S. Indian Service, with regard to the location of the permanent village and usual and accustomed fishing places of said Indians, as well as with regard to the manner in which said Indians live at the present time as well as prior to his birth;

That although he is a younger man than Johnny Buck, he can and does confirm the statements made by the said Johnny Buck as being true insofar as they relate to things which have occurred during his own lifetime and of which he has personal knowledge and recollection, and that as to the statements given with regard to things that happened prior to his birth, he can confirm them as being true for the reason that when he was a young man his parents, as well as the older members of the tribe, told him the very same things; that those things must be true because there was no reason for his parents to have not told him the truth nor did his parents or their parents have any occasion to tell their children other than the truth.

Affiant further deposes and says that most of the fishing by the Indians nowadays is done either with a spear or a gaff hook; that the nets referred to by Johnny Buck in his affidavit have not been used for several years because there are only four adult male members of the tribe and only affiant and Johnny Buck were capable of operating this particular fishing device; that for several years Johnny Buck has been too sick with rheumatism to assist him in operating the net;

That the fishing at *Wan-a-wish*, which place was referred to by Johnny Buck, is very poor compared to what it was when he was a young man; that in 1940 the Indians kept a record of the number of fish they caught, said record being kept by notching a stick each time a run was caught; that their white friends counted these notches and told them that their total catch was only 30 fish; that in 1941, the record kept [286] in the same fashion showed a total of 63 fish; that in 1939, the Indians only caught about 28 fish; that the Indians, despite what is said about them, don't catch fish before they have spawned for they know that if they do that, the fish would soon disappear.

Affiant further deposes and says that on the 11th day of June 1942, he was present when an affidavit containing the information previously given by Johnny Buck was read back to affiant and interpreted by Philip Olney, of the Yakama Indian tribe; that the information as originally given by the said Johnny Buck was contained in the said affidavit and said information is true to the best of affiant's knowledge and belief and he, therefore, executed the within affidavit.

Further affiant sayeth not.

(Sgd.) Cy J. Tomanawash his mark
Cy J. Tomanawash

Subscribed and sworn to before me this 11th day of June 1942.

(Sgd.) M.A. Johnson
H. A. Johnson, Superintendent
Yakama Indian Agency

AFFIDAVIT OF INTEPRETER

State of Washington }
County of Yakima }   }SS.

Philip Olney, being first duly sworn, upon his oath deposes and says:

That he is 61 years of age, a three-quarters blood Indian of the Yakama Indian tribe, and a citizen of the United States of America residing on the Yakama Indian Reservation, Washington;

That he is thoroughly conversant with the English language and with the language spoken by the members of what is known as the Priest Rapids Band of Indians; that the language spoken by said Indians is substantially [287] the same as that spoken by the Yakama Indians; that affiant can translate the English language into the language spoken by the Priest Rapids Indians and the language spoken by the Priest Rapids Indians into the English language;

That on September 29, 1941, at the Yakama Indian Agency, Toppenish, Washington, affiant, in the presence of Johnny Buck and Cy J. Tomanawash, members of the Priest Rapids Band of Indians, deponents in the foregoing affidavit, and Edward G. Swindell, Jr., U.S. Indian Service, did, at the request of Mr. Swindell, interrogate said Johnny Buck and Tananawash with regard to the location of the permanent village and usual and accustomed fishing places of the Priest Rapids Band of Indians, as well as with regard to the way in which those Indians and their ancestors obtained their livelihood; that he translated the questions of Mr. Swindell from the English language into the language spoken and understood by the said Johnny Buck and Tomanawash and that he translated the answers of said Johnny Buck and Tananawash to Mr. Swindell's interrogatories from the language spoken by them into the English language; that at that time Mr. Swindell made written notes of the information given by the said Johnny Buck and Tomanawash and reduced said information to the narrative form as given in the above and foregoing affidavit of the said Johnny Buck and Tananawash.

Affiant further deposes and says that on the 6th day of May, 1942, in the presence of Johnny Buck, and Mr. Swindell, he translated the information contained in the aforesaid affidavit from the English language into the language spoken by the said Johnny Buck, as said affidavit was read to affiant by Mr. Swindell; that the deponent, Johnny Buck, told affiant that the said narrative affidavit contained the information given by him to Mr. Swindell on September 29, 1941, and he had, therefore, signed said affidavit because the information contained therein was true.

Affiant further deposes and says that on the 11th Day of June, 1942, in the presence of Cy J. Tomanawash he translated from the English language into the language spoken by the said Tomanawash, who then told affiant that they contained the information [288] given by him and Johnny Buck to Mr. Swindell on September 29, 1941, and he had therefore signed said affidavit because the information contained therein was true.

Further affiant sayeth not.

(Sgd.) Philip Olney
Philip Olney, Interpreter

Philip Olney personally appeared before me and after having the foregoing affidavit read to him in my presence did acknowledge to me that the statements contained therein are true and that he executed same as his voluntary act.

Subscribed and sworn to before me this 11th day of June, 1942.

(Sgd.) M.A. Johnson
M.A. Johnson, Superintendent.
Yakama Indian Agency
[288A-89-90 fotos texts]

WY-YOW-NA

Primitive dugout hollowed out of tree trunk still in use by the remnants of the Priest Rapids Band of Sokulk Indians on the Columbia River located in SW/4, Sec. 17, T. 14 N., R. 27 E., near White Bluffs, Washington. This was and is in traditional fishing ground used during the fall run. Fish were speared after spawning or netted at night from dugouts

Drying shed at camp of Priest Rapids Indians at *Wy-Yo-Na.* Ordinarily the fish are dried by exposure to open air, but

shed had been enclosed at the time picture was taken since it had rained heavily during the preceding day and night.

Additional view of traditional fishing ground of *Wy-Yow-Na* showing Indian camp in center of  picture. In 1941 camp established about October 26 and disbanded November 18. [Locke Island *taq ʼʷt* u108] Only about 20 individuals, including children, ware encamped in 1941. All catch were reported with the condition of the fish poor. This is not located on a reservation and Indians fish here under special dispensation provided for in 1939 by Washington legislature (Sec.2451-2, Vol.1, Pierce's Code – Washington – 1939).

In left foreground note primitive Indian dugout with a modern touch added by patches from gasoline cans. [291]

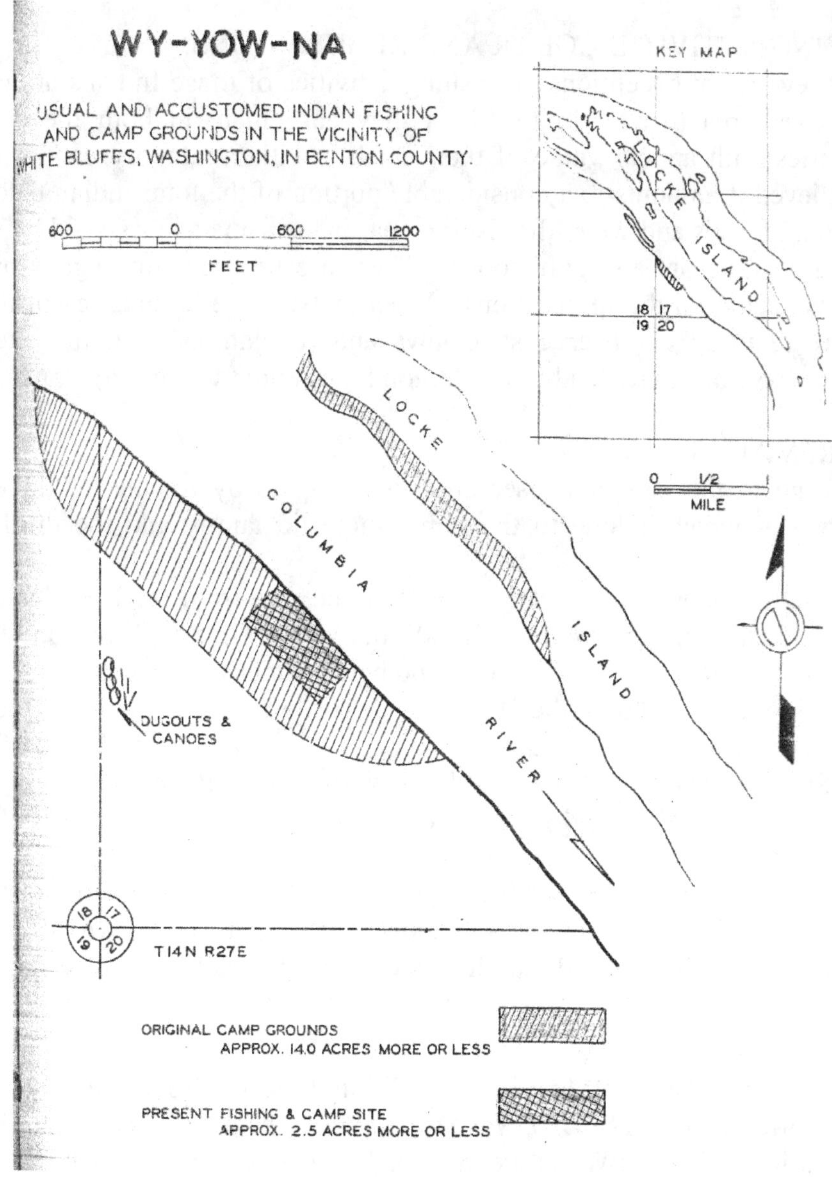

UMATILLA RESERVATION

AGENCY: - Umatilla - Pendleton, Oregon.
LOCATION: - Northeastern Oregon.
AREA: - 106,152 acres.
TREATY: - June 9, 1855, 12 stat.. 945; 2 Kappler 694 at Walla Walla, Oregon Territory.
INDIAN TRIBES: - Cayuses of the Waiilatpuan family and Walla Wallas and Umatillas of the Shahaptian family.[81]

LOCATION OF "U. and A." FISHING GROUNDS: -

Along the Columbia River on the east and south banks from the mouth of the Snake River to Cascade Rapids; also the Umatilla and Des Chutes rivers, including the headwaters of the Walls Walla and Grande Ronde rivers, Oregon. This area is similar in character to that ceded by the Yakamas and it too was crossed by many streams in which a plentiful supply of salmon was obtained each year. see General Area Map, ante p. 19.

PRESENT FISHING ACTIVITIES, GEAR AND REGULATIONS: -

With but few minor exceptions the fishing activities of those Indians are confined to the mid-Columbia River area (q.v.). In that area they participate in both the commercial and subsistence fisheries with annual value of their catch in either category cannot be ascertained although it is believed it amounts to a considerable portion of the total Indian catch in that area. With the exception of traps and weirs the fishing gear is the same as was used by their ancestors Viz. dip and bag nets, spears and gaff hooks. There are no regulations governing what little fishing activity as occurs on the reservations. When outside the boundaries of the reservation, these Indians are required to observe state laws and regulations with the exception of the concessions which have been granted by the Oregon legislature (ante p. 76). [292]

GENENERAL REMARKS: -

As above noted the Umatilla reservation is occupied by Indians of three separate and distinct tribes, two of which belong to the same linguistic family and the third being closely related thereto.

The Cayuse tribe's original habitat centered in the area from the Des Chutes River to the Blue Mountains including the headwaters of the Walla Walla, Grande Ronde and Umatilla rivers where the summer camping grounds at the root and berry patches were located.

The pre-discovery habitat of the Walla Walla (little river) people centered on the lower reaches of the river bearing the same name and along the east and south banks of the Columbia River, from the Snake river west to the Umatilla in Washington and Oregon.

The Umatillas originally resided on the Umatilla and the adjacent banks of the Columbia in Oregon.

All three of the tribes appear to have jointly utilized some of the numerous fishing places located in their respective domains as is evidenced by their respective affidavits. In this connection it should be borne in mind that there were no territorial lines of demarcation between

---

[81] [e#] = Eugene Hunn, E Thomas Morning Owl, Phillip Cash Cash Jennifer Karson Engum
     2015 *Čaw Pawa Laakni ~ They Are Not Forgotten ~* Sahaptian Place Names Atlas of the
     Cayuse, Umatilla, and Walla Walla Pendleton: Tamastslikt Cultural Institute.
 [u#] = Confederated Tribes of Umatilla and Noel Rude 2014 *Umatilla Dictionary* UW.

the territories claimed by the three tribes and further that it was customary for them to meet at various places during their summer travels for the purpose of trading and social intercourse.

After learning of the instant investigation, each of the three tribes selected delegates to accompany members of the staff of the Umatilla agency to the sites of the various fishing grounds and the camping grounds at the root and berry patches. A very complete record of the locations of such places was made and is on file at the Umatilla agency in Pendleton, Oregon. However, since practically all of them are of no present day value to the Indians on either account of destruction of the annual salmon runs or the restrictions of state law, such data, it was considered, would serve no useful purpose in this report nor was it considered advisable to endeavor to cover each location in detail in the affidavits. [293]

TYPICAL UMATILLA FISHING GROUNDS

Ho-pa-la-i-ya-ca-tats [*haawpala 'iyaakaatic* 'spearfish at rough water' e158]: A usual and accustomed fishing ground of the Indians of the Cayuse and Umatilla tribes now residing on the Umatilla Indian Reservation, Oregon. The place pictured is located near the confluence of Eagle and Patty Creeks, Oregon. It is no longer used. In the old days the Indians caught salmon and trout at this place through the use of grab hooks and spears.

Ya-we-shin-na [*yawišiinma* Ritter e146, e153]: A usual and accustomed fishing place

of the Cayuse and Umatilla Indians located near the northeast corner of the S¼ of Section 10, T. 9 S., R. 31 E., on the middle fork of the John Day River. In the early days the Indians were accustomed to acquire a considerable supply of salmon at this place through capturing them by use of a fish weir. The place is no longer used since Oregon conservation statutes outlaw that type of gear.

Koola-lool-pa [*kulk'uliipa* 'little bowl in ground' 3 Mile Falls Dam Hermiston e28]: Shows dam built on the Umatilla River, Oregon, which when constructed completely blocked the upstream passage of the salmon runs frequenting this stream, resulting in their ultimate extinction. Salmon trout and eels were taken at this point through the use of dip nets. Indian names furnished by Umatilla Indian Agency, Pendleton, Oregon.

[294 3 views] [295]

AFFIDAVITS OF GILBERT MINTHORN, GEORGE RED HAWK, AND MRS. YOUNG CHIEF
CAYUSE INDIANS
UMATILLA INDIAN RESERVATION, OREGON

STATE OF OREGON }
COUNTY OF UMATILLA } } SS.

Gilbert Minthorn, 66 years of age, and George Red Hawk, 80 years of age, each being first duly sworn and put upon oath, severally deposes and says:

That they are full blood members of the Cayuse Indian Tribe and citizens of the United States of America residing on the Umatilla Indian Reservation, Oregon; that they· have spent their entire life in the country formerly owned by the Cayuse Indians before it was sold to the Government in accordance with the Treaty of 1855; that they are personally familiar with the location of the usual and accustomed fishing grounds of the Cayuse Indians, as well as the location of the hunting districts and the root digging and berry gathering patches; that during the course of their lifetime they have visited these places, or practically all of them, and that as a result of the personal knowledge thus gained from actual observation and utilization of such places, they are in a position to give information with regard to the location thereof as well as how and when such places were used by the Cayuse Indians; that, in addition to the personal knowledge thus gained from actual observation, they were told when small boys and young men by their parents and the older members of the Cayuse Tribe that such places had always been used by the Indians of that tribe in obtaining their daily food throughout the year; that as a result of their age and position as leaders of their people, as well as for their personal knowledge of the situation, they were selected by the tribal council of the Umatilla Indian Reservation to give information with regard to such places in order that an appropriate record thereof could be made a part of the official Government records;

Affiants further depose and say that during the course of the autumn of 1941, that in company with Gilbert Conner and David Temple, members of the staff of the Umatilla Indian Agency, they visited the various herein above referred to places for the purpose of [296] pointing out the location thereof to said Gilbert Conner and David Temple and to advise them as to how the Indians are accustomed to using such places; that at that time the said Gilbert Conner and David Temple made a written record of the things they were told by affiants, and affiants understand that such record is now a part of the official agency records.

Affiants further depose and say that the Cayuse Indians prior to the coming of the white man, as well as thereafter until they had been permanently settled on the Umatilla Reservation, in accordance with the provisions of the treaty with the Government, were accustomed to roam throughout vast areas of what is now the State of Oregon; that due to the fact that it was difficult for them to obtain a sufficient supply of food at any one of a few places, it was necessary each year that they visit many places throughout the country occupied?*? by them at those times when they knew that fish, game, roots, and berries were available at such places; that as a result, they had no permanent villages although they were accustomed to spend the winter at various places along the streams throughout their country where the snow was not as deep as up toward the mountains;

That in the spring of the year when the snows had melted, the people in the various villages broke up in small groups for the purpose of visiting the various food supply places; that each group followed a well-established routine going from one place to another as the conditions were right at each for either fish or game and that ultimately they would all meet in the root and berry patches for visits and entertainment prior to returning in the fall to their winter camping grounds;

That the Indians knew when the salmon would be running in the various streams at the places where they were accustomed to catching them; that they would go to those places at those times and catch sufficient fish for their immediate needs as well as for the those of drying some to be put away for future use; that generally speaking, it was not possible to obtain sufficient fish at any one or two places which would permit them to have a sufficient supply for the entire year; [297]

That the Cayuse Indians were accustomed to catching their fish at the various usual and accustomed grounds by using spears or Indian fish traps consisting of weirs constructed across the streams; that when they had sufficient fish for the time being, they would remove the traps so that the fish would be permitted to go up to their spawning grounds; that in this manner there was sufficient fish each year at each of the places for the people who went there; that the salmon in the old days was much more plentiful than at the present time, and that for a number of years last past, the Indians have not been able to get as much fish for their food supply as they used to in the old days and which they would still like to obtain;

That the younger members of the tribe due to the change in the way they live, which has been brought about by reservation life, no longer fish like their ancestors did, although quite a few of them still go to Celilo for the purpose of fishing both for food and subsistence; that some Cayuse Indians had always been accustomed to visiting Celilo for the purpose of seeing their relatives and friends and either fishing for themselves or trading some of the things they had to the local people for fish which the local people at Celilo caught; that this was true even before the white man came to the country and that the trade amounted to quite a bit.

Affiants further depose and say that the Cayuse Indians were friends with the Indians of the Umatilla and Walla Walla tribes, which now reside on the reservation with them; that all three tribes have always intermingled and married amongst themselves and that the same is true with regard to the Indians that had permanent villages along the Columbia River.

Further affiants sayeth not.

(Sgd.) Gilbert Minthorn his mark.
Gilbert Minthorn
(Sgd.) George Red Hawk his Mark
George Red Hawk

Subscribed and sworn to before me this 8th day of May, 1942

(Sgd.) Dan Ohlerking
Notary Public for Oregon
My commission expires
Nov. 28, 1943 [298]

AFFIDAVIT

STATE OF OREGON }
COUNTY OF UMATILLA }   }SS.

Mrs. Young Chief, being first duly sworn, upon her oath deposes and says:

That she is 85 years of age, a full blood member of the Cayuse Indian Tribe, and a citizen of the United States of America residing on the Umatilla Indian Reservation.

That on September 2, 1941, she was present at the Umatilla Indian Agency, when Gilbert Minthorn and George Red Hawk, members of the Cayuse Indian Tribe and deponents in the foregoing affidavit gave information about Indian fishing and hunting districts and root digging and berry gathering patches to Edward G. Swindell, Jr., U.S. Indian Service, as well as with regard to the manner in which the Cayuses had been accustomed to live both prior and subsequent to the coming of the white people; that she listened carefully to the questions propounded by Mr. Swindell to the aforesaid deponents and also to the answers said deponents gave in response to such questions; that if such questions had been directed particularly to affiant, she would have given the same answers insofar as affiant was personally familiar with the location and manner of use of the various places from visits to same occurring throughout her lifetime; that as to events which occurred prior to her lifetime, affiant would have given substantally the same answers for the reason that when she was a small girl and a young woman, her parents and the older members of the tribe told her the same things that were told Mr. Swindell by the said Gilbert Minthorn and George Red Hawk; that as a consequence, affiant can and does confirm the statements of the said Gilbert Minthorn and George Red Hawk as being true to the best of her knowledge and belief. [299]

Further affiant sayeth not.

(Sgd.) Mrs. Young Chief Her Mark
Mrs. Young Chief

Subscribed and sworn to before me this 5th day of July, 1942

(Sgd.) Dan Ohlerking
(Seal) Notary Public for Oregon
My Commission expires
Nov. 28, 1943

AFFIDAVIT OF INTERPRETER

STATE OF OREGON }
COUNTY OF UMATILLA }   (SEAL)

Gilbert E. Conner, being first duly sworn, upon his oath deposes and says:

That he is 44 years of age, a three-quarters blood Indian of the Nez Perce Indian tribe and a citizen of the United States of America residing on the Umatilla Indian Reservation, Oregon;

That he was employed by the United States at the Umatilla Indian Agency, Oregon, and acted as official interpreter of the agency between members of the agency staff and the Indians of the various tribes residing on the Umatilla Reservation who are not able to speak the English language; that he is thoroughly conversant with the English language and with the language spoken by the members of the Cayuse Tribe of Indians now are allotted on the Umatilla Reservation; that he can translate the English language into the Cayuse Indian language and the Cayuse Indian language into the English language; [300]

That during the summer of 1941 affiant in the company of Gilbert Minthorn and George Red Hawk, members of the Cayuse Indian Tribe, and David Temple, Road Engineer or the Umatilla Indian Agency, did visit the various places which the said Gilbert Minthorn and George Red Hawk designated as the usual and accustomed fishing grounds, hunting districts and root digging and berry gathering patches of the Cayuse Indians; that at that time a written record of the location of such places was made and same was now a part of the official files of the Umatilla Indian Agency;

That on September 2, 1941, at the Umatilla Indian Agency, Oregon, affiant in the presence of the said Gilbert Minthorn and George Red Hawk, as well as in the presence of Mrs. Young Chief, and Edward G. Swindell, Jr., U.S. Indian Service, did at the request of Mr. Swindell interrogate the said Gilbert Minthorn, George Red Hawk, and Mrs. Young Chief, deponents in the foregoing affidavits, with regard to certain matters concerning the said usual and accustomed fishing, hunting, and other grounds of the Cayuse Indians, as well as with regard to the way in which those Indians and their ancestors obtained a livelihood; that he translated the questions of Mr. Swindell from the English language into the Cayuse Indian language which the said deponents speak and understand; that he translated the answers of the said deponents to Mr. Swindell's interrogatories from these Indian language into the English language; that at that time a written record vas made of the information given by the said deponents which information was then given has been reduced to the narrative form contained in the above and foregoing affidavits of the said deponents.

Affiant further deposes and says that on the 8th of May, 1942, in the presence of Gilbert Minthorn, George Red Hawk, Mrs. Young Chief, the aforesaid deponents, and Mr. Swindell, he translated the information contained in the aforesaid affidavits from the English language into the these Indian language as said affidavits were read to affiant by Mr. Swindell; that the deponents therein told affiant that the said narrative affidavits contained information previously given by them to Mr. Swindell on September 2, 1941, and that they had, therefore, signed said affidavit because the information contained therein was true. [301]

Further affiant sayeth not.

(Sgd.) Gilbert E. Conner
Gilbert E. Conner, Interpreter

Gilbert E. Conner personally appeared before me this 8th day of May, 1942, and after having the foregoing affidavit read to him in my presence did acknowledge to me that the statements contained therein are true and that he executed same as his voluntary act.

Subscribed and sworn to before me this 8th day of May, 1942.

(Sgd.) Dan Ohlerking
(Seal) Notary Public for Oregon
My commission expires
Nov. 28, 1943

AFFIDAVIT OF INTERPRETER

STATE OF OREGON }
COUNTY OF UMATILLA }   (SEAL)

Phillip Guyer, being first duly sworn, upon his oath deposes and says;

That he is 40 years of age, a Cayuse-Nez Perce Indian of the Umatilla Indian Reservation and a citizen of the United States residing on the Umatilla Indian Reservation, Oregon;

That he is thoroughly conversant with the English language and with the language spoken by the Cayuse Indians and can translate the English language into the Cayuse Indian language and the Cayuse Indian language into the English language;

That on June 5, 1942, in the presence of Mrs. Young Chief, a full blood member of the Cayuse Indian Tribe, he translated a joint affidavit of Gilbert Minthorn and George Red Hawk, of the Cayuse Indian Tribe, dated May 8, 1942, from the English language into the Cayuse Indian language, which the said Mrs. Young Chief speaks and understands; [302]

That on the same date, to-wit, June 5, 1942, affiant also translated to the said Mrs. Young Chief an affidavit, prepared for her signature, confirming the above referred to joint affidavit of Gilbert Minthorn and George Red Hawk;

That the said affidavit of May 8, 1942, above referred to contained information previously jointly given by Gilbert Minthorn and George Red Hawk to a Government representative relative to the location of the usual and accustomed hunting and fishing grounds of the Cayuse Indians, which were reserved to them in their treaty with the Government;

That the said Mrs. Young Chief did on June 5 tell affiant that the affidavit of May 8, 1942, above referred to contained the information previously given by said deponents Gilbert Minthorn and George Red Hawk to a Government representative on September 2, 1941, and that she had therefore subscribed to the affidavit prepared for her signature by affixing her thumb mark thereon because the information contained therein was true to the best of said Mrs. Young Chief's knowledge and belief.

Further affiant sayeth not.

(Sgd.) Philip Guyer
Phillip Guyer, Interpreter

Phillip Guyer personally appeared before me this 29th day of June, 1942, and after having the foregoing affidavit read to him in presence did acknowledge to me that the statements therein are correct and that he executed same as his voluntary act.

Subscribed and sworn to before me this 29th day of June, 1942.

(Sgd.) Henry Roe Cloud
Supt. Umatilla Indian Agency [303]

AFFIDAVIT OF JAMES KASH KASH

STATE OF OREGON }
UMATILLA COUNTY }   } SS.

James Kash Kash, being first duly sworn, upon his oath deposes and says:

That he is 79 years of age and a full blood member of the Cayuse Indian Tribe and a citizen of the United States of America residing on the Umatilla Indian Reservation, Oregon;

That he has spent his entire life on the Umatilla Indian Reservation, as well as traveling in the country formerly owned by these Indians before it was sold to the Government; that he is personally familiar with the location of the usual and accustomed fishing grounds of the Cayuse Indians, as well as the location of the hunting districts and the root digging and berry gathering patches; that during the course of his lifetime he has visited most of these places and that as a result of the personal knowledge thus gained from actual observation of the way the Indians utilized such places, he feels that he is qualified to give information with regard thereto; that in addition to the personal knowledge thus gained he was told by his parents when he was a small boy, and the other members of the tribe that these places had always been used by the Cayuse Indians in their effort to obtain a livelihood each year; that he was selected by the Cayuse Indians to give information to Government representatives with regard to the way the Indians used to live prior to the establishment of the reservation and subsequent thereto;

Affiant further deposes and says that he understands there was approximately 2,000 members of the Cayuse Tribe at the time of the treaty with the United States; that the great majority of these Indians would spend the winters in camps located at about the place where the city of Walla Walla, Washington, is located; that large numbers of them also had Winter Cams along the Walla Walls River near the present town of Milton, Oregon; that when spring came these people [304] would break up their winter camps for the purpose of visiting the various places where they knew they could obtain fish, game, roots, and berries; that when they left their winter camps, they followed the spring run of salmon as the run progressed upstream in the tributaries of the Columbia River; that the men would hunt and fish and the women would gather roots close to the hunting and fishing grounds; that as the year progressed, the Indians would have traveled further back toward the mountains and that ultimately and before returning once again to the winter camps, they would meet with the Nez Perce Indians for the purpose of trading the things that they had, such as roots and berries for buffalo robes and other things that the Nez Perce people had that could not be obtained by the Cayuse people; that this trade amounted to quite a bit.

Affiant further deposes and says that the Cayuse Indians cannot use their old fishing grounds for the reason that so many of the tributaries of the Columbia River are no longer used by the fish because they cannot ascend to the spawning grounds because the white people have constructed dams which they cannot get over; that in other streams the waste materials from mines is such that fish life cannot be supported; that aside from that, the habits of the younger generations are changing in that they are gradually adopting the white man's way of living and obtaining a livelihood either through farming or working on the sheep and cattle ranches;

That in addition to the foregoing, affiant recalls that when he was a young man a number of Cayuse Indians would go to Celilo on the Columbia River for the purpose of fishing the big salmon runs which were available at that point; that some of the Cayuse Indians, he understands, had always been accustomed to fishing at Celilo; that they were friends of the local people who lived there all the year around and that they did not have difficulty with regard to the use of the fishing stations located at that place; that the Indians who did not fish at Celilo would go there for the purpose of trading things that they acquired during the journey throughout the summer for things that the Celio residents had that could not be obtained in the Cayuse country; that this trading amounted to quite a bit. [305]

Affiant further deposes and says that it was customary for the Indians not to catch the salmon in the tributaries until after they had spawned for the reason that they knew there would be no salmon in the future if they did not permit the females to lay their eggs to be hatched and available in future years; that salmon was an important part of the food supply of the Cayuse Indians in the old days as well as at the present time, although he has noticed that the younger generations do not use as much salmon as their parents and ancestors were reported to have used; that he believes that this is the result of education to the white man's way of living, and since there are so few fish now as compared to what there were when he was a boy and what he understands was available prior to his birth, it is probably a good thing.

Further affiant sayeth not.

(Sgd.) James Kash Kash
James Kash Kash

Subscribed and sworn to before me this 8th day of May, 1942/3.

(Sgd.) Dan Ohlerking
Notary Public for Oregon
My commission expires
Nov. 28, 1943 [306]

AFFIDAVITS OF JAMES BILLY AND TOM JOE
UMATILLA INDIANS,
UMATILLA INDIAN RESERVATION, OREGON

STATE OF OREGON }
COUNTY OF UMATILLA } }SS.

James Billy, 63 years of age, and Tom Joe, 72 years of age, each being first duly sworn and put upon oath, severally deposes and says:

That they are full blood members of the Umatilla Indian Tribe and citizens of the United States of America residing on the Umatilla Indian Reservation, Oregon;

That they are Chiefs of the Umatilla Indians and were selected by the Umatilla Tribal Council for the purpose of giving information to Government representatives concerning the location of the fishing grounds, hunting districts, and root digging and berry gathering grounds of the Umatilla Indians as they existed prior to the coming of the white man and during affiants' lifetimes that they were selected for the purpose because during their respective lifetimes they have had occasion to visit practically all of such places, having lived and traveled about during their lifetimes throughout the country formerly owned by the Umatilla Indians prior to the coming of the white people; that as a result, they are personally familiar with the location of the various places and of the way they were used by the Indians ever since they were old enough to remember; that they are also familiar with the way the Indians used these places prior to their birth for the reason that when they were small boys and young men their parents and the older members of the Umatilla Tribe told them that these places had always been utilized by the members of their tribe; that it was customary for the Indians to pass this information along from generation to generation so that the young people would know the locations of the places as well as how and why they belonged to their tribe; that the things that were told them by their parents and others they believed to be true for the reason that there would have been no reason [307] for them to have told other than the truth with regard to these matters.

Affiants further depose and say that during the course of the summer of 1941, they, in company of David Temple and Gilbert Conner, members of the staff of the Umatilla Agency, visited such places for the purpose of giving the said David Temple and Gilbert Conner detailed information with regard to the exact location where the Indians established their camps; the places in the various streams where the fish were caught and the manner in which the fish were caught; that they also pointed out to the said David Temple and Gilbert Conner the location of the various hunting districts and root digging and berry gathering patches at the Umatilla Indians; that at that time the said David Temple and Gilbert Conner made a written record of the information thus obtained, which record affiants understand has been made a part of the official files of the Umatilla Indian Agency so that the information contained therein will be available after the older members of the tribe, who are the only remaining ones familiar with the location of all such places, have died.

Affiants further depose and say that prior to the coming of the white man and even when they were young men and had been removed to the reservation established by the treaty with the Government, the Umatilla Indians spent the major part of their time in the quest of fish, deer, elk, and roots and berries, which were their entire food supply at that time; that in those days and up until recent years the supply of fish available at the various places where the Umatilla Indians went each year was very plentiful; that in recent years as a result of settlement at the country and the destruction of fish by the white people, the supply is now very limited, although the Indians and especially the older ones depend upon fish to a large extent for their food supply;

That in the winter time the Indians would gather in large villages throughout the country roamed by them where they would remain until the snow had gone and it was time for them to start their journey to the various places to obtain food; that the Indians in these villages. would split up into smaller bands for the purpose at going to different places; that the main supply of their fish was obtained from the [308] Umatilla River and its tributaries; that the fish were caught with Indian traps and with spears and in some places small nets were used; that due to the number of Indians and the fact that they could not obtain enough fish or food at just a few of the various places they visited each year, it was necessary for them to split up into smaller groups so that each at them could obtain sufficient food along their line of march; that the Indians do not hunt and fish as much as they used to for the reason that the supply of game and fish has been so seriously depleted and also because when they leave the reservation they must obey the white man's law, which do not take into consideration the fact that the game and fish are only available at certain times in certain places; that the Indians still use roots and berries to supplement their diet, especially the older members of the tribe; that the younger members of the Umatilla Indians do not follow the same routine that their parents and their parents' parents did inasmuch as some of them farm their allotments or fish commercially at Celilo.

Affiants further depose and say that the Umatilla Indians have always been accustomed to going to the big Indian fisheries at the falls of the Columbia River, which is now known as Celilo; that they were friends of the Indians who lived at that place and that they visited them both for the purpose of fishing and for trading with them; that some of them were accustomed to visit and fish at Celilo each year, and that the trade amongst them even before the white man amounted to quite a bit for the reason that the Indians at Celilo were able to catch many more fish than those who remained in the Umatilla country and that they were anxious to trade their fish for the things that the Umatilla people were able to get that they were not in a position to acquire.

Affiants further depose and say that they, as well as the remaining few older members of the Umatilla Tribe, still obtain a considerable part of their food each year from the fish that they can catch at some of the old accustomed places; that they still go to the root digging and berry gathering patches to obtain supplies of these things which form a substantial part of the things they eat; that they would like to have the privileges which were promised to them at [309] the time they sold their lands to the Government kept by the white people so that they will always be able to enjoy living the way their ancestors did.

Further affiants sayeth not.

James Billy

Subscribed and sworn to before me this 8th day of May, 1942.

(Sgd.) Tom Joe
Tom Joe

Sworn to before me this 8th day of May, 1942

(Sgd.) Dan Ohlerking
(Seal) Notary Public for Oregon
My commission expires Nov. 28, 1943

AFFIDAVIT OF INTERPRETER

STATE OF OREGON }
COUNTY OF UMATILLA }   }SS.

Gilbert E. Conner, being first duly sworn, upon his oath deposes and says:

That he is 44 years of age, a three-quarters blood Indian of the Nez Perce Indian tribe and a citizen of the United States of America residing on the Umatilla Indian Reservation, Oregon;

That he was employed by the United states at the Umatilla Indian Agency, Oregon, and acted as official interpreter of the agency between members of the agency staff and the Indians of the various tribes residing on the Umatilla Reservation who are not able to speak the English language; that he is thoroughly conversant with the English language and with the language spoken by the members of the Umatilla Tribe of Indians who are allotted on the Umatilla Reservation; that he can translate the English language into the Umatilla Indian language and the Umatilla Indian language into The English language; [310]

That during the summer of 1941, affiant in the company of James Billy and Tom Joe, members of the Umatilla Indian Tribe, did visit the various places which the said James Billy and Tom Joe designated as the usual and accustomed fishing grounds, hunting districts and root digging and berry gathering patches of the Umatilla Indians; that at that time a written record of the location of such places was made and same was now a part of the official files of the Umatilla Indian Agency;

That on September 4, 1941, at the Umatilla Indian Agency, Oregon, affiant in the presence of the said James Billy and Tom Joe and Edward G. Swindell, Jr., U.S. Indian Service, did at the request of Mr. Swindell interrogate the said James Billy and Tom Joe, deponents in the foregoing affidavit, with regard to certain matters concerning the said usual and accustomed fishing, hunting, and other grounds of the Umatilla Indians, as well as with regard to the way in which those Indians and their ancestors obtained a livelihood; that he translated the questions of Mr. Swindell from the English language into the Umatilla Indian language which the said deponents speak and understand; that he translated the answers of the said deponents to Mr. Swindell's interrogatories from the Umatilla Indian language into the English language; that at that time a written record was made of the information given by the said deponents which information as then given has been reduced to the narrative form contained in the above and foregoing affidavits of the said deponents.

Affiant further deposes and says that on the 8th day of May, 1942, in the presence of James Billy and Tom Joe, the aforesaid deponents, and Mr. Swindell, he translated the information contained in the aforesaid affidavits from the English language into the Umatilla Indian language as said affidavits were read to affiant by Mr. Swindell; that the deponents therein told affiant that the said narrative affidavits contained information previously given by them to Mr. Swindell on September 4, 1941, and that they had, therefore, signed said affidavit because the information contained therein was true.

Further affiant sayeth not.

(Sgd.) Gilbert E. Conner
Gilbert E. Conner, Interpreter

Gilbert E. Conner personally appeared before me [311] this 8th day of May, 1942, and after having the foregoing affidavit read to him in my presence did acknowledge to me that the statements contained therein are true and that he executed same as his voluntary act.

Subscribed and sign to before me this 8th day of May, 1942.

(Sgd.) Dan Ohlerking
(Seal) Notary Public for Oregon
My commission expires
Nov. 28, 1943

AFFIDAVIT OF JAMES BILLY

STATE OF OREGON }
COUNTY OF WASCO }   }SS

James Billy, being first duly sworn and put upon oath deposes and says;

That he is 63 years of age and a full blood member of the Umatilla Indian Tribe and a citizen of the United States of America residing on the Umatilla Indian Reservation, Oregon;

That on the 8th day of May 1942, due to unavoidable causes, he was unable to be present at the Umatilla Indian Agency, Pendleton, Oregon, at the time the joint affidavit prepared for the execution of affiant and Tom Joe was read back to Tom Joe and interpreted from the English language into the Umatilla Indian language;

That on the 2nd day of June, 1942, however, the said above referred to affidavit was read back to affiant; that the information contained therein was translated from the English language into the Umatilla Indian language and it was the same information given by affiant and Tom Joe to Edward G. Swindell, Jr., U.S. Indian Service, under date of September 4, 1941, at the Umatilla

Indian Agency, Oregon; that said affidavit contained said information which is true to the best of affiant's knowledge and belief.

Further affiant sayeth not.

(Sgd.) James Billy
James Billy His Mark
Witness A.J. Barnhart [312]

Subscribed and sworn to before me this 2nd day of June, 1942.

(Sgd.) C.G. Davis
C.G. Davis
Special Examiner of Inheritance
U.S. Indian Service
The Dalles, Oregon

AFFIDAVIT OF INTERPRETER

STATE OF OREGON)
COUNTY OF UMATILLA) }SS

Andrew Barnhart, being first duly sworn, upon his oath deposes and says;

That he is 62 years of age, a full blood Indian of the Umatilla Indian Tribe and a citizen of the United States residing on the Umatilla Indian Reservation, Oregon;

That he is thoroughly conversant with the English language and with the language spoken by the Umatilla Indians and can translate the English language into the Umatilla Indian language and the Umatilla Indian language into the English language;

That on June 2, 1942, at The Dalles, Oregon, in the presence of James Billy, a full blood member of the Umatilla Indian Tribe, he translated an affidavit of Tom Joe, a Umatilla Indian Chief, dated May 8, 1942, from the English language into the Umatilla Indian language, which the said James Billy speaks and understands;

That on the same date, to-wit, June 2, 1942, affiant also translated to the said James Billy an affidavit prepared for the signature of said James Billy confirming the above referred to affidavit of Tom Joe;

That the said affidavit of May 8, 1942, above referred to contains information previously jointly given by Tom Joe and James Billy to a Government representative relative to the location of the usual and accustomed hunting and fishing grounds of the Umatilla Indians which were reserved to them in their treaty with the Government; [313]

That the said James Billy did on June 2 tell affiant that the affidavit of May 8, 1942, above referred to contained the information previously given by said deponents, Tom Joe and James Billy, to a Government representative on September 4, 1941, and that he had therefore subscribed to the affidavit prepared for his signature by placing his thumb mark thereon because the information contained therein was true to the best of said James Billy's knowledge and belief.

Further affiant sayeth not.

(Sgd.) Andrew Barnhart
Andrew Barnhart, Interpreter

Andrew Barnhart personally appeared before me this 8th day of July, 1942, and after having the foregoing affidavit read to him in my presence did acknowledge to me that the statements therein are correct and that he executed same as his voluntary act.

Subscribed and sworn to before me this 8th day of July, 1942.

(Sgd.) Henry Roe Cloud[82] [314]

AFFIDAVITS OF JIM KANINE, *IMOWTANIC*, AND FELICITE
WALLA WALLA INDIANS,
UMATILLA INDIAN RESERVATION, OREGON

STATE OF OREGON }
COUNTY OF UMATILLA} }SS.

Jim Kanine, being first duly sworn, upon his oath deposes and says:

That he is 70 years of age, a full blood member of the Walla Walla Indian tribe and a citizen of the United States of America residing on the Umatilla Indian Reservation, Oregon;

That he is what is known as the Principal Chief of the Walla Walla Indian Tribe and had been selected by the tribal council of the Indians of the Umatilla Reservation to give information with regard to the location of the usual and accustomed fishing grounds of the Walla Walla Indians; that he was selected for this purpose by reason of his position as head man of the tribe as well as the fact that during his lifetime he had occasion to visit a great number of the tribe's usual and accustomed fishing places; that, in addition to the knowledge he gained from personal observation at these various places, affiant was also informed with regard to their use by the Indians prior to the time of his birth through being told about such by his parents and the elder members of the Walla Walla Indian Tribe; that he was born along the Umatilla River, within the Umatilla Indian Reservation, and that he has spent his entire life on that reservation and traveling within the area formerly occupied by the Walla Walla Indians prior to the time of the creation of the reservation through treaty with the United States.

Affiant further deposes and says that prior to the coming of the white man he was informed that the Walla Walla Indian Tribe had roamed throughout a vast area in what is now the State of Oregon; that it was customary for the Indians to spend their winters in the valleys along the various streams within the country owned by the Walla Walla Indians; that with the [315] coming of spring the Indians from the various settlements would travel in the country owned by them throughout the spring and the course of the summer visiting not only the usual and accustomed fishing places where they each year obtained a supply of salmon for immediate use, as well as for preservation when the salmon were no longer in the river, but also the hunting, root digging, and berry gathering districts where they obtained deer and elk meat as well as roots and berries to supplement the fish which they caught in the various streams; that the routine of these Indians each year was substantially the same; that they would visit the various places at the proper times when they knew the fish would be available and that they would remain at such places until an adequate supply of fish had been obtained or the run had stopped, after which they would go on to other places where they knew the fish would soon appear; that in the course of the year they would of necessity have visited numerous places in order that they could have obtained an adequate livelihood; That when he was a boy, the Indians followed the same routine as did their ancestors even though in the course of time most of them received allotments on the Umatilla Indian Reservation; that this routine continued to be followed until the Indians as time passed were denied the right to utilize the various fishing places that had belonged to their ancestors or else the progress of white civilization had destroyed the run in the streams in which they were accustomed to obtain a supply of fish; that as time passed and the older members of the Walla Walla tribe died, the annual trips to these various places were made by a much smaller number of Indians than would do so when he was a boy; that the younger members of the tribe

---

[82] Henry Roe Cloud, Ho-Chunk with a Yale MA in Anthropology, divinity degree, and academy for native students, was by now posted to the NW at the end of his long career.

174

due to the change in their mode of living as a result of acquiring allotments on the reservation and the need to earn money so as to obtain the necessities of life from the white man's stores, did not care to visit the various places to obtain fish or to visit the hunting districts where their activities were subject to the strict laws of the white people;

That there are only a few of the older members of the Walla Walla tribe familiar with locations of all these places and some of them, when they are able to, still endeavor to go there to obtain food as they [316] used to; that they still go to the root and berry patches in the proper season to obtain a supply of these articles which form an important part of their food supply; that they still dry for future use as many fish as they can catch from the depleted runs which are still available to them; that the quantity thus obtained is not nearly sufficient for their needs but they make it serve as best they can; that the number of fish in the streams nowadays is very small compared to the number when he was a young man and prior to his birth, as he was informed with regard to the latter by his parents;

That in the old days the Indians caught their fish either with spears or by using Indian weirs or fish traps placed across the various streams; that the gear used at a particular place was determined by the conditions of the water; that he has fished using either of these methods at a large number of the old and accustomed fishing places; that the Indians did not catch more fish than they needed for immediate use and for drying in the future; that when they had sufficient fish for those purposes, they would remove the weirs from the stream so that the fish could go upstream and spawn; that the use of spears and weirs have been discontinued, the former having been replaced by grab hooks, which are used on the reservation, and in the latter, the white man's laws prohibit catching fish in that manner.

Affiant further deposes and says that the Indians of the Walla Walla Tribe prior to the coming of the white man were accustomed to making trips to the well-known Indian fishing grounds at the falls of the Columbia River, now known as Celilo; that they were friends and relatives of the Indians that lived at that place and they visited them for the purpose of trading some of the things they had for fish that the people at the falls had which were not obtainable on the Umatilla Reservation; that when they visited Celilo, they quite often caught fish themselves there with the consent of the people who lived at that place; that after the establishment of the reservation and the removal of all the Indians from their old homes to that place, the number who visited Celilo increased each year as the years went by, and the supply of salmon at the local usual and accustomed fishing places became smaller on account of the destruction of the spawning grounds by the white man through the construction of dams and in other ways; [317]

That the Indians of the Umatilla Reservation also used to exchange visits with the Nez Perce Indians living to the east; that these visits were for the purpose of renewing friendships and to trade amongst themselves for the things that were available to one group and not the other; that they would trade fish and roots and berries to the Nez Perces in exchange for buffalo robes, which could not be obtained very easily by the Walla Wallas; that the trade amongst the Indians amounted to quite a bit even long prior to the coming of the white man although, of course, no money was involved; the Indians only traded one kind of food for return in other kinds;

Affiant further deposes and says that during the Summer of 1941, in the company of *Imotanic*, a member of the Walla Walla Indian Tribe, and members of the staff of the Umatilla Agency, he visited the various usual and accustomed fishing places, hunting grounds, and root and berry patches of the Walla Walla Indians for the purpose of pointing out the location thereof to the members of the Agency staff; that, affiant during the course of his life actually camped at and used these various places for the purpose of obtaining a food supply; that the length of time the Indians would spend at each place would be determined by the amount of food available there; that ordinarily it would be from two to three weeks at a time, after which they would move on to the next place; that the order in which these places were used was in accordance with a well-organized procedure which the Indians had been following from as long back as they have any knowledge;

That at the time these places were visited with the members of the agency staff, comprised of David Temple, Road Engineer, and Gilbert Conner, such individuals made a written record of the exact locations of the old camping grounds used for fishing, hunting, root digging, and berry gathering; that he understands such record of the location of the places in question was made in order that it would be available in the agency files after the death of affiant and such other older members of the tribe who are the only remaining members thereof familiar with such locations.

Further affiant sayeth not.

(Sgd.) Jim Kanine
Jim Kanine [318]

Subscribed and sworn to before me this 8th day of May, 1942.

(Sgd.) Dan Ohlerking
(Seal) Rotary Public for Oregon
My commission expires
Nov. 28, 1943

AFFIDAVIT

STATE OF OREGON }
COUNTY OF UMATILLA } } SS

Imowtanic, being first duly sworn upon his oath deposes and says:

That he is 79 years of age, a full blood member of the Walla Walla Indian Tribe and a citizen of the United States of America residing on the Umatilla Indian Reservation in the state of Oregon;

That he was selected by the tribal council of the Umatilla Indians because of his age and personal knowledge to assist Chief Jim Kanine in giving information to Government representatives with regard to the location of the usual and accustomed fishing grounds of the Walla Walla Indians as well as the location of their hunting districts, root digging, and berry patches; that during the course of his life, he has had occasion to visit practically all of the various places formerly used by the Walla Walla Indians prior to the coming of the white man, some of which are still used by a few of the older members of the Walla Walla tribe; that during the course of the Summer of 1941, he, in company with the said Chief Jim Kanine and David Temple, and Gilbert Conner, members of the staff of the Umatilla Indian Agency, visited such places for the purpose of giving the said David Temple and Gilbert Connor detailed information with regard to where the Indians camped and fished and where they caught their fish; that at that time the said David Temple and Gilbert Conner made a written record of said information, which affiant understands has been made a part of the official files of the Umatilla Indian Agency, Oregon, so that the information contained therein will be available after the older members of the tribe, who are the only remaining ones familiar with the location of all such places, have died.
[319]

Affiant further deposes and says that on the 5th day of September 1941, he was present at the Umatilla Indian Agency, Umatilla Indian Reservation, Oregon, when the said Chief Jim Kanine gave certain information to Edward G. Swindell, Jr., U.S. Indian Service, with regard to the location of the various fishing grounds, hunting, root digging, and berry districts of the Walla Walla Indian tribe, as well as with regard to the manner in which said Indians lived ever since he can remember, as well as how they lived prior to his birth;

That he listened carefully to the questions propounded by Mr. Swindell to the aforesaid Chief Jim Kanine and also to the answers he gave in response to such questions; that if he had been asked the same questions, his answers so far as relating to things which occurred during his own lifetime and within his own personal knowledge would have been the same as those given by the said Chief Jim Kanine; that so far as the information given by the said Chief Kanine relates to things that occurred prior to his lifetime, his answers would have been the same for the reason that when he was a small boy and a young man, his parents told him substantially the same things;

That affiant therefore can and does confirm the statements made by the said Chief Jim Kanine as being true to the best of his knowledge and belief.

Affiant further deposes and says that on the 8th Day of May, 1942, he was again present with Chief Jim Kanine when an affidavit containing the information previously given by the said Chief Jim Kanine was read back to him by Mr. Swindell and interpreted by Gilbert Conner of· the Umatilla Indian Agency; that the information as originally given by the said Chief Jim Kanine was contained in the said affidavit and that said information is true; that the deponent therein, Chief Jim Kanine acknowledged such information as being that previously given by him and that he, therefore, executed said affidavit in the presence of affiant, the interpreter, Gilbert Conner, and Mr. Swindell.

Further affiant sayeth not.

(Sgd.) Imowtanic His Mark
Imowtanic

Subscribed and sworn to before me this 8th day of May, 1942.

(Sgd.) Dan Ohlerking
(Seal) Notary Public for Oregon
My commission expires
Nov. 28, 1943 [320]

AFFIDAVIT

STATE OF OREGON }
COUNTY OF UMATILLA }   }SS.

Felicite, being first duly sworn, upon her oath deposes and says:

That she is 79 years of age, a full blood member of the Walla Walla Indian tribe and a citizen of the United States of America residing on the Umatilla Indian Reservation, Oregon;

That on September 5, 1941, she was present at the Umatilla Indian Agency, Umatilla Indian Reservation, Oregon, when her husband, *Imowtanic*, and Chief Jim Kanine of the Walla Walla Indian tribe gave information about the fishing places, hunting districts, and root and berry gathering patches of the Walla Walla Indians to Edward G. Swindell, Jr., United States Indian Service; that she listened carefully both to the questions propounded by Mr. Swindell to the aforesaid Chief Kanine and *Imowtanic* and to the answers they gave in response to such questions; that the things they told to Mr. Swindell which related to events that occurred during affiant's lifetime are true as a result of a personal knowledge thereof and that as to the things which occurred prior to her lifetime, she believes to be true for the reason that when she was a small girl her parents told her substantially the same things.

Affiant further deposes and says that on 8th day of May, 1942, she was again present at the Umatilla Indian Agency in the presence of Chief Jim Kanine, *Imowtanic*, and Mr. Swindell when an affidavit containing the information previously given by the said Chief Kanine and *Imowtanic* was read back to them by Mr. Swindell and interpreted by Gilbert Conner of the Umatilla Indian Agency; that the said Chief Kanine and Imowtanic in the presence of affiant did acknowledge that the information contained in the said affidavits was the same information previously given and that they, therefore, executed said affidavit as their voluntary act. [321]

Further affiant sayeth not.

(Sgd.) Felicite Her Mark
Felicite

Subscribed and Sworn to before me this 8th day of May, 1942.

(Sgd.) Dan Ohlerking
(Seal) Notary Public for Oregon
My commission expires Nov. 28, 1943

AFFIDAVIT OF INTERPRETER

STATE OF OREGON }
COUNTY OF UMATILLA }   }SS.

Gilbert E. Conner, being first duly sworn, upon his oath deposes and says:

That he is 44 years of age, a three-quarters blood Indian of the Nez Perce Indian tribe and a citizen of the United States of America residing on the Umatilla Indian Reservation, Oregon; that he was employed by the United States at the Umatilla Indian Agency, Oregon, and acting as official interpreter of the agency between members of the agency staff and the Indians of the various tribes residing on the Umatilla Reservation who are not able to speak the English language; that he is thoroughly conversant with the English language and with the language spoken by the members of the Walla Walla Tribe of Indians who are allotted on the Umatilla Reservation; that he can translate the English language into the Walla Walla Indian language and the Walla Walla Indian language into the English language;

That during the Summer of 1941, affiant in the company of Chief Jim Kanine and Imowtanic, members of the Walla Walla Indian Tribe, and David Temple, Road Engineer of the Umatilla Indian Agency, did visit the various places which the said Chief Jim Kanine and Imowtanic designated as the usual and accustomed fishing grounds, hunting districts and root digging and berry gathering patches of the Walla Walla Indians; [322] that at that time a written record of the location of such places was made and same was now a part of the official files of the Umatilla Indian Agency;

That on September 5, 1941, at the Umatilla Indian Agency, Oregon, affiant in the presence of the said Chief Jim Kanine and Imowtanic, as well as in the presence of Felicite, wife of *Imowtanic*, and Edward G. Swindell, Jr., U.S. Indian Service, did at the request of Mr. Swindell interrogate the said Chief Kanine, Imowtanic, and Felicite, deponents in the foregoing affidavits, with regard to certain matters concerning the said usual and accustomed fishing, hunting, and other grounds of the Walla Walla Indians, as well as with regard to the way in which those Indians and their ancestors obtained a livelihood; that he translated the questions of Mr. Swindell from the English language into the Walla Walla Indian language which the said deponents speak and understand; that he translated the answers of the said deponents to Mr. Swindell's interrogatories from the Walla Walla Indian language into the English language; that at that time a written record was made of the information given by the said deponents which information as then given has been reduced to the narrative form contained in the above and foregoing affidavits of the said deponents.

Affiant further deposes and says that on the 8th day of May, 1942, in the presence of Chief Jim Kanine, *Imowtanic*, and Felicite, the aforesaid deponents, and Mr. Swindell, he translated the information contained in the aforesaid affidavits from the English language into the Walla Walla Indian language as said affidavits were read to affiant by Mr. Swindell; that the deponents therein told affiant that the said narrative affidavits contained information previously given by them to Mr. Swindell on September 5, 1941, and that they had, therefore, signed said affidavit because the information contained therein was true.

Further affiant sayeth not.

(Sgd.) Gilbert E. Conner

Gilbert E. Conner, Interpreter [323]

Gilbert E. Conner personally appeared before me this 8th day of May, 1942 and after having the foregoing affidavit read to him in my presence did acknowledge to me that the statements contained therein are true and that he executed same as his voluntary act.

Subscribed and sworn to before me this 8th day of May, 1942

(Sgd.) Dan Ohlerking

Notary Public for Oregon

(Seal) My commission

expires Nov. 28, 1943

PART III
APPENDICES "A" and "B"
CONSISTING OF MINUTES
OF
TREATY COUNCILS
AND
A DIGEST
OF
TREATY PROVISIONS

TRIBES OF MIDDLE OREGON

The minutes of the council held at Wasco, near The Dalles, Oregon Territory, June 22-25, 1855 between Joel Palmer, Superintendent of Indian Affairs, O.T., and the Wasco, Upper and Lower Des Chutes Bands of Walla Wallas, et al, known collectively as "The Tribes of Middle Oregon" have not been included. Those minutes were omitted for the reason that the non-reservation, fishing, hunting and miscellaneous rights of those Indians were subsequently relinquished by the Treaty of November 15, 1865, 14 Stat. 751, 2 Kappler 908. The council proceedings were substantially the same as those herein reproduced, i.e., the promises made the Indians were the same as was also the concern of the various chiefs and headmen regarding their right to continue to use traditional fishing and hunting grounds.

Indian Office file reference: "File Box – Indian Talks, Councils, etc." – Received in Indian Office, September 11, 1855. The original minutes, however, probably are now filed in the National Archives Building in Washington. [324 COPY]

******

Wash. W. 537/1855

RECORDS OF THE PROCEEDINGS OF THE COMMISSION
TO HOLD TREATIES WITH THE INDIAN TRIBES IN
WASHINGTON TERRITORY AND THE BLACKFOOT COUNTRY

1854 Olympia, W.T. December 7th Governor Isaac I. Stevens organized the Commission by appointing James Doty, Secretary, George Gibbs, Surveyor, H.A. Goldsborough, Commissary, and Frank Shaw, interpreter.

Col. M.T. Simmons, Special Agent for the Puget Sound District, was present.

The Commissioner read a letter addressed by him to the Secretary of the Interior concerning charges preferred against M.T. Simmons, Special Agent and containing extracts from a letter from Secretary C.F.H. Mason to the Commissioner upon the same subject in both of which letters the said charges were emphatically denied and refuted. The letter was ordered on file.

The Commissioner spoke of general operations among the Indian Tribes in Washington Territory and the necessity of speedily concluding Treaties with them and placing them on Reservations.

The Secretary then read Treaties lately concluded by the Commissioner of Indian Affairs with the Ottos [Otoe] and Missouri Indians and the Omahas, and their provisions were fully discussed, and the proper form for Treaties with Tribes west of the Cascade Mountains was considered.

After considerable discussion upon Reservations, Fishing Stations, Farms, Schools etc. the Commissioner directed Mr. George Gibbs to prepare a programme of a Treaty in accordance with the views of the Commission.

The question of employing a small schooner for the use of the Commission and transportation of Indian Goods came up, and it was decided to employ such schooner at $700 per month manned and victualled by the owner.

The Commission then adjourned to December 10th.

Dec. 10th – The Commission met and duly organized – Mr. Gibbs presented the outline Draft of a Treaty, which after [325 COPY 2] discussion and light modification was adopted as the basis of the Treaties to be held with the Tribes upon the Sound and the Pacific Coast, and is as follows:

"It is proposed that all the Indians to be first treated with, be seen and summoned [!!] to meet at the mouth of the Nisqually on the 24th inst. In the meantime the general purport of the assembly to be explained: The details to be settled there. The reserve to be agreed on and set apart. Gov. Stevens to be then notified that he may attend and conclude the treaty – he to read them an address and a feast then to be given.

"The first party to be composed of Indians from Ininity Prairie to the Puyallup – next, probably Hood's Canal, as Reserves will be located there – then the Dwamish and so on down the Sound to Bellingham Bay and the Straits – subsequently by land the lower coast, Cowlitz and Columbia Rivers."

Heads of Proposed Treaties.

Art. I The following named Tribes and Bands cede to the United States all their lands whatsoever.

Art. II There is however reserved to the use of said tribes the following tracts, viz: The rights of fishing at common and accustomed places if further secured [sic] to them: Proviso against Stated [Staked] or fenced claims.

May be removed from one Reservation to another on payment for improvements and cost of removal.

Art. III The Tribes agree to remove to and settle on the aforesaid Reserves within one year after ratification of the Treaty, or sooner if means are furnished them.

Art. IV In consideration of the cession the United States agree to pay the said Tribes etc. the sum of $ _____ (rate of $10. 00 for chiefs, $7. 50 for sub chief's, $5 for Tillicum, to be paid in annual installments decreasing at the rate of 5 per cent per annum). Note – The sum calculated on this principle to be stated in gross in the Treaty. Thus 650 Nisquallys at $5 per head is $3,250 or $32,500 in twenty years to be expended in such manner as the President shall direct. [326 COPY 2]

Art. V To enable them to move and settle on their Reserves to build houses for their chiefs, as also to indemnify settlers, if any, on lands reserved. The United States further agree to pay a <u>bonus</u> equal to the first years annuity.

Art. VI President authorized to divide their land and assign lots to heads of families. The United States to maintain at the Central Agency, an Agricultural School free to their children in common with other Tribes and provide Medical Attendance.

Art. VII The annuities not to be taken to pay debts of individuals.

Art. VIII The Indians agree to be on friendly terms with the whites. Depredations to be made good out of annuity money. The United States also to indemnify Indians for horses stolen by the whites.

     Not to make war on any other tribes but submit differences to agent. Depredations by one tribe against another to be paid out of annuities. Citizens of the United States may safely pass through their reserve. Roads may be run through them on compensation being made. Injuries committed by whites towards them not to be revenged, but on complaint being made they shall be tried by the Laws of the United States and if convicted the offenders punished. Injuries by Indians to whites to be in like manner prosecuted and punished by law.

     Every tribe to be responsible for offences committed by its people or by others in their lands. Chiefs in the first instance to be looked to and required to deliver up criminals at once – To be in return supported in the exercise of their lawful authority, by the Government.

Art. IX No white man shall be allowed to reside on any Reservations and Indians may at any time be compelled by Superintendent to stay there.

Art. X Liquor to be excluded from Reserves – If brought, any Indian or white man may seize and destroy it. A drunken Indian to forfeit his share of the annuities.

Art. XI Tribes may punish offenders of their own Tribe for any offence committed, according to their own laws, a majority of the Chiefs forming a court for the trial of all offenders. [327 4]

Art XII. They agree to free all slaves held at the time of the treaty, and to make no more.

Art XIII. System of Apprenticeship introduced.

Art. XIV. They agree not to trade at Vancouver Island, nor shall foreign Indians be permitted to reside on their lands.

"In regard to the Division or Tribes into Districts, and settling them upon Reserves, the following were to be considered as the utmost limits to be allowed."

PROBABLE RESERVES

                                      Souls

1. From Puyallup to Ininity Prairie   638

     Say three villages, Squawskin, Nisqually, Puyallup. Perhaps all may be removed to Squawskin.

2. D'Wamish, Suquamish etc.   454

     One village on East side of Hoods Canal

3. Snoquahoo and Snohomish

     One at mouth of Snohomish River

4. Skagit, Kikiallis etc.
       One near mouth of Skagit River
       One near mouth of
5. Lummy, Nooksaht etc.
       One on Samish   551
       One on Lumni
6. Sklallams, Chemacums and Skokomish   982
       One on Hood's Canal
       One on the straits
7. Makahs etc. on Coast   585
       Two Villages.
8. Cowlitz and Upper Chehalis
       Two Villages.
9. Chinooks and Lower Chehalis
       One on north side of Grays Harbor.
10. Quiniutt [Quinault].
       One on the River. [328 COPY 5]

"It is however proposed, if practicable to remove all the Indians on the East side of the Sound as far as the Snohomish: as also the S'Klallams to Hood's Canal, and generally to admit as few Reservations as possible, with a view of finally concentrating them in one.

December 24th – Governor Stevens left Olympia and proceeded to the Treaty Ground on the *She-na-nam* or Medicine Creek.

December 25th – The Programme of the Treaty was fully explained to the Indians present – At the evening session of the Commission the Draft – of the Proposed Treaty was read, and after a full discussion of its provisions by the gentlemen present, viz Messrs. Simmons, Gibbs, and Doty, it was ordered to be engrossed.

December 26th Treaty Ground. – Present Gov. Isaac I. Stevens, Commissioner, Hon. C.H. Mason, Secretary of the Territory, Mr. Doty – Secretary to the Commission, Mr. Gibbs, Surveyor, Lieu't W.A. Slaughter U.S.A, Col. M.T. Simmons, Special Agent and Frank Shaw, Interpreter. About 9 o'clock the Indians assembled to the number of 630 and Gov. Stevens addressed them as follows:

"This is a great day for you and for us, – A day of peace and friendship between you and the whites for all time to come. You are about to be paid for your lands, and the Great Father has sent me today to treat with you concerning the payment – the Great Father lives far off – He has many children – some of these children come here when he knew but little of them, or of the Indians, and he sent me to inquire into these things. We went through this County this last year, learned your numbers and saw your wants. We felt much for you, and went to the Great Father to tell him what we had Seen – The Great Father felt for his children – he pitied them and he has sent me here today to express those feelings and to make a Treaty for your benefit. The Great Father has many white children who come here, some to build mills: Some to make farms: some to fish – and the Great Father wishes you to have homes, pasture for your horses and fishing places, He wishes you to learn to farm and your children to go to a good school, and he now wants me to make a bargain with you, in which you sell your lands and in return be provided that all these things – You will have certain lands set apart for your homes and receive yearly payments of Blankets, axes, etc. – All this is written down in this paper which will be read to you. If it is good you will sign it, and I will then send it to the Great Father – I think he will [329 COPY 6] be pleased with it and say it is good: but if not, if he wishes it different, he will say so and send it back and then if you agree to it, it is a fixed bargain and payment will be made."

The Treaty was then read Section by Section and explained to the Indians by the Interpreter and every opportunity given them to discuss it.

Gov. Stevens then said: "The paper has been read to you, is it good? If it is good we will sign it: but if you dislike it in any point, say so now – After signing we have some goods to give you and next summer will give you more: and after that you must wait until the paper comes back from the Great Father – The goods now given are not a payment for your lands: they are merely a friendly present."

The Indians had some discussion, and Gov. Stevens then put the question, "Are you ready? If so I will sign it" – there were no objections, and the Treaty was then signed by Gov. I.I. Stevens and the Chiefs, Delegates and headmen on the part of the Indians and duly witnessed by the Secretary, Special Agent and seventeen citizens present.

The presents – goods and provisions were then opened and apportioned in the just ratio to the three chiefs of the Puyallup, Nisqually and Sqawkson Tribes, and were by them distributed to their people and the Indians present included in the Treaty.

Towards evening Mr. Swan arrived with 29 Indians of the Puyallup Tribe and reported twenty more on the way who, starting three days ago had been detained by bad weather. These forty-nine Indians not having received any presents, the Commissioner decided on sending them presents from Olympia in the ratio of l/12th of the goods given at the Treaty.

At any evening session at the Commission, all the members being present, the Treaty was very fully discussed and the provisions necessary to be incorporated in the further treaties to be concluded with Indians upon the Sound and Coast. The question of Reservations was considered and the number proper to he allowed. Messrs Simmons and Gibbs thought that several Reserves would be necessary for the remaining Tribes on the Sound on account of their differences in language and dispositions – and because they needed a number of fishing stations. [330 7]

The Question of a Central Agency, Farm and agricultural School was very fully discussed and unanimously voted as necessary for the civilization of the Indians and as no more than justice to them considering that they cede to the United States so large an amount of valuable land.

It was also thought necessary to allow them to fish at all accustomed places, since this would not in any manner interfere with the rights of citizens, and was necessary for the Indians to obtain a subsistence.

It was deemed absolutely necessary that slavery among the Indians on this Territory should cease, because it is a direct consequence of war upon neighboring Tribes, which by Treaty is prohibited.

Question of employing a physician to reside at the Central Agency, also Teachers, Artificers and Employees, was considered and voted necessary and the following estimate approved of.

One Township of Land to be Reserved for the Central Agency

One Surgeon at $1500 per year
One Teacher and wife   1500   "   "
1 Farmer   750   "   "
1 Blacksmith   750   "   "
1 Carpenter   750   "   "
Employees   1200   "   "
Medicines   1000   "   "
Support of 200 children   5000 @ $25 each
Necessary buildings   5000
Materials Tools etc. Making 2550
                            $20,000 for the first year and a yearly expenditure thereafter of.

The question of bringing all the remaining Tribes upon the Sound together in one Treaty, and if possible locating them upon one Reservation, was fully canvasied [canvassed] and different opinions entertained. Gov. Stevens and the Secretary thought it practicable – Messrs. Simmons, Gibbs and Goldsborough dissented – After considerable argument and explanation of the views of the Indian Department upon the question of Reservations, and after taking the opinion and advice of the gentlemen present, Gov. Stevens decided to bring all the Indians upon the East side of the Sound and the Islands into one Treaty to be held at the mouth of the Sno-ho-mish River on the 21st of January 1855, and in one week thereafter to treat with the Tribes on the West side of the Sound and upon the Straits, at some point on the west side of said Sound. [331 8]

Messrs. Simmons, Gibbs, Goldsborough and Shaw were accordingly directed to prepare and collect the Indians for the Treaties. ·

And then the Commissioner directed the Secretary to prepare a copy of all the proceedings of this Commission, to be forwarded with a copy of the Treaty to the Commissioner of Indian Affairs.

Where upon the Commission adjourned

(Signed) James Doty
Secretary [332 1]

Journal of the Expedition from the Conclusion
of the Treaty of Nisqually.

1854 Wednesday Dec. 21 Governor Stevens and Messrs. Mason and Doty returned to town in the morning – It was arranged that the remainder of the party should proceed with a preliminary reconnaissance of the reservations at the Meridian Line and on Commencement Bay, and that Messrs. Simmons and Shaw should thence proceed to call in the tribes for the remaining Treaties. Mr. Doty being directed to proceed to the Eastern side of the Mountains to prepare the Indians for future negotiations, George Gibbs was appointed Acting Secretary of the Commission. In the afternoon the party went on board the Schooner *R.B. Potter*, Capt. Fowler, which had been chartered for the trip and the vessel shifted her anchorage to opposite Shaw's House.

Thursday 28th Mr. Gibbs, assisted by F. Shaw and others of the party made a preliminary survey of the tract of land adjoining Shaw's Claim, and lying one mile west of the Meridian, within which the reserve was to be located – The form of the shore, not thoroughly understood when the Treaty was drawn up did not permit it being made in a square form as first contemplated – The following diagram exhibits the shore line in connection with the Section lines surveyed. The Reservation recommended to be adopted accordingly is thus described –

"The Northern half of Section 26, the North Eastern Quarter of Section 27, Fractional Section 23 – and the Eastern half of Section 22 – containing according to the U.S. Land Survey, twelve hundred and four acres, the whole in range one (1) west, township nineteen (19) north, and situated on the South side of Puget Sound, near the mouth of *She-nah-nam* or Medicine Creek, one mile west of the Willamette Meridian."

The Tract thus selected was duly approved by Gov. Stevens and adopted as a reservation under the Treaty and subject to the ratification thereof.

Friday Dec. 29th The state of the weather not permitting any further examinations at this time, and it being desirable to continue the preliminary surveys, the party proceeded in the Schooner to Commencement Bay. Stopping at Steilacoom, and anchoring at Swan and Riley's on the evening of Saturday 30th Jany – The next day tile weather [333 2] being stormy the Surveyor landed with a party to enable Messrs. Simmons and Shaw to proceed in the Schooner to Seattle – Major Goldsborough accompanied them, taking the steamer at that place for Olympia and the Schooner returned to Commencement Bay – The acting Secretary notified Governor Stevens by letter of the proceedings to this date.

Monday January 1st 1855 *Choche-oot-luts* Reservation. The Surveyor commenced the examination of the reserve on Commencement Bay beginning on the East line of Swan and Riley's Claim and running thence along the beach for a mile and a half in a South Easterly direction. It was found that the shore line, here, as in the first case precluded laying off the reserve in a square form as contemplated by the Treaty, and a settler having taken a claim on the West side of Point Harmon the line was not extended further – This reservation affords a good site for a village, with ground for potato patches and a small stream at which the Indians take their winter salmon, a high bluff, say 150 feet, rises a short distance back from the water at the western extremity, but approaches nearer the water and ranges along it at its eastern end. The woods being very thick and filled with underbrush, it was found necessary to employ Indians to cut in advance of the Surveyor – The next day (Jan. 2nd), therefore, a party was set to work, and a trail cut for half a mile through the woods on both the eastern and western sides. As the Indians will require the shore only, this tribe being exclusively fishing Indians, it was not seemed advisable at this time to continue it around the whole tract. The form of the reservation will appear from the diagram. The weather during all this time was very stormy, with squalls of snow and heavy rain and work in the woods was next to impracticable.

Description of Choche-oot-luts Reservation

Beginning at a point on tile beach, on the South side of Commencement Bay, marked by a large white fir tree, blazed on three sides and standing on the north east corner of Swan and Riley's Claim, thence along the beach and following its meandering one and a half miles in a south Easterly direction to a point marked by a fallen tree bearing the letters U.S.R. behind which three cedar trees are conspicuously blazed: thence south one and a half miles: thence west about one mile to a point due south or the place of beginning, and thence north about two and a half miles to said place of beginning – Containing in all about two sections or 1280 acres of land. [334 3]

This like the former was subsequently approved by Governor Stevens as a provisional reserve.

Some of the Puyallup Indians having been prevented by stress of weather from reaching the Treaty Ground, Gov. Stevens had directed a proportionate quantity of goods to be sent down and distributed to them. This was accordingly done at this place on Wednesday January 3d. And then having concluded its business embarked again and proceeded to Seattle.

For the purpose of exhibiting the forms of the several reservations as far as practicable the remaining one assigned to the tribes included in the first Treaty as found on the books of the Land Survey, is also herewith given.

A Copy Attest –
George Gibbs
Acting Secr. [335 1]

1855 Friday January 5th The Schooner reached and anchored at Seattle on Thursday, and to day Major Goldsborough returned in the steamer from Olympia the next day (Jan. 6) proceeded to Skagit had to take up Col. Simmons: but the wind being too heavy to permit a landing, went round and anchored at Point Elliott. On the 9th took Col. Simmons on board and proceeded with him to Port Gamble, where arrangements were made to bring in all the S'klallams, Skokomish, etc., at Point No Point, the week succeeding the convention of the other tribes at Point Elliott. I and other returned to Point Elliott and came to anchor.

January 9th Tuesday Major Goldsboro selected the place of encampment and the tents were sent ashore and pitched. The succeeding day the goods were landed and the party went into camp to enable Messrs. Simmons and Goldsborough to return to Seattle in the Schooner, the latter to purchase potatoes and other provision, and the former to talk with the Dwamish Indians. The Snoqualmoos under Patkanam were already upon the ground and the other tribes were expected in due time, but information had been received that the Dwamish had been influenced to remain at home, and insist upon treating upon their own ground. On Thursday, Mr. Shaw returned from Bellingham bay having been entirely successful in engaging the Lummis and other northern bands to come in, except the *hockshks* [Nooksacks], whose country was inaccessible from ice in the river.

Jany. 12th Friday Mr. Gibbs with a party of Indians examined the shore of Admiralty inlet from Point Elliott southward for some miles with a view to its fitness for a central reserve. The banks were found to be bluff with the exception of one or two small points and unfit for landing in canoes, an absolute requisite in choosing ground for the Indians. The country too was broken and very heavily timbered. In consequence, it was deemed proper to turn the examination in another direction.

The Skagits under their head Chief Goliah,[83] arrived to day and were received in great form by the Snoqualmoos. Each party drew up on the beach in single file and marched past the other, saluting with the sign of the cross & taking off their hats. They then counter marched, & broke into knots to exchange news. The whole was done with much ceremony & appearance of respect. [336 2]

---

[83] [An 1856 census by agent Robert Fay has Goliah at 6 feet, 55, slim, with 16 wards.]

Saturday Jan'y 13th The surveyor started in a canoe with Indians to examine the shore of Port Gardner and the mouth of the Snohomish. With the exception of the low flat at Point Elliott, which though very well suited for a single village, is not of sufficient extent for a general reserve, this shore does not afford a suitable location until reaching the bight formed by the point at the mouth of the Snohomish, where a low valley extends through to the river nor is this large enough for the purpose contemplated. The river itself was at this time very high, its banks which are low and covered with a forest of spruce & cypress were flooded. The stream very rapid and filled with draft. Upon such an examination as it was possible to give it at the season, Mr. Gibbs came to the conclusion that the peninsula lying between the Snohomish river and the inlet was unsuited to a general reserve, and that the anchorage and landing, being exposed to the northerly winds, formed a further substantiated objection. He accordingly turned his attention to the north side of the river and on

Tuesday January 16 being the first day that the weather permitted he crossed over to, and examined the country on the creek entering this bay from the North East. There is a flat of about 30 acres on the point on the north side of the Snohomish upon which there is a small village. The inner bay is about 1½ miles wide here, & the Creek enters through low marshy land. A short distance up however its banks rise above the level of freshet. It is a tide slough, into which a small stream enters. The Snohomish formerly had a village at this place, on the north or right bank, and the land behind it is level & the woods partially burnt off. Col. Simmons had crossed from here to the *skotuchwamish* river and reported that the country is of the same description the whole distance, and is very rich. Sufficient examination was given to satisfy the surveyor that for a special reserve this creek afforded an admirable situation, or that if it was considered desirable to establish the general reserve in this region, by the purchase of the claims & built at Tulalip bay, a position could be obtained of a township, fitted in all respects for an agency, having a harbor to which a vessel of ordinary size could have access, perfectly safe & with abundant good land for farms.

Wednesday Jan 17 The Lummi and some other northern bands were now in, & the Dwamish began to arrive. In the evening the Schooner returned from Seattle. [337 3]

Thursday Jan 18 A further examination was given to the land between Point Elliott & the Snohomish by penetrating some distance into the woods, the broken character of the country rendering the unfitness of that place certain.

Sunday Jan 21 The Snohomish & all the tribes expected at this place were now in. Governor Stevens arrived to day in the steamer *Major Simpkins*, accompanied by the Secretary Mason & Dr. C.H. Hitchcock of San Francisco. In the afternoon after receiving a verbal report on the country from the Surveyor and upon the views & feelings of the Indians from the Agent, he appointed George Gibbs, Secretary to the western Commission and directed a draft of a treaty to be made in pursuance of the principles contained in that made at *Shenaknam*. The subject of the reservations was fully considered and those selected which were embodied in the paper. A careful census of the Indians assembled and an estimate of the number of each tribe absent from the ground had in the meantime been made by Messrs. Simmons and Shaw on which the calculation of annuity might be based. The number on the ground reached 2300, and sticks were returned for 700 absentees, chiefly old men, women and children.

TREATY OF MUCKLETEOH ~ POINT ELLIOTT.

Monday Jan 22 The Indians were all convened, the four head chiefs, Seattle, Patkanam, Goliah and *Chowitshoot* being seated in front, the sub chiefs in a second line, and the various tribes in separate groups. Gov. Stevens then addressed them as follows:

Gov. Stevens: "My Children! You are not my children because you are the the [sic] fruit of my loins, but because you are children for whom I have the same feeling as if you were the fruit of my loins. You are my children for whom I will strenuously labor all the days of my life until I shall be taken hence. What will a man do for his own children? He will see that they are well cared for, that they have clothes to protect them against the cold and rain, that they have food to guard them against hunger, and as for thirst you have your own glorious streams in which to quench it. I want you as my children to be fed and clothed, and made comfortable and happy. I find that many of you are Christians, and I saw among you yesterday the sign of the cross, which I think the most holy of all signs. I address you therefore mainly as Christians, who know that this life is a preparation for the life to come. You want not simply a home on this earth where you and your children will be cared for, but you want a home for the next world. [338 4]

"You understand well my purpose, and you want now to know the special things we propose to do for you. We want to place you in homes where you can cultivate the soil, raising potatoes and other articles of food, and where you may be able to pass in canoes over the waters of the sound and catch fish, and back to the mountains to get roots and berries. The great Father desires this and why am I able to say this. There are two thousand men, women and children who have always treated white men well. Did I not come through your country one year twice? Were not many of you now present witnesses of the fact? (All said Gov. Stevens came) Did I then make promises to you? (All say he did not) I am glad to hear this because I came through your country not to make you promises but to know what you were, to know what you wanted, to know your grievances and to report to the great father about you. I have been to the Great Father and told him your condition. Here in this [Puget] sound you make journeys of three and four days, but I made a journey of fifty days to the Great Father on your behalf. You live on this shore but I went to the great shores of the East to report to the Great father about you. I told the great Father that I had traveled six moons in reaching this country and had never found an Indian who would not give me food, raimant [raiment] and animals to forward me and mine to the great country of the west. I told him that I was among 10,000 Indians, and they took me to their lodges and offered me all they had, and here I will pause and ask you again if you do not know that I have been absent several months on this business. (all shout yes) So you all know that I went to the Great Father, and you all know that I have come back. I went away but I left a good and strong man in my place. I call upon Gov. Mason to speak to you."

Gov. Mason now took the stand and addressed Indians as follows:
Gov. Mason: "My friends, when the Great Chief went away he left me as the Chief over all of you. Whenever you came to me and represented your wants and grievances, I did the best I could to remedy them. I did not have much to do with you, but I did for you all I could. You asked me where the great Chief had gone, and when he would return. I told all of you that came to see me that he had gone to see our Great Father at Washington. I told you that he would tell the Great Father all about your wants, and if it was good with the great Father, he would return and right them. I told you that he would treat with you about your lands. The great Chief has been to the Great Father and [339 5] he has returned to you he has called you together today and

you all know what he wishes to do for you (Cheer) I thank you for your expressions of good will.

Gov. Stevens continues: "My children. Though I went to the Great Father I left a father with you who will always take care of you, as his own children. You have also an older brother. (Gov. Stevens here pointed at the Agent Col. Simmons) a good man who has struck strong blows in your cause." Col. Simmons then addresses them in the Indian language as follows:

Col. Simmons:

"Nika Owh: Ilyas celi nika kumtux mesika, pe mesika kumtux nika. Kwahnesum close tuntun mesike kopah nika, pe ahucotti kopa konaway Boston. Alta Mesahche Boston chahko pe makcook tum Kopa Mesaiks, Kahkwa tilicum capercalla mesika dolla. pe chahko klhowyum siwash. Alta ikt ikt siwash maniook mesahche kopa Boston. Mika tuntun huu manook kahkwa, nika siwash tuntun. Close nika potlatch tumtum kopa Siwash alta. Mesika copet mahcook luiu kopam mesahche Boston, wake seli chahko close konaway siwash. Konaway mesika tenais chahko kahkwa Boston tenais Seli hyass kly nika tuntun kwahuesum. Boston wawa nika, Siwash kwahnesum capsusus yakka ictah, yakka whash, pussisse, shirt, sakoleeks, wappatoo, pe kwah nesum mesahche Boston kokshet siwash. Kwahnesum Siwash wawa, iko, ikt Boston mesahche kokshet nika. Kioshnesum kly nika tuntun alta. Pose Siwash copet muchkamuch him, kopet kltawa kopa mesahche Boston house, wake celi chahko close mesika siwash. Mesika Papa, kopa Boston makes wake yakka tuntun manook mesahche kopa siwash. Alko close namitch Siwash kwahuesum. Spose chee Siwash pe Governor Stevens snamook paper, mesika tyee yakka nomitch. Pose yakka Kumtux paper close, yakaka tchum yakka name hyas close kopa paper. Spose Yakka techum paper, chee paper kalipi, pa chahko mesika dolla kopa il1ahee.

O'kook octah mes ika iskum okcook sun, cultus potlatch konaway siwash kumtux nika tuntun slip Boston yukwa. Wake close nika ns wawa kopa Siwash? Close kopet alta. Alta mesika waver Governor Stevens pe siwash tyee."

ENGLISH (Translation)

"My Brothers: I have known you a long time, and you have known me. [340 6] Your hearts have always been good towards me, and formerly they were towards all Americans. Since then bad white men have come who sell you rum; so that people cheat you of your money and Indians become poor. Nowadays some Indians ill treat the whites. In my opinion rum is the cause of this – such is my real mind. I now give my true heart to you. Do you stop buying rum of bad white men and it will soon be well with all Indians. All your children will be like American children. My heart has cried for a long time. The whites tell me the Indians are always stealing their goods, their axes, blankets, shirts, pantaloons and potatoes, and bad white men are always beating Indians. The Indians are always telling me that some whiteman or other beats them. My heart is sick all the time. If you Indians will stop drinking liquor, stop going to the houses of bad white men, it will be good for you. "Your father in the American country – his heart is not to do ill to you. He will hereafter always take care of you. As soon as the Indians and Governor Stevens have agreed on the paper," One chief will see it. If he think the paper good, he will put his name to it. When he has signed it the paper will be returned and the money will be sent for your land.

"The goods that are given you to day are given as a present. You all know what my opinion was before other Americans came here. Did I not tell you the truth? I have done. Now the Governor will speak again &: then the Indian Chiefs." (Cheers).

Governor Stevens resumed:

"All this rejoices my heart, my heart is right and I am glad yours is, Our hearts are all the same. The Great Father wishes you to send him back a paper showing your desires & wishes. The great Father thinks you ought to have home as I before told you. The Great Father knows that you are Christians, looking to a future state, & that you have wives & children and he wants you to have a school where your children can learn to read and can be made farmers and be taught trades. He is willing that you should catch fish in these waters and get roots and berries back in the mountains. He wishes you all to be virtuous and industrious and to become a happy and prosperous community. Is this good and do you want this? If not he will talk further (All answer, "we do")

"My children: "I have simply told you the heart of the Great Father and what are his wishes and desires. But the lands are yours and we swear to pay you for them. We thank [341 7] you that you have been so kind to all the white children of the Great Father who have come here from the east. Those white children have always told you that you would be paid for your lands, and we are now here to buy them.

"The white children of the Great Father, but no more his children than you are, have come here, some to build mills, some to till the land and others to build and sail ships. My children, I believe that I have got your hearts, you have my heart. We will put our hearts down on paper, and then we will sign our names. I will send that paper to the Great Father, and if he says it is good, it will stand for ever. But you all know that God governs us in this world, and the Great Father may find something in that paper that is not right. If the Great Father thinks it is not right, he will send it back and tell me how he wishes it altered. If you agree to the alteration it will be a bargain & the paper will stand. I will now have the paper read to you and all I ask of you, two thousand Indians, men, women & children, is that you will say, first what you think, and if you find it good, that your chiefs and head men will sign the same." (Shouts)

Before the treaty was read the Indians sung a mass after the Roman Catholic form, and recited a prayer.

The paper not being quite ready for signature, Gov. Stevens invited the four head Chiefs to speak then.

"Does any one object to what I have said. Does my venerable friend Seattle object? I want Seattle to give his will to me and to his people."

Seattle: "I look upon you as my father. I and the rest regard you as such. All of the Indians have the same good feeling toward you, and will send it on paper to the Great Father. All of them, men, old men, women & children rejoice that he has sent you to take care of them. My mind is like yours. I don't want to say more. My heart is very good towards Dr. [David Swinson] Maynard[84] (a physician who was present) I want always to get medicine from him."

---

84 Thomas Prosch 1906 *David S Maynard & Catherine T Maynard*. Seattle: Lowman & Hanford. William Spiedel 1967 *Sons of the Profits*; 1978 *Doc Maynard*: The Man Who Invented Seattle. Nettle Creek Publishing Company, Seattle.

Gov. Stevens: "My friend. Seattle has put me in mind of one thing which I had forgotten. You shall have a doctor to cure your bodies and I trust your souls also. Now my friends, I speak to you as my friends though you are my children. [342 8] I want you if Seattle has spoken well to say by three cheers." (Three cheers were given) "Now we call upon Patkanam to speak his mind."

Patkanam: "To day I understood your heart as soon as you spoke. I understood your talk plainly. God made my heart & those of my people good and strong. It is good that we should give you our real feelings to day. We want every thing as you have said, the Doctor and all. Such is the feeling of all the Indians. Our hearts are with the whites. God makes them good towards the Americans." (Three cheers were given for *Patkanam*).

Chowitahoot was called for: "I do not want to say much. My heart is good. God has made it good towards you. I work on the ground (raise potatoes) and build houses. I have some houses at home. But I will stop building if you wish & will move to *Chah-shoo-sea*. Now I have given you my opinion & that of my friends. Their feelings are all good & they will do as you say hereafter. My mind is the same as Seattles'. I love him & send my friends to him if they are sick. I go to Doctor Maynard at Seattle it I am sick." (Cheers for *Chowitshoot*)

Goliah spoke: "My mind is the same as the Governor's. God has made it so. I have no wish to say much. I am happy at heart. I am happy to hear the Governor talk of God. My heart is good & that of all my friends. I give it to the Governor. I shall be glad to have a Doctor for the Indians. We are all glad to hear you & to be taken care of by you. I do not want to say more." (Cheers were given to *Goliah*).

Governor Stevens then announced that the treaty would be read to them. It should be mentioned that all the details except the sum to be given for their lands, had been fully explained by Col. Simmons, & Mr. Shaw, the Interpreter, in previous conversations with the Chiefs and head men and as is believed were fully understood. The chiefs also were consulted as to the fitness of the reservations finally adopted & approved of them. The talks were interpreted [343 9] into Chinook by Mr. Shaw and thence to the Indians by a Snohomish called John Taylor who also interpreted their replies into Chinook. Taylor like wise repeated the treaty, which he perfectly comprehended before hand, paragraph by paragraph. After it had been read' & translated, Gov. Stevens asked them if they were satisfied with it. If they were, he would sign it first, & then they should sign. If not he wished them to state in what they desired it to be altered. All having signified their approbation, it was signed first by him and afterwards by the Chiefs, headmen & so forth and is as follows:
*Note: See 12 Stat., 927; Volume 2, Kappler's Laws and Treaties, page 501.

The hour being late when the signing of the treaty was finished the distribution of the presents was deferred to the next day.

Tuesday January 23d – The Indians having re-assembled Governor Stevens inform them that he was about to distribute some presents. They were not intended as payment for their lands but merely as a friendly token of regard. He gave them but few things at this time but the next summer he should again give them a larger present when the goods intended for them arrived.

Seattle then on behalf of himself & the other Chiefs brought a white flag and presented it saying: "Now by this we make friends and put away all bad feelings if we ever had any. We are the friends of the Americans – all the Indians are of the same mind. We look upon you as our Father. We will never change our minds but since you have been to see us will be always the same, now. "Now! Do you send this paper of our hearts to the Great Chief. That is all I have to say."

The presents were then given to the Chiefs to distribute to their people, which was done and their own then given to them separately. [344 10]

The business at this place being satisfactorily completed the camp was struck and the party re-embarked. The steamer had been obtained for the purpose of expediting the preparations for the Treaty with the S'Klallams, and in the afternoon Gov. Stevens and Mr. Mason with some of the party went on board, but a heavy blow coming on, she lay to an anchor till morning. An Indian Express arrived today with news that the Indians were collected at Port Gamble awaiting the arrival or the Governor.

/s/ George E. Gibbs
Acting Secretary

Wednesday – January 24th Reached "Point No Point", and the steamer, (Leaving the schooner at anchor and the men on shore to form camp.) ran down to Port Gamble to bring up additional provisions and returned in the afternoon. The Indians began to arrive at the ground.

Thursday January 25th The weather was very strong but the Indians having assembled during the night, it was decided to go on with the Treaty. The Tribes consisted of the Clallums of S'Klallums, Chemakums, and Sko-komish or *Too-an-ho*och [Twana], and on a careful enumeration they were found not essentially to vary in number from 1200.

TREATY OF *HAHD-SKUS*, AT POINT NO POINT

The Indians having arranged themselves in a circle under their principal chiefs the Duke of York, or *Chits-a-mah-han* of the S'Kallams, *Nah-whil-lick* of the Sko-komish and *Kul-kah-han* or Gen. Pierce of the Chemakums. Gov. Stevens addressed them as follows:

My Children: – You call me your father, I too have a father, who is your great father. That great father has send me here today to pay you for your lands, to provide for your children, to see that you are fed and that you are cared for – the great father wishes you to be happy, to be friends to each other. The great father wants you and the whites to be friends, he wants you to have a home of your own, to have a school where your little children can learn. He wants you to learn to farm, to learn to use tools, and also to have a doctor. Now, all these things shall be written down in a paper. That paper shall be read to you. If the paper is good you will sign it, and I will sign it. I will then send the paper to the great father. If the great father finds that paper good he will send me word, and I will let you know. If the great father does not [345 11] find the paper good he will send it back to me, and say what alterations he wants in it – if you then agree to the changes, the paper is a bargain and will he carried out. The Great Father lives a great way off and some time will be required to hear from him. I want you to wait patiently till you hear from him. In the meantime the great Father has sent to you same presents simply as a free gift. Some of these presents I will give you today: but I shall give you more in the course of the summer. Your agent Mr. Simmons will give you notice of these presents. But besides these presents, you will have, to take care of you, your agent Mr. Simmons – you will also have a man you know, Gov. Leason [Mason ?] to take care of you. This you will have all the time and when the paper comes from the great Father then you will have your own houses and homes and your school. Now what have you to say – if good give your assent – if not say so." (Cheers of approbation.) "Now sit quiet a moment and the paper will be read."

The Treaty was then read and interpreted to the Skokomish by *Hool-hole-tan* or Jim, the first Sub-chief and to the S'Klallams and Chemakums by *Yaht-le-min* or Gen. Taylor – The reading being concluded Gov. Stevens asked if they had any thing to say.

Che-law-tch-tat, an old Skokomish Indian then rose and said: "I wish to speak my mind as to selling the land. Great Chief! What shall we eat if ·we do so? Our only food is berries, deer and salmon – where then shall we find these? I don't want to sign away all my land, take half of it, and let us keep the rest. I am afraid that I shall become destitute and perish for want of food. I don't like the place you have shown for us to live on. I am not ready to sign the paper.

L'Haii-at-scha-uk, To-an-hoock next spoke: "I do not want to leave the mouth of the river. I do not want to leave my old home, and my burying grounds. I am afraid I shall die if I do."

Mr. F. Shaw, the Interpreter, explained: to them that they were not called upon to give up their old modes of living and places of seeking food, but only to confine their homes to one spot.

Nah-whil-luk: The Skokomish head chief an old man rose and said, "I do not want to sell my land because it is [346 12] valuable. The Whites pay a great deal for a small piece and they get money by selling the sticks [lumber]. Formerly the Indians slept but the Whites came among them and woke them up and we now know that the lands are worth much."

It was explained that it was only by the labor laid out up on land that it became valuable and that his country was poor at best.

Hool-hol-tan or Jim: "I want to speak – I do not like the offers you make in the Treaty to us – you say you will give us land, but why should you give us the mouth of the river. I don't like to go on a reserve with the Klallams and in case of trouble there are more of them than of us and they will charge us with it. Before the Whites came among us we had no idea who made the land, but some time ago the Priests told us that the Great Chief Above made it, and also made the Indians. Since then the Americans have told us that the great Father always bought the land and that it was not right to take it for nothing – they waked the Indians up by this, and they now know their land was worth much. I don't want to sign away my right to the land. If it was myself alone that I signed for I would do it, but we have women and children. Let us keep half of it and take the rest. Why should we sell all, we may become a destitute. Why not let us live together with you.

Mr. Simmons: The agent explained that if they kept half their country, they would have to live on it and would not be allowed to go anywhere else they pleased. That when a small tract alone was left the privilege was given of going wherever else they pleased to fish and work for·the Whites. If you can cultivate more land than this, you can have it.

Jim resumed: "I am not pleased with the idea of selling all. I want you to hear what I have to say. All the Indians here have been afraid to talk, but I wish to speak and be listened to. I don't want to leave my land. It makes me sick to leave it. I don't want to go from where I was born. I am afraid of becoming destitute."

Chits-a-mah-han or the Duke of York: (The Duke stutters somewhat and dictated to *Soo-ich* one of his tribe.) "My heart is good. (I am happy) since I have heard of the paper read, and since I have understood Gov. Stevens, particularly since I have been told that I could look for food where I [347 13] pleased, and not in one place only. I will always be the same. My heart has lately been better. Formerly the Indians were bad towards each other, but Governor Stevens had made them agree to be friends, and I am willing he should act as he pleases. I think the more I know him, the better I shall be satisfied. Before the Whites came we were always poor, since then we have earned money and got blankets and clothing. I hope the Governor will tell the whites not to abuse the Indians as many are in the habit of doing, or ordering them to go away and knocking them down. We are willing to go up the Canal since we know we can fish elsewhere. We shall only leave there to get salmon, and when done fishing will return to our houses. I am glad to acknowledge you and the great father as our Father – (cheers.)

Governor Stevens: – "What are you now? What were you formerly? Have you not already been driven from your burial grounds? The great Father wants to put you where you cannot be driven away. The great Father besides giving you a home will give you a school, protect you in taking fish, break up your land, give you clothes and seeds. Was this good or not? I want an answer –"

Che-lan-teh-teel again spoke: – "What I want to say is to thank you. I have changed my mind. What you have said is good. I see that you mean well towards us. I look upon you as our father."

Spote-Xeh a Klallam: – "I have become satisfied since I have heard you. I know now that you are our father. I shall always be the same. I was once poor but now better off and shall always look to you for aid."

Kaht-ass-mehtt, or Mr. Stevens: – a subchief of the Klallams, "Why should my heart be bad. I will be the last to become bad. I feel that you should do as you think best. I am willing to submit. Such is my mind now and I don't think I shall change it." Cheers.

Governor Stevens then asked them what they wished to do about this signing of the papers – when the Skokomish chief said they would rather wait till tomorrow. They would talk it over and understand it thoroughly. Accordingly the Council was adjourned till the next morning.

Friday, January 26th – The Indians came up bearing white flags – Governor Stevens proceeded to address them as follows – [348 14]

"We meet here this morning – having a pleasant day – one sent by the *Sokali Tyee* [Above Lord], to accomplish a great work. I trust that from today on we shall all be good friends, and you prosperous and happy. The Treaty was read to you last night, you have talked it over, we will now consider it. I think the paper is good and that the Great Father will think so. Are you not my Children and also children of the great Father? What will I not do for my children and what will you not for yours? Would you not die for them? This paper is such as a man would give to his children and I will tell you why. This paper gives you a home. Does not a father give his children a home? This paper gives you a school? Does not a father send his children to school? It gives you mechanics and a Doctor to teach and cure you. Is not that fatherly? This paper secures your fish? Does not a father give food to his children? Besides fish you can hunt, gather roots and berries. Besides it says you shall not drink whiskey and does not a father prevent his children from drinking the fire water? Besides all this, the paper says you shall be paid for your lands as has been explained to you. In making this paper I know the great Father was good to his children, and did not wish to steal their lands. I think the Treaty is good, and your friend here who you have long known thinks so. Ask him! Is it good and are you ready for me to sign, and for yourselves, I think so. It is for you to say what you think right. It you have anything to say, say it now. I have done."

Duke of York – Wanted to speak: "His heart was white, so were those of his people and he will never stain it with blood or blacken it. It is the same as the Governors. He has talked all, he never talks much. Presents a white flag to Gov. Stevens who addressed him – "His heart grew big to him, at receiving this flag, and towards his people."

Nah-kwil-tuk – The Skokomish Chief – said: "His heart too had become white and he gave it to the Chief. He put away all his bad feelings. He would be as a good man, not stealing or shedding blood. He sent this word to the great Father. About what should we talk today. We have thrown away the feelings of yesterday, and are now satisfied. We want you to say so to him." He gives a flag to Gov. Stevens who says on receiving it, "I call you my son, but when I see your grey hairs, I should rather call you father. I thank you for this expression of your heart. I am sure you Will keep this feeling towards the agent, and those who succeed him. These children are my children. I hope you will always preserve them, and look with satisfaction [349 15] to this day.

Chim-a-kum – Chief *Hul-kah-had* or Gen. Pierce: – We talk to you, but what should we say, we can say nothing but what this flag tells. We give our hearts to you with it in return for what you do for us. We were once wretched, but since you come you have made us right. When the Americans came to my country they shall find my heart like this. Formerly other Indians did wrong to us. Since the Whites had come, we are free and have not been killed." Gave a flag – and Governor Stevens addressed him. "You are young. I hope your heart will be always white as your flag, and that you will be a father to your people. I too will take care of them and we will keep the record of the people on that flag and trust it will always be good."

Gov. Stevens once more asked them it they were satisfied to sign the Treaty. They all declared themselves so. It was accordingly signed, and a salute fired from the Steamer as a signal.

Some hostile feeling having previously existed on the part of the Chemakums towards the Klallams and Skokomish. Gov. Stevens now desiring that they should drop it forever, and that their hearts towards each other should be good as well as towards the whites. The three chiefs then on behalf of' their people shook hands.

The presents were then distributed to them as in the other cases, and in the afternoon the party re-embarked, Mr. Mason returning to Olympia in the steamer and Governor Stevens with the rest proceeding to Port Townsend in the Schooner on his way to Cape Flattery the next point of meeting.

George Gibbs.
Secretary.

The treaty is as follows: [attached]

NOTE: Here follows [ends] a treaty with the S'Klallam, January 26, 1855, 12 Stats. p. 933, Kapplers' Laws & Treaties, Vol. 2, p. 504.

TREATY OF NEAH BAY

Monday January 29th   The Schooner reached Neah Bay on the evening of the 28th, and today the tents, goods and men were landed and the Camp established. Governor Stevens, the agent [350 16] and interpreter lately put themselves in communication with the Indians of the Bay through the medium of Capt. E.S. Fowler, a Klallam Subchief called Captain Jack, who spoke the Makah language, and two Makahs men or Jefferson Davis and Peter who spoke Chinook. Expresses were immediately sent off to bring in the other Makah Villages and also if possible the tribes adjoining them on the Coast.

Tuesday Jan. 30 Gov. Stevens and the Secretary (George Gibbs) crossed the Peninsula of Cape Flattery to the Coast for the purpose of making a general examination of the country and selecting a spot suitable for the separate reserve of this tribe and such others as might be included with them. The Indians of the other Makah Villages arrived today but stated that the other tribes could not be called in until several days. It was accordingly determined to send for them to meet at Grays Harbor. In the evening Governor Stevens called a meeting of the Makah Chiefs on board the Schooner to hear the details of the proposed treaty more particularly. Being interrogated as to their relations with the tribes below them, they said that with the *Kive-deh-tut* or *Kwilleh-yeites* [Quileutes] they were on terms of amity, as also with the *Kwaaksat* or *Hooch* [*Hoh*], but that with the next band or tribe the *Kivites* or *Kahts ahuat*, they were not, that tribe having killed one of their people once years ago. They did not however desire to cherish any animosity, but did not know the feelings of that tribe towards them. They were directed to make a full return of each of their own villages the next day.

Governor Stevens then informally mentioned the principal features of the proposed treaty as follows. The Great Father had sent him here to watch over the Indians. He had talked with the other tribes of the Sound, and they had promised to be good friends with their neighbors and he had now come to talk with the Makahs. When he had done here he was going to the Indians down the Coast and would make them friends to the Makahs. He had treated with the Sound Tribes for their land, setting aside reserves for them and had stipulated to give them a school, farmer, etc., and a physician, when he had finished.

Kal-chote of Neah Bay spoke: "Before the big Chiefs (*Kleh-silt*, the White Chief, *yallacoom* or Flattery Jack, and *Heh-ike*) died he was not the head chief himself, he was only a small chief, but though there were many Indians there, he was not the least of them. He knew the country all around and therefore he had a right to speak. He thought he ought to have the right of fish and take whales and get food where he liked. He was afraid that if he could not take halibut where he wanted, he would become poor." [351 17]

Koh-chook of the Stone House [Tatoosh Island] followed: – "What *Kal-chote* had said was his wish. His country extended up to *Hoke-ho*. He did not want to leave the salt water."
Gov. Stevens informed them that so far from wishing to stop their fisheries, he intended to send them oil, kettles and fishing apparatus."

Klah-pe-at-hoo of Neah Bay: Since his brother died, he had been sick at heart (his brother was the late 3d chief.) He was willing to sell his land: all he wanted was the right of fishing.

Tse-heu-wrl: – He wanted the seal. What was his country if whales were killed and floated ashore, he wanted for his people the exclusive right of taking them and if their slaves ran away, they wanted to get them back."

Governor Stevens replied that he wanted them to fish but that the whites should fish also. Whoever killed the whale was to have them if they came ashore. He added as a reason for buying their land that many whites were coming into the Country and that he did not want the Indians to be crowded out."

Kalchote resumed: – "He wanted always to live on his old ground and to die on it. He only wanted a small piece for a house and would live as a friend to the whites and they should fish together."

Klah-pe-at-hoo: – "He and Kalchote lived together. They did not want to leave their old Home."

Tse-kaw-wtl: – said the same thing. He too only wanted his house.

Ke-bach-sat of *Tso-yess:* – "My heart is not bad but I do not wish to leave all my land. I am willing you should have half, but I want the other half myself. You know my country. I want part for my village. It is very good, I want the place where the stream comes in."

Heatse: his brother was of the same mind.

It-an-daha of *Wa'atch:* – "My father, my father! I now give you my heart. When any ships come and the whites injure me I will apply to my father and will tell him of my trouble and look to him for help, and if any Indians wish to kill me. I shall still call on my father, I shall submit all my difficulties to him; my wish is like the rest, I do not wish to leave the salt water. I want to fish in [352 18] common with the whites. I don't want to sell all the land. I want a part in common with the whites to plant potatoes on. I want the place where my house is. I do not want to say much, we are all of one mind. I have no particular country myself, mine and that of the *Tse-kaw-wtl* are the same."

Kal-chote again: – "I do not want you to leave me destitute. I want my house on the Island (Tatooch Island, commonly called the Stone House.)

Governor Stevens asked "whether if the right of drying fish where ever they pleased was left them, they could not agree to live at one place for a winter residence and potato ground explaining the idea of sub-division of lands and he desired them to think the matter over during the night. They were also directed to consult among themselves upon the choice of a head chief. As they declined doing this on the ground that they were all of equal rank. He selected *Tse-kow-wootl,* the Ozette Chief as the head. A choice in which they all acquiesced with satisfaction.

Temporary papers in lieu of commissions were then issued to *Kal-chote,* and *Klah-pe-at-hu* of Neah Bay, *Keh-tchook* of the Stone House (Tatooch Is), *It-an-da-ha* and W'aatch *Haatse* and *Kebach sat* of *Tsooyess* as sub chiefs.

Col. Simmons then explained to them that "these papers were given them as evidence that they were chiefs, that as such they must take care of the people, and that bye and bye the great papers would be given them. On his former visit they had declined to receive papers, but now they were evidently much valued." The general council was then adjourned to the next day.

January 31 Wednesday – The heads of the Treaty had been adjusted and on the morning the Indians were again assembled. Two additional sub-chiefs received papers, vis: *Tah-a-kowtl* of Ozett and *Kats-kussum* of the Stone House. The number of the whole tribe was found to be 600.

Governor Stevens then addressed them: "My children I have seen many other of my children before you. They have been glad to see me and to hear the words of the great Father. I saw the great Father a short time since and he sent me here to see you and give you his mind. The whites are crowding in upon you and in the great Fathers wishes to give you your homes. He wants to buy your land and give you a fair price but [353 19] leaving you enough to live on and raise your potatoes. He knows what whalers you are, how you go far to sea to take whales. He will send you barrels in which to put your oil, Kettles to try it out, lines and implements to fish with. The great Father wants your children to go to school and learn trade and this will be done if we agree today. I am now about to read you a paper. If you like it, we will sign it. If it is good I shall send it to the great Father and if he likes, it he will send it back with his name. If he wants it altered he will let you know, when it is agreed to, it is a bargain [deal]."

The treaty was then read to them, interpreted clause by clause and explained.

Governor Stevens then asked if they were satisfied. If they were to say so. If not to answer freely and state their objections.

Tse-heu-wrl – brought up a white flag and presented it saying: – "Look at this flag, see if there are any spots on it. There are none and there are none in our hearts."

Kalchote presented another flag: – "What you have said was good and what you have written is good."·

The Indians gave three cheers or shouts as each concluded. The governor then signed the Treaty and was followed by the Indian chiefs and principal men.

The Treaty is as follows: [attached]

NOTE: Here follows the Treaty with the Makahs on January 31, 12 Stat. p. 939; Vol. 2. Kepplers Law & Treaties, p. 510.

The presents were afterwards distributed and in the evening the party re-embarked. Owing to the wind the vessel did not reach Port Townsend till the 3rd of February. The next day (February 4th) Gov. Stevens left with some of the party in the steamer *Mayor Tompkins* for Victoria in order to confer with Gov. Douglas on the subject of the Northern Indians and on the 5th returned to Port Townsend and reached Olympia on that night of the 6th. [354 20]

Council with the Upper and Lower Chihalis, Lower Chinook,
Cowlitz and Quinaiutl Indians.

February 20th Tuesday Mr. Simmons, Indian Agent and Mr. Gibbs, Secretary, with the employees of the party rendezvoused at Judge Fords on the Chehalis River and proceeded down in canoes to the place previously selected for the council ground, the claim of the Pilkinton, a few miles above the entrance of the Chihalis into Grays Harbor, which they reached on the 22nd. Mr. Frank Shaw, one of the interpreters and special agent had previously been sent by way of the

199

Cowlitz and Columbia Rivers to act in connection with Mr. Tappan sub agent for the district in bringing in delegations from the tribes living on those waters. Governor Stevens reached the grounds on Saturday the 24th and Mr. Tappan the same night. The Indians now began to assemble from different points and on Sunday a count was made of the tribes present and their report obtained of the number of individuals absent. This was done in the usual manner, each band a village giving in a bundle of sticks corresponding to the individuals left behind.

The tribes thus counted were:
       The Upper Chihalis numbering in all - - - -   216
       The Lower Chihalis numbering in all - - - -   217
       The Quinautl and sub band of Kwehtsa - - -   158

To which were added upon the arrival of Mr. Shaw - Delegates from the others, to-wit:

       Lower Chinooks, numbering as before - - - - -   112
       Cowlitz -   140
Giving a total of 370 Indians present, representing tribes and bands, whose total numbers are
       - ~ - - -   843

The excepting the Upper Chinooks and a part of the Klikatats Tribe who were not summoned to treat at this point were supposed to constitute all the remaining Indians of the Territory west of the Cascade Range. It was now however found that the Quinaults did not occupy the whole country between the Chehalis and the Makahs, but that another and distinct tribe, the Kwillehyates were intermediate. This was perceived upon collecting vocabularies of the languages for comparison, that of the Kwillehyates proving to be distinctly different, and upon pursuing the inquiry it was further ascertained that the Messengers sent up the Coast had for this reason not notified them of the Council. [355 21]

Being wholly unrepresented therefore, they were necessarily omitted [omitted] in the intended negotiation but their numbers are ascertained to be about ••• 300.

The necessity of Ethnological inquiry in concluding arrangements for treating with or locating an Indian is strikingly shown in this instance.

Mr. Shaw arrived on Monday with the delegation of Cowlitz and Chinook Indians. The time had meanwhile been occupied by Col. Simmons and the Interpreters present in explaining the details of the Treaty proposed to be made to the several chiefs that it might be told in advance to their people.

Tuesday February 27th – The Council was opened, and Col. Simmons announced its object. The Indians were then addressed by Gov. Stevens as follows:

"My children, I have seen many Indians in the Last two months. None better clothed nor apparently better clothed than you. You have seen the whites for years. You have heard of the great Father, yours, and the father of the whites. That great father has many white children and they are coming here, the great Father wishes that his white and red children should be friends, and you are friends now, what is your state now though? Do you now own all your old burying grounds and potato patches, have you not been told by the whites "Let us have these places and the Great Father will pay you for them?" The whites now have these lands, but you have not got your pay, and the great father has sent me here to talk with you and know what he should pay you for them, and He also thinks you should have homes where no white man would go without your wish. You want homes where you can live happy all your days and gather roots, berries, and fish, and shall have them. You have many children. We want those children you to have trades, and to farm, etc. Some times you are sick and need a physician, you also want ploughs and tools to raise crops, and you want also an elder brother, as agent who shall be your brother and take care of you. This is the heart of your great Father, it is my heart, that of your older brothers, Mr. Simmons, Mr. Tappan, and Mr. Shaw.

(Spoke to the Chinooks and Cowlitz.) "You will ask me my friends how you can know it. These three years ago treaties were made with you by Dr. Dart, and the great [256 22] Father did not like them. More papers did not do enough, did not take care of you. If we put one man here, another one there, and so on, how can the agents take care of you? How can you be friends in that case? You are friends away from the Chinooks, Cowlitz, Upper Chihalis, etc. and we want you to remain so. Now we want to make a paper that shall protect you all as friends, that shall save you from whisky. "My children, whiskey is your great bane. There was once a time when the Indians did not drink whiskey and they were numerous and strong. We want you to quit whiskey and you will become so again, and the bad white men as you know are the ones who beat and ill treat you. We want you to take fish where you have always done so and in common with the whites. We want your animals to feed on the prairies. We also want this, if any of you want to go to Shoalwater Bay to dig oysters for pay, we want you to do so. We want you (Cowlitz) to continue to run your canoes in the rivers and be paid for it. We want you (Chihalis) to work where you wish. If any of you want to go to Olympia, etc., to buy goods or work, good, but in doing all this you must not drink whiskey. You must be always good men. Not interfere with the whites. You can have all this provided you will agree to a permanent home where we can prevent bad white men from injuring you. Have one home where the agent will live, and then go and work out and let your children go to school. Now I have put my mind on a paper which will be read to you. It will be carefully explained to you, and if you like it we will all sign it. I will then send it to the great Father and I think he will find it good. If he finds it good he will send me word and it will be a bargain. If he wants it altered he will send me word and if you agree to the alteration it is fixed. Then you will be paid. I think he will find it good and I will tell you why. I came to this country a year ago. I saw your wants, I visited you and was determined to be your friend. I went back over seas and mountains traveling two moons and I saw the great Father. The great Father heard me and sent me back with his heart. He knows all about you and in the paper which will be read to you has done what he thinks will be for your good. One thing about your payments. You will not get them till the paper comes back. I shall, to be sure, give you somethings now and more next summer, but those are not to pay but only a gift. I have no more to say now, but I want you to tell me your minds.

The draft of the proposed Treaty was then read and translated to them. [357 23]

Governor Stevens: "You have now heard the Treaty. Is it good? If not, say wherein it is not."

Yowannus [*yawniš*] – Head Chief of the Upper Chihalis: "Thought it very good. Today was the first time, he knew the Governor's mind, and his heart was long to hear it. They were nearly destitute, and he was glad to hear such liberal promises. Formerly they were many, but now they are few and poor."

"We believe (said he) you are now really going to do something for us. That you are going to take care of us. It is for you to say where we shall go to select one home for us. I am rejoiced to think I can live where I please. I think I ought to have some place, and want the privilege of taking some place to live on. My mind is that it is good for you to take part and leave a part for us to live on.

"The reason that I wish to select my land is that I know there are some bad white men and I am afraid to sell all without reservation. The country is a large and good one for cultivation. I want out of it the Mound Prairie and another below it. (Smiths Prairie) That is all I have to say."

Governor Stevens explains: "The great Father knew his wants and his country. He knows that it is a good country. But there is a good country elsewhere, where he would be as comfortable as here. We want the great Father to select the place for him, to do for him as he would do for his own children. There was on the coast a place where there were plenty of fish and good land. I think the great Father will think well of this and will probably select it. Think over it and later say what you like."

Ta-ho-la, Head Chief of the Kwinai-utl: "He wanted his country. His children lived there and wanted food. He wanted them to get it there, did not want to leave it. The river he did not want to sell near the salt water, nor the sand beach mouth, but that part above the mountains and off the river he would sell. He has but one heart. It is good. He says but one things, has not two mouth[s] and don't want to say much."

Governor Stevens: "He has not said many words, but he has said much. I know what he means. He wants him to have the salt and fresh waters and fish, knows exactly how he lives, his country, and that north is a good country and we want to put other Indians there. I want him to let [358 24] the great Father say where his home shall be. Where he shall have the water and get food. Nothing will be done about their lands till the paper comes back. Perhaps a year and a half. You know Mr. Simmons. He will soon go to your country and see it so that the great Father will know fully all about it."

Tu-heh-uk, Head Chief of the Lower Chihalis: "I am indeed glad to 'hear what you have said. The great Father was indeed his, and he was of the same mind as the Governor. All his people felt the same about the great Father. All of same mind. No dissent. Our father has talked to us about our land and we think as he does. We are very proud to think we have a father. I give up all my land but what I claim for my self and that I don't want the whites to take. I want to take and dry salmon and not be driven off. I want three miles above and below "*Wahmoolchie*" for a reserve on the Chihalis. This river was all mine. While looking for food on it and fishing I do not want to be driven off. I want the river for a fishing place and down below (Chehalis) for a reserve. There was grass there for my horses. I want the breach. Everything that comes ashore is mine. (whales and wrecks.) I want the privilege of the berries (Cranberry Marsh). I want a paper showing the bounds of the reserve. So that when a white man took it, I could show him. I want a place where whites could not settle. Wanted to know what could be done with the land if his slaves were turned loose. I would have no one to work for me. They were like my people."

Gov. Stevens: "He (*Tuleh-uk*) sees that we write down all that he says. That speech of his I send to the great Father who will know exactly what he wants. That paper (the Treaty) was the heart of the Great Father which he thought good. It said he should have the right to fish in common with the whites, and get roots and berries. He saw that settlers were coming in and what was wanted was to prevent the Indians and whites from interfering with one another. As to the Cranberry Marsh, he can get berries there, but if a settler should drain it, he would want to keep it. What he says about wanting a place there and up the river will be told the great Father, but I want them to leave it ·to the great Father to say where their homes should be. Settlers were very glad to have good Indians around them to work for them. The great Father wants him and the rest to have one permanent home, but during the Summer to go where they pleased to work, and meanwhile could live anywhere if no objection made by settlers. As to his [359 25] slaves he could do as the whites did, if they wanted to stay with him, good. For the rest he could make his own bargain. The reason that a large payment was made them, was because they gave up their land and slaves to [so] because they gave up much. They were to be paid much. If they did not sell, they would not get it. The great Father thought their conditions would be bettered."

Kish-Kok head chief of the Cowlitz: "The French, Hudson's Bay People first came among them against their will and did not use them well. When Mr. Shaw came he told them a straight story and they hurried to come along. Mr. Shaw had told them they would have an agent to look out for them and a doctor. When the Bostons (the Americans) came they were glad to see them and wanted them to settle in their country. Wanted now to know where they themselves where to have a piece of land. He described the bounds or his country as in the report. They wanted a strip of country crossing the Cowlitz and taking in a small part of the "Puget Sound" farm. That where the Kammas [camas] ground was."

Ow-hye – a Cowlitz delegate: Formerly the King Georges (English) came. They a paid them a shirt to go from Cowlitz to Vancouver. The Indians were very much ashamed at their treatment. They just now find out what the land was worth by seeing the French sell to the whites. Several hundred Dollars for a small piece with a house on it. It was northern land, but the Indians after all, they were willing to put up with a very small piece of land but they want it at that place. When the Americans came, they first saw money and knew its value. They have been paid well for everything they had done. <u>Women</u> as well the men. When they went back they could show their Commissions as chiefs, and they wanted one to show where their grounds were so that the French would know. As soon as they got back to the Cowlitz, they would gather their people up and make them live in one place. They were now scattered everywhere. He wanted the same ground with *Kish-Kok* because there was a fishery on it. Where they could go in winter and to go on the prairie to live for their houses. He wanted Davis, an American settler to live near him as he worked for him. Davis treated him like a brother and gave him flour and he gave Davis salmon. He wanted· to stay there till he dies. All his children have died there but one. [360 26]

Governor Stevens: "This paper has to go to the great Father and it will be a long time before it will get back. I cannot give a paper showing where their land is till it does. We will send all they had said to the great Father, who would fix the reserve for them. The great Father has many red children and has tried many ways to take care of them, and he finds the paper (Treaty) the best. He wants them to have a home and an agent among them to look after them and for their children to go to school. A great many white people, when their boys grow large send them out to work with their friends and learn, and when they have grown up and made some money, they come home and marry, and he wanted the Indian Children to do the same. The great Father wanted another thing, when they got on their permanent home that each should take a small field and improve it as his own, as the whites did. It would be eighteen months before the paper would come back in the meantime they could live where they liked provided it was not on a settler's claim."

Nah-kot-ti and *Moosmoos* – Chinooks: "They feel very good in their hearts. They have become clear as the sun as to the Governors words, formerly their minds were dark like night. Now they understand him. They have become enlightened. Now about their lands. He wanted to put his house on the Nasal [Naselle] River (Shoalwater Bay) Where his dead were buried. In the summer he wanted to go to the *Wap-a-loo-chie* (a stream emptying into Baker's Bay) to dry salmon and then return to the Nasal to put in his potatoes. He did not want settlers to come to his land. The Bostons should take salmon as before at Chinook. When anything came ashore on the weather beach, whales or anything they wanted one half. Wanted to fish in Shoalwater Bay as before. As also to take oysters. Was willing to have the whites take winter salmon also, but did not wish them to live on their reserve. They wanted also to get cranberries and sell to the whites. He had done. He also wanted a paper to show what his reserve was."

Governor Stevens: "Was glad to hear what they wanted, and where they got their living but he wished them to leave it to the great Father to say where their land should be. They of course were to fish etc. as usual. As to whales they were theirs, but wrecks belonged to the owners and if the Indians found them they were to tell the wreckmaster and they would be paid a share of what they saved. They must not hide the things. One of the reasons why the former [361 27] Treaties were rejected was that they gave the same sort of little reserves as they now wanted. The great Father had tried many ways and he thought this Treaty the best. He wanted many Indians to be in one place where they could be taken care of. They were to think over this and make up their minds."

Chah-lat a Sub chief from the North side of Grays Harbor: "He wanted to speak of his land. The chiefs talk was good and had made them happy. They did think they were going to be driven off to some other country, and were glad to hear they were not. They were formerly very numerous, now but few. Were glad to think they had a great Father to take care of them. Their hearts were those of the whites. They would do what ever was wanted. They would not forget what had been told them. They wanted to build their houses on the north Point, and there was a small creek they wanted to fish in. When whales came ashore they wanted them. It was their food. That point was their only place for fishing. There was a tide prairie there for their horses. If they go to Shoalwater Bay they don't stay long. As soon as they have done working for the whites any where they go back. Formerly when they went to Shoalwater Bay, the Americans (some of them) treated them badly, beat them, and knocked them over. That little creek was the only place he cared for, as he always got his salmon there and he liked the place. On the in shore he wanted only a small place for his house but wanted a scope on the beach where things floated up of which he got a good deal.

Governor Stevens: "The paper secured him the right to fish and pasture. Also berries and roots, where they pleased. The Treaty provided an agency, school etc. and it was necessary in order to take care of them that they should be together. A large body of them in one place. The paper would be sent to the President and when he saw it he would decide where that place should be. Wanted him to think it over and talk with his people, and bye and bye he would speak to them again."

Tee-whit of Satsop and *Squatsen*: "There were not many of them left, they have died off on their land. He wanted part of his land, would give up part to the whites. He wanted to give the land above the road on Satsop to the Bostons. Below that and up the Chehalis to the drift he wanted himself. It was a very good country." [362 28]

Governor Stevens: "If we made that bargain we could not keep the settlers out of his land nor protect him. We want him to leave it and go to another place equally good for him. He had but few people and they could not cultivate it. He would still have the privilege of going to old place whenever he wanted to fish. Wanted him to leave it to the great father to select a place for him and the others where he could be taken care of."

Squatsen: "All his people were of one mind. The part he was willing to give up was a large one."

The Council was then adjourned till after dinner.

Afternoon Governor Stevens addressed the Council as follows. "My children you have told me your hearts. My son of the Upper Chihalis, and the Satsop chief have told me what land they wanted. The Quinaielt chief has expressed his wants. Also the chiefs of the lower Chihalis and the northern Shore have pointed out their small spots. And the Cowlitz and Chinooks have said what they wanted. What each of you has said, has been written down and will be sent to the great Father. The great Father has many children away to the rising sun and knows what is good or them. If we gave you all the little spots you want, the great Father could not be your father, though he desires to be so for he could not take care of you. His white children are coming here in great numbers. He cannot stop them and they will crowd upon you, to take care you, you must have a winter home. Each band must have their own spot on the general reserve and that should be fenced. There must be with you an agent who can be always on the ground to take care of you. You already know about the school and about your children coming there to learn. I want you to see that the paper is right in this matter. Now Col. Simmons has been longer in the country than I, you know him better than you know me. His heart and mine are one. I want Mr. Simmons to speak to you."

Col. Simmons addressed them in the Chinook Language: "I know many of your faces. I have known many of you a long time. My heart is well disposed to you. You never have done ill to me, why should I to you? When I first came to Olympia, there were no Bostons, you were then many and we were few. I know that about six years ago the measles came and many of you died and my heart was sick. The Indians were wretched. There was no doctor to cure them. This paper will give you a doctor to cure you. This paper promises [363 29] to make your children know how to read. You say you want a little piece of ground here and there. Why don't you know that if you have it, the Chief can do nothlng for you? He cannot run around to every man's house. I think the paper good for you. It will prevent the whites from injuring you. You are half asleep. You don't understand the paper. Do you suppose the chief would make a bad paper for you. It will be about eighteen months before this paper comes back. Till it does it is nothing. That he gives you now is a mere present. In the summer he will give you more. These are not for payments. (This referred to the idea what had got abroad that the presents on the ground were intended as a full payment for their lands.) Many of you know the whites well. Some of them are good to the Indians, they never ill treat them or give them rum others are bad. They want you to work, they want your money. They trade you rum and then you complain of them and they beat you."

"If you like this paper Governor Stevens will sign it and your chiefs shall. If the great Father likes it, you will get your money when it comes back.

Mr. Tappan and Mr. Shaw the sub agent and Interpreter when successively spoke to the same effect.

Governor Stevens: "I want you to be entirely satisfied. If things don't suit you I want you to say so, and we will talk longer. If you are ready to sign I will sign it now."

Yowannus being called, said: "What has been said is good. He understand it very well. He does not want to sign till he knows where he is going to. He wants to stay in his own country and not be moved elsewhere. All their chiefs and people have died then and he wants Governor Stevens to give them that land. It would be better even if we should all die there. He wants some of the old places. Where he has lived long ago and to divide with the whites."

Col. Simmons asked if he would be willing to keep a piece of that land and be confined to it. Explained that if he had a winter home elsewhere he could still travel but if he insisted on a reserve, that he would be obliged to stay there.

 (Question by Yowannus: "What are my horses to do?" Col. Simmons replies that his horses would do like those of the whites, "pasture on the commons."

Governor Stevens finding that the subject of the horses caused much trouble explained that this reserve should be large enough to afford pasturage for their horses and a road which would enable them to reach the settlements. Think of this tonight and tomorrow we will talk again.

Adjourned [364 30]

Wednesday February 28th Gov. Stevens addressed the Indians assembled: "My children. You have had time to consider what I said to you yesterday. I think you understand the paper now. You understand that you will be placed where you will have food and grass for an1mals. Where you will be able to communicate with the settlements and get work. You understand that to find the place a survey will be made and the ground known. And that your place will be picked out by your great Father, and that I shall send to him every thing you have said. You know that he is your great father and your good father, and that he will take good care of you. You understand all this and I have no more to say. I am ready to sign the paper if you think it good."

Tu-leh-uk Head Chief of the Lower Chihalis: "The chief is our father, we are glad to think we have a father. He is now the father of all the Indians. We are glad to think that you are about to prepare a good place for us to live in. To have a portion of the land saved to us, so that we can always have a claim to it."

Governor Stevens directed the interpreter, Mr. Shaw, to repeat again that the Treaty intended that they should sell all their land and go on to such a reserve as the President should select.

Tu-leh-uk replies: "He wants his own ground. He wants it very much."

206

Governor Stevens. My children. I supposed you understood the wishes of the great father in regard to his children. It is his wish that you be his children that you be under his protection. The great father desires to cure you when you are sick that your children should learn the great father wants you to have food and your animals grass. The paper provides for all that. But it stipulates that the great father shall select the place where you ought to live. I take it for granted that you want the care and protection of your father and that you are thankful for the payments which this paper provides. This cannot be done for you as it should be unless the place is fixed by him. Are you ready to leave it to him. In all that you have said to me you have expressed your confidence in the great father and in myself. I spoke yesterday of the many children that he has, and today I speak of the many that I have and have seen, and I say to you that the place which we propose to provide for you shall be one that will be good [365 31] for you, and where you will be happy. Remain on the places which you have pointed out to me and you will be swept away. You cannot be protected there. Each house would require a man to take care of you and we have not got them. Where are your lands now? Who has them? You or the white settlers and yet they were few when you were many. Now you are few and they are many and more coming. Whose grounds is this? Who built that house and planted the potatoes? Did you? But don't you want such a place where you cannot be driven off. This is what the great father wants you to have. The paper states that you shall fish in common with the whites. That you can visit the rivers and put up your summer houses. That you can travel and work. What more can can [sic] a father do? What less? I ask you again will you leave the place to be fixed by him. Now my children you can do as you please. I have put it on a paper. It is for you to say whether you will have the care etc, and the payment promised by it. You know that no man can have all he wants. That he must be satisfied if he gets what will make him comfortable. It ill for you to decide whether you will sign or not."

The *Kwinai-utl* chief now came forward accompanied by the principal men of his tribe and expressed his willingness to sign the Treaty and Governor Stevens accordingly signed it first and was followed by Tahola.

Annan-ata sub chief of Upper Chihalis: "This chief is our father. We want a piece of land in our own country. A small piece. We won't go to the Kwainaiutl. We will die on our ground."

Governor Stevens told them that the paper did not say they should go to Kwinai-utl.

Annanata said: They want the Innitie prairie, and Smiths Prairie.

Governor Stevens said that they should be placed where they could reach their old ground in a few days, perhaps in one. He wanted them to leave it to the great Father to select the place.

Annanata: They were fixed in what they had said.

Mr. Shaw and Judge Ford then represented to them the position in which they now stood with regard to their lands that their wishes would be communicated to the President, and [366 32] that he would act as he saw fit. But that the whites were constantly increasing and pushing them off of one piece and another of land and that unless some arrangement was made they would be driven away from those grounds altogether.

Tu-leh-uk and his sub chief came up to say that they were all agreed in their feeling towards the Governor and satisfaction at his sentiments but that they do not wish to move.

A long desultory explanation ensued. Cowlitz came up and Chinooks were willing to sign themselves as soon as the others did but as the Upper Chihalis had come first they ought to sign first. It was now evident that great difficulty would be found in bringing these bands together. Not only was each very much averse to quitting its own soil, but the jealousy of each other was very apparent further adjournment was made till afternoon.

Afternoon. Governor Stevens: "After what you have said today, I think the paper had better be read to you again. Listen carefully to it. If you don't understand it, say so plainly.

Treaty again read, and the Indians requested to say if there was anything they desired to have explained farther.

Governor Stevens: My children the paper has been read and explained. If you want it further I will do it. This paper has my heart in it and I believe it to be that of the Great Father. I believe that he will agree to it and that no alteration will be necessary. Now I have thought carefully over your wants. I have been sent here to be your father and I intend to be so. After hearing your wants patiently, I have done what I think best for you. You are offered a price for your lands which you have asked for long and I have provided a home for you. A father who loves his children does not change his mind without reason. It will be so with me because I am satisfied it is for your good. If your hearts are with it you will sign it. If not I cannot buy your lands.

"Now go back till tomorrow and then finally give me your answer."

March 1st Thursday Governor Stevens again addressed the Indians assembled. "My children. Yesterday I told you my [367 33] mind, what I believe was for your good, that when a father had made up his mind as to what was good for his children he could not change. If he did, he ceased to be a father. You have all said you were glad to have one, to have me for father. That did my heart good and I determined to be henceforth, and as such I can only look to your good. But he is always patient and listens patiently, for their good. He does not strike or beat or force his children. I as your father shall not force you. A father listening to his children if they are good can always satisfy them and I think I can satisfy you. I want you to be satisfied that I propose to select will be for your good. We have agreed upon all points but that you want to have food, to be furnished with clothing and tools, to be cured if sick, we only differ as to the place where you are to have this. A father however always listens to his children and I will to you."

Anannata Sub chief Upper Chihalis: "My father, I have many people. I speak for the Cowlitz and Satsop too. We will give up all our lands to you except from opposite the mouth of Black River down to the lower end of Smith's Prairie. That is the spot we have chosen. They are very proud at the promises made them but don't want all to come together. They did not want to unite with the others."

Kwonesappa Cowlitz sub chief: "They were all of one mind there. Would not forget what had been promised, were willing to give up all their lands on that river and come down on the Chihalis. It was good for them to go so far but did not want to go below. He was glad they would be made as white people. He had long wished for this. He wanted the privilege of travelling as (you) have said. They are much rejoiced to be clothed and enjoy these benefits. It makes their hearts good."

Yowannus: "Last night we came to this conclusion and now only ask for a small piece of land. We are glad to have united. We are afraid of belief driven among different people whose language we did not understand. We have finally settled on a place for these five bands, the Cowlitz, Upper Cowlitz, Upper Chihalis, Satsop, and Mountain Indians (a remnant of the *Kwalk wi o quas*) [*Swaal*]. We have heard all our Father has said patiently. It is all good except the place he proposes as our reserve. We don't like the idea of going among other people speaking a different language."

Tu-leh-uit: We are very proud all of us. We have made you our father. We give up all our lands to you but a [368 34] small piece. We Kwinai-utl speak a different language. All those on this river from *Wan ool chie* down are willing to go together. I want but a small piece of ground where my horses can eat. We are pleased to raise potatoes. We want to raise them on a small piece of our own ground. This land on the river now belongs to the Americans. We only want to fish here."

Mak-an-hu, Northside of Gray's Bay: "He wants the Big chief to look out for those north of the Chihalis. They are willing to give up their lands and go ever on the west side with *Tu-leh-uk*. They have four rivers on the Northern side which they give up."

A Satsop sub chief: "There are no whites on our lands but we are willing to give them up, and go with the Upper Chihalis etc., on to the piece they asked for. They only speak for a small reserve from mouth of Black River to Smith's Prairie" (10 miles).

Cowlitz Chief, *Ow hys*: "We are very proud of our Father. He has but one tongue. We are the same in face, and are willing to come together (with the Upper Chihalis, etc) We are now willing to give up our land. We want the privilege of going to our old grounds and want a paper to show that we may do so. We are glad to think that the roads are open to us, that we may go where we wish. We are very glad to see the first Americans who came among us, are glad we can still visit them."

Nah-kotti, Chinook: "Wants to live on the Nasal on Shoalwater Bay where he lives in winter and gets his salmon. If he was two days without salmon his heart failed him. There was a road on the Peninsula called *Nah-kotti*'s Road and landing. He gave away this and his land but wanted to go over it to get salmon. Wanted the same privilege as the white men as to travel and labor, to pick up wrecks etc. on the beach, would give up half he found."

A young Indian on behalf of *Skemaqus*, the Head Chief of Wah-kiakum (who was sick and could not come.) The old man told him to come up here and say that he wants to die on his ground. All his children lay there and he wanted to be buried there too. Wanted the two creeks by his house where the salmon came, would give up all the rest.

Ta-ho-la, Kwinai-utl chief: "Wanted the mouth of their river. Would give up the Upper part. There was no whites [369 35] there. He don't want to lie to the white chief. He had heard what the governor says, and will remember it."

Kah-kow-en: a very old chief of the Lower Chihalis "He has already given the white chief his ground. He was once a great chief and owned all the ground. He likes the Boston Chief, the great chief very much. It was raining and very bad weather. He was glad to hear that they were to stop, that Gov. Stevens was to go up the river (to Olympia) and he would go down. He had not many people now and he was very glad that their lands should become American. He wants to keep a small part of it. The whites would not be likely to come there. *The sea beach was his country*. He did not want to leave it. He was an old man and would soon peg out, and he should not know much more about the whites. He wants to be heard but was done talking.

Mo-te-lis a sub chief from north side of Gray's Harbor: "He now listens to the young men talking. He has not much to say himself. He just looks on, is so old that his heart is dried up. He owns a large country the small rivers round the North side Grays Harbor and wants to stay there till he dies."

Governor Stevens: "I have listened with much pleasure to you this morning. I see that good is working its way with you. Yesterday and the day before the Cowlitz wanted a place on their river. They wanted two places, the Satsops their place, but you have thought over my words and talked together and having now talked it over you who wanted five places are now satisfied with one. And the Chinook only want a place to fish and plant their potatoes and the Kwinai-utl are satisfied with the mouth of their river. So that you now want only four places instead of eight. Now there are old men here, and they know how many there were of you formerly. Then you found you could live even on the Kwinai-utl River. There used to be as many as all of you now. Now this paper does not say you all shall be placed on that river. It only says you shall be placed between Grays Harbor and Cape Flattery. You know Gray's Harbor, that you have to work a whole winter's day to cross it, and it is all salt water. You know there are a number of streams north of Grays Harbor. On the Copalis there is a prairie, now there used to be twice as many Indians as there are here North of there and they could not sell salmon, oysters and cranberries to the settlers for there [370 36] were none. Well you can now not only sell these things but you will besides be furnished yearly with clothing, tools, etc. I want you to agree to a paper which will be good for you, and that the great Father shall select this country where twice as many used to live and where all of you now shall. You say you speak different languages. We know it but I have told you how many children the great Father has, and Indians speaking different languages are often placed together. Do you have any difficulty now? You live near each other and talk together, without difficulty. Now I made treaties with the Sound Indians. *Kow-Kow-en* knows the Klallams, Chemakums and Skokomish spoke different languages, and were once at war. They all came together[,] made same obligations, and I told them to agree together, talk it over. They did and were finally satisfied, but we told them as we did you that we would separate their respective grounds. They finally agreed on it. So with you, we will put each of you on a good place for itself within this reserve; but you are afraid you cannot get to the settlements. How can Col. Simmons get to you, or I? But you can have a road, you can go to Shoalwater Bay and to Chinook already. I want you to think it over. I am sorry that you are homesick and that *Kow kow·en* wants to get home. We must take time for this, and if you want the paper read again it can be.

Adjourned till afternoon.

Evening Governor Stevens remarked "that they had got part way this morning and he hoped they had come together this evening. That he could not consent to their proposition of this morning. They professed to regard him as their father, but they always went back to the same thing and did not trust his promises. Informs them as to the course pursued as to the California Indians where a great many small tribes with no heads. No treaties were made with them, but reserves were established and they were moved on to them. Mr. Shaw the interpreter illustrated the condition of things in California by his own observation there. The great Father does it for them because they have no will of their own. They do not go voluntarily, but are yet satisfied when they get there. Asked which was best for them, to consent voluntarily to this Treaty and put themselves under his protection or to be moved in this way. They are now diminishing in numbers and in the present way are like to become fewer still, every year. I have taken pains to bring with me white men whom you have long known as your friends, and who understand everything about you, your interests, and we are all of one opinion.

Annantata: "The Governor knew that they had always lived near the whites and they wanted to continue to do so. [371 37]

Gov. Stevens: "They were not to be moved for two years at any rate and even then those whom the whites wished to have remain with them could do so."

Ke-heh-uk: "Has been all the way up the Coast to Cape Flattery. There is no good land. It was all stones."

Gov. Stevens: "Indians had told him there where tide prairies down on the Coast for their horses, but besides that they had the privilege of grazing their horses everywhere on open and common lands."

Annantata: "Refers to the Reserves on the Sound. Other Indians had reservations in their own country. Why not they.

Gov. Stevens: "The reasons here were different. The Reserves there were very small. The Indians picked them out and when they were examined, two proved to be very poor. Proposed to give them a large place. On the other hand he had put all the Klallams, Chim a cums and Skokomish on one place who were twice as many, as all the present tribes.

Annantata: "They had already yielded a great deal. Five bands who knew but little of one another had all agreed to come to one place."

Kish-kok: He knew very little of these other people, but he gave up his own country, the whole of it, (and it was a very good one) to come to the Satsop Country. There were many of the Cowlitz and so on of the others and they had given up much. He never saw Mr. Shaw but once, he never told any one before what he told him. The Governor called the Indians his children, and he thought all they could do was to yield to their father all their land and to come down with the Mountain people as far as the Satsop. Supposed he would be satisfied with it. He gave away the whole of his country at all events. It was all first rate land. He thought to please the great father by doing so. When Mr. Shaw saw him he told him the Governor would be glad to have him give up his lands and he now did so, and wanted one Boston to live with them and take care of them. If they moved and settled at the mouth of Satchall, he wanted a white man to stake it out and put down corner Stakes. When they came down the Cowlitz, *Yack-kannan* (an old Chief) was mad at him for coming to make the trade. He however adhered to what he said. [372 38]

Gov. Stevens was glad to hear him say how well he was disposed. Why not let his great Father choose for him.

Yowannus: is heart was good.   Mr. Governor had given him a paper on Mr. Ford recommendation. He gave up all the good country that had belonged to him and came down to the Satchel, and wanted the place to extend to a small creek below it for the five or six bands he had spoken of.

Gov. Stevens understood him fully, but he could not put that in the paper. There was a saw mill and two settlers on that creek and two settlers on the prairie. They had cut a road which he could not take away. I want them to listen to what I say. They don't listen but repeat the same thing. Settlers would come still further down the river and make roads and what then would be their position. The great Father was constantly sending settlers here. The Boston country was full and he had to send them away.

Annantata: "They were good friends of Mr. Fort [Sidney Ford], Mr. Goodell, Mr. Armstrong and Mr. Strall, they wanted them to live near them. If either of them told him to do anything he went and did it."

Gov. Stevens: "Would they like to have the California system carried out where they did not ask them, but put them on a reserve?"

Annantata: "No. Indeed!"

Gov. Stevens: "What will you do then? Will you leave it to President by Treaty, when the paper promises you a good place, or is he to select it himself without? For it comes to that finally."

Tu-leh-uk: "We cannot understand anything about it."

Council broke up suddenly.

Friday March 2nd Indians again convened. Col. Simmons announced that when the Governor had done talking it was all done.

Governor Stevens: "We have now been here a week. I have heard you all. Only one band the *Kwin ai utl* have [373 39] hearts like mine, but the paper is nothing without all signs. The *Kwin ai utl* alone leave it to the great Father. There can therefore be no Treaty and I shall not call upon you again to treat, but next Summer I shall send Col. Simmons through that country to examine it and when a good place is found I shall say to the great Father put these people upon it. There will then be no treaty, no promises but you will be in the hands of the great Father to do as we please. We shall recollect however the willingness of the Kwin ai utl and the good behavior of the Cowlitz, Chinook and Upper Chihalis. In regard to the lower Chihalis, I have a word to say to their chief *Tu-leh-uk*. *Tu-leh-uk* come here! bring your paper! (Takes his commission and reads it.) A man who cannot control his people is no chief. You have not prevented your people from drinking. You brought some rum here and your father was drunk here. I reproved you for it at the time, and passed it over, but last night you behaved disrespectfully, you let your people defy me. (They had fired their guns during the night) You are no longer a chief. (Tears [up] the paper.) I have only one word. There has been no treaty. I therefore give you no presents but the Kwin ai utl will hereafter receive presents when Mr. Simmons comes to their country. You will all have your potatoes and return home."

Broke up the Council.

Saturday March 3rd. It having been found impracticable to bring the Indians voluntarily upon one reservation, Governor Stevens dismissed them and this morning started on his return. The rain of the last week continued and the heavy rise in the river impeded the canoes so much that the party did not reach Fords till the afternoon of the 15th. On the 7th the Governor and Secretary returned to Olympia.

The following is a copy of the Treaty prepared with the expectations of its being adopted and was signed by Gov. Stevens, and the Kwin-ai-utl Chief, but which was not finally concluded for the reasons above shown.

Articles of Agreement and Convention, made and concluded at *Ki-seh-mah*, near the mouth of the Chihalis River, in the Territory of Washington, this __ day of February Eighteen hundred and fifty five, by Isaac I. Stevens, Governor arid Superintendent of Indian Affairs of said Territory on the part of the United States, and the undersigned Chiefs, head men and delegates of the different tribes and bands of Cowlitz Upper and Lower Chihalis and Quinaielt Indians, on the part of said tribes and bands and duly [374 40] authorized thereto by them, and is as follows:

NOTE: This treaty was ultimately adopted, See "Treaty with the Quinaielt, etc., 1855, 12 Stats. 971; Vol. 2 Kappler's Laws and Treaties." [375 1]

Official Proceedings at the Council held at the
Council Ground in the Walla Walla Valley
with the Yakama Nation of Indians and which resulted in the
conclusion of a Treaty on the 9th of June 1855.[85]

May 28th 1855.

At 11 a.m. *Kamaiakun, Owhi & Skloom*, Yakama Chiefs came to the Council Ground; they had been greatly delayed on the road by continued heavy rains and consequent high water in the streams. But few of their people accompanied them as it is the season for digging Roots and catching Salmon. The Yakamas were so accompanied by Delegates from the *Pahwanwappam*, *Pisqouse* [*Psk^waws*], *Wenatshappam* and Palouse Indians, all Tribes or Bands acknowledging *Kamaikun* as their Head Chief and there were present Representatives from the Bands living on the Columbia River down to the White Salmon River.

Gov. Stevens addressed them briefly, welcoming them; offering them provisions as his friends and guests; and inviting them to meet tomorrow in council at this place and hear what the Commissioners wished to say to all the Indians in this County.

---

[85] [See portraits on last page, each correctly spelt name is in index]

The next day, the 29th the Yakama Chiefs attended at the Council and listened to an explanation of the objects had in view by the Governor in proposing to Treat with them. They continued to attend from day to day and Gov. Stevens stated to them fully the terms of the Treaty he proposed to conclude with them; the amount to be paid for their lands and the manner of payment; the Extent of the Reservation to be set apart for them and that upon the Reservation he wished to place the Yakamas, the Colvilles, the *Pisquoise & Oakinakanes* and the Bands on the Columbia River below the Mouth of the Umatilla as low down as the mouth of the Cowlitz River; The Yakama Chiefs made no reply to these propositions until the 8th of June when upon the request of Gov. Stevens that he would speak his mind, Kamaiakun spoke briefly saying in effect that most of his people had left their country, some gone to the Caloopooyer Country, some to Nisqually and some to the *Taih*. He wished the Americans to settle in his country on the Waggon Road. He spoke for his people not for himself alone. He wished no Goods for himself. He was tired talking and waiting here and wished to get back to his Garden. [376 2]

Skloom and *Owhi* spoke but only in a general manner and the Council adjourned it being understood that the Yakama Chiefs had determined to return home the next day.

In the evening Gov. Stevens had a lengthy interview with Skloom which did not result in anything conclusive: but in the morning, June 9th, at an early hour Kamaiakun visited Gov. Stevens and announced his determination to return home that day: Gov. Stevens endeavored to convince him that it was better to reflect well upon the course he, the Head Chief of his Nation, was about to pursue; whether it would result in good or Evil to his people and advised him to remain until the conclusion of the Council with the Nes Perces and others, and try to make up his mind to a Treaty which would certainly be beneficial to his people.

Kamaikun said he was tired of hearing so much talking; he himself did not wish to talk: Why did not *Owhi* and *Skloom* speak? He Kamaikun did not wish to be Head Chief, but, since they all said he must talk; must be the Chief; well let it be so. He would now speak: He would make the Treaty proposed; he liked the Reservation and wished to collect there all his people; they were much scattered, as he had before said, and he desired to have them sent home. He then gave a statement of the Indian Tribes and Bands who considered him their head Chief, viz: The Yakamas proper the Palouse, *Pisquouse, Okinakanes* and Methows, the *Pshawnwappam* and all the Bands on the Columbia below the Umatilla as far as the White Salmon River and these he would undertake to govern; <u>He was satisfied with the Reservation in his country, but desired a small piece of land at the place called *Wenatshapam* – where the Indians take many fish – for the Pisquouse & Methows</u>. He wished the papers written so that he might sign them today and go home. This was all. During the interview several Head men of the Palouse, Pisquouse & Methows were present and unanimously assented to *Kamaikun*'s decision.

Kamaikun was present at the General Council during the day but did not speak; and in the evening immediately after the adjournment of the Council he called upon Gov. Stevens for the Treat[y] and signed it: *Owhi* and *Skloom* did the same, as also the Palouse Chief *Kahlatoose*, and all the Chiefs present named by *Kamaiakun* as being under his jurisdiction. Several Chiefs of the Bands at Dalles and above, who were in attendance during the first days of the Council, had returned home to catch their usual supply of Salmon, these, *Kamaiakin* said, as also all that he had named would sign the Treaty whenever it was presented to them if Gov. Stevens thought it necessary. [377 3]

The Treaty was then duly witnessed and the Council with the Yakamas declared adjourned *sine dei*.

On Monday the 11th The goods, presents for the Yakamas were portioned out and Kamaiakun although he would not take any goods for himself superintended the division among his people.

Kamaikun said he had never taken goods from the whites as presents: he did not wish them now but when the Treaty was pronounced good by the President then he would live on the Yakama Reservation and accept his share of the annuities and other payments.

The Chiefs were entertained at Gov. Stevens' Table and throughout their stay here appeared to have the most friendly feelings towards the whites.

Towards evening, Kamaikun, Owhi and Skloom and their people started on their return to the Yakima Valley.

I hereby certify the above to be a true record of the proceedings at the Yakama Council.

(Sgd.) James Doty
Secty. Treaties W.T.

Approved and for further detail, see record of the Joint Treaty Official Proceedings

(Sgd.) Isaac I. Stevens
Gov. & Supt Ind Affairs Washington Terr'ty [378 4]

Council Grounds. Camp Stevens
Walla Walla Valley June 13th 1855

Hon. Geo. W. Manypenny
Commissioner Indian Affairs
Washington D.C.

Sir.

We as joint Commissioners have made treaties with the tribes common to the two Territories of Washington and Oregon, of which we are respectively the Superintendents, and herewith have the honor to enclose the Treaties and the record of the official proceedings.

The tribes with whom treaties have thus been made are the Nes Perses, Walla Wallas, Cayuses and Umatillas, of whom 2,650 are estimated to be in Washington Territory and 1,350 in Oregon as per following Table.

	Washington	Oregon
Nes Perses	1,950	550
Walla Wallas	550	250
Cayuses	150	350
Umatillas		200
	2,650	1,350

The lands ceded by these Tribes are as follows:

	Washington	Oregon	Total
Nes Perses	12,320 sq. miles	11,818	24,138
Walla Wallas			
& Cayuses			
& Umatillas	2,903	3,362	6,270
Total	15,228	15,180	30,408

The Indians have been placed on two Reservations. The Nes Perses in their own country and mostly in the Territory of Washington and the remaining Tribes on a single Reservation in

Oregon.   Separate Treaties have accordingly been made with the Nes Perses, and with the confederated tribes and bands of the Walla Wallas, Cayuses and Umatillas.

The reserves of these two Treaties are as follows.

Nes Perses	22 sq. miles
Walla Wallas, Cayuses	
& Umatillas	800
Total estimate of country included in reservations	5,922. [379 5]

All the above numbers and estimates may be corrected hereafter, in taking a census of the Indians in their own country, and locating and surveying the reservations. The census of the Nes Perces has been furnished by the chiefs of the several bands. They have 2,133 persons at home, 16% in Washington and 463 in Oregon, and they estimate 300 to 500 at Buffalo [hunting in Plains]. (We have assumed 357 at Buffalo.) 8% from Oregon and 280 from Washington. The Census will be taken by Looking Glass on his return thither.

The reservations may seem to be large especially that of the Nes Perses [Perces] tribe.

All these tribes own large bands of horses and cattle and have small farms.

The Nes Perses country is well described by Lawyer in his speech in council as poor and barren, and with the provision that other tribes not exceeding the aggregate number of the Spokanes, Walla Wallas, Cayuses and Umatillas may be placed upon the reservation, it is not believed it can be objected to. The Nes Perses own some 15,000 horses and cattle and the Cayuses, Walla Wallas, and Umatillas some 20,000.

The Cayuse reservation is decidedly limited and is simply adequate to their wants.

The initial proceedings in collecting the Indians were taken by the Superintendent of Washington Territory who in January dispatched Mr. Doty to the Indian country for that purpose. On learning from Mr. Doty that there was a probability that treaties could be effected the Superintendent of Oregon was invited to join in the operations as a joint commissioner and at a meeting at Vancouver on the 4th April the arrangements were made for their joint action and on the 7th of April the 20th day of May was fixed upon for opening the Council. Instructions were given accordingly to the proper Indian officers.

A copy of the official journal of the Superintendent of Washington will give somewhere in detail the operations of Mr. Doty the Sec'ty of the Washington Superintendent in establishing the camp for the Treaty and in collecting the Indians. The information has already been partially communicated officially to the department. The Supt. of Oregon despatched Agent Thompson to the Indian country, who also gave notice to the chiefs of the Walla Wallas, Cayuses and Umatillas and conferred with Mr. Doty on the Council ground. [280 6]

In the general operations of the commissioners the Indians of the Yakama Nation and those of Oregon below the Umatillas were also assembled at the Council Ground to embrace the largest possible field, and to promote the great ends of peace and friendship between the different tribes, the Supt. of Washington deemed it best to commence the negotiations with the Yakamas in open council with the Tribes common to the two Territories to which arrangement the Sup't of Oregon assented. They were consummated in a separate and special council.

The commissioners deemed it their duty on reaching the Dalles to make a requisition on Major Hains [Raines] to despatch a military force to the Council ground. A copy of their letter to him is herewith enclosed, which sets forth the reasons for their action. It is due to *Pee-o-pee-mox-a-mox* the Walla Walla chief to state that on receiving from Mr. Doty information of the turbulent conduct of five young men of the Cayuse Tribe and a request that he as the only real chief in the valley should restrain them, he executed his authority immediately and no further trouble was given by them. These five young men had previously much annoyed the settlers entering their houses in a threatening manner, breaking down their enclosures and indicating a bad spirit.

The commissioners reached the Treaty Ground on the 21st May. The Nes Perses on the 23rd May, the Cayuses on the 25th, the Walla Wallas and the Yakamas on the 27th and the council was opened on ·the 29th of May.

At the time of opening the Council the Cayuses, Walla Wallas and Yakamas refused both tobacco and provisions as did the Salmon band of the Nes Perses tribe.

The official journal will show the peculiar phases of the negotiations, and the complete concurrence of all the Indians in the arrangements finally agreed upon.

Looking Glass a prominent Nes Perses chief reached the council ground on the 9th of May, seven days from the St. Marys Valley and on Saturday endeavored by a bold stroke to depose Lawyer the Head Chief, assume authority in his stead and dictate other terms. The council was adjourned, the Tribe refused to recognise his authority and on yesterday Looking Glass signed the Treaty next to the Head Chief entirely satisfied with the terms. The Cayuses whom the unexpected course of Looking Glass had encouraged to resisting their positive agreement with equal cheerfulness signed the Treaty. [381 7]

Thus has ended a most difficult and protracted negotiation. The council ground was in the Cayuse country near the place consecrated by the blood of the missionary Dr. Whitman and his family who were killed in 1847 by the Indians of the Cayuse tribe.

Its effects on the peace of the country hardly admits of exaggeration, and no Treaty been effected there would probably have been blood shed and open war the present year. Its effect upon the Snakes will be great and it will save a large expenditure in consequence, in the military operation of the present year to chastise that tribe for its atrocities last season.

The official proceedings will show the effects made to place all the Indians of the joint Treaties on one Reservation. To effect treaties the commissioners had no alternative than to agree to two Reservations. It was deemed due both to the Indians and settlers that the provision for a waggon road should be inserted in the joint treaty providing for a reservation in Oregon.

The official journal is so full that no further elaboration of the matter seems called for in this communication, a map is enclosed showing the country ceded and the lands reserved.

In regard to administration, the commissioners are of opinion that from the present time it would be impolitic to have the Indians of the same Tribe under two jurisdictions, accordingly we have made arrangements from this time that the Nes Perses shall be under the jurisdiction of the Sup't of Washington and the Walla Wallas, Cayuse under that of the Supt't of Oregon.

Each Superintendent will accordingly at the proper time furnish the necessary information to the Department in all matters appertaining to the execution of the Treaty and the future government of the Tribes.

The reservations will be particularly examined and reported upon to the Department.

We are
Very Respectfully
Your Obedient Servants
Isaac I. Stevens
Governor & Supt. Indian Affairs
Washington Territory
Joel Palmer
Superintendent Indian Affairs
Oregon Territory [382 8]

A true copy of the record of
the official proceedings at the Council in the Walla Walla Valley,
held jointly by Isaac I. Stevens Gov. & Supt. W.T.
Joel Palmer Supt. Indian Affairs O.T.
On the part of the United States
with the Tribes of Indians
named in the Treaties made at that Council
June 9th and 11th 1855 [383 9]

PROCEEDINGS AT INDIAN TREATIES IN WASHINGTON TERRITORY EAST OF THE CASCADE MOUNTAINS

Programme of operations at the Walla Walla Council decided upon by the Commissioners Gov. Isaac I. Stevens and Superintendent Joel Palmer, May 22nd A. D. 1855

Present – Indians common to both Territories, Oregon and Washington, viz. Nes Perses, Cayuse and Walla. Tribes in Oregon from the western boundary of the Snake Tribe to the Cascades of the Columbia.

Tribes in Washington from the Bitter Root to the Cascades, except the Spokanes, Coeur d'Alenes, Colvilles, and Pend D'Oreilles.

Gov. Stevens and Gen'l Palmer Superintendent of Washington and Oregon to act jointly for the Nes Perses, Walla Wallas and Cayuse common to the two Territories. To agree upon the terms of treaty. To sign jointly. Each acting for the Indians the above tribes in his own jurisdiction.

Gen'l Palmer sole commissioner for the Oregon Indians proper present at the council.

Gov. Stevens sole commissioner for the Washington Territory Indians proper present at the council.

Gov. Stevens to preside at the council.

The proceedings to be carefully recorded for the Tribes common to the two Territories separately by the Secty of Gov. Stevens and the Secty of Gen'l Palmer.

The two records to be carefully compared and certified jointly by the commissioners. [384 10]

Each commissioner to appoint an agent and commissary.

Gov. Stevens for the Washington Nes Perses, Cayuses and Walla Wallas. Gen'l Palmer for the Oregon Nes Perses, Cayuses and Walla Wallas. Goods and provisions to be distributed to the Nes Perses, Cayuses and Walla Wallas, by the Superintendents in proportion to the Indians under the jurisdiction of each.

OFFICERS OF THE JOINT TREATY

Gov Stevens } Commissioners
Gen'l Palmer }
James Doty, Sect'y for Washington Territory
Wm McCoy,   "   "   Oregon   "
H.A. Crosbie, Commissary for Washington Territory
C. Olney,   "   Oregon
Agent R.R. Thompson, in charge of Oregon Nes Perses, Cayuses and Walla Wallas.
Wm. Craig, Interpreter, Washington Territory

N. Raymond,   "   "
_____ Leaufoher, interpreter, Oregon Territory
John Flette   "

Census of the Nes Perses, Cayuses and Walla Wallas.

	Washington T	Oregon T	Total
Nes Perses	1400	400	1800
Cayuses	150	350	500
Walla Wallas			
including Umatillas 600		200	800

This census to be revised on the Indians reaching the ground.

A public table for the prominent chief's under charter of agents Landsdale, Thompson and Bolon.

Gov. Stevens details Palmer and F. Genitto.

Sup't Palmer also details one or two men.

Col. Crosbie to take personal charge of issues for public table, or issues of provisions to Indian tribes, and goods distributed. Provisions and goods to be turned over to the agents, and issued under their direction. [385 11]

May 28th, Monday.

Agent Bolon with an interpreter went to meet the Yakamas who are supposed to be near at hand, and returned at 10 a.m. having seen *Cam-i-ah-kum* [*Kamaiyakin*] and also the Chief *Poe-o-pee-mox-a-mox*.

The latter had said to Mr. Bolon, "that someone had informed him that the chiefs and others in the Commissioners camp had said that he was unfriendly to the whites. That his heart was with the Cayuses whose hearts were bad. He was very sorry to hear this. He had always been friendly to the whites and was so now. He should go today to see the Commissioners, and ask why such things had been said of him."

The Commissioners and Sec'ty Doty visited the Lawyer at his lodge, as he was unable to walk without great difficulty. An old gun-shot wound received at the battle of Pierres Hole, having broken open again causing much pain.

The Lawyer explained a map of the Nes Perses country which he had drawn for Gov. Stevens. Several chiefs came in and suddenly *U-u-sune-mel-o-can*, one of the chiefs, said:

"The Cayuses wish us to go to their camp and hold a council with them and *Pee-o-pee-mox-a-mox*."

What have we to say to the Cayuses or *Pee-pee-mox-a-mox*? What are their hearts to us? Did we propose to hold a council with them or ask them for advise? Our hearts are Nes Perses hearts and we know them. We came here to hold a great council with the Great Chief of the Americans, and know the straight forward truth to pursue and are alone responsible for our actions. Three Cayuses came last night and spoke to Jim and two other head men urging them to come to a council at the Cayuse camp, to meet *Pee-o-pee-mox-a-mox* and *Cam-i-ah-kum*. He did not wish to go; they insisted; then I said to them; You had best say no more. His mind is made up.

What do you come here for and ask these chiefs to come to a council when to the Head Chief and the rest you say nothing! Have we not told your messenger, yesterday, that our hearts are not Cayuse hearts? Go home! [386 12]

Our chiefs will not go. We have our own people to take care of, they give us enough trouble, and we will not have the Cayuse troubles on our hands. This is my heart."

Lawyer opened a book containing in their own language the advice left to them by their Great Chief Ellis, and read as follows:

Ellis said: "Whenever the Great Chief of the Americans shall come into your country to give you laws, accept them! The Walla Wallas heart is a Walla Wallas; a Cayuse heart is a Cayuse; so is a Yakamas heart a Yakamas; a Nes Perses heart is a Nes Perses heart; but they have all received the white law. They are all going straight, yes! While the Nes Perses are going straight, why should they turn aside to follow others who are going straight? Ellis, advise is to accept the white law. I have read it to you to show my heart."

The Commissioners were glad to hear what had been spoken. They knew the Nes Perses were always friendly to the whites. Lewis & Clark had said this and all white men. The Commissioners were friendly to all Indians, and when they come together would tell them so, and show it by what they propose to do. They had no more to say now because when they spoke they wanted all the Indians to hear. The Commissioners then returned to camp.

At 11a.m. *Pee-o-pee-mox-a-mox, Cam-i-ah-kum, Owhi, Skloom* and a number of Walla Wallas and Yakamas rode into camp, and having shaken hands in the most friendly manner, with the Commissioners and agents, seated themselves under the arbor in front of the Commissioners tent and indulged in a smoke; using their own tobacco exclusively although other was offered them.

Gov. Stevens then said to them: "My friends, we are glad to see you. We are glad to see all the Indians around here, and what we say to one is the same to all. You will see that what we say to one tribe is spoken to all the tribes. When you are ready to come into council, when the council is opened, we will speak to you of the important business for which you have been called together. We have near to our hearts the prosperity of the Indians and the propositions to be made to you will prove this.

We shall endeavor to clearly explain the wishes of the Government, in order that you may fully understand them; as it is our desire you should. [387 13]

If it is convenient to you we will suggest tomorrow at noon as the time for opening the council. We look upon you as friends, shall so speak to you; as one friend speaks to another, and wish you to reply as such.

Gen'l Palmer said: "I am equally pleased with Gov. Stevens to see you. Many years ago I met you and considered you friends and I look upon you as the same now, and hope our meeting will prove this to be true.

We come here to promote peace and happiness among you, leaving behind all that was bad, bringing only that which was good; thus we have but one heart. When you understand this then there will be no difficulty but we will all work together for the best.

As all the chief are not here we will not speak of important business but wait till all are present.

I want to know if the time fixed by Gov. Stevens for opening the council is good, and if you will meet.

Pee-o-pee-mox-mox said: "I want more than one interpreter at the Council that we may know they translate truly."

Gen'l Palmer said: "You may have any one who can comprehend what he is told to interpret, and who will suit you. We wish you to understand clearly what is said. Will you designate a interpreter whom you have confidence in?"

The Chief said: "I do not wish my boys running around the camps of the whites as these young men do. (alluding to some young Nes Perces who were lounging about our camp feeling quite at home as they knew themselves to be among friends.)

Pee-o-pee-mox-mox said: "We have rode over today merely to see the Commissioners. [388 14]

Gov. Stevens said: "Come and see us as our friends and guests. *Cam-i-ah-kum* knows that our people have been in his country, and eaten of his food. So of *Pee-o-pee-mox-mox* and the Nes Perses. We always give food to our friends when they visit us, you have been invited to come and are welcome to whatever we have.

We have a public table at which we are glad to have all our friends sit, and share that which hospitality induces us to offer.

We have provided plenty of food, and have already given beef, corn and potatoes to those on the ground. They were invited and wish them to have plenty to eat.

I was glad to hear that my friend *Skloom* had been so kind to Mr. Tinkham one of my party who crossed the mountains. He was in want and Skloom gave him provisions and clothing.

The Chiefs then took their leave. [389 15]

PROCEEDINGS AT THE COUNCIL HELD AT CAMP STEVENS WALLA WALLA VALLEY, ON THE 29TH DAY OF MAY 1855

Col. Stevens, Superintendent of Indian Affairs in Washington Territory, and Gen'l Joel Palmer, Superintendent of Indian Affairs in Oregon Territory, with the following named chiefs, delegates and head men present at the Council, and representing their respective tribes and bands of Indians as below stated:

For the Nes Perses: Lawyer, Joseph, *U-u-sune-mal-o-can*, James, Timothy, Red Wolfe, Spotted Eagle, Three Feathers, Jason, Jacobs, *Cow-pook*, *Is-coh-tim*, *Kay-kay-map*, *Tu-per-lan-its-a-kum*, Billy, *Toh-ton-mel-a-wot*, The Snipe, Bold Eagle, and others.

For the Cayuses: The Young Chief, *Stsachus*, *Camaspilo*, and others
For the Walla Wallas: *Pee-o-pee-mox-a-mox*
For the Yakamas: *Cam-i-ah-kun*, *Ow-hi*, *Skloom*, *Kow-was-say-ic*, *Si-ry-was*, *Skin-pah*
For the Palouses: *Kah-lat-toose*
For the Spokanes: Gerry
For the Pisquoise and Methow: ?? ??
For the Oak-kin-a-kanes: ??

On May 29th, at 2:02 p.m. the Council opened. Present: the commissioners, officers of Treaties, the Indian agents, and some fifty citizens.

Besides the Indian chiefs already mentioned and some others, about 1800 Indians, Nes Perses, Cayuses, Walla Wallas, Yakamas, Dalles Indians and others on the Columbia above were assembled.

After the pipe had been smoked sometime, Gov. Stevens said: "My Children: Before entering upon the council we [390 16]   must have good and faithful interpreters. We want men who will state truly and exactly all that is said; we want men that you know to be good men; men that you can trust; we want no others.

We propose as interpreters for the Nes Perses: William Craig, this man, (pointing to Mr. Craig) who has long lived with you, also McDauphin and Delaware Jim.[86]

For the Cayuses: Mr. Pembrom [Pembrun] and Mr. Olney.

For the Walla and Yakamas: John Whitford.

Thus for each language we propose to have two and three interpreters. Now I ask you, do you want others added to the number? Are you satisfied with these men? If you have any others you wish to propose, speak out, for we wish you to be satisfied.

Stachus, a Cayuse said: We know of no others whom we would wish. There may be some words hard for them to make us understand, but we think the arrangement good as it is.

Gov. Stevens said: When you cannot understand what we say to you, stop us and we will repeat it.

Each interpreter will now be sworn to be a faithful interpreter.

Gov. Stevens then administered to the interpreters the following oath.

You solemly swear in the presence of Almighty God, that you will well and truly interpret to the best of your ability what may be said by the Commissioners for the United States holding this council on the one part; and the chiefs and head men of the tribes and bands of Indians here present on the other part. So help you God.

Gov. Stevens then said: My children, the interpreters have each taken a solemn oath in the presence of Almighty God, to be true and faithful interpreters. I will now read the form of the oath. (and it was read as above)

Gov. Stevens continued: My children; I have much to say to you; my brother here Gov. Palmer will have much to say to you. We want you to listen and be comfortable [391 17] at the same time. We want clear skies, we want the ground to be dry. We will meet tomorrow with a clear sun and the day before us. Then we will open the whole subject, and will see if our hearts and your hearts will not come together.

We have met as friends today, tomorrow we will meet as friends and then enter upon our business. I therefore adjourn the council till 10 o'clock a.m. tomorrow. The weather is rainy and bad, tomorrow we hope the skies will be clear and you will all be able to be present. Should it rain tomorrow we will meet when it clears up.

One word on another point, you have come here by our invitation and are our guests. I have entered, and so has my friend here Gen'l Palmer, many an Indian lodge, and they always gave us to eat and drink. We therefore have brought provisions which we offer to you as a friend to a guest; and we therefore trust you will all feel free to receive the provisions we have brought to furnish you with as our guests.

I propose to the Walla Wallas, Cayuses and Yakama that you take two oxen, drive to your camp and slaughter for yourselves.

Young Chief replied: We have plenty of cattle, they are close to our camp. We have already killed three and have plenty of provisions.

Gov. Stevens said: We are much pleased to hear you are so well provided for, but we have plenty of provisions and you are welcome to them.

---

[86] [Delaware Jim was among many Lenape, then living in Kansas (1830-67), who actively explored the West, including as scouts of Fremont's explorations and Black Beaver, from the Texas Delawares now at Anadarko, Oklahoma. Like Cherokee explorers, they provided early warnings to Northwest natives of American duplicity.]

Young Chief replied: We have plenty at present. We do not throw away your offer. If we want any we will come to you.

Gen'l Palmer (to the interpreter): say to the Yakamas: You have come a long ways. You may not have provisions. If you want any we have them and you are welcome.

Young Chief said: *Cam-i-ah-kun* is supplied at our camp.

Gov. Stevens said: There will be no more said today unless you wish to say something. [392 18]

Young Chief said: We have nothing to say today; the weather is bad, rainy. We do not throw away your offer. When we are done talking you will know our hearts. We will talk slow not all in one day. No snow falls at this season of the year. There will be time for you to go anywhere you wish.

The council then broke up and nearly all the Indians returned to their camps.

Pee-o-pee-mox-a-mox and *Cam-i-ah-kun* dined with the Commissioners and remained in their tent sometime smoking in a friendly manner.

Timothy, a Nes Perses chief acted as crier for his nation and he will also record in their language the full proceedings each day of the council and this will be preserved among the archives of the nation and handed down to future generations.

May 30th Wednesday.

At 1 o'clock P.M. the Indians began to assemble and at 1¾ P.M. the Council opened. Present same as yesterday.

Gen'l Palmer Said: My friends. I am glad to see so many of you here today: Yesterday the council was organized and Interpreters sworn to repeat to you what we say. To day my brother in Council will speak to you the great desire that our Chief has to promote your good.

I know that our Great Chief has a good heart. I know that my brother Gov. Stevens has a good heart that they both desire to do and act for your good. I hope then you have come here with good hearts to listen to what he has to say. We both come here to talk to you as men and not as boys; We throw behind us everything that is bad, and come to you with one heart: we hope you have done the same; you are men able to judge between good and bad: and when my brother speaks to you, you can judge whether it be good or bad.

For the present I am done, and my brother will speak to you. [393 19]

Gov. Stevens Said: My Children, The sky is clear, the ground is dry, my heart is glad to day. Our hearts are glad. You are men! You have families: You have the means to live.

You have all of you been friends to me and mine; Two years since I came among you: Two years only have I known you; I come from the great waters beyond the mountains, across the mountains, and you have all been friends to me.

The Nes Perses. Lawyer fed my men driven out of the mountains by snow: the Cayuses and Walla Wallas received my men kindly; *Pee-o-pee-mox-a-mox* saw us in his country and gave us guides: the young chief and his people had nothing but smiles and kindness for us; and yesterday *Cam-i-ah-kun* showed me a paper from Capt. McClelland saying that he furnished guides and welcomed them on their way.

So to the North and East; there sits a Flat Head and there a Coeur D'Alene on the route across the Bitter Root; there are Poulouses and Colvilles and Spokanes away to the North; there are also men from both sides the river, from far down; all were kind, and I brought a message to all from a tribe beyond the mountains: I have been among the Black-feet and have brought word that they would meet you in Council, and that war should cease.

I met you in the trail, I saw your people in the Buffalo country: I met your people on the road to the Buffalo country: My heart said peace in the Buffalo country, peace here; peace is here now: peace between yourselves, peace between us. So for your kindness to me I am your friend, and I came from the Great Father to be your friend.

The interpreters yesterday took a solemn oath to speak truly. I took a solemn oath and my brother took a solemn oath to be your friends.

The Great Father has learned much of you. He first learned of you from Lewis and Clarke; *Pee-o-pee-mox-a-mox* remembers Lewis and Clarke, the Lawyer does: they came through your country finding friends and meeting no enemies.

I went back to the Great Father last year to say that you had been good, you had been kind, he must do something for you. My brother wrote to the Great Father in like manner. [394 20]

He told the Great Father, these men have farms; the Great Father said I want them to have more and larger farms; I told him you had cattle and horses; he answered that he wanted your horses and cattle to increase: I told him some of your grown people could read and write: He answered, I want all the grown people and all the children to learn to read and write; I told him that some of you were handy at trades; he answered that he desired to give all who choose the means to learn these trades;

Why did the Great Father answer in this way? Why did he send my brother and myself here this day, to say this to you? Because you are his children; his red children are all dear to him as his white children; his red children are men, they have hearts, they have sense; they resent injury: we want kindness on the one side and kindness on the other; we want no injuries to resent.

The Great Father has been for many years caring for his red children across the mountains; there (pointing East) many treaties have been made. Many councils have been held; and there it had been found that with farms and with schools and with shops and with laws; the red man could be protected.

Why do I saw [say] laws? What has made trouble between the white man and the red man? Did Lewis and Clark make trouble? They came from the Great Father; did I and mine make trouble? No! but the trouble had been made generally by bad white men and the Great Father knows it, hence laws.

The Great Father therefore desires to make arrangements so you can be protected from these bad white men, and so they can be punished for their misdeeds; and the Great Father expects you will treat his white children as he will make a law they shall treat you. We are now in council to see if we can arrange the terms which will carry this into effect.

Let us go back to old times across the mountains and see what was there done; the red man received the white man gladly; but after a while difficulties arose; the blood of the red man was spilled and the blood of the white man; there was cold; there was hunger; there was death. But a man came, William Penn, and said I will see if my white children and my red children cannot be friends, and they were friends: Wm Penn and the Indians came together as [395 21] we now come together; they made a Treaty: there was peace; and no white mans blood and no red mans blood had been shed, and there has been peace to this day; this was in olden times.

Oh! these people said we too will make treaties; we too will live in peace. They tried various plans, a plan that worked well when there were but few whites, did not work well when there were many. It was found that when the white man and the red man lived together on the same ground, the white man got the advantage and the red man passed away.

The Great Fathers name at that time was Andrew Jackson: he said I will take the red man across a great river into a fine country where I can take care of them; they have been there twenty years; they have their government, they have their schools, they have their own laws; their Chief John Ross knows as much as my brother or myself and a great deal more; he is what you call a Lawyer: he is an Indian, a Cherokee. When he goes to see the Great Father, the President, he sits with him at table as you sit with us at table.

Before you met my brother and myself in council, you have your own council: and the Great Father when he acts has his council also. He has his chiefs.

When I saw the Great Father he called his chiefs together, and had a council about you. He has two chiefs who have the care of the red men, their names are Gen'l Orr and Robert Johnson, I want you to remember them. Robert Johnson lives near John Ross; they both told me that what had been done for John Ross should be done for you, and more, as I will tell you.

As we grow older, we learn more and grow wiser; so of the Great Father and his chiefs; they did much for John Ross and his people twenty years ago; they have learned much since and know better what to do; they find one thing however the same now as then.

They gave John Ross and his people a tract of land into which no white man could go without their consent; they sent them an agent, they had schools, they had mills, they had shops, they had teachers, they had farmers, they had doctors. I repeat again no white man could go there unless the red man consented to it. [396 22]

North of that tract of land the whites are going in but they cannot enter it: South of that tract of land the whites are going in but they cannot enter it; that tract of land is the Indians home; his home and the home of his children.

There are other tracts of land East of the mountains set apart for the red mans home: for there are many tribes. Those tracts the white man can not enter without the consent of the red man. On all these tracts the red man has schools and farms and mills: they have teachers and physicians and an agent.

Now listen carefully: On these tracts the land was all in common: there were one or more larger fields for the tribes but no man had his special field: the Great Father and his chiefs now think that is not good: the Great Father said, the white man has his farm, his cattle and his horses: the Great Father says that when on that tract of land an Indian has his field, that field should be his.

This brings us now to the question. What shall we do at this council? We want you and ourselves to agree upon tracts of land where you will live in those tracts of land we want each man who will work to have his own land, his own horses, his own cattle, and his own home for himself and his children. On each tract we want an agent to live who shall be your brother, and who shall protect you from bad white men. I shall speak more of this subject by and by.

On each tract we will to have one or more schools: we want on each tract one or more blacksmiths; one or more carpenters; one or more farmers; we want you and your children to learn to make ploughs, to learn to make waggons, and every thing which you need in your house. We want your women and your daughters to spin, and to weave and to make clothes. We want to do this for a certain number of years.

Then you the men will be farmers and mechanics, or you will be doctors and lawyers like white men; your women and your daughters will then teach their children, those who come after them to spin, to weave, to knit, to sew, and all the work of the house and lodges, you will have your own teachers, your own farmers, blacksmiths, wheelwrights and mechanics besides this we want on each tract a saw mill and a grist mill. [397 23]

Now we want you to agree with us to such a state of things; You to have your tract with all these things; the rest to be the Great Father's for his white children.

Besides all these things, these shops, these mills and these schools which I have mentioned; we must pay you for the land which you give to the Great Father; those schools and mills and shops are only a portion of payment. We want besides to agree with you for a fair sum to be given for your lands, to be paid through a term of years as are your schools and your shops.

Now these payments are something you will have to think much about. Whatever is done is done with your free consent; I have more to say about these payments, about the agent, and about your doing better, as I think you will if we can agree.

I am tired of speaking; you are tired of listening. I will speak tomorrow. My brother will now say a few words to you.

Gen'l Palmer said: I shall say but little to you today; It is not expected we can come together with one day's talk; nor do we expect you can understand with what has been said all that we want. You will not make up their mind until you hear all we have to say.

Tomorrow my brother will say something more to you; when he is through then I will speak to you. Sometimes when people have a matter to settle they commence way off; but as they understand each other they come together. With us, if we commenced way off, I hope we are a little nearer now, and by and by I hope we shall come quite together.

As we expect you are tired sitting, and as we do not wish to say too much at once, we will speak no more.

We will meet tomorrow if you like, at an earlier hour say 10 A.M. and you can come without our sending for you. If any present wish to say anything, we are ready to listen to it.

No reply was made by the Indians and the Council then adjourned as [at] 4½ P.M. [398 24]

May 31st Thursday
The Indians assembled at 11½ A.M. and at 12 M. the council commenced.

Gov. Stevens Said: "My children. I said to you yesterday we want you to agree to live on tracts of land, which shall be your own and your children's; we want you to sell the land you do not need to your Great Father; we want you to agree with us upon the payments for these lands; we want you to have schools and mills and shops and farms; we want you to have teachers and millwrights and farmers and artisans; we want your people to learn to read and write; your men and boys to be tanners or millwrights or mechanics, or to be of some profession as a lawyer or a doctor. We want your wives and daughters to learn to spin and to weave and to make clothes and all the labor of the house; this for a number of years as we may agree.

"I said yesterday this would only be a part of the payment. We want also for a certain number of years to furnish you with some clothing, clothing for your men, your women and your children.

"I will mention only some of the principal articles; there will be blankets and cloth for leggings, clothes made, shirts and other articles for the men and boys; there will also be blankets and shawls and calicos and shirting and other articles for the women and girls. The particular articles however will be agreed upon between yourselves each year; you may want certain articles one year, and different articles the next.

"Besides clothing we would wish to furnish you with tools and implements for the shops; for the blacksmith; for the wheelwright for the tin-smith and such other tools all you might need; we also want to provide you with tools for your farms, with ploughs and hoes and shovels and when you get further advanced with reapers and all the implements white men have; we want in your houses plates and cups and brass and tin kettles; frying pans to cook your meat and bake ovens to bake your bread, like white people.

"I have told you about the mill to grind wheat and corn, and about the mill to saw boards and lumber, and that we should employ carpenters in your service. [399 25]

"We want you by and by to live in houses and we shall furnish you with a mill to saw lumber, and with carpenters, and your own people by and by will become carpenters and then you will have houses; all this for a term of years. Then we hope that all your people, every family will have its farm, its cattle, its horses, and I trust, its sheep; then I said you will have your own teachers and your own schools; you will have your own smiths, your own wheelwrights, your own carpenters, your own physicians and lawyers and other learned men.

"I told you of John Ross. As your fathers and your friends we think this will be good for you.

"In thinking over the matter we want you to bear in mind what you have seen and what you know what venerable old man Jim recollects when he first saw a house in this country; you all of you recollect when you first saw cattle, now you count your horses and your cattle by thousands.

"The horse carries you wither you wish to go, yourself, your wife, your children; and your packs, and he works in your fields; your cattle now furnish you with a portion of your food; your cows furnish you with milk and you already know how to make butter; we trust you will make butter and cheese, and that your women will all have churns. Formerly you raised no wheat, no potatoes. Now you have both grain and vegetables. Is not this a great change? A change which you all have seen? Has it not been for your good?

"Let us look at it now in a different way. My brother said yesterday he would have much to say today.

"We do not want you to agree not to get roots and berries, and not to go off to the Buffalo; We want you to have your roots and to get your berries, and to kill your game; we want you if you wish to mount your horses and go to the Buffalo plains, and we want more; we want you to have peace there. What has disturbed you on those plains? The Blackfeet tribe of Indians who stole your horses and murdered your grown people and your children; we want that to cease forever.

"The Blackfeet are not all bad people; they have some good chiefs among them and some good men; a part of them promised me two years ago not to make war upon you, and those have kept their promise; I could not see all, and [400 26] those I could not see have since given trouble. But I left with them a man who spent a whole year with them; a man whom you have seen here; a man who writes at that table. He traveled all through their country. sometimes alone sometimes with two or three men; he saw them all, he talked to them about you, and they promised to meet you in council this year and make a peace with you, to murder no longer your people, to steal no longer your horses.

"The Blackfeet have now began to think if will stop stealing horses from the Indians this side of the mountains, what will become of our bands of horses? They will pass away. Raise your own horses says Mr. Doty as do the Flat Heads, the Nes Perses, the Cayuses, the Walla Wallas, the Coeur D'Alanes, the Spokanes, the Yakamas and so back to the Flat Heads again. The Blackfeet then said, the Buffalo are not as plenty as formerly, we have to cut too many old bulls.

"Doty then talked about you, said you had your fields, horses and cattle, and raised your own milk, meat and vegetables; the Blackfeet then said we too would like to have farms; we would like to have cattle and milk and bread.

"The Blackfeet and other tribes who live in the Buffalo country see that the Buffalo cannot subsist there forever; they feel that unless they change their mode of life, they will soon pass away.

"They desire to change their mode of life. We shall help them provided they agree not to molest you.

"When you see the Blackfeet at the Council they will ask you many questions, they will want you to tell them when you first had horses and cattle, and when you first had crops. If we agree at this council they will ask you all about that; and you will tell them you have not as much game as you once had, and the time is coming when you will not have dressed skins for your clothing; you will tell them the Buffalo is passing away, and the time will come when we will not have robes for our tents and lodges; we have already changed and found it for our good, and we are determined to make another change in good season; we have made a bargain with the Great Father; we will have instead of tents of lodge skin when there are no Buffalo, houses of boards and of lumber; when the elk and the deer and the buffalo pass away, then we will have clothing, every man and woman and child like the white man; we have enough now to do to get roots and game and berries for our children; but we intend then to raise enough for our women and children, when their numbers have increased, and roots and berries and game are no longer to be found. [401 27]

"If we can agree here, this you will be able to say to the Blackfeet, and the Blackfeet will say, we will cut old bulls no longer, we will not starve, we will not die of cold, we will do as you have done we will be friends, we will chase the Buffalo together on the plains, we will be friends forever.

"I have spoken of an agent, I will speak more. If we agree at the council we have many things to do for you; the agent will live with you and see that it is done; if you think we have not done our part go to the agent and tell him so, and he will see that we do do it. If we think you have not done your part the agent will go to the chiefs and say so frankly and arrange it with them; he will be your elder brother, and will see that you are not wronged, and that the bargain is carried out.

"I have much more in my heart to say but not now, there will be time enough by and by; my brother Gen'l Palmer has to speak, he is your friend as I am but he has known you longer, and be can speak to you better than myself; he feels for you and you will find that every word which he says comes from a desire to serve you.

"It you wish to hear him now he is ready to speak."

Gen'l Palmer said: "My friends, I do not wish to tire your patience too long, I have something to say to you, if you will listen1 a little longer I will speak.

"My brother here speaks truly, when he says I desire to speak and act for your good.

"In order to explain more fully the course pursued by the government towards the Indians on the other side of the mountains I will tell you of it; my brother here has reference to that subject and I may perhaps have to repeat his words.

"He has told you something about our first settlements among the Indians over the mountains; those settlements were made over three hundred and sixty years ego. First came a chief with several of his brethren in three ships across the ocean, they found many Indians in that country who received them kindly, they gave to them food and received in return beads and various trinkets; that chief after traveling over a great extent of country and visiting many villages left a part of his people and returned home.

"After having been absent some time he returned and many [402 28] others, upon arriving at the point where he had left his children none could be found. After the Chief left, these people began to quarrel among themselves and with the Indians.

"There were many causes for this; a portion of the Indians whose hearts were not good, stole the property belonging to these people; the whites retaliated by whipping and ill treating them. That was the first offense on the part of the Indians; the whites had long been without women and they often took forcibly the women of the Indians; this induced them on their part to retaliate; these difficulties continued from bad to worse until finally there was war; our people were but few, the Indians many; our people were all killed; there were also many Indians killed. Upon seeing our Chief return with his vessel and other vessels and so many people they fled; they knew they had done wrong as well as the whites, and they expected they would be punished for it; this time our Chiefs brot' with them their women and children and cattle and horses, and tools to work with.

"The Indians seeing they were not interfering with them returned and for a while they lived together in peace; but they lived indiscriminately together, a white man here and an Indian there; but they could not long live this; their customs and mode of life was a different, they did not understand each other; they continued a number of years with little difficulties occurring, occasionally killing one another until it finally broke out with another war; peace would sometimes be made and last for a little time, but finally they would get foolish and their hearts would get bad; as it is said in this country sometimes; in this part of the country by the young men they are few we are many let us wipe them out.

"They finally made war, a council was held, speeches and harangues were ma and they declared war, a few white men were killed and many Indians were killed; there were more Indians killed than white men because we had better arms and know how to make them. This war continued some time but finally they had peace; the whites brought with them and made after they arrived here whiskey; this the Indians were very fond of and like all other persons after drinking it were foolish; they quarreled among themselves and killed each other and some whites in their drunken frolics; our chief saw this condition and desired to do them good; he saw that the Indians and the white men could not live peaceably together: he [403 29] called the Indians together in council; he proposed as we propose in this council, to purchase their country and select a place for them to live; he proposed to have a district of country set aside for the Indians to live in that no whiteman should live there; but the Indians said No! why should we leave the bones of our fathers and go to a strange land; we have plenty of elk, deer, bear, berries, and roots; we like you let us live together, we don't want to cultivate the soil you are welcome to occupy it; they were told that the wild game, the roots and the berries would not last always; they said they were a great and numerous people, they knew what was best for them and did not want our counsel; they quit talking, the whites went to their houses and Indians to their lodges; our people continued coming; every year vessels came until our people got so numerous as the leaves on the trees.

"It was but a few years before their game was all killed off; for the white man killed the game as well as the Indians; the Indians had no food in his lodges, the women and children were hungry; at last they commenced stealing our peoples property and plundering their houses; our people were forced to retaliate by whipping and shooting some of them. The Indians again sent messengers to the surrounding tribes to call them to make war; they resolved in council to exterminate the whites, kill them off; they commenced by burning houses, murdering woman and children, and killed a good many of our people; finally our warriors were collected and they had war; they did not understand our mode of warfare and thousands of Indians were killed and but few of our people were killed in the battles. This continued for a long time and the tribes finally concluded they had been acting foolish, and that they would receive the talk of our chief.

"Those that were left finally agreed to meet our chief in council; they did so and there was peace. In that council it was agreed by the Indians that they would reside on a certain district, set aside for them certain limits, certain bounds; they agreed in that council to live in peace with the whites, and to commit no depredations on them and to live at peace with other tribes; our chief agreed that we would build them mills black smith shops, carpenters shops and supply them with all necessary fixtures.

"Our chief directed his agents to build those mills and school houses and shops, and he employed teachers and [404 30] smiths and millers and sent the among them. They supplied them with cattle and horses and oxen and ploughs and wagons and every variety of farming tools. These Indians then began to see that they had acted very foolish, and that when the supposed they know enough for them and did not want any of our counsel, they knew nothing, they were as blind men; they have since been learning and continued to learn and prosper, and are now a great happy and good people; there were a few tribes who refused to go into that council, who refused to treat. What was the condition of that people? Those who thought themselves very wise and refused to take the advice of the white people those who continued to make war upon our people? Their game was all killed, they had nothing to eat, they fled to the mountains then they continued to live but a few years of miserable existence, until they were finally overtaken by more powerful tribes and all killed. There were other tribes in other districts of country, who heeded the advice of the chief and were set aside in districts of country belonging to themselves.

"In all cases where they have entered into a treaty and agreed to reside upon tracts set apart for them our chief has aided them. All who have settled upon these tracts have not done well, for they are lazy and have foolishly thrown away what has been paid them.

"But you as a people know how to appreciate these advantages and would not throw them away; all experience we have had with Indians these Three hundred and sixty years shows us that the white man and the red man cannot live happily together; although we may live near together there should be a line of distinction drawn so that the Indians may know where his land is and the white man where his land is; you are all able to judge for yourselves by the constant difficulties that are occurring here among you, between the whites and the Indians.

"We have some people whose hearts are bad, who violate our law; we have men who are afraid to live in the settlements, they seek opportunities to go among people at a distance, among the Indians; as an evidence of that I need only refer to matters that have transpired within the past four weeks in your own country; a few men had formed a plot by which they were to get your horses: their plan was this: part of those men went over into your bands and if they found any horse branded took a description of it, wrote it down in a book; when they had visited all your bands and got the description they would go away. [405 31]

"Sometime after they would take their book and give one of their party a description of these horses and an order to get them; when they gather up all these horses they will drive them off to the Grand Ronde or some place in the Blue Mountains they contemplate when they had got the stray horses coming back and driving all your horses to Salt Lake; but a short time ago Mr. Thompson came up and learned the trick: he went below and took out a warrant for them and these soldiers came up to try to arrest them.

"It is these men I am told who would rob you of your property, who are giving you advice not to treat with us; whose counsels do you prefer to take? These men who would rob you, or ours who come to befriend you? These men who came here are strangers to you with smooth tongues, they care nothing about the truth. I don't mean to say that all who come among you are bad men; I am afraid there are a few of these young men who come to live among you and wish to get your women, not because they desire your women but because they want your horses; they will come and remain among you a few years, get a woman and raise children, but when they get a band of horses around them, they will be off and leave the women and children without anything; I have been told that one of these men has been in your camp since we have been holding this council, advising you to have nothing to do with us; these men you cannot tell always who they are, but all such men need watching; you will now be able to judge who are your friends, such men, or myself and my brother who have come here to act for your good.

"We have been talking a good while and you have been listening. You are tired sitting. I have more to say to you but I will leave it untill tomorrow and say no more at present."

The Council then adjourned at 3½ P.M.

In the evening the Young Chief sent a message to the Commissioners to the effect that he should be pleased if no council should be held tomorrow, as his people desired to make a great Feast and have a general holiday. To which request the Commissioners acceded. [406 32]

Lawyer, *Pee-o-pee-mox-a-mox*, Young Chief and *Cam-i-ah-kun* dined at Gov. Stevens table with Gen'l Palmer and the gentlemen of the party.

June 1ˢᵗ Friday.

All about the Treaty Ground was very quiet, all the principal Chiefs dined at Gov. Stevens table.

The day was extremely warm and to have held a council would have been most uncomfortable.

June 2ⁿᵈ Saturday

The Indians began to collect at 11½ A.M. Some delay was occasioned by the non appearance of *Cam-i-ah-kun* and *Ow-hi*. But at 12 M. all the chiefs being present the council opened.

Gen'l Palmer Said: My friends, we have met here today to continue the talk; I shall try and speak so that you may understand me.

I have said that the white man and the Indians could not long live together in peace, a few may do so but where there are many we cannot do it. It your Chiefs are unable to restrain your people where there are but few, how can our Chief prevent his people from doing wrong when they are so many and scattered over so large an extent of country.

It is but fifty years since the first white man came among you, those were Lewis and Clark who came down the Big River – the Columbia. Next came Mr. Hunt and his party, then came the Hudson Bay Co, who were traders. Next came missionaries; these were followed by emigrants with waggons across the plains; and now we have a good many settlers in the country below you.

It there were no other whites coming into the country we might get along in peace: You may ask, why do they come? Can you stop the waters of the Columbia river from flowing on its course? Can you prevent the wind from blowing? Can you prevent the rain from falling? Can you prevent the [407 33] whites from coming? You are answered No! Like the grasshoppers on the plains; some years there will be more come than others, you cannot stop then. Our chief cannot stop them, we cannot stop them, they say this land was not made for you alone, the air that we breathe, the water that we drink, was made for all. The fish that come up the rivers, and the beasts that roam through the forests and the plains, and the fowls of the air, were alike made for the white man and the red man.

Who can say that this is mine and that is yours? The white man will come to enjoy these blessings with you; what shall we do to protect you and preserve peace? There are but few whites here now, there will be many, let us like white men, act so as to prevent trouble.

And now while there is room to select for you a home where there are no white men living let us do so. I have made treaties with all the Indians tribes in the Willamette Valley, with all in the Umqua Valley, with all in the Rogue River and Shasta country; they have agreed to remove to such tracts as shall be selected for them; they have agreed to be friendly with the whites and all other Indians; they have sold us all their country except the reservations; we have agreed to build them mills, blacksmith shops, waggon makers shop, to erect a tin shop and gun smith shop, to build a school house and hospital, to employ millers, mechanics, school teachers, doctors and farmers, all these expenses to be paid by the government for twenty years.

Do you want these things? Do you want a saw mill to saw the timber to build your houses? You have a few lodges now, how long will they last? by and where will you get your hides to make lodges? Gov. Stevens told you that the Blackfeet said the Buffalo are not as plenty as they were once; it is but a few years since there were a plenty of Buffalo at Fort Hall. Mr. Craig here has seen many of them there and probably others of you have; where are they now? All gone;

Do you want mills to grind your wheat and your corn? Do you want blacksmiths to make your ploughs and harrows? to make your axes, hatchets, hoes, knives, and to shoe your horses? Do you want a gun-smith to mend your guns when broken? Do you want a tinner to mend your kettles, your pans and cups? Do you want a carpenter to build your houses and a waggon maker to make your waggons? Do you want a shoe maker to make your boots & shoes? Do you want a doctor to [408 34] attend to the sick and give them proper medicines? Do you want farmers to assist you and show you how to raise wheat, corn and potatoes? Do you want school teachers to teach your children how to read and write? Is it not good that these men can write down what is said here and understand what it is? It would make my heart glad if you could all do so. It would make my brother's heart glad if you could all do so; would it not be good if you wanted to talk with my brother, or if you wanted to talk with our Great Chief? If you knew how to write and wanted to talk you could send it to him on paper and he would know your heart: would it not be good then to have schools among you?

Do you want to have plenty of provisions for your women and children? Do you want to have plenty of blankets and clothing? The deer skin and the elk skin cannot always be had to make your clothing; do you always want to live at peace with all persons? If you want all these things we are ready to give them to you; when we know your hearts then we shall know whether you want these things or not.

You have often been told that by and by our Great Chief would send some person to buy your country; I suppose you have been looking for that person a long time; Dr. White came here. What did he do? He may have talked very well to you but what use? Mr. Walpole came, what did he do for you? My brother and myself have come, we have not only come to talk but to do something. Will you receive it or will you throw it behind you? We did not come here to scare you or to drive you away, but we came here to talk to you like man, and to make such arrangements as to preserve peace and protect you. Our agents have tried to protect you in all your rights: but I am fearful they will not always be able to do so, if you continue to live in this scattered condition.

I see here a good many old people. I expect you have left a good many of your old people at home; we want to do them some good while they yet live, and if you enter into a treaty with us as we can then do them some good and do you all good; if we enter into a treaty now we can select a good country for you; but if we wait till the country is filled up with whites, where will we find such a place? My heart is that it is better for you to enter into a treaty now with us. I know that my brother has a good heart and wants to do you good, but we do not know how long we can act for you. Perhaps it may not be [409 35] long before other agents will come; the next that come may not have such good hearts and do as much for you as we will.

If we make a treaty with you and our Great Chief and his council approves it, you can rely on all its provisions being carried out strictly. My heart is that it is wise for you to do so. I will not speak any longer.

Gov. Stevens Said: My Children, my brother and myself have opened our hearts to you, we want you to open your hearts to us.

Five Crows Said: "We are tired."

Gen'l Palmer Said: We are not expecting to say any more today.

Five Crows Said: I have a little to say. Do you speak true that you call brother? We have but one Father in Heaven; it is He (pointing above) who has made all the earth; He made us of earth on this earth: He made our Fathers; when he gave us this earth. He gave no gardens.

He created our Fathers when he created Adam; we were divided into different countries; It was He, the Almighty that passed the law; He is the same God that made the Ten Commandments; He said my Children, you must do no evil, you must not steal, you shall not take any thing without payment; the Great Father says he will send the thief into fire – into hell

The Commissioners said will you speak now or on Monday?

Pee-o-pee-mox-a-mox Said: Why not speak tomorrow as well as today? We have listened to all you have to say, and we desire you should listen whom any Indian speaks. It appears that Craig knows the hearts of his people, that the whole has been prearranged in the hearts of the Indians; that he wants an answer immediately without giving them time to think; that the Indians have had nothing to say so far it would appear that we have no chief.

I know the value of your speech from having experienced the same in California, having seen treaties there. We have not seen in a true light the object of your speeches; as it there was a post set between us, as if my heart cried from what you have said; as if the Almighty came down upon us here this day; as if He would say, What are you saying? Look at yourselves your flesh is white mine is different, mine [410 36] looks poor, our languages are different. If you would speak straight then I would think you spoke well; we have come together to speak about the earth and not of God; you were not afraid of the Devil!

You see this earth that we are sitting on; this country is small in all directions. Why should you fear to speak on Sunday? Should I speak to you of things that have been long ago as you have done? The Whites made me do what they pleased, they told me to do this and that and I did it; they used to make our women to smoke; I suppose then they did what was right: when they told me to dance with all these motions that are here then I danced. From that time all the Indians became proud, and called themselves chiefs.

On another subject I have something else to say. Now how are we here as a post? From what you have said I think you intend to win our country, or how is it to be? In one day the Americans became as numerous as the grass; this I learned in California; I know that is not right. You have spoken in a round about way; speak straight. I have ears to hear you and here is my heart. Suppose you show me goods shall I run up and take them? That is the way we are, we Indians, as you know us. Goods and the Earth are not equal; goods are for using on the Earth. I do not know where they have given lands for goods.

We require time to think, quietly, slowly. I see Americans in all countries, it is not the country to think about, we may think about another; there is the Mission (Catholic Mission) it is right there and it is right it should be there. You have spoken in a manner partly tending to Evil. Speak plain to us. I am a poor Indian, show me charity; if there was a chief among the Nes Perses or Cayuses, if they saw evil done they would put a stop to it and all would be quiet; Such chiefs I hope Gov. Stevens and Gen'l Palmer are. I should feel very much ashamed if the Americans should do anything wrong. I had but a little to say, that is all. I do not wish you to reply today, think over what I have said.

Com-os-pi-lo Said: in substance as follows, it was addressed to his people and rendered by the Interpreters after the conclusion of his speech.

He reproved the young men for laughing and talking; said they considered him of no account any longer; they had knocked off his horns and his teeth were worn out; once he had horns and he could hook; teeth and they were sharp [411 37] and he could bite; you young men think yourselves very smart by and by you will learn; now I am tired of your conduct; I am not speaking to Gov. Stevens or Gen'l Palmer, I am speaking to you young men, as my children, to listen and behave yourselves.

Gov. Stevens Said: "We are ready to hear, my friends, anything you have to say today. If you desire not to speak today the council will adjourn till Monday. We do not wish to speak on Sunday because our Great Chief does not want us to do business on that day, unless it is a matter of necessity. We think that most of our red brethren do not wish to do business on Sunday."

The Council is adjourned till Monday at 10 A.M.
And the Indians then dispersed at 3 P.M.

June 4th at 12½ P.M. the Indians began to collect and 1½ P.M. the council opened.

Gov. Stevens Said: "*Pee-o-pee-mox-a-mox* said on Saturday, he had listened patiently to all we had said, and hoped we would listen patiently when any Indian spoke. We listened patiently on Saturday, we shall listen patiently today; we want you to open your hearts and speak freely.

After a long pause the Lawyer said: "If you will designate some one to speak first we will speak. If you do not they will sit here all day without speaking."

Gov. Stevens Said: "We expect the Head Chiefs know the hearts of their people. We will be glad to hear the Lawyer speak."

The Lawyer Said: "My Chiefs and people, I will now speak, listen (to Commissioners) I ask good for these poor people; I think my chief about what you have been speaking; It is from the man that made us, My Chief, or is it from your own people? that is the reason of my asking, where is it from you have spoken My Chief? Although I think it is from the white people; from where the white people is they have been dying and dying, and are yet dying, and also the whites are living all from the same people. The same thing of our people our red people that are younger and from the same root; and here you see these many of us yet and still living, old men and children. [412 38]

"The Supreme Being our maker listens to the white people who are dead and also to those who are living; the same thing with the red people, they listen to the dead and also the living.

"And this that the President has made up his mind for us poor people; he has thought we were a poor people and says go and see them and learn them straight; and that is the reason you have told them you would learn them to read and write and all those other things you have spoken of; and that is the reason I have understood what you have spoken from the President: for that reason you have been asking us questions, and now we are asking questions from you.

"It was not for nothing I have been listening to you. My country is poor it is a trifling country. You see the map the marks of our country, one stream runs one way another runs another way, it is all rock. My Chief, but the Big Chief from the Light (the East) said to you go and talk to these people and you have done it, he says go there to take care of your white people and your red people and you have done it. As long as the Earth stands take care of the people; he said to the white people and the red people all as one let us listen to the laws, when the earth is done away with there is the end of the law, and that is the reason you see us good and we see you good.

"My Chief that is all I have to say at the present, there are a good many men here who wish to speak. Let them speak."

The Commissions requested *Pe-at-tan-at-tee-miner* to speak, who replies. You have heard what I have to say. My mind is the same as the Lawyer has spoken. What I had to say he has said, he has spoken my mind, I have nothing to say, he has said all, for my land it is for you and for me. I shall do you no wrong and you do me none, both our rights shall be protected forever; <u>it is not for ourselves here that we are talking, it is for those that come that we are speaking. This is all I have to say at this present time.</u>

Cam-i-ah-kun was invited to speak and said: I have something different to say than the others have said. It is young men who have spoke: I have been afraid of the white man, their doings are different from ours. Your chiefs are good, perhaps you have spoken straight, that your children will do what is right, let them do as they have promised. This is all I have to say. [413 39]

Pee-o-Peo-mox-a-mox was next invited and said I do not wish to speak. I leave it to the old men.

Gen'l Palmer said: "We do not know who of them desire to speak; let their old men speak if they desire to do so.

Gov. Stevens Said: "If *u-u-Sin-mull-e-cun* would like to speak we would be glad to hear him. He replied. I do not wish to speak now let those who have already spoken speak. What the Lawyer has said is my heart, it is not necessary for me to speak.

The Commissioners called upon *Staachas* to speak, who said, how is a chief's language? How is the Big Chief talk? Where has their talk sprung from? That they have spoken straight on the part of the Indians; the Lawyer although young has spoken well for me. Who is it that is going to speak straight for all of us. Now I want the whites and the Indians to show all their hearts; you know and we all know life while we are living, and I ask you my friends to speak straight and plain to us, as if I spoke to the President I say Yes. I would wish that the President was here so that we might all listen to him; he would enlighten us, he would give us life, he would make us to live as we ought to live, we would give each other our hands to hold always.

Lawyer spoke first and he will have more to say about this we are now speaking of. Lawyer has asked you to speak plain. I make the same request. I have nothing more to say.

Pee-o-pee-mox-a-mox Said: "I do not know what they (the interpreters) have said. My heart was heavy, my heart has to separate so, that was my heart. I do not know for what lands they (the Interpreters) have spoken. If they had mentioned the lands that had spoken of then I should have understood them. Let it be as you propose so the Indians have a place to live, a line all though it was fenced in, where no white man can go.

"If you say it shall be so then all these Indians will say yes. Although that you have said the whites are like the wind: you cannot stop them, you make good what you have promised.

"You have spoken for lands generally. You have not spoken of any particular ones, your words are here (at this place). If you spoke as the watch goes, then we would say yes; the manner in which you have addressed the whole of [414 40] us has made my heart heavy. I had nothing to say: like you Americans; and I like the Hudson Bay Co. people by which means I am led this way and that way; I do not know as yet what lands these Indians have spoken for but when they mention the lands then I shall know.

Fah-hah-tsil-pilp ?*? or the Red Bear said: "I am not ashamed of any of my friends, for why should I be ashamed? If there was something above that I should be ashamed of, then I should be ashamed; I am not ashamed of any people that are sitting around, we have spoken here with our brothers. This is the first time I have ever seen my brothers here.

"I like your talk very much as I have heard it, and that is the reason I have listened to you well. And here where we see each other face to face we will talk straight. We shall know if you shall like my talk that I am now talking as I have like yours. I wonder if we shall both tell the truth to each other.

"This is what I think my Brothers, that one time more we will talk, we will not say yes from what has yet been said.

"Now my younger brother there will speak." Being thus called upon,

Tip-pee-il-lan-ah-cow-pook, or the Eagle from the Light arose and said: "Yes my friends you see where the Sun is. He hears me. It is from beyond where the Sun is that sent you here to talk.

"The red people are put on this earth. A white man was sent on this earth from the Light (meaning the East). The red man was sent from the west, and now the big Chief from the Light has sent his talk here to the red people.

"The President has spoken to me through you and I hear it. He likes us. He has fixed places for us to sit on and love one another, and I also like the white people as the President likes us.

"On a road ready finished, he has sent you here. Look at the face of the earth, there is a road to travel on. Roads up the valleys and roads on to the end of the earth. From the time you started, you found a road till this time.

"You are now come to join together the white man and the red men. [415 41]

"And why should I hide anything? I am going now to tell you a tale. I like the President's talk; I am glad of it when I hear it here and for that reason I am going to tell you a tale.

"The time the first white men ever passed through this country, although the people of this country were blind, it was their heart to be friendly to them. Although they did not know what the white people said to them they answered yes, as if they were blind. They travelled about with the white people as if the people that said that had been lost, and those lost people said to them, yes.

"I have been talked to by the French and by the Americans, and one says to me, go this way, and the other says go another way; and that is the reason I am lost between them.

"A long time ago they hung my brother for no offence, and this I say to my brother here that he may think of it.

"Afterwards came Spalding and Whitman. They advised us well and taught us well, very well. It was from the same source, the Light (the East). They had pity on us and we were pitied. And Spalding sent my Father to the East – the states – and he went. His body was never returned. He was sent to learn good counsel and friendship and many things. That is another thing to think of.

At the time, in this place here, when there was blood spilled on the ground, tho there was blood upon the earth we were friendly to the whites and they to us. At that time they found it out that we were friends to them. My chief, my own chief said, I will try to settle all the bad matters with the whites and he started to look for council to straighten up matters; and there his body lies, beyond here. He has never returned.

At the time the Indians held a grand Council at Fort Laramie. I was with the Flatheads and I heard there would be a council this side, next year. We were asked to go and find counsel, friendship and good advice. Many of my people started and died in the country. Died hunting what was right. There was a good many started there on Green River, the small-pox killed all but one. They were going to find good council in the East; and here I am looking still for counsel, and to be taught what is best to be done.

And now look at my peoples' bodies scattered everywhere hunting for knowledge, hunting for someone to teach them to go straight. [416 442]

And now I show it to you, and I want you to think of it. I am of a poor people. A preacher came to us, Mr. Spalding. He talked to us to learn, and from that he turned to be a trader, as though there was two in one, one a preacher and the other a trader. He made a farm and raised grain and bought our stock, as though there was two in one; one a preacher the other a trader.

And now from the East has spoken and I have heard it. And I do not wish another preacher to come and be both a trader and preacher in one. A piece of ground for a preacher, big enough for his own use, is all that is necessary for him.

Look at that, it is the tale I had to tell you, and now I am going to hunt friendship and good advice.

We will come straight here – slowly perhaps, but we will come straight.

Gov. Stevens said: My brother, if any of you wish to speak today, I will still be silent. Is there anyone who wishes to speak now? If not, I will go on. We have listened to you carefully. We think we know your hearts.

You are willing to make a bargain. You want to know exactly the terms. We have promised mills, shops, schools, teachers, farmers, and all the other things for a term of years. You want to know how many years. We have promised you as the other part of the payment clothing for yourselves, your wives, and your children; tools and implements for your farms and shops and articles for your house.

You want to know how much clothing. How many implements and tools and articles for your farms, your shops, and your houses; and how many years will you have them?

Before I answer that, I will answer another question which you have asked me. You want to know where your Reservations are to be. What is the ground we have in view for you? I will explain this matter freely.

Here are Nes Perses, Cayuses, Walla Wallas, Yakamas, and Umatillas and bands on both sides of the Great river to below the Dalles.

Tribes northwards: Colvilles, *O-kin-a-kune*, Paluse.

For the principal tribes here present, We have thought of two Reservations. One Reservation in the Nes Perses country [417 43] and one in the Yakama country. The Reservation in the Nes Perses country, to extend from the Blue mountains to the spurs of the Bitter Root, and from the Palouse river to part way up the Grand Ronde and Salmon River.

On this Reservation we wish to place the Spokanes, the Cayuses, the Walla Wallas, as wall as the Nes Perses, and also the Umatillas. That will be something for them to think about to see whether they can agree to it.

The Yakama Reservation to extend from the Attannun river to include the valley of the Pisco river – and from the Yakama river to the Cascade Mountains. On this Reservation we wish to place the Colvilles, *O-kin-a-kunes*, *Palouse*, *Pesquouse*, *Klit-a-tats*, and the bands on the north side of the river below the Walla Wallas as far as the Kuth la poodle [*Cathlapoodle*] river, near the Cowlitz. All these as well as the Yakama as on that Reservation.

There is a third Reservation East of Mr. Jefferson's which will be explained to you by Gen'l 'Palmer; there it is proposed to place the bands below the Umatillas.

We want you to think about this and see it you like it. You may think the Reservations are not good. If not you will say so. The Cayuses, the Walla Wallas, the Umatillas, may prefer the Yakama to the Nes Perses Reservation, and they may not like either.

I will give briefly the reason for selecting these two Reservations. We think there are large enough to furnish each man and each family with a farm, and grazing for all your animals. There is especially in winter grazing on each Reservation. There is plenty of Salmon on these Reservations, there are roots and berries. There is also some game. You will be near the Great Road and can take your horses and your cattle down the river and to the Sound to market.

Though near to the great roads, you are a little off from them, and you will not be liable to be troubled by travellers passing through.

We can better protect you from bad white men there. We can better prevent the trader and the preacher all in one man going there. We can better prevent bad men telling you to dance, and cheating you with lies. We can better stop the thief who comes to steal your horses. Your horses will be saved to you and there will be no thieves to throw into hellfire. [418 44]

You may ask, why so many tribes on one Reservation, and how is it proper to place them on the Reservation?

We want as many tribes together as can be taken care of by one agent. We can do more with the same means; this is a matter I wish to explain fully, and also about the payment in clothing, etc., which I mentioned in the first part of what I said, I will speak no more today, but speak tomorrow. Think over what I have said and hear the rest tomorrow.

Gen'l Palmer said: I shall say nothing to you tonight. You have been sitting a long time and you are tired. We want you to come tomorrow morning early. We want you all to come. You have heard but part, we want you to hear the whole, and when you hear all I think you will say it is good. I have nothing more to say to night.

The Council then adjourned at 6 P.M.

June 5th, Tuesday.

The Indians began to collect at 11½ A.M. and at 12 M. the Council opened.

Gov. Stevens said: "My Children, I stated yesterday that we wished to place you on two Reservations and that as regards the tribes below the Umatillas. There was a third Reservation which would be explained by my brother, Gen'l Palmer. I stated we wanted as many tribes as could be taken care of by one agent.

"I will now explain this matter more freely. We wish to put the Spokanes, the Nes Perses, the Walla Wallas, the Cayuses, the Umatillas on one Reservation in the Nes Perses country.

"Here (showing a draft on a large scale) is a map of the Reservation. There is the Snake River. There is the Clear water river. Here is the Salmon river. Here is the Grande Ronde river. There is the Palouse river. There is the *El-pow-wow-wee*.

"We commence where this river, the Palouse, comes from the mountains, and down the river to the mouth of the *Ti-not-pan-up*, then to the Snake river 10 miles below the mouth of the *El-pow-wow-wee*, then to the source of the *El-pow-wow-wee*. Thence along the crest of the Blue Mountains to the Grande River below the Grande Ronde, thence along the ridge between the *Wall-low-low* river crossing the Snake [419 45] River 15 miles below the mouth of Powder river, thence to the salmon river a little above the crossing, thence by the spurs of the mountains to the source of the Palouse river at the place of beginning.

"<u>This is a large Reservation. The best fisheries on the Snake river are on it; there are the fisheries on the Grande Ronde river. There are fisheries on the *Os-ker-wa-wes*, and the other streams. There are cumesh [root] grounds here at this place (pointing to the large cumash grounds of the Nes Perses</u>. We feel it we put you on this Reservation our agent can visit you all and take care of you all.

"Each tribe will have its own place on the Reservation. The Spokanes will have their place and their home. The Nes Perses their place and their home. The Walla Wallas their place and their home. The Cayuse and the Umatillas their place and their home.

"The Spokanes will have a blacksmith, a school, and a farmer. The Walla Wallas will have a blacksmith, a school, and a farmer. The Cayuse and Umatillas will have a blacksmith, a school, and a farmer. The Nes Perses are more numerous, they will have two blacksmiths, two schools, and two farmers.

"Three schools are the first schools where your children will learn to read and write. The agent will live in some central place where there will be an agricultural and industrial school common to all the tribes. To this school all the tribes will send such of their children as wish to study more than in the first schools, and to learn trades. Here where the agent lives will be the tinner, and the tin shop. There will be one for all the tribes. There will be the waggon maker and wheel right; there will be one for all the tribes.

"For the four tribes there will be two saw-mills and two flouring mills in proper localities. Thus all the tribes will be on an even footing, and each will have the same provision made for them.

"You will see that you will be better taken care of all on one reservation; each tribe having its own place, than if the Spokanes were on one reservation with the whites all around them, the Nes Perses on one reservation with the whites all around them, the Cayuses and Umatillas on one reservation with the whites all around them. [420 46]

"Here (showing the map) you will be on one Reservation with equal rights under one Agent, and the same provisions for your welfare. But each tribe has its head chief. A chief takes care of his people. His people listen to him. He devotes his time, his very life to their good. We want you chiefs to be such men, we expect them to know about you and to see that we do our part. They will not work for themselves, they will work for you. Who shall therefore give the Head Chief of each tribe Five Hundred Dollars a year for 20 years to be paid in cash.

"We shall build for each Head Chief a good house to live in. The Agent will have his house and he will be paid. The Head chiefs shall have their houses and be paid. They will all labor for the good of the Indians.

"You will be allowed to pasture your animals on land not claimed or occupied by settlers, white men. You will be allowed to go on the roads, to take your things to market, your horses and cattle. You will be allowed to go to the usual fishing places and fish in common with the whites, and to get roots and berries and to kill game on land not occupied by the whites; all this outside the Reservation.

"My friends, I have held four councils on Puget Sound, I have made treaties with all the Indians on that sound. They number more than all the tribes here present. They have all agreed, should the President decide, to go on one Reservation. That Reservation is only about one fiftieth part as large as this; they have, however, few horses and cattle. They have not three hundred hear [here]. They take Salmon and catch whale and make oil. They ask for no more land. They think they have land enough. You will be farmers and stock raisers and wool growers and you need more.

"Now I will tell you the payments that will be made provided you are placed on one Reservation. If you go on different Reservations different provisions will be made. Well, you all go on one Reservation, Spokanes, Nes Perses, Walla Wallas, Cayuses and Umatillas; we shall spend a certain amount in moving you onto the Reservation, in breaking up and fencing your farms, in building houses for your chiefs, your sub-chiefs and your people, in cooking utensils for your houses, in milk pans and churns, in a good supply of blankets and clothing. In all these things we will expend for you, One Hundred Thousand Dollars. This will be done the first year you go on the Reservation. [421 47]

"Now if any man gives up a tract of land in going onto the Reservation, he will have the same thing done for him that is done for all the rest and he will have, in addition, his improvements made good to him on the Reservation or the value of them paid to him in cash, as he may desire.

"The other payments extend through twenty years. Two Hundred and Fifty Thousand Dollars. We do not want to spend this amount or much of it in cash, and I want my friend *Pee-o-pee-mox-a-mox* and the other chiefs to listen while I give the reason. I ask all the chiefs to hear my reasons and think of them.

"We can furnish you with nearly twice as many goods with the same amount of money as you can get from the Traders. We shall buy the things you want in New York and San Francisco at cheap rates and good articles. The expense of getting them to you will not come out of your money; it will cost you nothing. You now pay Eight or Nine Dollars for a blanket at Fort Walla Walla, we shall furnish you two such blankets for lefs [less] than that sum, say from six to seven dollars. At Fort Walla Walla a flannel shirt costs three dollars, we will give you three shirts for three dollars. You pay for a calico shirt at Walla Walla one and a half and two dollars. We can furnish calico shirts for fifty cents a piece. If we furnish the goods therefore, you will get three blankets, three flannel shirts and three calico shirts for the same money you now pay for one blanket, one flannel shirt, one calico shirt and have to make a long journey for them besides. We can furnish four hoes for a dollar and a half. You know what you have to pay for a single hoe at Fort Walla Walla and the Dalles. We want the payments to do as much for your good as possible. We don't want half of it to go into the pockets of Traders.

"I ask the chiefs to listen to me again.

"There will be a certain sum each year for their people. We want them each year to consult their people and tell us what things they want. We want them to make out a list how many blankets they want and what kind of blankets, the number of flannel and calico shirts they want, and so for every article of clothing for their men, women and children. Also the tools they want for their farms, their house and their shops. In [422 48] short we want the chiefs to tell us how they want the money spent. The list to be made out every summer for the pay of the next year. If you want part of the pay made in money, we want you to give the reasons and state the sum each year. We will send your reasons to the President and let him decide. There are many of you we would be willing to give a part of the payment in money, but not to the men who drink whiskey, and not to the man who do not take care of their wives and children. Let, therefore, your chiefs each year make out a list of how much money and we will send it to the President.

"I have now a few words to say in regard to the Yakama Reservation; the same provisions as regards schools, farms and shops will be made as in the case of the Nez Perses Reservation.

"Here is the Yakama Reservation, commencing with the mouth of the Attanum river, along the Attanum river to the cascade mountains, thence down the main chain of the Cascade mountains south of Mount Adams, thence along the Highlands separating the Pisco and the Sattass river from the rivers flowing into the Columbia, thence to the crossing of the Yakama below the main fisheries, then up the main Yakama to the Attanum where we began.

"We propose to place there the Colvilles, the *O-kin-a-kunes* and *Pisquouse* Indians (they now send their cattle and horses there in winter), also the Bands on the Columbia River below the Walla Wallas down to the mouth of the *Kuth 1a poodle* river, also the Klicatat around Mount Adams and Mount St. Helens. These Klicatats and these bands on the Columbia originally came from here or further north.

"We will give one blacksmith, one farmer and one school for the Colvilles, one of each for the *Pisquouse* and *O-kin-a-kunos*, one of each for the Yakamas, one of each for the Yakamas including the Palouses, one of each for the remaining bands. They shall have the agricultural and industrial school as in the other Reservation. They shall have the same mechanics, gunsmith, plough and waggon makers. There children shall be taught and they shall learn trades like the children on the other Reservation. They shall have the same liberties outside the Reservation to pasture animals [423 49] on land not occupied by whites, to kill game, to get berries and to go on the roads to market. Payments to be made in the same way as in the Nez Perses Reservation. One Hundred Thousand Dollars to be expended the first year. Two Hundred and Fifty Thousand Dollars, the next twenty years.

"I need say nothing more. It is designed to make the same provision for all the tribes and for each Indian of every tribe. The people of one tribe are as much the people of the Great Father as the people of another tribe; the red men are as much his children as the white men.

"We think this plan will be for your good. We want you to think of it. I have tried to talk plain and to speak straight out. My Brother will now speak."

Gen'l Palmer Said: "My Brothers, my brother here has said as much perhaps as could be said. He has told you what we desire to do for you; it is for you to say whether you will receive it or throw it away; we have but one heart; he has been speaking of something which interests you; it is the duty of your chiefs and your men to think well of it. It was said by this man (Young Chief) the other day that we were not acting wholly for these that are here now, but for those who come after us; it is the duty of a parent to provide for his children. You may not understand all the advantages of the propositions that have been made to you; but they are for your benefit and those who come after you; as a chief desiring to promote your interest, I say it is good; that I would not deceive you; the Great Spirit who knows the heart of all men knows that I desire to promote your good.

"We expect it will take at least two years to prepare these reservations for you to go onto. If we make a bargain and sign the papers, my Brother and myself and all the Head Chiefs and Head men, that paper must go to Washington. Our Chief and his council will examine it: if they approve it they say yes, and give us the money to expend in accordance with its provisions.

"My brother has stated that you will be permitted to travel the roads outside the Reservation. We have some kind of roads which perhaps you have never seen; we may [424 50] wish to make one of the roads from the settlements east of the mountains to our settlements here: they may desire to run that road through your Reservation; if we desire to do so we wish that privilege; that kind of road we call a railroad. I will try and explain to you the way in which we make such roads. We first lay on the ground sticks of timber, we then lay other sticks across in that way, unite them together and run a strip of iron on the top of them, we then place a waggon on those tracks and instead of having horses or oxen hitched to the waggon we build a fire; some of you have seen a steamboat; they have on this waggen a boiler filled with water, the fire heats the water and produces steam, which propels the machine. I am unable to explain all the machinery or the way in which it works but they will travel faster than your swiftest horses can run, all the time. If we start from here at sunrise we can be at Wascopen [*Wascopam*] by the middle of the day. We sometimes attach twenty of those waggons together and one of those Engines draws the whole, they will take waggons enough to draw more people than are here. We call the waggen in which they have the fire and water a Locomotive: I have rode on those waggons many a time so have our people here all or nearly all of them. Now if our chief desires to construct such a road through your country we want you to agree that he shall have the privilege. You would have the benefit of it as well as other people.

"We have another improvement that I wish to speak to you about, it is called a Telegraph. We may possibly desire to make such an improvement through your country. We set posts into the ground 15 or 20 feet high, and as far from here as that house; when the posts are set we place a wire on the top about as big as that; this wire extends as far as we wish to make the road if it is 100 or 1000 miles.

"If my brother is at Oregon City and desires to speak to the Great Chief he speaks to him if the wires extend that far; the man at the other end of the land will know what he says as quick as I who stand beside him; if the instrument which is attached to this wire should be in your country and a man should steal your horse, and you desired to send work [word] to the Willamette Valley, you would tell this man and he would work the machine and the man in the Willamette would understand you had lost a horse, and before the thief could reach [425 51] there they would know it, arrest him before he came. You may not understand them now, but when you know as much as the white man you will.

"Now as we give you the privilege of traveling over roads, we want the privilege of making and traveling roads through your country, but whatever roads we make through your country will not be for your injury. I told you yesterday I would explain to you another Reservation, but that Reservation is for the people who live below here; there are but few of them here; and as I expect to hold a council with them when I return, and as that Reservation does not particularly interest you, I need not explain it now.

"Now I want you all to talk among yourselves and think about what has been said to you, and I want you to think of it like men. When you think of it if you say that what we have said is good and that you receive it, you can express it to us and we can soon write out the Treaty.

"You are now tired, you have been long sitting, you know our hearts, and if there is anything you do not fully understand before you make up your minds come and inquire end we will explain. If any of you wish to speak now we will listen to you. Or if you can make up your minds so as to give us an answer this evening come and do so and we will be ready to receive it."

Stachas Said: "My friends I wish to show you my mind, interpret right for me. How is it I have been troubled in mind? If your mothers were here in this country who gave you birth, and suckled you, and while you were sucking some person came and took away your mother and left you alone and sold your mother, how would you feel then? This is our mother: this country, as if we drew our living from her.

"My friends, all of this you have taken. Had I two rivers I would be content to leave the one and live on the other.

"I name three places for myself, the Grande Ronde, the Touchet towards the mountains and the Tucannon.

That is all I have to say." [426 52]

After a long pause –

Gov. Stevens Said: My brothers, if you do not feel inclined to speak today, we will come together again tomorrow.

We want the chiefs and the people to speak freely as *Stachus* has done. We will think of what *Stachus* has said. We could give our reasons now but we are all tired. We will tomorrow after you have spoken, state what we think. Come early in the morning and let us see if we cannot agree before night.

The Council is adjourned till 9 0'clock tomorrow.

Five Crows Said: "I am as it were without thinking yet. I require time to think and then I will answer."

Council then adjourned at 4½ P.M.

Thursday June 7th.

Council met pursuant to adjournment – at 12 o'clock – Present as before.

Gov. Stevens Said: "My brothers we expect to have your hearts today, let us have your heart straight out.

Lawyer Said: "My friends you have been speaking to me a poor people. This Earth is known as far as it extends. This earth has red people on it and it has had as far as it extends. The people are lost, they don't think whose talk has come to us poor people. On the other side of the big water there is a large country. We also know that towards the east there are a great many different kinds of people: there are red people and yellow people, and black people, and a long time ago the people that travelled this country passed on the waters. And there is that country on that other side of the big water and here is this on this side. On the other side of the big waters they have their laws. Yes, they have their laws there. We now hear the laws they have there, and we now know they have those laws there. We also know the white people pass about on the waters as they wish to. I do not know what they find in travelling about on these waters or [427 53] what they are hunting, whether it is timber, leaves, grass or what. It was the Spaniards in that direction that just travelled about in their ships, they were the ones who first discovered this country and it was in that way they travelled to look for things, in that way they travelled when they found this country; the red people that along the shores to the big waters, these were the people, and at this place they landed to see those poor people. At that place the red man started to run off, or a part of them did because they did not know the people who came to see them, and the rest come [came] and met them, there is where the white people first placed their children when they first come into the land. From this country they took back samples of rich earth, of flowers, and all such things: they also reported they had found a country. And it was known that there was a new country found. And one of the head men said, I knew there was a country therebefore. Columbus the discoverer said Can you make an egg stand on end. Although he tried he could not do it, he did not understand how, it fell over: than Columbus showed them all that he could make it stand, and he did it, he made the egg stand. After they saw it done they could all do it.

"Those children that he had placed in this country among the red people, from them the blood ran on both sides: that is when the laws come into this country to those poor people: there were a great many white people come back to that place: that is the reason the red people traveled off further and from that they kept still travelling on further as the white people came up to them and this man's (Delaware Jim) people are from the same people: they have come till they are here to us now, and from that country some central part came Lewis & Clark, and that is the way the white people travelled and came in here to my forefathers. Where they came into our country they named that stream *Kooskooski*: it was then they knew us poor people. They passed through our country and knew all our country and all our streams, and on their return my forefathers used them well: as well as they could.

"From the time of Columbus and from the time of Lewis & Clark we have known our friends: we poor people have known you as brothers although we were a poor people, a people knowing nothing when we first saw the white chiefs Lewis & Clark. From these poor people there were [428 54] some of them that started in that direction (east) and of these there is only one now living (Spokane Gerry) they want to be taught, they returned after they could see a little and told us about the Great Spirit; they told us the laws for the poor people; they had seen and heard them. My Chief said our old laws are poor, the new laws we are getting are good laws, are straight. We said there were these laws, the laws of the Commandments; our old laws the laws of our forefathers and the new laws are getting shown to us and when the French and American traders first came to us they told us there were laws and those laws should be sent to us.

Ellis our Chief spoke strait for the white people; the President has sent you here to us poor people. Yes! the President has studied this and sent you here for our good. This is the reason I said on Monday use us well my Chief we are a poor people.

"The Governor has said the President has sent him to take care of his children; it was you that had spoken thus my brothers (Gov. Stevens and Gen. Palmer) I want the President to see what I a poor man has said. I have got your talk here (pointing to his note book) and although a poor man I can look at it from time to time. I can take care of that; my brother, we have been talking a long time and are all tired.

"I think on the stream just below where Mr. Craig lives will be a good place for one mechanic or one of the ranches you have shown me. I also think perhaps in the country where I live may be good place for some more of them, in case they were crowded below it would be a good place where I live.

"Now my friends I have spoken; those things that have been talked of, you know, I have shown you my heart. You have said to them all you had to say. I have also given you all I had to say.

"Then my friends I have spoken; those things that have been talked at you know. I have shown you my heart. You have said to them you have said all you have to say. I also have said also all I have to say.

"You spoke of a road through my country (the Reserve) it is a bad country, to make roads in, but perhaps it may go through, that is the reason I think we have both [429 55] talked. 'Tis all our talk. Our Father Chief has said take care of one another. There is no reason that I should speak long although I have more to say. That is the reason I say take care of us well: that is all I have to say at this time, my brethren. I will have one word more to say when we are about to part.

Gov. Stevens: "We have the heart of the Nez Perces through their Chief, their hearts and our hearts are one. We want the hearts of the other people through their Chiefs.

Young Chief: "Us Indians are blind the reason we do not see the earth well, the Lawyer sees clear. The reason that I do not know anything about this ground is I do not see the offer you have made us yet. If I had the money in my hand then I would see: the country is very large is the reason this land is afraid. I wonder if this ground has anything to say: I wonder if the ground is listening to what is said. I wonder if the ground would come to life and what is on it: though I hear what this earth says, the earth says, God has placed me here. The Earth says, that God tells me to take care of the Indians on this earth: the Earth says to the Indians that stop on the Earth feed them right. God named the roots that he should feed the Indians on: the water speaks the same way: God says feed the Indians upon the earth: the grass says the same thing: feed the horses and cattle. The Earth and water and grass says God has given our names and we are told these names: neither the Indians or the Whites have a right to change those names: the Earth says, God has placed me here to produce all that grows upon me, the trees, fruit, etc. The same way the Earth says, it was from her man was made. God on placing them on the Earth during then to take good care of the earth and do each other no harm. God said, You Indians who take care of a certain portion of the country should not trade it off unless you get a fair price.

I am as it were, blind. I am blind and ignorant. I have a heart but cannot say much, that is the reason the Chiefs do not understand each other right. They stand apart. Although I see your offer before me I do not understand it and I do not yet take it. I walk as if were in the dark and cannot therefore take hold of what I do not see. Lawyer sees and he takes hold. [430 56]

When I come to understand your proposition then I shall take hold. I do not know when. Tis all I have to say."

Five Crows Said: "I will speak a few words. My heart is just the same as the Young Chief."

Gen. Palmer: "We know no chief among the Walla Wallas but *Pe-pe-mux-mux*; if he has anything to say we should be glad to hear it.

Pe-pe-mux-mux: "I thought these Indians were all the same as one, all alike (beckoning the Indians he said). Why do you speak to one another? listen to me. That is the way with your Chiefs, you white people. When you show us something then we think it good, treating us as children, giving us food. I do not know what is strait. I do not see the offer you have made to the Indians. I never saw these things with my father. My heart cried very hard when you first spoke to me, the same as if I was a feather. I flew, then I thought the same as if you were talking to a feather. I thought what will I do? I have seen everything on both sides of the river. You are all talking together, we are all talking together. If you were to separate as we are now and appoint some other time we shall have no bad minds. Stop the whites from coming up here till after this talk, not to bring their axes with them, the same as if I saw my heart above.

I hope the President will not think I say or mean anything bad, there is no difficulty in sending letters about; this that I have said to you I do not know in what light you have taken it, whether I have spoken straight or wrong. The whites may travel in all directions through my country was shall have nothing to to [sic] say to them providing they do not build houses on our land. Now I will speak about Lawyer.

I think my friend has given his lands, that is what I think from his words. You hear both of you what I say, it is why that I request another meeting, whenever it shall be. It is not only by one meeting that we can come to a decision. I have listened to you in a friendly way. It you come again with a friendly message from the President I shall see them at this place, tomorrow I shall come to see you, and towards [431 57] evening I shall go home. You have spoken to us in a friendly way and I speak to you in the same way, slowly. Gov. Stevens and Gen. Palmer I cannot give you a direct answer, perhaps you will not think of my words. I beg you will leave me in this way for today. Tomorrow I will give you answer. I do not know; that is all I have to say."

Gen Palmer: "I wish to say a few words to these people, but before I do so if *Kam-i-ah-kan* wishes to speak he can do so."

Kam-i-ah-kan Said: "I have nothing to say."

Gen. Palmer: "I would inquire whether *Pe-pe-mox-mox* or the Young Chief speaks for the Umatillas. I wish to know if they are of the same heart.

Owhi: "I have nothing to say about this land today. God gave us day and night, the night to rest in, and the day to see, and that as long as the earth shall last, he gave us the morning with our breath; and so he takes care of us on this earth: and here we have met under his care. Is the earth before the day or the day before the earth. God was before the earth, the heavens were clear and good and all things in the heavens were good. God looked one way then the other and named our lands for us to take care of. God made the other. We did not make the other, we did not make it, he made it to last forever. It is the earth that is our parent or it is God is our elder brother. This leads the Indian to ask where does this talk come from that you have been giving us. God made this earth and it listens to him to know what he would decide. The Almighty made us and gave us breath: we are talking together and God hears all that we say today. God looks down upon his children today as if we were all in one body. He is going to make one body of us: we Indians present have listened to your talk as if it came from God.

"God named this land to us that is the reason I am afraid to say anything about this land. I am afraid of the laws of the Almighty, this is the reason I am afraid to speak of the land. I am afraid of the Almighty that is the reason of my hearts being sad: this is the reason I cannot give you an answer. I am afraid of the Almighty. Shall I steal this land and sell it? or what shall I do? this is the reason that my heart is sad. [432 58]

"My friends, God made our bodies from the earth as if they were different from the whites. What shall I do? Shall I give the lands that are a part of my body and leave myself poor and destitute? Shall I say I will give you my lands? I cannot say. I am afraid of the Almighty.

"I love my life is the reason why I do not give my lands away. I am afraid I would be sent to hell. I love my friends. I love my life, this is the reason why I do not give away my lands. I have one word more to say.

"My people are far away they do not know your words, this is the reason why I cannot give you an answer now. I show you my heart, that is all I have to say."

Gov. Stevens: "Now will *Kam a ah kan* and *Skloom* speak.

Kam-a-ah-kan: "What have I to be talking about?

Gen. Palmer: "We have listened and heard your Chiefs speak. The heart of the Nez Perces and ours are one. The Cayuses, the Walla Wallas and these other people say they do not understand us. We were in hopes we would have but one heart. Why should we have more than one heart? The Young Chief says he does not see what we propose to give them. *Pe-pe-mox-mox*, says the same. Can we bring these saw mills and these grist mills here on our backs to show these people? Can we bring these blacksmith shops, the wagons & tools on our backs to show them at this time? Can we cause farms of wheat and of corn to spring up in a day that they may see it? Can we build these school houses and these dwellings in a day? Can we bring all the money that these things will cost that you may see it. It would be more than all the horses of any one of these men could carry. It takes time to do these things. We come first to see you and make a bargain. We brought but a few goods with us to give you but whatever we agree to give you you will get.

"How long will these people remain blind. We came to try to open their eyes they refuse the light. I have a wife and children, my brother has also a wife and children. I have a good home, fields of wheat, potatoes, [433 59] oats, peas and beans. Why should I leave them and come so far to see you? It was to try and do you good but you throw it away. Why is it that you do so? We all sometimes do wrong. Sometimes because our hearts are bad, and sometimes because we have bad council. Your people have sometimes done wrong. Our hearts have evil. Our hearts will cry, but if you will try and do right we will forget it. How long will you listen to this bad council and refuse to receive the light?

"I too love the earth where I was born. I left it because it was for my good. I have come a long way. We ask you to go but a very short distance. We don't come to steal your lands, we pay you more than it is worth. Here in this little valley and the Umatilla valley that affords a little good land, between these two streams and all around it is a parched up plain. What is it worth to you or to us? Not one half of what we have offered for it. Why do we offer you so much? It is because our Chief has told us to take care of his red people. We come to you with his messages to try and do you good. You throw his words behind you. Why do you do it? Because you have listened to bad council.

"I told you the difficulties that existed between the whites and the Indians beyond the mountains. If the whites and the Indians live together here as they did there, it would be the same. Our Chief know this and be sent us here to see you and to talk with you, this we do before there are many whites here."

Pe-pe-mox-mox says: "let us part and appoint another day". Before the day would arrive we might have a great deal of trouble. Gold has been found in the country above yours. Our people are very fond of it. When our people hear this they will come here by hundreds, among these who come there will be some bad people, those bad people will steal your horses and cattle. There are but few of you, you cannot prevent it when you are scattered over a great extent of country, you cannot prevent it: but it you are living in these reservations we can protect you and your property. Then why should you refuse to receive our talk and refuse to allow us to protect you? Your refusal to receive it is not such talk as should come from Chiefs desirous of promoting the interest of their people. I want you [434 60] to think more of this tonight and if you act like wise men I think you will arrive at a different conclusion.

"We expect to perfect the arrangements with the Nez Perces perhaps tomorrow. We have but one heart, we expect it will always remain so. We want the Walla Wallas, the Cayuses and the Umatillas to unite with us and have but one heart: we want you to stop your ears against bad council and receive that which is good. We do not come among you as traders we come bearing the words of our Great Chief. If you refuse to receive it our hearts will be sad. Our hearts will be sorry for these chiefs for we like them. Our hearts will be sorry and bleed for all these old men. Our hearts will be sorry and bleed for these young men. Our hearts will be sorry and bleed for these women and children.

"We want to help you to put food into your lodges and homes. We want to help you to get clothes and blankets to cover you from the storm; we want to help you to get arms and ammunition to kill game; we want to open your eyes and give you light that you may see. We want to make you a good people.

"Will you receive our talk or will you throw it behind you. My heart will be glad tomorrow if you come and say we are all of one heart.

"What I have said is for your good: think of it. I have nothing more to say."

Cam an pello: "It is true you have mercy on us. I think it is true what you have been saying: if you were to send me into a mountanous country still I would say you have mercy on us. What would I be glad for? I was glad to hear the first talk by the Governor, that was the reason I was glad to hear what they said. I would be very glad if he had said to me stop over on one side, then I would be glad.

"What would I be glad about if I were to take a thing and throw it away? That is the reason my heart cries. If you would show me fine lands and I were to see them then I would be glad and go to them. How do you show your pity by sending me and my children to a land where there is nothing to eat but wood? That is the kind of land up there, that is the reason I cry. [435 61] Look at my hands! An old man. I have but them by hard work: then I ask myself have I labored in vain? What have I to be glad for?

"The white man first showed me and aided me in making my garden and every mile I have been laboring. Will God think nothing of the labor I have bestowed on my garden? Do you do this to me in pity? I am really pitiable and therefore I pray night and day till I am tired. I have no books. The missionaries told me if I had no books I had a book in my heart which enabled me to pray to God. They told me in taking water to drink I should think of God, this I have not learned of myself, it is what they have taught me and I keep it. The laws of God are not alone for you, they are for me as well."

Woa-lish-wam-pum: "I have got only two things to say. I have listened to your speech without any impression. I did not understand it. I know this. We are the same. You have life and breath you white people; we red people have life and breath. I think the old laws are straight, that they should still exist.

"The Nez Perces have already given you their land. You want us to go there. What can we think of that? What is the reason I cannot think of leaving this land to go there. Your words since you came here have been crooked. That is all I have to say."

Gen. Palmer: "I desire to say a few words in reply to *Cam an pello*, he says he "is an old man, he has worked hard in his garden." We have said that any man who has a garden or a field and who left it to go to this reservation should have as much improvement made there for him, or be paid for it in money as he chooses. We will go farther and say he shall have a better improvement: it shall have a better fence, be ploughed well. We will not take them there to starve, they shall live better than where they are and if there is not good land enough in the reservation to make them farms we will make it larger.

Gov. Stevens Said: "Although you are all tired, my friends, I must say a few words. My Brother and myself have talked straight? Have all of you talked straight? Lawyer has and his people have. And their business will be done tomorrow. [436 62]

The Young Chief says: he "is blind and does not understand". What is it that he wants?

Stickuss says: his "heart is in one of the three places, the Grand Ronde, the Touchet, and the Tu-kan-on".

Where is the heart of the Young Chief?

Pe-Pe-mox-mox: "Cannot be wafted off like a feather." Does he prefer the Yakama reservation to that of the Nez Perces'? We have asked him before, we ask him now where is his heart?

And *Kam-a-ah-kan* the great Chief of the Yakamas has not spoken at all. His people have had no voice here today. He is not ashamed to speak – he is not afraid to speak – then speak out.

But *Owhi*: is "afraid lest God be angry at his selling his land" Owhi, my brother, I do not think God will be angry if you do your best for yourself and your children. Ask yourself this question to night. Will not God be angry with me if I neglect this opportunity to do them good? *Owhi* says his people are not here. Why did he promise to come here to hear our talk. I do not want to be ashamed of *Owhi*. *Owhi* has the heart of his brother *Teayass* and his people; we expect him to speak straight; out.

We expect to hear from *Kam-a-ah-kan*, from *Skloom*. The papers we will have drawn up tonight. You can see them tomorrow. The Nez Perces must not be put off any longer, their business must be dispatched.

I hope the hearts of all the others and our hearts will agree. They have asked us to speak straight, we have spoken straight. We have asked you to speak straight, but we have yet to hear from you.

Gen. Palmer: "This man (*How-lish-wam-pum*) says the reason he does not want to go to the Nez Perces' country is that they have given it to us. If he and his people go on that Reservation it will belong to them as much as to the Nez Perces. They will all be served alike, every man will have his farm, it will be his.

Pe-pe-mox mox: says "we have met as friends let us say nothing that is bad, let us part friends. We have been friends a long time". I hope we shall always remain friends and as brothers. When we part we will part as friends. Then let us act as friends and as wise men. [437 63]

Five Crows: "Listen to me you Chiefs. We have been as one people with the Nez Perces heretofore; this day we are divided. We the Cayuses, Walla Wallas, and *Kam-a-ah-kane* people and others will think over the matter tonight and give you an answer tomorrow.

Owhi: "*Kam-a-ah-kan* is the man who is to speak about these lands. I have nothing to say about them. We will settle the matter among ourselfs.

Gen. Palmer: We have heard what Five Crows has said. We want all this people to have one heart, they ought not to have two hearts. Our Great Chief looks upon them all as his children and I hope you will think on what is here said to you.

Gov. Stevens: "My Friends, we will meet in the morning again, we have to get through the business of the Nez Perces so that they may get home, they have a long journey before them. We shall meet as friends I hope. Your hearts and ours will be united I trust. We want every person to come early. If any person wishes to speak, speak now or otherwise we shall meet in the morning. [438 64]

Council met at [?*?]

Gov. Stevens Said: "My friends, judging from your faces, I think you see your way clear. The paper of the Nez Perces is nearly ready and soon will be read to them. We expect that the Young Chief, that *Peo-Peo-mox-mox* and *Kamiakan* will speak now, and we hope that with them the business may be concluded today. Let us know what they want, we are here for that purpose.

The Young Chief Said: "We have been tiring one another for a long time. We did not know our hearts, we did not understand each other on both sides, about this country. We have so many horses and cattle in the country is the reason we were troubled. Your marking out the country is the reason it troubles me so and has made me sit here without saying anything. You Americans, your forefathers are dying in your own country, as many of your people are wealthy in stock it requires a large tract to keep them. Those that have large bands of cattle marks each one a tract for himself. The reason why we could not understand you was that you selected this country for us to live in without our having any voice in the matter. We will think slowly over the different streams that run through the country, we will expose the country and think over it slowly. I cannot take the whole country and throw it to you. If we can agree this country will furnish food for the whites and for us. The whites and ourselves will be compelled to have equal privileges in getting timber from the mountains to build our houses and fences; then we shall love one another. The good of you white people is foremost, the bad is behind, it is the same with us Indians; we keep the bad with us behind us. You embraced all my country, where as I to go, was I to be a wanderer like a wolf. Without a home, without a house I would be compelled to steal, consequently I would die. I will show you lands that I will give you, we will then take good care of each other. The reason for my uneasiness is for my stock which is running all over the country. Perhaps we will be compelled to divide with our stock, one taking one way the other another way, perhaps out there (pointing South) it would be well to draw a line to divide us. This is the reason why I think we should stop a while that we may come to an agreement. We will see when you make another offer whether we can agree to it. Wait, we may come to an agreement when we see your offer, if any people come send good people; those of the settlers [439 65] who are here now it is well they should stay. I think the land where my forefathers are buried should be mine; that is the place that I am speaking for. We will talk about it, we shall then know, my brothers, that is what I have to show to you, that is what I love the place we get our roots to live upon (meaning the Grand Ronde). The Salmon comes up the stream – that is all.

Gen. Palmer Said: "My brothers, when we quit talking yesterday your minds were very much troubled, you were unwilling to go to the Nez Perces reservation. We have thought of your words. The Nez Perces have a great many horses & cattle, you too have a great many horses & cattle, perhaps you might not agree together quite so well; your people appear to be much divided where to go. We asked you to give us your hearts and tell us where it was, the Young Chief (We ***) [??] has given us his heart, the Grand Ronde Valley. We have thought of the Umatillas. Many of your people died there. It is a good country for your horses and cattle. We desired first to have you go all to one place, but to show you that we wish to do you good I will make you another proposition. I propose to designate for the Cayuses, the Walla Wallas & the Umatillas – to commence on the Columbia river (this is the Columbia river pointing to the map) this is the Umatilla river, this is the Agency, this is McKay's place, this is Wild Horse Creek. Now I propose to select a reservation commencing at the mouth of Wild Horse Creek and running up this creek to the mountains to the head waters of *Hou-te-nic* Creek, now down that creek till you strike Mr. McKay's claim, now across from his claim to the Umatilla river, then up to the mouth of the Wild Horse Creek, leaving Mr. McKay's claim out of the reservation. This will include all your farms, your houses and gardens within the reservation. You will have sufficient grazing for your stock and land to make farms but your stock will have the privilege of grazing on any lands not claimed by the whites. If the Whites should settle near to the reservation their stock might sometimes go onto the reservation while yours might go off it; if they should do so we would not want you to quarrel about it. We would build at suitable points on the reservation a saw-mill and a flouring mill; we would employ millers to attend them for you for twenty years, and by that time you would be able to attend them yourselves. We will have a blacksmith shop and employ a blacksmith for 20 years; [440 66] we will have a plow and wagon-markers shop and employ mechanics for that for twenty years; we will have a carpenter and cabinet makers shop and employ mechanics for that for 20 years – we will have at least two school houses and employ teachers for at least 20 years; we will build a hospital and furnish a doctor and medicines for twenty years; we will build a good house for *Peo-Peo-Mox-Mox*, and a good house for the Chief of the Cayuse; we will build a house for *Peo-Peo-Mox-Mox*'s son, we will plow and fence ten acres of land for *Peo-Pee-Mox-Mox*; we will plow and fence the same for the chief of the Cayuses; we will plow and fence five acres for *Peo-Peo-Mox-Mox*'s son; we propose to do more for him and for his son because he leaves his country and goes to another place. We will give him as soon as he goes down to the Dalles for it $500, in money – we will give him a yoke of oxen, wagon and two plows – we also give him some other things which it is not necessary to mention. We give him a salary and also the chief of the Cayuses of $t500 a year, in money, this to continue for twenty years – the same as is to be given to the Lawyer, the head chief of the Nez Perces. We give these salaries because they are the head chiefs, and are expected to labor for the good of their people, and in the event of the death of the head chief their successors get the salaries. Now in addition to these things we will expend fifty thousand dollars in the first and second years after the treaty is ratified. This money is to be expended in building houses, opening farms, buying teams and waggons and paying persons working for them, and in any way that the President may deem best calculated to promote their interests. In addition to this there will be expended for you eight thousand every year for five years, for the next five years six thousand dollars a year, the next five years four thousand dollars a year, for the next five years two thousand dollars a year – this makes twenty years, and the amount to be expended one hundred thousand dollars ($100,000). This amount will be expended as the President may direct; we should consult you every year as to how you wanted it paid – part in money – part in goods. You will not be required to go onto this reservation till our chief the President and his council sees this paper and says it is good; and we build the houses, the mills, and the blacksmith shop. But we want you to allow the white people to come and settle in the country anywhere outside of the reservation. The President will have this [441 67] reservation surveyed and marked off, so that every man that has a piece of land will know which is his. <u>You will be allowed to go and catch fish and dig roots the same as the whites</u>; and if any of our people do wrong to you you are not to shoot them, but to go to the Agent. We expect the chiefs to restrain their young men from doing wrong. We have a few goods here for you, those that we give you will be in addition to these payments, we charge you nothing for them. I have given you now my heart; I have offered you more than your country is worth – more than you know how to count. How long will it take you to decide? If you say it is good the papers can be arranged tonight, tomorrow they can be signed; we would then give you these goods and you could go home with a good heart. We have been here a good many days talking – we are all tired; we commenced far apart; it is for you to say now whether we shall come together. This I say to the Cayuses, the Walla Wallas & Umatillas those people are all interested; *Pee-Pee-Mox-Mox* being the first chief I want to hear from him. I have nothing more to say.

Pee-Pee-Mox-Mox said: –The young ·chief has nothing more to say; he has said all he had to say, as if it was I that put obstacles in the way. Our hearts should not be otherwise than one. I have already spoken all that I have to say – I and Gen. Palmer this morning. They have already written all that we have said. I spoke this morning about having a little house, a place to sell my cattle on the other side of the Columbia where my cattle range for a trading post when the Americans pass. I have nothing to talk about; I have only a few words more. <u>I said to Gen. Palmer that I desired permission to get fish there while I lived</u>; when I learn that the house is made, (meaning the reservation) then I shall go there; when we have settled all things then you have your presents for these Indians. Now that we have made up our minds if you think proper you may give us some provisions; sometime tomorrow in the afternoon we will go home; you are now tired – that is all I have to say.

Gen. Palmer Said: "That we have agreed that *Pee-Pee-Mox-Mox* shall have the privilege of building a house at the mouth of the Yakima and catching fish for five years. I should like to have all the chiefs and head men of the Umatillas, Cayuses and Walla Wallas and also the name of every man on this paper that the President may see every man's name and know that they have given their consent.

Gov. Stevens Said: – "My friends. I am glad Looking Glass one of your chiefs is coming, he is a friend of *Kamiakun*; we have now got nearly round the circle; our [442 68] hearts are almost together; I call upon *Kamiakun* to say whether we shall get entirely around. My friends, Looking Glass is close by; – he has come away from the Blackfeet – the buffalo country across the mountains; there is war; here is peace and friendship; let his first glance be upon you sitting here; when he is close by two or three of us will go and take him by the hand and set him down by his chief in the presence of his friend *Kamiakun*. Let us now have *Kamiakan*'s heart.

Kam-i-ah-kan Said: "The place that I am from there are but few Indians, all have gone to the Calapooya country. Some are at Nisqually and some at Taih – that is the reason I have deferred speaking till I see my Indians. I wish the Americans to settle on the wagon route; we do not confine them to the road; they may settle about the road so that the Indians may go and see them. I do not speak this of myself it is my people's wish. *Owhi* and *Teias* and the chiefs. I, *Kamaiakan* do not wish for goods myself. The forest knows me, he knows my heart he knows I do not desire a great many goods. All that I wish is for an Agent, a good Agent who will pity the good and bad of us and take care of us. I have nothing to talk long about. I am tired, I am anxious to get back to my garden. That is all I have to say.

Joseph, Nez Perce: "These are my children (looking around). I see them all sitting there: talking slowly: is good. It is good for old men to talk straight; talk straight on both sides and take care of one another. It is not us, it is those of our children who come after us. It is good for the old people to talk together good and straight on account of our children on both sides to take care of each other till the last day: without speaking I am going. It is not anything bad that I am thinking that I am going without speaking, no, it is not anything bad, it is a place to live, a place for our good to live there. Think for year after year for a far way ahead. I wonder what you think if I could see your thoughts. It is not that there is anything bad that I speak. I hear you speaking to my children, and they have many hearts. I am going without talking and you don't know my talk. At the Grand Ronde I saw my children on both sides; we have been talking and finished your talk; this is all I have to say. [443 69]

Gov. Stevens Said: "If anybody else wishes to speak we shall be glad to hear them.

Red Wolf Said: "I have only one or two things to speak. I want Mr. Craig to stay there in the Nez Perce country, and not go away. The reason why I wish Mr. Craig to stay there is because he understands us, he speaks our language well; when there is any news that comes into the country we can go to him and hear it straight; the same for us when anybody comes to speak to us he will sit down with us and we understand them. It is good for him to stay there to interpret on both sides so that each can understand the other.

Gov. Stevens Said: "We wish to hear from Scloom [*Skloom*], one of the Chiefs of the Yakamas.

Scloom said: "What I have to say is about this the earth: it is long since the earth was made and the trees were made to grow out, and there was one there, a very small boy, I do not know what he knew but he took an axe and cut a tree, and make it as if he has made a watch, he went to the tree and looked up and saw a star, he took a line and measured the land from that tree; all the land he had measured he plowed; about half way on the line he threw the tree across. For this country that he had plowed up he got $800 for each mile; That is the reason the Indians like the place where they have their gardens; for the reason there was such a price paid for them; the land uncultivated where there are no gardens is not worth as much, it might be sold for $40 a mile. Why should I speak a great deal? We are not bargaining for lots; you know your own country above, you select your piece of land and pay a price for it. There it is the same and have choice. My friends, I have understood what you have said; when you give me what is just for my land you shall have it. This is all I have to say.

Gov. Stevens Said: "I have a word to say in answer to the remarks of Skloom. Proposals have been made for the lands of the Yakamas and their neighbors; a place has been pointed out for the Indians to live in; outside of this place the gardens and farms are to be paid for in money at a fair value. The price paid will probably be a good deal more than the price he has mentioned for those gardens. I say to *Skloom*, we do sell good lands for eight hundred dollars a mile, but not in this country. [444 70] We do not expect to! sell any of this land. Skloom probably knows that. I ask *Kamiahkan* and I ask *Skloom*, make your own propositions. I also say to *Owhi*, let us know what you think your lands are worth and where you want your home. We shall meet again in the morning, I want *Kamiakun* and his chiefs to make their own proposition.
Looking-Glass is coming. We shall meet tomorrow morning."

Saturday June 9th

The Council was opened at 2 o'clock P.M. when Gov. Stevens Said: "My Friends, Today we are all I trust of one mind. Today we shall finish the business which brought us together. Yesterday the Yakamas had not made up their minds fully. Today they and ourselves agree; the papers have been drawn up. A paper for the Nez Perces: they live on one Reservation. A paper for the Walla Wallas, Cayuses and Umatillas, they have their Reservation on the Umatilla. And a paper for the Yakamas, they have their Reservation. These papers engage us to do exactly what we have promised to do.

"My brother explained yesterday to the Walla Wallas, Cayuses and Umatillas what would be given in their paper. It has been given to them in the paper.

"In the paper for the Yakamas we have included the tribes to acknowledge *Kam-i-ah-kan* for their head chief. The *Piscouse*, the *Swan-wap-um* and *Palouse*, the Yakamas and all the

Bands on the Columbia below the Walla Walla down to the White Salmon River. <u>They have their reservation and fishing stations which I understand is satisfactory.</u>

"The Nez Perces have their reservation as was shown them in Council and in the paper everything was set down which was promised them. They all know what was said.

"The money, the payment intended for the Nez Perces, the Walla Wallas, the Cayuses and Umatillas has been divided. We have given two parts or a $150,000 to the Walla Walla, Cayuses and Umatillas. We have given the Nez Perces three parts or $200,000.

"In the Yakama reservation we have not placed as many tribes as we expected. We have thrown out the [445 71] *Okan-ah-gans* and Colvilles and the Tribes below the White Salmon. Their numbers are about the same as the Nez Perces. We have given them the same amount. There is the paper for the Nez Perces (holding it up), here is the paper for the Yakamas. My brother will show the paper for the Walla Wallas, the Cayuses, the Umatillas.

"It is stated first in all the papers the Indians who signed the paper, then your lands are described. We have got the descriptions from yourselfs. Then your reservations are pointed out, those you all know.

"You will not be called according to the paper to move on the Reservation for two or three years; then is secured to, you your right to fish, to get roots and berries, and to kill game; then your payments are secured to you as agreed; then your schools, your shops, and physician and the other things we have promised you are secured; then the salaries, the houses and the ten acre farms of your chiefs are secured to him.

"Then there is another article if any of you get into debt then payment cannot be taken for your debts, every Indian must pay his own debts.

"Then you promise to be friendly with other tribes and the whites.

"Last you are to drink no whiskey and do all you can to prevent others doing it; and also those who drink whiskey will not be paid their annuities.

"I have thus given the substance of the different Treaties. Shall it be read over in detail? You have already heard it not once but two or three times. It can be read over Article by Article and the Interpreters can state to you whether it is what you are promised. If there is anyone present who wishes to speak let him do so before we go on with this business, Let Looking Glass speak."

Looking Glass Said: "I am now going to speak. From those who have been speaking, they have been listening to us from above and from the ground. A long time ago the Great Spirit spoke to my children. I am from the body of my parents and I set on a good place. The Great [446 73 no 72] Spirit spoke to his children the Laws, will track on the ground strait and after that there have been tracks on my ground and after that the big Chief, the President, his ground was stept on in the same way and for that reason I am not going there to trouble on his grounds and I do not expect anyone to tramp on mine.

"I have great respect for my friends, he sees your eyes and your hearts, and that is the reason all this people are his children. Why do you want to separate my children and scatter them all over the country? I do not go into your country and scatter your children in every direction.

"It is for me to speak for these people my children, that is what I say. The Big Chief speaks to his children and I also speak to my children and tell them what to do; and that is what we are talking about; you see where the Sun is. I never go where the whites are and mix with them and talk with them.

"I am already named from above, by the Supreme Being, my heart is with the country. I live upon and head [lead], that is the reason my heart tells me to say where my children shall go. I want you to look well to what I have shown you.

"I want to know if an Agent will stay up in my country?

Gov. Stevens: "As long as there are people."

Looking Glass: "Will the Agent be there that long to keep the whites from pushing into our country?"

Gen. Palmer said: "Certainly."

Looking Glass: "Will you mark the piece of country that I have marked and say the Agent shall keep the whites out?"

Gen. Palmer: "None will be permitted to go there but the agent and the persons employed, without your consent."

Looking Glass: "It is not for nothing I am speaking to talk strait, it is just as if I [447 74] were to see the President and talk to him it would be straight, that is just what I want, that you talk straight from the President. Look at my talk. I am going to talk straight. When I hear your talk it goes to my heart. I am not like those people (pointing about) who hang their heads and say nothing. We will have a short talk, not a long one. (after a silence of a few minutes the)

Young Chief Said: "That is the reason I told the Governor to let it be till another time, till we know what the Looking Glass would say. I heard that Looking Glass was coming.

Governor Stevens: "I will say to the Young Chief, let Looking Glass have time to think, he is thinking now in order that he may speak, he will speak straight and from his heart. We will wait now till we have heard Looking Glass speak.

Looking Glass: "The line of the Cayuse Reservation will be where the trail crosses the Walla Walla, there in a straight line to the Umatilla below Mr. McKay's house, from thence north of the butte, straight to John Day's River. The reason why that shall be the line is that they want more room for their horses and cattle. (After a pause of a few moments he continued) By what time will you build the mill?

Gov. Stevens: "The year they move on, when the President approved the Treaty.

Looking Glass: "Yes! Now we will talk. We have talked before. You said you would send this talk to the President and if he says yes, then it is right. Yes. And I will listen to what the President says and if he says yes, then we will talk.

Billy: "This is just putting it off further and making us more tired. You have no pity on us.

Three Feathers: "We cannot understand back here. Why don't he speak louder. Looking Glass is speaking, we look upon him as a Chief.

Billy: "I thought we had appointed Lawyer our head, our head Chief and he was to do our talking, that is the reason why I have spoken. [448 75]

Gov. Stevens: "I will say to my brother the Looking Glass that everything we say and do is sent to the President. What Looking Glass has said and what I say now goes to the President, but can I send anything to the President unless you agree to it? Can the President act? We have met that we may agree upon something then it goes to the President. The Pres't. has sent me and my brother to make this very agreement. We must agree upon something then it goes to the President and if he thinks it is good then he approves of it. I ask L. Glass to look upon it and see that it cannot be done any other way.

Gen. Palmer: "Our great Chief, the President, directed me and my brother to come here. We have been here 19 days, we have been talking a great deal. That talk has been for your good. We came here to talk straight, we have shown you our hearts, we will not lie to you. Yesterday we made a bargain with the Cayuse, the Walla Wallas and the Umatillas and the day before with the Nez Perces. The Looking Glass was not here but we did not forget him. We know that when he understands it all he will say yes. This morning we made a bargain with the Yakamas, they with these others all say yes. We expect the Looking Glass and his people will all say yes. We have told these people and it is so said in the paper that their horses and cattle would be allowed to graze outside of the reservation the same as our people when it was not occupied by whites. It we change the line to where he says we would have to stay here two or three days more to arrange the paper. We are all tired. You are tired. Shall we say one thing today and another thing tomorrow?

"They have said yes! My heart says yes to the line that was shown yesterday and today. All things will be done as we told you. Shall we do so. My heart says yes. I have nothing more to say."

Looking Glass: "Yes! Let it be so."

Eagle from the Light: "When I spoke to you before I said that I should speak slowly and I have been thinking about what to say, but I don I know yet what to say. These people have been talking among themselfs as though there was two and when I heard what they had to say I said very well; let us go as two.

Looking Glass: "What I showed these people when I came here. I spoke beyond it (referring to the map) and you have said that this talk you would send to the President and he will see it. [449 76]

"You see my body it is not divided, it is one body as these are all my children (pointing about). They have all got horses and cattle that is the reason I made it larger.

I want you to talk plain just like the light [Light] and then I will say yes. That is all I have to say now."

Gov. Stevens: "I will ask of Looking Glass whether he has been told of our council. Looking Glass knows that in this reservation settlers cannot go, that he can graze his cattle outside of the reservation on lands not claimed by settlers, <u>that he can catch fish at any of the fishing stations, that he can kill game and can go to Buffalo when he pleases, that he can get roots and berries on any of the lands not occupied by settlers</u>. He knows what the Reservation is; that we promise him two mills, a saw and a grist mill, two schools and a blacksmith; that we give him a physician, and all the other things that have been spoken of; the people all know it, it has been read over two or three times.

"This Reservation is in his own country. I ask Looking Glass is not this talking straight? We send all this to the President and besides this we pay a certain sum of which you all know; we have been looking for him ever since we have been here; Lawyer will recollect that I have been enquiring when will Looking Glass come? We wanted him to come.

"Those who go to the Buffalo are all my children. I am going to see the Blackfeet next moon. The Blackfeet had stolen some of his horses, but he got them back again. I heard the story last night. He killed some of their men. I know that Looking Glass wants me to go and made peace in that country. Let us first agree here.

Gen. Palmer: "We buy your country and pay you for it and give the most of it back to you again."

Looking Glass: "You have said to me that the whites shall not go over that line, none shall go into that country and this you said and it is said: And you will show to the President what we <u>have</u> said. [450 77]

Gov. Stevens:. "I understand Looking Glass has consented with the other Chiefs. The papers are now ready to sign: here I will particularly speak to *Kamahkan* or the head Chief of the Yakamas. Are you ready?

Young Chief: "What the Looking Glass says, I say.

Gov. Stevens: "I ask you whether you are ready to sign? I stated that whatever the Looking Glass said and we said would go to the President. We agreed upon a line yesterday and the day before. The papers are drawn: we ask are you now ready to sign those papers and let them go to the President.

Looking Glass: "That he said yes to his line.

Gov. Stevens: "Looking Glass is satisfied with the Nez Perce line, the young Chief and *Pe-pe-mox-mox* yesterday agreed to the Umatilla reserve.

Looking Glass: "I said yes to the line I marked myself, not to your line.

Gov. Stevens: "I will say to the Looking Glass, we cannot agree.

Gen. Palmer: "I would say to the Looking Glass, what use is it to purchase his country and give it all back again. We did not come here to talk like boys. We don't wish to part with a misunderstanding."

The Nez Perces, the Walla Wallas, the Cayuses and the Umatillas agree to the boundaries as we have marked. Do you wish to throw all we have said to you behind you. Shall we like boys say yes today and no tomorrow? *Pe-pe-mox-mox*, Young Chief and the Nez Perces say yes! None of their people say no! Why do we talk so much about it? I have done.

Young Chief: "The President is your Chief and you do what he tells you. That is the reason the Looking Glass marked out the line he wanted: he is the head Chief.

Looking Glass: It was my children that spoke yesterday and now I come and hear them speak. I asked my children what was their hurry? They knew that I was coming. Why did they run and speak till I came: that [451 78] is the reason I marked it bigger. I wanted to talk with you and have you talk with me. And after that. Your talk and my talk will go to the President.

Gen. Palmer: "I will say to my brother that I did not know that he was absent when we made our minds to come here, and set the time. My brother and myself come here and we came a long way. We have been here a long time. We were not in a hurry, these people wanted to go home, they had fields of wheat, and of potatoes, the weeds were growing up, they wanted to go home, there was no one at home to take care of the fields. We have other persons to see besides these.

"My Brother has to go to the Blackfoot country and make peace. He wanted to say to them. You shall not steal these peoples horses: you shall not make war upon them; these are the reasons we talk. We talk because our Great Chief told us.

"The papers have not been signed, they had not forgotten him nor had we. Shall all our efforts to protect them be destroyed? Shall our talk be thrown away? If the Looking Glass is a Chief I hope he will act as a Chief acts for the good of his people.

"If we were to say yes to his line our Chief would say No! but if we shall say the line we have marked we believe our Chief will say Yes. Which will you do, take that line or have it all thrown away? Let us act like wise men and not part without doing good for each other.

Looking Glass: "I am not going to say any more today.

Gen. Palmer: "If the Nez Perces are not ready they can talk among themselfs and come tomorrow.

"If the Cayuses, the Walla Wallas and Umatillas are ready to do what yesterday they said they would, then the paper is ready for them to sign, and tonight they can get their goods and go home when they please.

"The paper is also ready for the Yakamas if they choose to sign it they can do so."

Gov. Stevens: "The Council will now adjourn till Monday morning and I trust by that time Looking Glass will have thought the matter over and we will be able to agree. [452 79]

Monday June 11th

Council opened at 11 o'clock.

Gov. Stevens said: "My children, we have met today for the last time. Every man here present has agreed to a treaty in council. The Nez Perces agreed to a treaty. Not one man spoke against it. All agreed that the head Chief would speak for you. You were all called upon to speak. I called upon Joseph to speak and he spoke: "I have a good heart," says Joseph, "what the Lawyer says let it be".

The Eagle-from-the Light said: "the head chief Lawyer had spoken so be it."

The Red Wolf said: "What the Lawyer has said be it so, he is our head chief."

Said *U-ute-sin-ma-le-kin*: "my chief has spoken for me."

Every man Said: I say again, "Lawyer is our chief." "I agree to the treaty." So said the Cayuses, the Walla Wallas, the Umatillas and the Yakamas. The Young Chief and *Stickuss* said, "We pledged our words, we agree."

We all expect that you all will do what you promised to do. We don't believe you will break your word and make us ashamed of you. I don't believe we shall have to say to the President, "You have promised, and then broke your promise."

No! We know that you will keep your word. First the Nez Perces, – I shall call upon Lawyer the head chief, and then I shall call on the other chiefs to sign.

Will Lawyer now come forward. (he then came forward and signed the Treaty) Now I call upon Looking Glass and Joseph to sign the Treaty. (After they had affixed their names James and the other chiefs and head men put their names to it.)

Gov. Stevens: "My Brothers, the Treaties have now all been signed. They will be sent to the President. All the speeches on both sides will be sent to the President. The President will see that everything has been fairly explained and agreed upon between us. He will see that you have all noted like men here. He won't find any fault even with Looking Glass. [453 80]

"Looking Glass came back after a long absents [absence] and asked time to look at the treaty. Time was given him to think it over. He was satisfied and we find his name next to his head chief's.

"I think the President will approve what we have done. We will let you know when we hear from him, which will be sometime next year.

"We have some few presents to give you which will be distributed upon your leaving the ground. They are designed for those who need them most. You will dispose of them in that way.

"Thenceforth you will have me for your Great Chief, Mr. Tappan for your Agent, and Mr. Craig for your Interpreter.

"The Yakamas will have Mr. [AJ] Bolon for their Agent.

"The Walla Wallas and Umatillas will look to Gen'l Palmer hereafter.

"There is another point which I wish to speak about from my heart. It is the Blackfoot Council. My brother, the Looking Glass, knows that we want peace on those Buffalo plains. You all know it. I think I can I make peace there.

"Nez Perces! Nearly one fourth of your people live there. I want some chiefs of courage and character, and one hundred of your braves to go to that council. I say to Lawyer, the head chief, of the Nez Perces, I would be glad to have him go, I would be glad to have Looking Glass go. Arrange this among yourselfs. I hope and trust that Mr. Craig will go with you.

"The Cayuses, Walla Wallas, Umatillas, and Yakamas, I would like to have some of them also.

"We shall have chiefs and braves from the Flatheads [Selish], the Cour de lains [Coeur d'Alene], Coo-too-mey's [Kootenay] and I hope from the Spokanes. The Blackfeet have promised to meet you there in council and when we meet there will be peace among you. Think this matter over and decide for yourselfs."

Gen'l Palmer: "My brothers, I wish to say a few words before we part. When we came here we didn't know the hearts of your people. We have been together a long [454 81] time and have talked a great deal. We have listened to what you have said, and you have listened to what we have said. ___ you have sometimes been afraid that we were not working for your good. Your willingness to come forward and sign the Treaty is evidence that you have decided that we intended to do you good. We have shown you our hearts and you have shown us yours. We commenced a long way apart but now we are together. We are one. I hope we shall always remain as one and have but one heart.

"From this time we expect that we and you will always be at peace. We not only want you to be at peace with all whites but we want you to be at peace with yourself. We didn't come here to divide you or to induce one to against another. You may live at separate place, but your hearts would be as one and help each other. We chiefs and old men should give good council to their young people. The young men should listen to the old men and be advised by them. The young people should strive to assist the old people. Take care of them. It is the duty of the old people when they see these boys act foolish to council them. It is the duty of all to take care of your women and children, furnish them with food and with clothing.

"I say again! Take care of your old people, supply their lodges with provisions, for you will soon be old yourself and will need help.

"We expect you will all leave this ground with good hearts and if there are any among you that have bad hearts, advise them to throw them away. If your people are foolish and do wrong it is your duty as chiefs to punish them for it. We shall try and prevent the whites from doing wrong to the Indians, and you must prevent your people from doing wrong to the whites.

"The Treaty provides that if an Indian steals the property of the whites it may be paid for from the annuities. It also provides that if your people steal other tribes it will be paid for in the same way. We also provide that if the whites take the property of an Indian it must be paid for. The Agent who is the proper person to apply to in case an injury is done you and when any of your people do wrong to the whites, then it is the duty of the chiefs to punish the offender. If one does wrong to an individual he is not to redress his own wrong but he is to submit it to the chiefs or his council, or to the Agent and abide by their decision. [455 82]

"It is to be hoped that your people will do no wrong. Let us try and prevent it if we can. We expect the chiefs to look to this and if there is any of their people who have stolen property and have it on hand it is my heart they should give it up to their Agent, and the Agent will do all he can to return your property.

"We have, my brother, told you that we had a few goods to give you. Your people are not all here to receive them. We have been here a long time and cant remain to see you all. We shall therefore give these goods into the hands of the chiefs and we expect the Head Chiefs to call his chiefs and see them distributed justly.

"My Brother, Gov. Stevens, will furnish the Nez Perces with goods. Mr. Thompson and myself will furnish the Cayuse, Walla Walla and Umatillas with goods. And when we get through talking the head chiefs of the Cayuses, Walla Wallas, Umatilla will go receive the goods and take care of them.

"We have not got a great many goods but when this paper goes to the President and he says it is good then we will supply you with other goods, and we shall do all things that we have agreed upon. Mr. Tompson will be the Agent for the Cayuses, Walla Wallas, and the Umatillas.

"When we part we will all go to our homes with good hearts towards each other. When we have built the blacksmith shops, saw mills, and chiefs home[s] and other things we have agreed to. Then we expect you will go upon the reservation, and when you go and if you leave your little farms and improvements they will be valued and you will be paid for them.

"I shall go home with a good heart towards all your people, and I shall be very sorry if I hear your people have done wrong. I have nothing more to say at present.

"If any of you have anything to say we are ready to listen to you.

Gov. Stevens: "I will say to the Nez Perces, I hope to visit them in their own country when I come back from the Blackfoot Council. I hope also to visit the Yakamas on my return.

"The Cayuses, Walla Wallas and Umatillas will look to Gen. Palmer hereafter. They will also look upon me as their friend. [456 83]

Tin-tin-meet-see: "I understand you well. We are never the beginners in doing wrong to the whites. All Indians here understood well what has been said. When your white children come into this country they do things at random (to the Indians) You have heard all that has been said and now let us go home and do right.

Eagle of the Light: "My forefathers are all dead, I only am left, there is but the encampment remaining, it is good to hear and think of each other. We have heard good words spoken from the President to take care of us poor people well. His children's way you have come here to see. For days our bodies have been together, also the night and also for years, also for winters. You have shown that he likes his red children. I do not want our hearts to come together wrong, but right, and remain so as long as we are a people, and we will stop the bad people on both sides. The lord will reward us both when our hearts are good that we will look and care for each other, – The old and the young will go right and then all will be right – from little could come great difficulties – that is the reason we speak from small things to big ones – that is all at present.

James Said: "It is not from anything bad that I have not spoken. It is as though the man I speak of is not of the party. When the white people came to my country Mr. See told me when he came there he was coming for good and not for bad. When the white people come and they would come in great numbers do not do anything bad to them. I have never done bad to them. I wish Mr. Craig to stay with us and hear the Indians speak for he could speak to our people and they could understand him – therefore I wish him to stay.

Red Grizzly Said: "I like your talk – you talk well. When you have finished I like it still, this you have brought us from the President. I like that talk my friends. From the time I spoke here I have been sick at heart. This man who has just now spoken, he spoke a little longer because he knows how to speak and there is also another who has just come, the Looking Glass, they speak straight and friendly. You have also spoken friendly, and shown them your heart plainly – not that I am a good man that I like it. My heart is glad as though I see your heart when I hear your words. What I have good to speak I have not spoke yet. (here he was interrupted by the Indians when the Red Owl said the Young Chief wished to say that he wanted you to stop the whites from taking their horses or cattle and if my horses go across the line of the reservation which is a small one I do not want these horses and cattle to be taken off because they are over the line). [457 84]

Gen. Palmer said: "My brethren. This man has said from little things grow great ones. It is true, it is so – a single word spoken unkindly leads to a difficulty. It would be better if we always would not do or say bad things, but if little things are done wrong we should try and forget them. I have been told that there are sometimes difficulties among the Indians in reference to their mode of worship. That is a thing that we do not interfere with. We are willing to let the people worship God as they please. We do not say do this or do that. If their heart is to sing or pray and preach it is good, if others say it is not our heart to pray and to preach it is good, but we want all people to be good people. If those who sing and pray think it is good, let them to try to convince others. Talk kindly, treat them kindly and convince them they will do right. Some will worship one way and some will worship another – do not quarrel about it but worship or not worship, we want you to have good hearts. I have done. –

Looking Glass Says: "As so many are now writing, some other time you and I will have a heart. I have a good head and a good heart, by and by we will have a talk.

Council Adjourned sine die at three o'clock.

We hereby certify the above to be a true record of the proceedings.

SS James Doty
Sect'y to Treaties in N. [W.] Terr'y.
SS Wm. McKay
Sect'y to Treaties in O.T.

Approved

Isaac Stevens
Gov. & Supt. W.T.
Joel Palmer
Supt. Ind. Affairs
for O.T. [458]

Digest of Treaty Concluded at Medicine Creek, Territory of Washington,
between Gov. Isaac I. Stevens, Superintendent of Washington Territory,
and the Nisqually, Puyallup, etc.

DATE: Dec. 26, 1854; RATIFIED: March 3, 1855
STATUTE REFERENCE: 10 Stat. 1132; 2 Kappler 661
TRIBES INVOLVED: Nisqually, Puyallup, Steilacoom, Sqawskin, S'Homamish, Stehchsss, T'Peeksin, Squi-aitl, and Sa-heh-wamish, and other bands around head of Puget's Sound, treated with as one nation for purposes of treaty.

Article 1

Cedes to United States certain described lands occupied by said tribes in Territory of Washington.

Article 2

Describes boundaries of three separate tracts of land within ceded territory to be reserved to the exclusive use of the said Indians.

Provides no whites shall be permitted to reside upon reserved areas without permission and that the tribes will settle thereon within one year after ratification of treaty.

Provides that if necessary for public convenience, roads may be run through their reserves; also reserves right-of-way to Indians to nearest public highway.

Article 3

"The right of taking fish, at all usual and accustomed grounds and stations, is further secured to said Indians in common with all citizens of the Territory, and of erecting temporary houses for the purpose of curing, together with the privilege of hunting, gathering roots and berries, and pasturing their horses on open and unclaimed lands: Provided, however, That they shall not take shellfish from any beds staked or cultivated by citizens" *
* Verbatim [459 2]

Article 4

Provides for payment by the United States of $32,500 over a 20 year period, same to be expended under direction of the President upon beneficial objects. The Superintendent of Indian Affairs, or other proper official, shall each year inform the President of the wishes of said Indians in respect thereto.

Article 5

Provides for expenditures by United States of $3,250 for settlement of reservations and breaking up sufficient land for cultivation.

Article 6

President may remove Indians from reservation to some other suitable place or places within territory (when interests of territory may require, and the welfare of said Indians be promoted) on remunerating them for improvements and expenses of removal, or may consolidate them with other friendly tribes.

President may cause survey and assignment of lots to individuals or families as permanent home.

Substantial improvements made by Indians and abandoned in consequence of treaty shall be valued and payment made therefor.

Article 7

Provides annuities shall not be used to pay debts of individuals.

Article 8

Indians acknowledge their dependence on the United States Government and promise to commit no depredations on property of United States citizens or other Indians.

Payment by those proven responsible in the event depredations occur.

Indians promise not to make war on any other tribe except in self-defense.

Indians agree not to shelter offenders against laws of the United States. [460 3]

Article 9

Provides for withholding of annuities from those drinking liquor or procuring same for others.

Article 10

Provides for establishment of an agricultural and industrial school to be supported by the Government for 20 years, same to be free for children of said tribes.

Provides that the United states employ a physician to reside at central agency.

Expenses of above not to be deducted from annuities.

Article 11

Provides for abolishment of slavery and prohibition of future acquisition of slaves.

Article 12

Indians agree not to trade outside of the United States; nor shall foreign Indians reside in reservation without consent of superintendent or agent.

Article 13

Treaty to become effective as soon as ratified by President and Senate.

****

Digest of Treaty Concluded at Point Elliot, Territory of Washington,
between Gov. Isaac I. Stevens, Governor and
Superintendent of Indians Affairs for said territory,
and the Dwamish, Suquamish, etc.

DATE: Jan. 22, 1855: RATIFIED: Mar, 8, 1859
STATUTE REFERENCE: 12 Stat. 927; 2 Kappler 669
TRIBES INVOLVED: Dwamish, Suquamish, Sk-tahl-mish, Sam-ahmish, Smalh-kamish, Skope-amish, St-kah-mish, Snoqualmoo, Skai-wha-mish, N'Quentl-ma-mish, Sk-tah-le-jum, Stoluck-wha-mish, Sno-ho-mish, Skagit, Kik-i-allus, [461 4] Swin-a-mish, Squin-ah-mish, Sah-ku-mehu, Noo-wha-ha, Nook-wa-chah-mish, Mee-see-qua-guilch, Cho-bah-ah-bish, and other allied and subordinate tribes occupying certain lands in Territory of Washington.

Article 1:

Cedes to the United States certain described lands occupied by said tribes in Territory of Washington.

Article 2:

Describes boundaries of four separate tracts of lands within ceded territory to be reserved to the exclusive use of the said Indians,

Provides no Whites shall be permitted to reside upon reserved areas without permission of tribes and superintendent.

Provides that if necessary for public convenience, roads may be run through the said reserves and Indians compensated for any damages thus sustained.

Article 3:

Provides for reservation of one township of land for the purpose of establishing thereon an agricultural and industrial school and having in view the ultimate settlement thereon of all Indians living west of the Cascade Mountains.

Article 4:

Provides that tribes shall settle on reserved areas described in Article 2 within one year after ratification of treaty.

Article 5:*

"The right of taking fish at usual and accustomed grounds and stations is further secured to said Indians in common with all citizens of the Territory, and of erecting temporary houses for the purpose of curing same, together with the privilege of hunting and gathering roots and berries on open and unclaimed lands. Provided, however, that they shall not take shellfish from any beds staked or cultivated by citizens."

*Verbatim [462 5]

Article 6:

Provides for payment by the United States of $150,000 over a 20 year period, same to be expended under discretion of the President upon beneficial objects. The Superintendent of Indian Affairs, or other proper official, shall each year inform the President of the wishes of said Indians in respect thereto.

Article 7:

President may remove Indians from reservation to some other suitable place or places within territory (when interests of territory may require, and the welfare of said Indians be promoted) on remunerating them for improvements and expenses of removal; or may consolidate them with other friendly tribes.

President may cause survey and assignment of lots to individuals or families as permanent home.

Substantial improvements made by Indians and abandoned in consequence of treaty shall be evalued and payment made therefor.

Article 8:

Provides annuities shall not be used to pay debts of individuals.

Article 9:

Indians acknowledge their dependence on the United States Government and promise to commit no depredations on property of United States citizens or other Indians.

Payment from annuities of those proven responsible in the event depredations occur.

Indians promise not to make war on any other tribe except in self defense.

Indians agree not to shelter offenders against laws of United States.

Article 10:

Provides for withholding of annuities from those drinking liquor or procuring same for others.

Article 11:

Provides for abolishment of slavery and prohibition of future acquisition of slaves. [463 6]

Article 12:

Indians agree not to trade outside of the United States; nor shall foreign Indians reside in reservation without consent of superintendent or agent.

Article 13:

Provides for expenditure by United States of $15,000 for settlement of reservations and breaking up sufficient land for cultivation.

Article 14:

Provides for establishment and support for 20 years of an agricultural and industrial school, same to be free for children of said tribes.

Provides that the United States employ a physician to reside at the central agency.

Expenses of above not to be deducted from annuities but to be defrayed by the United States.

Article 15:

Treaty to become effective as soon as ratified by President and Senate.

Digest of Treaty Concluded at *Hahdskus* or Point No Point, Suquamish Head,
Territory of Washington, between Gov. Isaac I, Stevens, Governor and
Superintendent of Indian Affairs for said territory,
and the S'Klallam Indians.

DATE: Jan. 26, 1855;
RATIFIED: Mar. 8, 1859
STATUE REFERENCE: 12 Stats. 933; 2 Kappler 674
TRIBES INVOLVED: Various villages of the S'Klallams, viz: Kah-tai, Squah-quaihtl, Tch-queen, Ste-tchtlum, Tsohkw, Yennis, Elh-wa, Pishtat, Hunnint, Klat-la-wash, and Oke-ho, and also of the Sko-ko-mish, To-an-hooch, and Chem-a-kum tribes. [464 7]

Article 1

Cedes to the United States certain described lands occupied by said tribes in Territory of Washington.

Article 2

Describes boundaries of tract of land within ceded territory, comprising six sections or 3840 acres situated at head of Hood's Canal, to be reserved to the exclusive use of the said Indians.

Provides no whites shall be permitted to reside upon reserved areas without permission of tribes and superintendent.

Provides that if necessary for public convenience, roads may be run through the said reserves and Indians compensated for any damages thus sustained.

Provides President at liberty to place other friendly tribes upon reserve.

Article 3

Provides that tribes shall settle on reserved area described in Article 2 within one year after ratification of treaty.

Article 4*

"The right of taking fish at usual and accustomed grounds and stations is further secured to said Indians, in common with all citizens of the United States; and of erecting temporary houses for the purpose of curing; together with the privilege of hunting and gathering roots and berries on open and unclaimed lands. Provided, however, That they shall not take shell-fish from any beds staked or cultivated by citizens."

* Verbatim

Article 5

Provides for payment by the United States of $60,000 over a 20 year period, same to be expended under direction of the President upon beneficial objects. The Superintendent of Indian Affairs, or other proper official, shall each year inform the President of the wishes of said Indians in respect thereto.

Article 6

Provides for expenditure by the United States of $6,000 for settlement of reservation and breaking up of sufficient land for cultivation. [465 8]

Article 7

President may remove Indians from reservation to sane other suitable place or places within territory (when interests of territory may require, and the welfare of said Indians be promoted) on remunerating them for improvements and expenses of removal; or may consolidate them with other friendly tribes.

President may cause survey and assignment of lots to individuals or families as permanent home.

Substantial improvements made by Indians and abandoned in consequence of treaty shall be evelued and payment made therefor.

Article 8

Provides annuities shall not be used to pay debts of individuals.

Article 9

Indians acknowledge their dependence on the United States Government and promise to commit no depredations on property of United States citizens or other Indians.

Payment from annuities of those proven responsible in the event depredations occur.

Indians promise not to make war on any other tribe except in self-defense.

Indians agree not to shelter offenders against laws of the United States.

Article 10

Provides for withholding of annuities from those drinking liquor or procuring same for others.

Article 11

Provides for establishment of an agricultural and industrial school to be supported by the Government for 20 years, same to be free for children of said tribes.

Provides that the United States employ a physician to reside at the central agency.

Expenses of above not to be deducted from annuities but to be defrayed by the United States.

Article 12

Provides for abolishment of slavery and prohibition of future acquisition of slaves. [466 9]

Article 13

Indians agree not to trade outside of the United States; nor shall foreign Indians reside in the reservation without consent of superintendent or agent.

Article 14

Treaty to become effective as soon as ratified by President and Senate.

* . * . * . * . *

Digest of Treaty Concluded at Neah Bay, Territory of Washington,
between Gov. Isaac I. Stevens, Governor and
Superintendent of Indian Affairs for said Territory,
and the Makah tribe.

DATE: Jan. 31, 1855; RATIFIED: Mar. 8, 1859
STATUTE REFERENCE: 12 Stat. 939; 2 Kappler 682
TRIBES INVOLVED: Makah tribe, viz: Neah, Waatch, TsooYess, and Osett.

Article 1

Cedes to the United States certain described land occupied by said tribes in Territory of Washington.

Article 2

Describes boundaries of tract of land within ceded territory to be reserved to the exclusive use of the said Indians.

Provides no whites shall be permitted to reside upon reserved areas without permission of tribes and superintendent.

Provides that if necessary for public convenience, roads may be run through the said reserves and Indians compensated for any damages thus sustained.

Provides President at liberty to place other friendly tribes upon the reserve.

Article 3

Provides that tribes shall settle on reserved area described in Article 2 within one year after ratification of treaty. [467 10]

Article 4

"The right of taking fish and of whaling or sealing at usual and accustomed grounds and stations is further secured to said Indians in common with all citizens of the United States, and of

erecting temporary houses for the purpose of curing, together with the privilege of hunting and gathering roots and berries on open and unclaimed lands; Provided, however, That they shall not take shell-fish from any beds staked or cultivated by citizens."
          * Verbatim

Article 5

Provides for payment by the United States of $30,000 over a 20 year period, settle to be expended under direction of the President upon beneficial objects. The Superintendent of Indian Affairs, or other proper official, shall each year inform the President of the wishes of said Indians in respect thereto.

Article 6

Provides for expenditure by the United States of $3,000 for settlement of reservation and breaking up of sufficient land for cultivation.

Any substantial improvements an Indian is forced to abandon shall be valued and payment made therefor.

Article 7

President may remove Indians from reservation to some other suitable place or places within territory (when interests of territory may require, and the welfare of said Indians be promoted) on enumerating them for improvements and expenses of removal; or may consolidate them with other friendly tribes.

President may cause survey and assignment of lots to individuals or families as permanent home.

Article 8

Provides annuities shall not be used to pay debts of individuals. [468 11]

Article 9

Indians acknowledge their dependence on the United States Government and promise to commit no depredation on property of United States citizens or other Indians.

Payment from annuities of those proven responsible in the event depredations occur.

Indians promise not to make war on any other tribe except in self-defense.

Indians agree not to shelter offenders against laws of the United States.

Article 10

Provides for withholding of annuities from those drinking liquor or procuring same for others.

Article 11

Provides for establishment and support for 20 years of an agricultural and industrial school to be free for children of said bands.

Provides that the United States employ a physician to reside at the central agency.

Expenses of above not to be deducted from annuities but to be defrayed by the United States.

Article 12

Provides for abolishment of slavery and prohibition of future acquisition of slaves.

Article 13

Indians agree not to trade outside of the United States; nor shall foreign Indians reside in reservation without consent of superintendent or agent.

Article 14

Treaty to become effective as soon as ratified by President and Senate. [469 12]

Digest of Treaty Concluded at Camp Stevens, Walla-Walla Valley,
Oregon Territory, between Gov. Isaac I. Stevens and Joel Palmer,
Superintendent of Indian Affairs for Washington and
Oregon Territories, respectively, and the Walla-Wallas, etc.

DATE: June 9, 1855; RATIFIED: Mar. 8, 1859
STATUTE REFERENCE: 12 stat. 914; 2 Kappler 694
TRIBES INVOLVED: Walla-Wallas, Cayuses, Umatilla, also other bands of Indians occupying lands in Washington and Oregon territories treated with as one nation for purposes of treaty.

Article 1

Cedes to the United States certain described lands occupied by tribes situated in Washington and Oregon territories.

Describes boundaries of lands within ceded territory to be reserved to the exclusive use of the said Indians.

Provides no whites shall be permitted to reside upon reserved area without permission and that the tribes will settle thereon within one year after ratification of treaty.

*"Provided, also, That the exclusive right of taking fish in the streams running through and bordering said reservation is hereby secured to said Indians, and at all other usual and accustomed stations in common the citizens of the United States, and of erecting suitable buildings for curing the same; the privilege of hunting, gathering roots arid berries and pasturing their stock on unclaimed lands in common with citizens is also secured to them."

Provides for diminishing of payments in event any bands claiming any portion of said ceded area do not accept treaty provisions.

Provides for payment of value of any substantial improvements made by any individual Indians compelled to abandon same to comply with removal provisions.
       * Verbatim

Article 2

Provides for payment by the United States of $100,000 over a 20 year period, same to be expended under direction [470 13] <Article 2 continued> of the President for buildings, land subjugation, purchasing stock, farming equipment, clothing, etc.

Article 3

Provides for expenditure by the United States of $350,000 for erection of buildings on reservation, etc., during first and second years after treaty ratification.

Article 4

Provides for erection and maintenance of mills, hospital, and other shops in addition to above specified consideration; also for employment of certain specified skilled personnel for a period of 20 years.

Article 5

Provides for erection by United States of dwelling houses for head chiefs of each of the three principal bands; also the clearing and fencing of 10 acres of land for each chief and payment to each of $500 a year in cash for 20 years.

Provides for opening of a new wagon road to be used by immigrants in lieu of the then present road passing through area reserved to Indians.

Article 6

Provides for allotment of lands to individual Indians at the discretion of the President; the issuance of restrictive patents thereon and the cancellation thereof in the event Indians fail to occupy and cultivate same.

Article 7

Provides annuities shall not be used to pay debts of individuals.

Article 8

Indians acknowledge their dependence on the United States Government and promise to commit no depredations on property of United States citizens or other Indians paid from annuities of those proven responsible in the event depredations occur. [471   14]   <Article 8 continued>

Indians promise not to make war on any other tribe except in self defense.

Indians agree to submit to all rules and regulations of the Government.

Article 9

Provides for withholding of annuities from those drinking liquor or procuring same for others.

Article 10

Right-of-way reserved for highways and railroad through reservation when same considered necessary in the opinion of the President.

Article 11

Treaty to become effective as soon as ratified by President and Senate.

* * *

Digest of Treaty Concluded at Camp Stevens, Walla-Walla Valley,
Oregon Territory, between Gov. Isaac I. Stevens, Governor and
Superintendent of Indian Affairs for Territory of Washington,
and the Yakama, etc.

DATE: June 9, 1855; RATIFIED: Mar. 8, 1859
STATUTE REFERENCE: 12 Stat. 951; 2 Kappler 698

TRIBES INVOLVED: Yakama, Palouse, Pisquouse, Wenatshapam, Klikatat, Klinquit, Kow-was-say-se, Li-ay-was, Skin-pah, Wash-ham, Shyiks, Oche-chotes, Kay-milt-pah, and So-ap-cat – confederated tribes who for the purpose of this treaty are to be considered one nation, "Yakama".

Article 1
Cedes to the United States certain described lands occupied by said tribes in the Territory of Washington. [472 15]

Article 2
Describe boundaries of tract of land within ceded territory to be reserved to the exclusive use of the said Indians.
Provides no whites, excepting those employed in the Indian Department, shall be permitted to reside upon reserved area without permission of tribes and superintendent.
Provides that tribe shall settle on reserved area within one year after ratification of treaty.
Substantial improvements made by any Indian and abandoned in consequence of treaty shall be evalued and payment made therefor prior to actual abandonment.

Article 3
Provides that if necessary for public convenience, roads may be run through the said reserve, and, on the other hand, right-of-way secured to Indians to nearest public highway, as also right to travel public highways in common with citizens of the United States.
*The exclusive right of taking fish in all the streams, where running through or bordering said reservations, is further secured to said confederated tribes and bands of Indians, as also the right of taking fish at all usual and accustomed places, in common with the citizens of the Territory, and of erecting temporary buildings for curing them; together with the privilege of hunting, gathering roots and berries, and pasturing their horses and cattle upon open and unclaimed land.
* Verbatim

Article 4
Provides for payment by the United States of $200,000 in addition to goods and provisions distributed at treaty council. Of this amount, $60,000 will be paid the first year for settlement of reservation, construction of homes, and breaking up of sufficient land for cultivation. The remainder to be paid over a 20 year period; all to be expended under direction of the President upon beneficial objects. The Superintendent of Indian Affairs, or other proper official, shall each year inform the President of the wishes of said Indians in respect thereto. [473 16]

Article 5
Provides for establishment of two schools; one of which shall be an agricultural and industrial school, same to be supported and maintained by the Government for 20 years and to be free to the children of said confederated tribes.
Provides for erection of two blacksmith, one tinsmith, one gunsmith, one carpenter, and one wagon and plow maker shops, and the employment of necessary personnel to operate same and instruct the Indians.
Provides for erection of saw and flour mill.

Provides for the erection of a hospital and the employment of a physician, same to be maintained and supported by the Government for 20 years.

Provides for the erection of a house, the clearing and fencing of 10 acres of land, and a payment to said tribes of $500 per annum for 20 years, all for the use and benefit of their head chief.

Article 6

President may cause survey and assignment of lots to individuals or families as permanent homes.

Article 7

Provides annuities shall not be used to pay debts of individuals.

Article 8

Indians acknowledge their dependence on the United States Government and promise to commit no depredations on property of United States citizens or other Indians.

Payment from annuities of those proven responsible in the event depredations occur Indians promise not to make war on any other tribe except in self-defense.

Indians agree not to shelter offenders against laws of the United States.

Article 9

Provides for withholding of annuities from those drinking liquor or procuring same for others.

Article 10

Provides for the reserving and setting aside of an area of not to exceed one township of six miles [474 17] <Article 10 continued> square, situated at forks of the Pisquouse or Wenatshapam River, and known as "Wenatshapam Fishery", which shall be subject to same provisions and restrictions as other Indian reservations, said tract to be surveyed and set aside wherever the President may direct.*[87]

---

[87] *NOTE: The Wenatshapam Fishery was duly surveyed and set apart in 1893. By agreement dated January 8, 1894, set forth in full in the Indian Department Appropriation Act for the Fiscal Year 1895, dated August 15, 1894 (28 Stat. 286, 320), the Yakama Nation of Indians ceded and relinquished all their right, title and interest in said fishery. The basis for such action on the part of the Indians as set forth in the agreement was the fact that they had "found the said right of fishery and the said fishery * * * of little use or benefit to them". The consideration for the cession was $20,000 and the promise that the Indians known as the Wenatshapam [Pskʷaws] Indians could have allotments of land in severalty in the vicinity in which they then resided, or elsewhere, as they may select. [475 18]

[Though ceded in the Yakama Treaty, the Wenatshapam Fishery was a mainstay of the Interior-Salish-speaking Pskʷaws, known as Wenatschapam in Sahaptian, featuring a sockeye run now encouraged by a hatchery at Leavenworth. Misplaced surveys proposed a Pskʷaws reserve with these salmon, but confused federal authorities, often in DC, dealt with Yakamas, who sold off this Salish fishery and used the money to start their 1894 irrigation system. In a famous quote by a bemused native:

"Does the Great Father in Washington think a salmon is an eagle that lives on top of a mountain, or does he think a salmon is a deer that lives in the woods and hills, or does he think

Article 11
Treaty to become effective when ratified by President and Senate.
* * * * *

Digest of Treaty Concluded at Camp Stevens, Walla-Walla Valley,
Oregon Territory, between Gov. Isaac I. Stevens and Joel Palmer,
Superintendents of Indian Affairs for Washington
and Oregon Territories, respectively,
and the Nez Perces.

DATE: June 11, 1855; RATIFIED: Mar. 8, 1859
STATUTE REFERENCE: 12 Stats. 957; 2 Kappler 702
TRIBES INVOLVED: Nez Perce tribe of Indians

Article 1
Cedes to the United States certain described lands occupied by said tribe partly in Oregon and partly in Washington territories.

Article 2
Describes boundaries of tract of land within ceded [475 18] <Article 2 Continued> area to be reserved to the exclusive use of the said Nez Perce tribe and other tribes and bands of Indians in Washington territory.

Provides no whites, excepting those employed in the Indian Department, shall be permitted to reside upon reserved area without permission of tribe and superintendent.

Provides that tribe shall settle on reserved area described above within one year after ratification of treaty.

Substantial improvements made by any Indian and abandoned in consequence of treaty shall be evalued and payment made therefor prior to actual abandonment.

Article 3
Provides that if necessary for public convenience, roads may be run through the said reserve, and, on the other hand, right-of-way secured to Indians to nearest public highway, as· also right to travel public highway in common with citizens of the United States.

Use of Clearwater and other streams through reservation secured to citizens of United States as public highway.

---

a salmon is a mountain goat that lives among the rocks of the snow-covered mountains."

When sale of these 23,000 acres was discussed with Yakama, $.50/acre was suggested since the land had forest, water, and some farm land not yet taken by settlers. By comparison, land there along the railroad right of way sold for $5/acre. During the 6 January 1894 sales meeting, Psk^waws were snow bound, so only Yakamas attended and sold off their land. A few Psk^waws took homesteads around Cashmere to stay in their homeland, where, on 4 July 1937, still pleading injustice, Chief John Harmelt and his wife, both blind, burned to death in their cabin, and remaining Psk^waws moved to the Colville Reservation. In 1965 they were awarded money in final recognition of their ownership, but, as they say, "You can't count on money to return each year to feed you, the way you can with salmon."]

*"The Exclusive right of taking fish in all the streams where running through or bordering said reservation is further secured to said Indians; as also the right of taking fish at all usual and accustomed places in common with citizens of the Territory; and of erecting temporary buildings for curing, together with the privilege of hunting, gathering roots and berries, and pasturing their horses and cattle upon open and unclaimed land."   *Verbatim

Article 4

Provides for payment by the United States of 200,000, in addition to goods and provisions distributed at treaty council. Of this amount $60,000 will be paid the first year for settlement of reservation, construction of houses, and breaking up of sufficient land for cultivation. The remainder to be paid over a 20 year period; all to be expended under direction of the President upon beneficial objects. The Superintendent of Indian Affairs, or other proper official, shall each year inform the President of the wishes of said Indians in respect thereto. [476 19]

Article 5

Provides for establishment of two schools; one of which shall be an agricultural and industrial school, same to be supported and maintained by the Government for 20 years and to be free to the children of said tribes.

Provides for erection of two blacksmith, one tinsmith, one gunsmith, one carpenter, and one wagon and plow maker shops, and the employment of necessary personnel to operate same and instruct the Indians.

Provides for erection of saw and flour mill.

Provides for the erection of a hospital and the employment of a physician, same to be maintained and supported by the Government for 20 years.

Provides for the erection of a house, the clearing and fencing of 10 acres of land, and a payment to said tribes of $500 per annum for 20 years, all for the use and benefit of their head chief.

Article 6

President may cause survey and assignment of lots to individuals or families as permanent homes.

Article 7

Provides annuities shall not be used to pay debts of individuals.

Article 8

Indians acknowledge their dependence on the United states Government and promise to commit no depredations on property of United States citizens or other Indians.

Payment from annuities of those proven responsible in the event depredations occur.

Indians promise not to make war on any other tribe except in self-defense.

Indians agree not to shelter offenders against laws of the United States.

Article 9

Provides for withholding of annuities from those drinking liquor or procuring same for others. [477 20]

Article 10

Tract of land occupied by William Craig, a proven friend of the Nez Perce, shall not be considered a part of the reservation, except it shall be subject in common with lands of reservation to operations of intercourse act.

Article 11
Treaty to become effective when ratified by President and Senate.

* * * *

Digest of Treaty Concluded at Wasco,
near the Dalles of the Columbia River, Oregon Territory,
between Joel Palmer, Superintendent of Indian Affairs for Oregon,
and the confederated tribes of Middle Oregon.

DATE: June 25, 1855; RATIFIED: Mar. 8, 1859
STATUTE REFERENCE: 12 Stats. 963; 2 Kappler 711
TRIBES INVOLVED: Tribes residing in Middle Oregon, to wit: *Taih* or Upper De Chutes band of Walla-Wallas, *Wyam* or Lower De Chutes band of Walla-Wallas, Tenino band of Walla-Wallas, Dock-spus or John Day's River band of Walla-Wallas; Dalles band of the Wascoes; Ki-gal-twal-la band of Wascoes; and Dog River band of Wascoes.

Article 1
Cedes to the United States certain described land occupied by said tribes in Territory of Oregon.

Describes boundaries of tract of land within ceded territory to be reserved to the exclusive use of said Indians.

Provides no whites shall be permitted to reside upon reserved area without permission of the superintendent and agent.

Provides that tribes shall settle on reserved area within one year after ratification of treaty. [478 21] <Article 1 continued>

Provides further, however, that if the designated three principal bands involved decide before removal to said reserve and before any improvements thereon are made, that they wish another reservation to be selected for them, the same shall be done if agreement between Indians and Superintendent as to location can be reached.

*"Provided, also, That the exclusive right of taking fish in the streams running through and bordering said reservation is hereby secured to said Indians; and at all other usual and accustomed stations, in common with citizens of the United States, and of erecting suitable houses for curing the same; also the privilege of hunting, gathering roots and berries, and pasturing their stock on unclaimed lands, in common with citizens, is secured to them."/1/[88]

In event any band or bands shall not accede to treaty, then the bands becoming parties hereto agree to receive payments in proportion that their aggregate number has to whole number of Indians residing in and claiming entire ceded area.

Substantial improvements made by any Indian and abandoned in consequence of treaty shall be evalued and payment made therefor.

---

[88] 1/ The rights under this proviso were relinquished by treaty of November 15, 1855 (14 Stat. 751; 2 Kappler 908) digest of which follows.

* Verbatim

Article 2

Provides for payment by the United States of $100,000 over a 20 year period, same to be expended under direction of the President upon beneficial objects, such as advancement in civilization, moral improvement and education, building, opening and fencing farms, providing of stock, agricultural implements, seeds, etc.

Article 3

Provides for additional expenditure by the United States of $50,000, less the value of articles advanced the Indians at the time of the signing of the treaty and prior to their removal to the reservation, for [479 22] <Article 3 continued> the erection of buildings, subjugation of farms, and the furnishing of necessary subsistence and farming equipment.

Article 4

Provides that in addition to the above specified considerations, the United States will erect one saw mill and one flour mill, suitable hospital building, a school house, and other shops, and for the employment of the necessary personnel for certain specified periods.

Provides for the erection of a house, the fencing and plowing of 10 acres of land for the head chief of the confederated bands, and the chief of each of the three principal named bands; also, a payment to the head chief of said confederated band of $500 per annum for 20 years.

Article 5

Provides for allotment of land to individuals in accordance with specified schedules; the issuance of restrictive patents thereon, and the revocation or cancellation thereof in the event any family shall famil [fail] to occupy and cultivate its allotment.

Article 6

Provides annuities shall not be used to pay debts of individuals.

Article 7

Indians acknowledge their dependence on the United States Government and promise to commit no depredations on property of United States citizens or other Indians.

Payment from annuities of those proven responsible in event depredations occur.

Indians promise not to make war on any other tribe except in self-defense.

Indians further agree to submit to laws and regulations prescribed by United States for government of said Indians.

Article 8

Provides for withholding of annuities for those drinking liquor or procuring same for others. [480 23]

Article 9

Provides that if necessary for public convenience, roads may be run through said reserves.

Treaty to become effective as soon as ratified by President and Senate.

Digest of Treaty Concluded at the Warm Springs Agency, Oregon,

between J. W. Perit Huntington,
Superintendent of Indian Affairs for Oregon
and the Confederated Tribes and Bands of Middle Oregon.

DATE: Nov. 15, 1865; RATIFIED: Mar. 2, 1867
STATUTE REFERENCE: 14 Stat. 751; 2 Kappler 908
TRIBES INVOLVED: Same as in original treaty digested immediately preceding this.

Article 1*

"It having become evident from experience that the provision of article 1 of Ute treaty of the twenty-fifth of June, A. D. eighteen hundred and fifty-five, which permit said confederated tribes to fish, hunt, gather berries and roots, pasture stock, and erect houses on lands outside Ute reservation, and which have been ceded to the United States, is often abused by the Indians to the extent or continuously residing away from the reservation, and is detrimental to the interests of both Indians and whites; therefore it is hereby stipulated and agreed that all the rights enumerated in the third proviso of the first section of the before mentioned treaty of the twenty-fifth of June eighteen hundred and fifty-five – that is to say, the right to take fish, erect houses, hunt game, gather roots and berries, and pasture animals upon lands without the reservation set apart by the treaty aforesaid – are hereby relinquished by the confederated Indian tribes and bands of Middle Oregon, parties to this treaty.
   * "Verbatim"

Article 2

Tribes agree to hereafter remain upon reservation and also agree that when called upon by superintendent or agent they will assist in pursuing and returning those members of said tribes who do leave or attempt to leave the reservation. [481 24]

Article 3

Provides that if necessary for any Indians to leave reservation, superintendent may issue written pass limited to a short period. Any Indian staying out of reservation for longer period than designated on the pass shall be deemed to have violated this a treaty.

Article 4

Provides violation of treaty shall subject guilty Indians to a deprivation of their share of annuities and to such other punishment President may direct.

Article 5

Provides that United States as a consideration for relinquishment of rights herein enumerated shall expend $3,500 for teams, agricultural implements, and seeds to advance civilization of said confederated tribes.

Article 6

Provides that United States shall allot to head of each family in confederated tribes a tract of land sufficient for his use, possession of which shall be secured to said family and heirs thereafter forever.

Article 7

Indians agree to report all infractions of liquor laws and to use under direction of superintendent or agent, all proper means to secure identification and punishment of persons unlawfully furnishing liquor to Indians.

* * * *

Digest of Treaty Concluded between Gov. Isaac I. Stevens,
Superintendent of Indian Affairs of ?? for Washington Territory,
and the Quinaielt, etc., on the Qui-nai-elt River,
July I, 1855, and at Olympia, January 25, 1856.

DATE: July 1, 1855 & Jan. 25, 1856; RATIFIED: March 8, 1859
STATUE REFERENCE: 12 Stab. 971; 2 Kappler 719
TRIBES INVOLVED: Qui-nai-elt and Quil-leh-ute Indians [482 25]

Article 1
Cedes to the United States certain described land occupied by said tribes in Territory of Washington.

Article 2
Provided for setting aside of tract or tracts of land within ceded territory to be sufficient for their needs and reserved to their exclusive use.
Provides no whites shall be permitted to reside upon reserved areas without permission of tribes and superintendent.
Provides that tribes shall settle on reserved areas within one year after ratification of treaty.
Provides that if necessary for public convenience, roads may be run through the said reserves and Indians compensated for any damages thus sustained.

Article 3
*"The right of taking fish at all usual and accustomed grounds and stations is secured to said Indians in common with all citizens of the Territory, and of erecting temporary houses for the purpose of curing the same; together with the privilege of hunting, gathering roots and berries, and pasturing their horses on all open and unclaimed lands. Provided, however, that they shall not take shellfish from any beds staked or cultivated by citizens; * * *
* Verbatim

Article 4
Provides for payment by the United States at $25,000 over a 20 year period, same to be expended under direction of the President upon beneficial objects. The Superintendent of Indian, or other proper official, shall each year inform the President at the wishes of said Indians in respect thereto.

Article 5
Provided for expenditure by United States of $2,500 for settlement of reservation and breaking up sufficient land for cultivation.

Article 6

President may remove Indian from reservations to some other suitable place or places within territory (when interest of territory may require, and the welfare of said Indians be promoted) on remunerating them for [483 26] <Article 6 – continued> improvements and expenses of removal; or may consolidate them with other friendly tribes.

President may cause survey and assignment of lots in reserve to individuals or families all permanent homes.

Substantial improvements made by Indians and abandoned in consequence of treaty shall be evalued and payment made therefor.

Article 7

Provided annuities shall not be used to pay debts of individuals.

Article 8

Indians acknowledge their dependence on the United States Government and promise to commit no depredations on property of United States citizens or other Indians.

Payment from annuities on those proven responsible in the event depredations occur.

Indians agree not to make war on any other tribe except in self defense.

Indians agree not to shelter offenders against laws of the United States.

Article 9

Provides for withholding of annuities from those drinking liquor or procuring same for others.

Article 10

Provides for establishment and support for 20 years of an agricultural and industrial school, same to be free for children of said tribes.

Provides that the United States employ a physician to reside at the central agency.

Expenses of above not to be deducted from annuities.

Article 11

Provides for abolishment of slavery and prohibition of future acquisition of slaves.

Article 12

Indians agree not to trade outside of the United States; nor shall foreign Indians reside in reservation without consent of Superintendent or agent.

Article 13

Treaty to become effective as soon as ratified by President and Senate.

'' '' * '' * '''

Chehalis Meeting Notes

1-30-42
EGS:lg

Chehalis. A collective name for several Salishan tribes on Chehalis r, and its affluents, and on Grays harbor, Wash. Gibbs states that it belongs strictly to a village at the entrance of Grays harbor, and signifies 'sand." There were 5 principal villages on the river, and 7 on the N. and 8 on the S. side of the bay; there were also a few villages on the N. end of Shoalwater bay. By many writers they are divided into Upper Chehalis or Kwaiailk (q.v.), dwelling above Satsop r., and the Lower Chehalis from that point down. The following subdivisions are mentioned, some of which were single villages, while others probably embraced people living in several: Chiklisilkh, Cloquallum, Hoquiam, Hooshkal, Humptulips, Kishkallen, Klimmim, Klumaitumsh, Nickomin, Nooachhummilh, Noohooultch, Nookalthu, Noosiatsks, Nooskoh, Satsop, Wynooche, Whiskah. The Satsop speak a dialect distinct from the others. In 1806 Lewis and Clark assigned to them a population of 700 in 38 lodges. In 1904 there were 147 Chehalis and 21 Humptulips under the Puyallup school superintendent, Wash.

Box 1828
c/o US Courthouse
Seattle, Washington

1358-E Federal Building
Los Angeles, Californi
November 25, 1941

Mr. Ernest Beckwith,
Chairman, Chehalis Indian Tribal Council,
Oakville, Washington.

Dear Friend:

In keeping with my promise previously made to you, I am writing to let you know that I expect to visit you and the other Chehalis people on Thursday, December 4, for the purpose of obtaining information about the usual and accustomed fishing and camping grounds of the Chehalis Indians situated outside the boundaries of the reservation.

I expect to arrive about ten o'clock in the morning and I presume that the arrangements previously made for the use of the school house are still applicable. In the event the meeting will be held elsewhere, will you please have someone meet me at the school house so as to take me where the meeting will be held.

I am sending copies of this letter to the individual whose names appear below in order that they also will be advised of the forthcoming meeting and will make arrangements to be present, in view of the fact that they have been selected to give me information I desire.

Sincerely yours,
Edward G. Swindell, Jr.
Associate Attorney

EGS/lg

cc: Taholah Agency
Silas Heck
Peter Heck
Dan Secena
Andrew Sanders

Box 1828
c/o US Attorney
1020 US Courthouse
Seattle, Washington

Taholah Indian Agency
Hoquiam, Washington
October 30, 1941

Mr. Ernest Beckwith, Chairman,
Chehalis Indian Tribal Council,
Oakville, Washington.

Dear Mr. Beckwith,

I have just received telegraphic instructions to proceed to Washington for a conference in connection with certain questions which have arisen concerning features of the hunting and fishing matters now being surveyed. Since I am leaving at once, it is necessary that our meeting arranged for this coming Thursday, November 6, be postponed until such time in the future, I can again arrange to meet with you and the others who were selected to give me certain information. Will you please see that word of this postponement is conveyed to all the others.

Sincerely yours,
Edward G. Swindell, Jr.
Associate Attorney

Mr Peter Heck
Oakville, Wa

Tah-[ho]-lah Ind[ian] Agency
Hoquiam, W^a

Dear Sir:

Received your letter wanting to know where to hold the meeting concerning fishing ground.

I believe the same place where the other meeting was held would be the best place for this meeting at the School House.

If people come and listen it would be all right. If they are interested enough.

Yours Truly
Peter Heck
Oakville, Wa

Oakville, Wa
Nov 3, 1941

Mr EG Swindell,
Just to let you know that the meeting for the fishing & camp grounds at the 6th of November will be at the community hall again, "school house." That is where we have our meetings.

Sincerely yours,
Andrew Sanders

Oakville, Wash
Nov 1, 1941

Edward G. Swindell, Jr.
Associate Attorney
c/o US Attorney
1020 US Courthouse
Seattle,

Dear Friend:
In reply to your letter concerning a meeting place.
The most convenient place for you to meet would be at the Community Hall where we had the first meeting. Should they decide to change the meeting place Silas Heck will meet you at the Community Center and notify you.

Yours Truly
Ernest Beckwith,
Chehalis Tribal Chairman
P.S. The meeting will be just with Dan Secena, Peter Heck and Andrew Sanders and Silas Heck interpreter.

Box 1828
c/o US Attorney
1020 US Courthouse
Seattle, Washington

Taholah Indian Agency
Hoquiam, Washington
October 30, 1941

Mr. Ernest Beckwith, Chairman,
Chehalis Indian Tribal Council,
Oakville, Washington.

Dear Friend:

You will recall that at the conclusion of out meeting on the evening of October 17, I promised to return to the Chehalis Reservation to take the statements of those individuals who had been selected to give me information concerning the usual and accustomed fishing and camping grounds of the Chehalis Indians outside the boundaries of the present reservation.

This is to let you know that I would like to and am planning upon meeting these people on Thursday November 6. The following are the names of those who were selected to give me this information.

Peter Heck

Andrew Sanders

Dan Secena

It was also decided that Silas Heck would meet with us to interpret if necessary. I am sending each of them a copy of this letter for their information and I do hope that all can attend as it is doubtful whether I could again return for the same purpose.

I expect to arrive about 10:00 or 10:30 in the morning and am planning to devote as much of the balance of the day as is necessary in obtaining the information in question.

I am leaving the selection of where we will all meet to your judgment and would like you to immediately write me as to what place has been selected so that I will known where to come. If no other place is available we could meet at the school house where we had our first meeting. In any event please let me know promptly where we are to meet so that there will be no delay – also be sure and let the others known of the place that will be used.

As I explained before, I believe we will accomplish more in a shorter time if we do not have a big meeting like the last one.

Should my plans for some unforeseen reason be changed, you will be promptly notified.
Sincerely

Edward G. Swindell, Jr.

Associate Attorney

EGS/reb
Cc to Taholah Agency
Silas Heck
Peter Heck
Dan Secena
Andrew Sanders

EGS:lej

2/25/42

Transcript of testimony given by Dan Secena and Andrew Sanders at the Chehalis Community House, Chehalis Reservation, Washington, on December 4, 1941:   <with additions from handwritten notes marked between angle brackets>

The questions and answers were interpreted by Silas Heck.

The witness stated that he is a full-blooded Chehalis Indian, and that he is about 84 years old, <June 1857> having been born about in June 1857.

He is familiar with the old fishing places of the Chehalis people.

LINCOLN CREEK

Says that there was an Indian fishing place and village at the mouth of Lincoln Creek where it enters the Chehalis River.

The Indian name was Nah-<Eha>Cha-Thlah-Loat-Sun<Son>, and that the name means "mouth of creek".

Has seen Indians living there when he was a small boy. At that time there was one big house for the Chief and a number of small houses situated around the Chief's house. These comprise the old Indian community. There were many people living at this place.

In addition, there were a number of small settlements located all along the river.

This place was one of the principal fishing places for the late fall fish.

Says that the only people who fished at this place were those who live there.

Pointed out that the Indians did not stay in one place all the time but would move around to the root <camas> and berry grounds to get roots and berries when in season.

The Indians that lived here were able to get enough fish from the fall run to last them all the year.   1001783

Stated that he has never actually fished there himself but has seen Indians fishing there. The Indians caught the fish with traps, spears, and gaff hooks. They sometimes used a net to get <dip> the fish out of the water.

The trap was so made that the fish in swimming upstream and attempting to get over the trap would be thrown back into a basket.

There were lots of people and lots of fish. Some of the people got their fish from the traps and others got them with hooks and spears.

The fish were dried by smoking them over a fire.

<u>Peter Heck</u> says he never did see this place but heard about it from his father although what he heard was only about the trap and not the other things.

<u>Andrew Sanders</u> says he never saw this place but heard about it from his father. He heard that it was a gathering place for Indians of various tribes, that there were plenty of camas (roots) on the nearby prairie and that the Mud Bay, Squally, and Tenino-Chehalis groups used this place. In addition to the fall salmon caught here, the Indians were also accustomed to catching salmon in the spring runs. They also caught eels, and when the fish and eels stopped running, in about June, they would move to Skookumchuck. (Note: this latter camp was about 4 or 5 miles from Scatter Creek.)

SCATTER CREEK

Says that there was an old Indian village and fishing place at the mouth of scatter Creek where it enters the Chehalis River.

The Indian name for this place was Wah-Thlah-Lin-Nah-Loat-Sun<Son>. Does not know what this means in English, although the final syllables refer to the fact that it was the mouth of a creek, the same as the previous one discussed.

Does not remember ever seeing any Indians living here but understands that people of the Chehalis tribe did live there before he was born. The fact that there [2 1001784] were no people living at this place when he was born was probably brought about by the fact that the inhabitants were wiped out by the smallpox plague, which was brought into the country by the white men.

He understands that there was quite a number of people living at this village.

The creek is a small creek and the Indians caught the salmon by spearing them. To do this, they placed pickets across the creek, which stopped the fish as they were coming upstream and gave them an opportunity to use the spears.

He has visited there many times but when he visited there, the Indians <he> used <iron> gaff hooks made of iron.

The first time he visited there was when he was a young boy. He has not visited there for a long time, however, due to the fact that the salmon no longer came up the stream <disappeared>.

When myself and the other Indians fished at this place, we remained until the salmon run was over. The salmon that were not eaten fresh were dried by smoking them. These smoked salmon would last all winter.

The people who used to live at this village considered it their permanent residence, whereas I and the other Indians who fished there only stayed there temporarily.

The Indians did not sell the fish they caught at this place although some times they would give fish as presents to the white settlers.

<Peter Heck – never saw it – got mad and quit>

Andrew Sanders – says the Indians within his memory also fished at this place <also Scatter Creek> in the winter time for silver side salmon and that this run usually occurred about Christmas time.

He has fished there himself with a spear and gaff hook.

In the early part of the year, or in about May, the Indians would fish for trout, using a small trap<s> which they would move from time to time from the mouth of the creek clear up to the head of the lake.

The Indians would smoke the surplus trout that they caught.

The Indians used to stay at this place about two or three weeks at a time.   [3 1001785]

RAINBOW FALLS

Andrew Sanders says that the Indian name for this place is Wah-Moss <Wah-mŏs> and that he does not know what it means.

This was ^not^ a permanent village although the Indians used to go there each year for the purpose of catching eels.

This place is situated near Pe Ell on the Chehalis River.

The Indians would camp at this place for about a month each year during which they would also hunt elk.

He remembers about twenty to thirty Indians camping at this place at different times during his life time.

The eels were caught by hand as they hung to the rocks at the falls.

MUD BAY - ELD INLET (?)

Andrew Sanders. This place was called Squi-Eyelth, which also was the Indian name for the Chehalis people, including the Indians living at Mud Bay and Eld Inlet.

This was once one of the permanent villages of the Chehalis Indians but there was no village there when he first visited the place as a young man.

This was a good place to catch clams and dog salmon.

The clams not eaten fresh were dried for future use. The salmon were caught by hand in the shallow water.

Has not been to this place for four or five years on account of the game wardens who molest the Indians.

SQUAXIN

Andrew Sanders. The Indian name for this place was Qui-Tse-Lay-Chen, which meant "center of where people live".

This was one of the clam-~~catching~~ digging places of the Upper Chehalis Indians, and, although I have never been there, I have heard and been told that it always had been used as a clam-catching place by the Indians. <Dan Secena – never been there.>   [4 1001786]

SKOOKUMCHUCK

<u>Andrew Sanders</u>. The Indian name for this place was Tow-A-Tin, which means "fording place". The Indian village was located about a mile above the mouth of the creek on the north side of the river, which is near the present city of Centralia, originally known as "Centerville".

When I was a small boy, quite a few Indians lived there.

The Indians fished in Skookumchuck Creek with spears and gaff hooks. They did not use a trap as the water was too swift for that purpose.

Has fished there many tines, the first time being about forty years ago, but has not fished there since he got married. Does not think there has been a village there·for about eighty years, or more, or since the white people crowded them out.

The Indians dried the fish they caught here and they also dried the salmon eggs by packing them in fish skins. <Dan Secena doesn't know anything about this place.>

MICHIGAN HILL

<u>Andrew Sanders</u>. The Indian name for this place was Yah-Lookt<lŭkt>-Un, which means "place to fall down". This place received its name as a result of an old Indian legend in which some animals <fox or coyote> were pushed over a cliff which was there. ·

There was no permanent village at this place. The Indians would come down early each year from Skookumchuck to catch fish <easily> which could be found resting in the still water before proceeding farther upstream.

This was not a permanent village because the people were afraid to live there due to the fact that it was believed to be haunted.

This place was located about six miles from Skookumchuck and the Indians used to go back and forth in canoes. It is located about a mile below the mouth of Lincoln creek; that is, about a mile north of Lincoln Creek, or in the direction of Gray's Harbor.   [5 1001787]

GRAND MOUND

<u>Dan Secena</u>. The Indian name for this place was Klah-Ky-Icklth and it meant "long prairie". There was a big permanent village at this place and it was here that I was born.

I was told that many more Indians lived here before I was born but they were killed off by the epidemic.

The old village was on the Chehalis River and it was situated within the borders of the present State School for Girls.

The Indians speared the fish they caught here and they also caught salmon with a trap.

This was the main village <band> of the Upper Chehalis.

Ha doesn't know whether the Indians ever sold the fish they caught at this place but he knows he never sold any. <Andrew Sanders nothing to add.>   [6 1001788]

EGS:lej
2/25/42

Transcript of testimony given by Lucy Sanders (Mrs. Andrew Sanders) at the Chehalis Community House, Chehalis Reservation, Washington, on December 4, 1941:

States she is a full-blooded Chehalis Indian and that she is about 67 years old.·

In addition to the information given me by Andrew Sanders and Dan Secena, which she confirms as having either been within her [own] knowledge or told to her by her parents or the old people, she wished to add the following:

That there was a permanent Chehalis Indian village at the mouth of Black River on the upstream or east side thereof.

That the Indian name of this village was Sah-tsah-ulth, which meant "river coming from the lake". She said that <both> the lake and the river had the same name.

She further advised that she was born in this particular village <upstream east side>. When she was a little girl, the Indians fished there, using spears, hooks, and also a trap constructed at the mouth of the river.

She also advised that there was an Indian village known as Thla-qah-mish but that she did not know what it meant in English. This is now near Cedarville, Wash.

The village was located across from the mouth of Cedar Creek above the City of Cedarville and that this was a permanent village of the Chehalis and that they had always lived there. <no handwritten notes>   [1001789]

Handwritten hw >>

Chehalis Community   12/4/41
House – Chehalis Resn

<u>Present</u>

Peter Heck	Michael Hansen
Dan Secena	Ralph Heck son John
Mr & Mrs Walter Klatush	Andrew Sanders
Ruth Pete	Lucy Sanders, Mrs Andrew
Virgie Case	George Sanders
Silas Heck	
	Visitors from Cowlitz
	John Ike

hw Dan Secena – born at Grand Mound near present state school for girls.

Peter Heck – born at Indian village about 2 miles above Lincoln regular Indian Village – Over 70 years

Andrew Anders – at Tenino – about 80 years old

* Gathering place for Indians of various tribes in the prairie full of camas Squally, Mud Bay group & Tenino Chehalis spring salmon caught as well as eels when fish eels stopped in June they would move to Skookumchuck Not this camp was about 4 or five miles Scatter Creek.

19 Dan Secena hw

20 Peter Heck hw

21 Andrew Sanders hw

25 Lucy Sanders

Chehalis Reservation
Cowlitz People present

10/17/41
Community Hall
Open   31 present

Chairman Mr Ernest Beckwith
Chief John Ike Kinswa – Cowlitz

Andrew Sanders – interpreted by Silas Heck
<Upper Chehalis distinguished from Lower down around Gray's Harbor>
1 mouth of Lincoln Creek where it runs into channels Chehalis River
2 Scatter Creek – mouth of Scatter Creek
3 Rainbow Falls near Pe Ell on Chehalis River – eel fishing
4 Mud Bay – Oyster Bay either Budd or Eld Inlet – clam grounds <p22 squi-eyelth – name of Chehalis people [tribe] also the Indian group at Mud Bay ~ Eld Inlet – for clams & salmon – clams dry – and fish caught by hand in shallow water – There had been a permanent village there but it was gone when I first went there as a young man – Haven't been up for 4 or 5 years – account game wardens. Dan Secena never was there.>
5 Squaxon Island – clam fishing
6 Skookumchuck – south of Centralia
7 Michigan Hill – just below mouth of Lincoln Creek
8 Grand Mound – Chehalis River   Black River
        witnesses Peter Heck Andrew Sanders Dan Secena

Peter Heck

 Satsop fat fish – Cosmopolis near Aberdeen   10/17/41
3 Cedarville – trap
4 Lincoln Creek – Chehalis River
5 Chehalis River – length throughout – caught with spears
                        Peter Heck
1 hunted ^elk^ where Cosmopolis over hills to North River for Elk. – Where cached 6 canoes
2 Garrad Creek – elk hunting grounds
3 head of Lincoln Creek – elk
4 Willapa – elk
5 Black Hills – Deer Hunting
6 La Quay to [Claquato] near Chehalis
7 Ball Hill about 12 miles from Chehalis

Lower → Cowlitz Indians
1 Cowlitz mouth to Columbia River – smelt sturgeon
2 Touttle River mouth to Cowlitz – 2 traps one Touttle one in Cowlitz
3 Olequa Creek –
4 Salmon Creek – close to present town of Toledo
5 Iron Rock – above salmon Creek near Knan??
6 Baker Rock – main fishing ground

7 Tilton River – where entered Cowlitz

29 map Received 10/17/41 from John Ike

Cowlitz

8 Dunn's canyon near Harmony
9 Falls of Cowlitz River – Way up near Kanst
10 also all the way up to Packwood –

Chehalis Indian Reservation

Hunting and Fishing Accustomed Grounds and Villages

The Chehalis Indians have a promise of the treaty which was stated that as long as the sun rises they could trap and as long as the river flows and there is fish in the river they can fish and that they can hunt as long as there are hills to hunt in and as long as there is an Indian living. ---- <some of this is questionable EGS>

Gov Stevens came to Fords Prairie and promised them a Reservation there, twenty two (22) miles long and four (4) miles wide each side of the river, which would run from Skookumchuck to the mouth of Cedar Creek. The Indians agreed, providing they could keep their fishing and hunting ground and also the places they went to pick berries and dig roots. Gov Stevens said he didn't want the berries and roots and that they could also have their game and fish.

The Indians went to the mouth of the Chehalis River, located near Aberdeen and Hoquiam to get st?? meat ?? At Cosmopolis was a large Indian village, where in the mountains they hunted for bear and deer, and went to the head of Johns River to hunt for elk.

At Sandy Island they hunted for wild game, as bear, deer, and they also fished here.

Next Village was located at Melborn, where they hunted and fished. Then from the mouth of the Wynoochee River to the "Poor Farm" was also a place for hunting and fishing. Then along the Black Creek they hunted and fished. About (12) miles up the Wynoochee River was another Indian village where they fished, hunted, and trapped. The next place was at the Mouth of the Satsop river was another large Indian Village, and they hunted, fished, and trapped along here, on up to Newman Creek. Up the Satsop to it's source, many villages were located, where they fished and hunted. At the head of the Wynoochee and Satsop rivers the Indians hunted for Elk.

From South Elma to Clucullum were also Indian Villages and on up Bush Creek where they hunted and fished. At Gibson Creek was located another village. From the mouth of Cedar Creek to Cedarville was also a place for the Indians to hunt and fish. <OK had a trap> They went up to Garrad Creek in the hills to hunt. At the mouth of Garrad creek they hunted for Elk. Williams Creek for deer, bear, and fishing. Independence Creek for the same, also trapping. At Jamestown fishing and hunting from the mouth of Scatter Creek, up to Grand Mound. Up Scatter Creek were many villages, which went on to Tenino where there was a large village when they hunted, fished and trapped. Also roots and berries. Then to Lincoln Creek which was a very large village. Tribes came from elsewhere to gather their berries, roots, and to fish and hunt. At the heads of Lincoln Creek, over to North River they hunted Elk. Next place was at Skookumchuck, which ran on up to Centralia, where they hunted and fished, berries and roots – same as Lincoln Creek. Many villages on up to Bucoda, where another large village was located. The next large place was across from Chehalis, where hunted and fished extensively.

The next was Cluquato, where they hunted. At Ball Hill they hunted bear and deer and trapped. Above Chehalis was another village where they hunted and fished. Up to the Forks of the Chehalis, about four miles from the other large village was located another, where another large village was located. TheN [2] on up for about seven miles, on the main Chehalis River, to the Whon e [xʷone]. Fish and trapped which still stand there is the place where many villages were located and they hunted and fished, trapped etc. Then to below Dryad is the Rainbow Falls where the Indians caught eels. Next is Pe Ell Prairie where a large village was located and they hunted, fished, and trapped, dug roots and picked berries.

They also fished and hunted along the Black River and at Mimia [Mima] Prairie. They fished at Little Rock too.

<sgd> George Sanders

Counsel

Portland Area Office
Portland 18, Oregon

Reference Librarian   November 18, 1952
Documents Division
Tacoma Public Library
Tacoma 3, Washington

Dear Madam:

Reference is made to your postcard of October 25, 1952, concerning request for a copy of the Report on Source, Nature and Extent of Fishing, Hunting and Miscellaneous Related Rights in Washington and Oregon. We have just been granted authority by the Commissioner to make the Report available to certain individuals or groups and are transmitting herewith a copy for the use of the Tacoma Library.

In the use of the Report it should be understood that the conclusions of law are those of the compiler and Report has not been approved or disapproved by the Bureau of Indian Affairs or the Department of the Interior. It has not been edited since it was submitted August 26, 1942, consequently some of the laws quoted may have been amended or repealed. The material contained in the affidavits, of course, is factual insofar as the affiants are concerned.

Sincerely yours,
(Sgd) Edward G. Swindell, Jr.
For E Morgan Pryse
Area Director

US Department of Interior
Office of Indian Affairs
Field Service
Portland Area Office
Portland 18, Oregon

Ruth S. Reynolds
Librarian   November 18, 1952
Whitman College Library
Walla Walla, Washington

Dear Miss Reynolds:

Reference is made to your letter of November 4, 1952, addressed to the Office of Indian Affairs at Los Angeles, California concerning request for a copy of the Report on Source, Nature and Extent of Fishing, Hunting and Miscellaneous Related Rights in Washington and Oregon. The letter was forwarded to my attention and as we had just been granted authority by the Commissioner to make the Report available to certain individuals or groups and are transmitting herewith a copy for the use of the Whitman College Library.

In the use of the Report it should be understood that the conclusions of law are those of the compiler and Report has not been approved or disapproved by the Bureau of Indian Affairs or the Department of the Interior. It has not been edited since it was submitted August 26, 1942, consequently some of the laws quoted may have been amended or repealed. The material contained in the affidavits, of course, is factual insofar as the affiants are concerned.

Sincerely yours,
(Sgd) Edward G. Swindell, Jr.
For E Morgan Pryse
Area Director

Enclosure

Name Index

A

B

C

D

E

F

Place Name Sources

[b#] = William Elmendorf and A L Kroeber
  1992 The Structure of Twana Culture, with comparative notes on Yurok Culture. Pre-White tribal lifeways on Washington's Hood Canal. Pullman: WSU Press. [1960]

[d#] = M Dale Kinkade
  1991 Upper Chehalis Dictionary. University of Montana Occasional Papers in Linguistics #7.

[e#] = Eugene Hunn, E Thomas Morning Owl, Phillip Cash Cash Jennifer Karson Engum
  2015 Čaw Pawa Laakni ~ They Are Not Forgotten ~ Sahaptian Place Names Atlas of the Cayuse, Umatilla, and Walla Walla Pendleton: Tamastslikt Cultural Institute.

[j#] = Jay Powell
  2008 Quileute Dictionary La Push. [1976]

[k#] = Timothy Montler
  2012 Klallam Dictionary. UW

[l#] = Dawn Bates, Thom Hess, Vi Hilbert
  1994 Lushootseed Dictionary. UW.

[m#] = Ann Renker & Maria Parker Pascua
  1989 Makah Traditional Cultural Property Study. Olympia: Office of Archaeology and Historic Preservation.

[s#] = Marian Smith
  1940 The Puyallup-Nisqually. NY: Columbia University

[u#] = Confederated Tribes of Umatilla and Noel Rude
  2014 Umatilla Dictionary UW.

[v#] = Virginia Beavert & Sharon Hargus
  2009 Yakama Sahaptin *Ichishkiin Sinwit* Dictionary. UW

[w#] = William Bright
  2004 Native American Placenames of the United States. OU

Please Help Fight Typo Gnomes!

Sold @ Amazon.com

IV ~ Portaits

KAM-I-AH-KAN, YAKIMA HEAD CHIEF
(undated)

PEU-PEU-MOX-MOX
WALLA WALLA HEAD CHIEF, JUNE 7

LAWYER, NEZ PERCE HEAD CHIEF
MAY 25

LOOKING GLASS, NEZ PERCE CHIEF
JUNE 9

OWHI, YAKIMA CHIEF, JUNE 3

OLD JOSEPH, NEZ PERCE CHIEF
MAY 29

TIMOTHY, NEZ PERCE CHIEF, JUNE 7

YOUNG CHIEF, CAYUSE HEAD CHIEF
JUNE 8

YUM-HOW-LISH, CAYUSE CHIEF
JUNE 11

JAMES, NEZ PERCE CHIEF, MAY 29

SPOKANE GARRY, SPOKANE HEAD CHIEF
MAY 27

SIX NEZ PERCES TAKE NOTES OF THE COUNCIL PROCEEDINGS (See text p. 102)
Former students of Spalding, they were able to read and write their language.

FIVE CROWS, CAYUSE CHIEF, JUNE 11

www.ingramcontent.com/pod-product-compliance
Lightning Source LLC
Chambersburg PA
CBHW081608250726
48657CB00009B/2498